Teaching Primary English

Teaching Primary English is a comprehensive, evidence-informed introduction designed to support and inspire teaching and learning in the primary school. Written in a clear and accessible way, it draws on the very latest research and theory to describe and exemplify a full and rich English curriculum. It offers those on teacher training courses, as well as qualified teachers who are looking to develop their practice, subject knowledge and guidance for effective, enjoyable classroom practice.

Advice and ideas are supported by explicit examples of good teaching linked to video clips filmed in real schools, reflective activities, observational tasks and online resources. Each chapter includes suggestions for great children's literature, considers assessment throughout and offers support planning for diversity and special educational needs. Key topics covered include:

- spoken language for teaching and learning
- storytelling, drama and role play
- reading for pleasure
- early reading, including phonics
- poetry
- writing composition
- spelling and handwriting
- grammar and punctuation
- responding to and assessing writing
- multimodal, multimedia and digital texts.

With a focus on connecting all modes of English, the global and the local, and home and school experience, this detailed, uplifting book will support you in developing a curious, critical approach to teaching and learning English.

Additional content can be found on the fantastic supporting website. Features include:

- video clips from within the classroom to demonstrate English teaching techniques
- audio resources, including an interactive quiz, to check understanding and provide real-life examples and case studies
- downloadable resources to support teaching and incorporate into lesson plans.

Eve Bearne became Project Officer for the National Writing Project after working for twenty years in schools and colleges. When the Project ended, she was appointed to Homerton College, Cambridge, UK, as a Senior Lecturer in Language, before being appointed Assistant Director in Research. Eve was President of the United Kingdom Reading Association from 2003 to 2005 and currently oversees *Publications* for UKLA. Eve has written and edited many books on English, literacy and children's literature.

David Reedy is General Secretary and a past President of the United Kingdom Literacy Association (UKLA). He was Co-Director of the Cambridge Primary Review Trust until 2017. From 2010 to 2014 he worked as Principal Adviser for primary schools in the London Borough of Barking and Dagenham. He has also been a Visiting Fellow at the Institute of Education, University of London, UK. Currently, David works with schools and teachers nationally and internationally to develop effective pedagogical practices, particularly in English. David's most recent publications include *Guiding Readers: A handbook for teaching reading comprehension to 7–11 year olds* (UCL IoE Press, 2016) and *Teaching Grammar Effectively in Key Stage 1* (UKLA, 2016); he has also contributed to *Teaching English Creatively* 2nd edition (Routledge, 2015).

Teaching Primary English

Subject Knowledge and Classroom Practice

Eve Bearne and David Reedy

Routledge
Taylor & Francis Group

LONDON AND NEW YORK

First published 2018
by Routledge
2 Park Square, Milton Park, Abingdon, Oxon, OX14 4RN

and by Routledge
711 Third Avenue, New York, NY 10017

Routledge is an imprint of the Taylor & Francis Group, an informa business

© 2018 Eve Bearne and David Reedy

British Library Cataloguing-in-Publication Data
A catalogue record for this book is available from the British Library

Library of Congress Cataloging-in-Publication Data
A catalog record for this book has been requested

ISBN: 978-1-138-68155-2 (hbk)
ISBN: 978-1-138-68156-9 (pbk)
ISBN: 978-1-315-17480-8 (ebk)

Typeset in Din Schriften
by Fish Books Ltd.

Visit the companion website: www.routledge.com/cw/bearne

To Lesley, for constant support.
David

To Peter, for always being there.
Eve

CONTENTS

FIGURES

WEBSITE RESOURCES

Please visit the companion website at www.routledge.com/cw/bearne for access to video clips, audio resources and downloadable resources for classroom use.

WI.1   Long-term English plan

WI.2   Planning and teaching sequence

WP1   Standard English quiz

W1.1   My language family tree

W1.2   Perceptions survey – spoken language

W1.3   Background paper for discussion of the language deprivation debate

W3.1   'The Fairy Tree' story

W3.2   *The Button Story*

W3.3   Stegosaurus story

W3.4   Helen Bromley article 'Storyboxes'

W3.5   Drama conventions

W3.6   Role play scenarios

W3.7   Case study: Using a picture book as a basis for drama

W4.1   Guidance and format for observing spoken language

W4.2   Case study: *Three by the Sea*

W4.3   Case study: *The Slodge* using the planning and teaching sequence

W4.4   Planning for spoken language – transcript

W4.5   Scale of Progression in Spoken Language

W5.1   Case study: Rivers of Reading

W5.2   River of Reading format

W5.3   Personal Reading Profile

W5.4   'Texts I Like'

W5.5   Some of the best short stories for children

W5.6   Case study: Guided reading

W6.1   Pennac's 'Rights of a Reader'

ACTIVITIES

In each chapter you will be asked to carry out activities to enhance your subject knowledge. There are different types of activities:

- *Reflective:* a chance for you to mull over ideas and keep notes on a blog/in a journal, so that you can relate your own experience to the classroom, share insights with others or build cumulatively to a summary of what you have learned.
- *Paired/group discussions:* to clarify and share ideas.
- *Classroom observations:* to identify aspects of teaching and build your own professional development plans.
- *Planning for teaching:* to begin planning to teach specific aspects of English.
- *Gathering ideas/information:* to build your own repertoire of texts to support your teaching.

The following grids show how the activities are designed to contribute to your developing professional expertise.

Part One: Spoken language

Chapter	Activity	Subject knowledge
Introduction to Part One	**P1I.1 Standard English quiz** A short quiz to test your understanding of the difference between Standard English and dialect/accent/register variation.	**contextual:** developing awareness of cultural attitudes to language use **linguistic:** learning about grammar
Chapter 1 Developing talk	**1.1 Early language experience – reflective journal/blog** A reflection of your own home language experience, how it might have influenced your language or literacy as an adult and how it relates to the spoken language curriculum.	**textual:** of the different spoken texts learned in homes and communities

Chapter	Activity	Subject knowledge
Chapter 1 Developing talk	**1.2 Language family tree – reflective journal/blog** Further reflections on home language and literacy experience to identify the language assets you bring from your home to the classroom and how these will help you model spoken language in the classroom.	**linguistic:** about how you have learned to vary your spoken language according to audience and purpose **pedagogical:** how to use your linguistic knowledge in teaching
	1.3 Adult intervention in children's language development – discussion Viewing a video to observe how adults induct children into the language patterns and expectations of their communities.	**contextual:** noting some social and cultural aspects of early language development
	1.4 Perceptions survey: Spoken language – reflective journal/blog Asking children about their perceptions of talk and using the information to help plan for teaching spoken language.	**contextual and pedagogical:** investigating how attitudes to spoken language can impact classroom teaching
	1.5 The teacher's role – discussion (pairs or small groups) Summarising jottings from the reflective activities in the chapter to identify what these suggest for the teacher's role in developing spoken language in the classroom.	building **pedagogical** subject knowledge
	1.6 Observing young children's language: Implications for classroom practice – discussion/reflective journal/blog Reading and viewing background material to compare these with your own experience of young children's language observed in the classroom and consider the implications for classroom practice.	**contextual, linguistic and pedagogical:** identifying how differing views of children's language development contribute to professional understanding
Chapter 2 Spoken language for teaching and learning	**2.1 Principles of dialogic teaching – reflective journal/blog** Comparing transcripts of classroom dialogue with your own classroom observations about how principles of dialogic teaching are evident in the classroom and making notes for future classroom observations.	**textual:** how dialogue works to move thinking forward **linguistic:** how language varies according to purpose and audience **pedagogical:** how these insights can be deployed to improve learning
	2.2 Talk moves – discussion pairs/small groups Reading about the 'talk moves' that can be taken to develop productive classroom discussion and using them as a basis for observation and future planning for teaching.	**textual:** how dialogue can be organised to support learning **pedagogical:** using observations for future planning for teaching

Chapter	Activity	Subject knowledge
Chapter 2 Spoken language for teaching and learning	**2.3 Observing dialogic teaching – reflective journal/blog** *This Activity is in two parts.* 1 Reading an article outlining practical essentials of classroom dialogue, identifying implications classroom practice and planning to try out different kinds of teaching and learning talk to extend your own repertoire. 2 Viewing Video 1 to observe the repertoire of effective dialogic teaching.	**linguistic:** how language is deployed to formulate and exchange ideas and develop thinking **pedagogical:** drawing on reading and observation to build professional expertise
	2.4 Thinking together – discussion pairs/group Using teaching resources from the Thinking Together Project to support primary-age children in developing their own ground rules and to plan how they might be used in a forthcoming teaching unit.	**contextual:** noting how classrooms are culturally developed places for learning **pedagogical:** using these insights to plan for teaching
Chapter 3 Storytelling, drama and role play	**3.1 Anecdote from childhood – pairs/ small groups** Using personal anecdote as a starting point for more structured storytelling and viewing a video of a poet telling an anecdote/story.	**textual:** looking at the structure of personal anecdotes in comparison with more formal story structures **linguistic:** how language can be varied to entertain and engage an audience
	3.2 What is the story? – pairs/small group Using a short sentence as the basis for building a story and using a frame to help recall key events for storytelling.	**textual:** learning to build a story with key events **pedagogical:** using a framework/prompt for storytelling in the classroom
	3.3 Making a story frame – individual/ pairs Listening to a story on a sound file/reading a story resource on the website and drawing a map or other frame to help retell the story in the classroom. An important aspect of this activity is to reflect on your experience of telling the story and the children's responses as a means of building your own storytelling expertise.	**textual:** adding to your repertoire of known story structures **linguistic:** manipulating language for effect **pedagogical:** developing your professional expertise as a classroom storyteller
	3.4 What children know about telling stories – individual/pairs Watching a video of a 5-year-old storyteller, noting how a young child structures a story and considering how you might support him in developing his story making.	**textual:** noting how story structure develops as children grow older **pedagogical:** identifying ways of helping children develop the storytelling aspect of spoken language

Chapter	Activity	Subject knowledge
Chapter 3 Storytelling, drama and role play	**3.5 Personal memories of drama/role play – reflective journal/blog/pairs/group** Noting memories of drama or role-play activities in your own school experience to build a composite list of the range of formal and informal practices and opportunities that drama offers the learner.	**textual:** noting the variety of forms of drama/role play activities **pedagogical:** extending personal experience of classroom drama and role play
	3.6 Opportunities for role play – pairs Noting the different role play areas/scenarios you have seen in classrooms and starting to compile a list of books and resources that can be used for role play and drama in the classroom.	**textual:** building a list of resources to support drama teaching **pedagogical:** developing a range of approaches to drama/role play in the classroom
	3.7 Scenarios and problems for role play – pairs/group Adding possible characters and problems to the list of scenarios for role play (to be collated as a group resource) and considering opportunities for Teacher in Role.	**textual:** continuing to build resources to support drama teaching **pedagogical:** extending a personal repertoire of drama approaches
	3.8 Finding resources for storytelling and drama – individual to group Finding picture books, videos, CD ROMs, sound files, information about local theatre groups or storytellers and library services that offer storytelling/drama sessions and sharing these ideas with colleagues.	**textual:** building resources for storytelling and drama and awareness of what is available locally
	3.9 Planning for storytelling, role play and drama – individual to pairs and group Using a picture book as a starting point to plan to include some aspects of storytelling, role play and drama in the first phase of a teaching sequence.	**pedagogical:** planning to use storytelling and drama/role play to enhance teaching and increase the personal spoken language repertoire
Chapter 4 Planning for, developing and assessing spoken language	**4.1 Decisions about groupings – reflective journal/blog/group discussion** Observing and enquiring about how teachers make decisions about grouping the children in order to note ideas to help you decide how best to groups children for learning.	**pedagogical:** increasing awareness of how best to organise the classroom for learning
	4.2 Evidence about spoken language – reflective journal/blog/group discussion Noting how teachers observe and keep evidence of children's spoken language, including involving the children in assessments and making some personal observations of children.	**contextual:** considering the principles used to make decisions about assessment **pedagogical:** adding to a personal store of observations to feed into making assessments

Chapter	Activity	Subject knowledge
Chapter 4 Planning for, developing and assessing spoken language	**4.3 Planning a teaching sequence focusing on spoken language – individual/pairs** After reading an account of a teaching sequence, using the format provided to plan a teaching sequence using a range of spoken language opportunities. These plans can be shared to become part of a group resource.	**pedagogical:** developing a wider range of spoken language opportunities throughout a teaching sequence
	4.4 Observing two children and noting their achievements in spoken language – reflective journal/blog Selecting two children to observe for two or three weeks and, in discussion with the teacher, note their achievements on the Scale of Progression for Spoken Language in order to consider how to move their spoken language forward.	**contextual:** building on principles used to make decisions about assessment **textual:** noting the different kinds of spoken language and behaviours children have at their disposal **linguistic:** developing knowledge of how children use language to express their own intentions in spoke language **pedagogical:** developing expertise in making assessments

Part Two: Reading

Chapter	Activity	Subject knowledge
Chapter 5 Perspectives on reading	**5.1 Reading autobiographies – reflective journal/blog/pairs/group** Making your own River of Reading, noting memories of reading from as early as you can remember. What were some of the key reading experiences at home and at school? Sharing and comparing memories of reading with colleagues. Reflecting on the principles and noting personal principles about teaching reading.	**contextual:** developing awareness of how experiences of reading affect attitudes to reading **textual and linguistic:** noting the different kinds of reading you did from an early age **pedagogical:** considering implications for the principles underlying reading pedagogy
	5.2 Personal Reading Profiles – reflective journal/blog/pairs/group Completing the Personal Reading Profile and the questions about reading behaviours in website resource W5.2 and noting any patterns in your reading preferences. Sharing and comparing profiles and responses with a colleague considering the implications for the classroom and for the diversity of readers in any classroom.	**contextual:** developing awareness of the range and repertoire of reading, including reading behaviours and preferences **pedagogical:** considering implications teaching and learning reading

Chapter	Activity	Subject knowledge
Chapter 5 Perspectives on reading	**5.3 'Texts I Like' – individual to group** Using the examples given in website resource W5.4, beginning to compile a list of texts that might be useful for the classroom.	**textual, linguistic and pedagogical:** building subject knowledge of good texts to support reading, writing, talk and drama/role play and considering how these might be used in the classroom
	5.4 Reading aloud – individual to small group Choosing a short passage and practising reading it aloud to a small group of colleagues before reading to a class. Reflecting on the experience and considering the value of fluent and expressive reading aloud to a teacher of reading.	**contextual:** developing the skill of reading aloud with expression **textual and linguistic:** noticing how language features influence reading aloud **pedagogical:** identifying the value of reading aloud in the classroom
	5.5 Reflective journal/blog/pairs/group Guiding reading. Reading the case study in website resource W5.6. Considering the functions of different kinds of questions. Observing group reading in order to focus on questioning.	**linguistic:** noticing the effects of different kinds of questions **pedagogical:** developing a sense of how to use questioning to move children's reading on
Chapter 6 Reading for pleasure	**6.1 Reflecting on personal reading for pleasure – reflective journal/blog** Making a quick list of voluntary reading (of any kind) over the last few days and considering how long it took to read it, the purpose for reading, how hard it was to read, whether it was on screen or on paper, recommended or self-chosen. Noting the difference between intrinsic and extrinsic motivation to read.	**contextual, textual and linguistic:** building awareness of the complex interrelationships between contexts for reading, reading behaviours, texts and meaning
	6.2 Rights of a Reader – reflective journal/blog/pairs/group Individually at first, reading website resource W6.1 Pennac's 'Rights of a Reader', in pairs or small groups discussing them and amending Pennac's list in the light of these discussions. Considering the relationship between the reflections in Activity 6.1 and these discussions and their implications for being a Reading Teacher.	**contextual and textual:** developing awareness of the contextual and textual factors that might influence a reader's choices and preferences **pedagogical:** identifying the importance of sharing reading preferences with young readers and creating an environment of opportunity and choice
	6.3 Keeping up with books for children – pairs/group/reflective journal/blog Visiting websites which draw attention to and review children's books, browsing the resources, reviews and interviews, noting on the 'Texts I Like' record (website resource W5.4) new ideas about books to use in the classroom.	**textual and pedagogical:** building subject knowledge of texts for classroom use

Chapter	Activity	Subject knowledge
Chapter 6 Reading for pleasure	**6.4 Children's views on reading – pairs/group/reflective journal/blog** Viewing videos of groups of children talking about their reading for pleasure and considering the implications for classroom practice.	**contextual, textual and pedagogical:** identifying key features of children's comments about their preferences and reading habits, particularly in relation to home and popular cultural influences on reading, and considering the implications for classroom practice
Chapter 7 Early reading including phonics	**7.1 A 3 year old reading – reflective journal/blog/pairs/group** Viewing video of a 3 year old 'reading' a Mr Men story to identify the knowledge he has about reading before being able to decode the words and what concepts about print he will need to be taught.	**contextual, textual and pedagogical:** noting pre-reading strategies which feed into more formal reading and identifying further steps for a beginner reader
	7.2 Teaching phonics – reflective journal/blog/pairs/group Viewing video of a discrete phonics session, identifying the different elements of a phonics teaching session which are being covered.	**textual and pedagogical:** building subject knowledge of the elements of discrete phonics teaching
	7.3 Onset and rime – reflective journal/blog/pairs/group Using website resource W7.2 Onset and rime. Attempting to make as many words as possible in one minute as an indication of the value of onset and rime to generate vocabulary knowledge.	**textual, linguistic and pedagogical:** adding to subject knowledge of how to build vocabulary
Chapter 8 Comprehension	**8.1 Making sense of texts – individual/ pairs/group** Reading a short text as an example of using multiple sources to gain meaning including grammatical knowledge, knowledge of other texts, knowledge of other languages and wider knowledge of the world.	**contextual linguistic and textual:** raising awareness of the complexity of sources readers draw on to make sense of texts
	8.2 Formulating questions – pairs/group Choosing a short story or section/chapter from a book that could be used with a guided reading group and with a partner devising three different kinds of question: looking, clue and thinking. Considering how to extend the children's answers by response. Planning to use these as soon as possible.	**contextual, linguistic, textual and pedagogical:** formulating questions that will require young readers to read for deeper meaning as well as what is literally clear and trying out the effect of thoughtfully planned questions

Chapter	Activity	Subject knowledge
Chapter 8 Comprehension	**8.3 Planning a reciprocal teaching session – individual/pairs** Choosing a short story or section/chapter to use with a guided reading group and planning a reciprocal teaching based session using predicting, questioning, clarifying and summarising. Noting the effectiveness of dialogue in developing the children's ideas.	**contextual, linguistic, textual and pedagogical:** identifying how dialogic questioning can help to extend children's comprehension of texts
Chapter 9 Describing and assessing progress in reading	**9.1 What a good reader can do – individual journal/blog to pairs/small group** Using Traves' list of 'What a Good Reader Can Do', identifying parts of the list that the children in a known class are already tackling and comparing what has been noted with a colleague who has experience of a different age range to consider what might be barriers to children becoming good readers.	**contextual, textual and pedagogical:** reflecting on the aspects of reading that children bring from their out of school reading contexts, and considering the role of the teacher in providing opportunities for children to develop as readers
	9.2 Range and repertoire: Teacher surveys – individual journal/blog to pairs/group Completing surveys about the personal knowledge of children's texts, comparing the findings with colleagues and considering the impact of subject knowledge of children's texts on the ability to provide a range of reading experiences in the classroom.	**contextual, textual and pedagogical:** developing awareness of the role of a teacher's subject knowledge of children's texts in supporting children's successful progress as readers
	9.3 Children's perceptions of themselves as readers – individual/group Asking some children to complete a reading perceptions survey and using their responses to consider how these perceptions help in assessing the child as a reader.	**contextual, linguistic, textual and pedagogical:** identifying children's achievements as readers as reflected by their self-perceptions
	9.4 Miscue analysis – individual journal/blog In discussion with the class teacher, identifying a reader who is giving cause for concern over reading to carry out a miscue analysis (or running record if the child is very young), and planning some intervention next steps to support the child's reading development.	**contextual, linguistic, textual and pedagogical:** analysing a child's reading in order to identify how best to offer support

Chapter	Activity	Subject knowledge
Chapter 9 Describing and assessing progress in reading	**9.5 Noting achievements in reading – reflective journal/blog to pairs/group** *There are three parts to this Activity.* 1 Watching video footage of one girl talking about her reading, and using Reading Progression Scales in website resource W9.12, to note her achievements in terms of engagement and response. 2 Watching video footage of a group of readers chosen from either 6 to 7 year olds, 7 to 8 year olds or 9 to 10 year olds, noting their achievements and bringing together these observations to consider progress in engagement and response over several years. 3 Observing children in the classroom and noting their achievements on the Reading Progression Scales in order to consider ways forward.	**contextual, linguistic, textual and pedagogical:** analysing video footage of a reader to note achievements in engagement and response Observing groups of readers and using these reflections to note progress over several years Noting the achievements of children in the classroom in terms of Engagement and response in order to consider how to help move these readers forward
Chapter 10 Poetry	**10.1 Memories of poetry – reflective journal/blog to group** Recalling poems, rhymes, jingles, songs from childhood to consider what they offer in terms of rhyme, rhythm and language play.	**contextual:** considering the importance of early experience of poetry in all its forms in childhood **textual and linguistic:** noting the ways that poetic texts of all kinds contribute to an understanding of how language can be used for pleasure and purpose **pedagogical:** relating personal reflections to classroom work
	10.2 Children's perceptions of poetry – reflective journal/blog to group and classroom Comparing children's perceptions of what poetry is with definitions offered by poets and starting to compile a list of what makes a poem a poem.	**contextual:** noting the different ways that poets have defined poetry over the years **textual and linguistic:** considering form, style, vocabulary, rhyme and rhythm in poetry **pedagogical:** starting to establish a sense of poetry as a different and distinct form of text that can cover the range of human experience

Chapter	Activity	Subject knowledge
Chapter 10 Poetry	**10.3 Auditing the poetry provision of the classroom – reflective journal/blog to group** Investigating the provision of poetry texts available in the classroom and making efforts to expand the repertoire. Making opportunities to enjoy poetry every day in the classroom and planning for an extended teaching sequence involving poetry.	**textual:** extending the repertoire of texts in the classroom **linguistic:** playing with poetry in the classroom, enjoying the sound and meaning of a range of poems **pedagogical:** creating an environment conducive to the enjoyment analysis and composition of poetry
	10.4 Close reading of a poem – pairs/group – classroom activity Reading a poem analytically and looking for clues to meaning as a basis for classroom work on poetry analysis.	**contextual:** noticing how experience of other texts or life experiences might inform children's interpretation of a poem **textual and linguistic:** analysis of the different contributions made by form and language to meaning **pedagogical:** developing awareness of how children interpret and appreciate poetic texts
	10.5 Planning and teaching poetry – pairs/whole group Watching videos of Lee, a teacher of 8 to 9 year olds, teaching a narrative poem then discussing his planning and evaluation.	**textual and linguistic:** observing how a teacher focuses on language in a narrative poetry lesson **pedagogical:** planning to teach poetry and evaluate the children's learning
	10.6 Policy about responding to poetry – reflective journal/blog to group Finding out about the school's policy on responding to poetry writing as a basis for drawing up a personal list of ways to support children as they compose and improve poems.	**pedagogical:** adding to subject knowledge about how to promote, support and move children's poetry compositions on

Part Three: Writing

Chapter	Activity	Subject knowledge
Chapter 11 What writing involves	**11.1 Rivers of writing – reflective journal/blog/pairs/group** Making your own 'writing river', noting your writing experiences so far and comparing your writing history with a sound file of three young teachers talking about their experiences of writing at home and at school. Using these insights, noting the classroom implications for teaching writing.	**contextual:** developing awareness of how experiences of writing affect children's attitudes to and confidence with writing **textual and linguistic:** noting the different kinds of written texts in any one person's writing history **pedagogical:** considering how classroom approaches to writing can affect confidence, motivation and achievement
	11.2 Writing diary over a few days – reflective journal/blog/pairs/group Noting all the different kinds of writing you have done over a few days considering how the purpose and the readership for writing might make a difference to the way people write. Adding to notes about classroom implications.	**textual:** noting the different types of writing, audiences and purposes of written texts in any one person's everyday writing repertoire **pedagogical:** adding to awareness of implications for classroom practice
	11.3 Discovering children's perceptions about writing – reflective journal/blog Asking children about their perceptions of writing in the classroom and using the information to help plan for teaching writing.	**contextual and pedagogical:** investigating how attitudes to writing can impact classroom teaching
	11.4 From early mark-making to forming accurate words and sentences – pairs/group Looking at children's writing to observe principles of writing development in the early years. With these notes in mind, considering the writing curriculum statements, and the implications for teaching writing in the early years.	**contextual:** awareness of the principles which govern children's early writing development **textual and linguistic:** learning how children's writing develops into recognisable script **pedagogical:** considering the implications of children's early writing for classroom practice which will foster sound writing development
	11.5 Identifying diverse needs – reflective journal/blog Noting individual children's differences and needs and adding to notes about implications for practice, thinking they might be supported and extended.	**contextual:** drawing on principles about diversity to identify specific needs **pedagogical:** developing expertise about how to plan for teaching a diverse range of learners

Chapter	Activity	Subject knowledge
Chapter 12 Writing composition	**12. 1 The classroom as an environment for writing – reflective journal/blog** Noting how the physical environment in a classroom signals support for young writers and how the 'environment of possibility' affects how children learn to write fluently and with assurance.	**contextual and pedagogical:** awareness of how principles about managing classrooms and teaching affect children's ability to learn to write effectively
	12.2 Children's narratives – individual/ pairs/group Viewing a highly competent 10 year old reading her own story and noticing how she draws on different kinds of experience for her narrative writing, highlighting strengths in her writing and thinking of how she might be helped to improve.	**textual:** noting how narrative reflects a range of experience drawn from texts read and heard, from everyday experience and from the imagination **linguistic:** developing awareness of how children deploy language for specific effects **pedagogical:** applying observations to developing expertise in responding to children's writing
	12.3 Planning to teach story structure – reflective journal/blog to small group Using a collection of stories to plan a forthcoming teaching sequence to teach story structure. These plans can be shared with the group as a useful resource.	**textual and pedagogical:** developing knowledge of a range of story structures and applying this to planning, teaching and evaluating
	12.4 Building a library of non-fiction texts – reflective journal/blog to group Gathering examples of: instructions, non-chronological reports, recounts, persuasive texts, discussion, explanation and evaluation which might be shared as a group resource.	**textual:** building knowledge of different kinds of texts through gathering and sharing resources
	12.5 Gathering and organising ideas – reflective journal/blog to group Noting successful ways to gather and organise information and ideas quickly and efficiently and sharing these ideas with the group to build a repertoire of useful frames, scaffolds and diagrams to use in the classroom.	**textual and pedagogical:** building a repertoire of useful frameworks and scaffolds for writing and planning to use and evaluate them

Chapter	Activity	Subject knowledge
Chapter 13 Spelling and handwriting	**13.1 Our history as spellers – reflective journal/blog/pairs/group** Noting memories of learning to spell and being taught spelling and identifying factors which help and hinder successful learning of spelling.	**linguistic and pedagogical:** developing awareness of how correct spelling can best be developed in the classroom
	13.2 Generating correct spellings using onset and rime – individual/pair/group Using a resource article, generating words by combining different onsets and rimes and considering what this suggests about how children might be helped to generate correct spellings by using the analogies offered by onset and rime.	**linguistic and pedagogical:** adding to awareness of how children can be helped to spell correctly
	13.3 Morphemes – group discussion (very brief) Noting how pronunciation and spelling do not always go hand in hand.	**linguistic:** expanding knowledge of the English spelling system
	13.4 Investigating language – reflective journal/blog to pairs/group Using the examples in the text, developing spelling challenges for the age group you are most familiar with.	**linguistic** and **pedagogical:** applying knowledge of the English spelling system to ways of teaching spelling successfully
	13.5 Handwriting – individual/pairs Writing with your eyes closed illustrates that although vision is important, the essential component of turning a composition into a text is through muscular movement. Considering the implications for teaching handwriting.	**contextual and pedagogical:** understanding how theories of cognitive and physical development affect learning handwriting and applying this to teaching
Chapter 14 Grammar and punctuation	**14.1 Definitions of 'grammar' – reflective journal/blog/pairs** Reflecting on personal views about grammar and memories of being taught grammar and identifying implications for teaching grammar effectively.	**contextual, linguistic and pedagogical:** discovering how attitudes to teaching grammar can help or hinder effective teaching
	14.2 Implicit knowledge about language – individual/pairs A fill-in-the-gaps activity demonstrates that everyone has implicit knowledge of the structures of sentences in their own language.	**linguistic:** learning how implicit linguistic knowledge can be built on for later grammatical development
	14.3 Grammar quiz – individual Completing a grid on the website to identify knowledge – and gaps – about grammatical definitions.	**linguistic:** building a repertoire of grammatical terminology and knowledge

Chapter	Activity	Subject knowledge
Chapter 14 Grammar and punctuation	**14.4 Punctuation – individual/pairs** Working at first individually, then in pairs, to establish current knowledge of punctuation marks and giving examples of their use so that gaps in knowledge can be filled.	**textual and linguistic:** adding to knowledge of how punctuation affects the sense of a text
Chapter 15 Responding to and assessing writing	**15.1 Differentiation – reflective journal/ blog** Investigating how teachers provide for diversity and differentiate resources, activities, support and response as a basis for planning a teaching sequence which pays attention to diversity.	**contextual and pedagogical:** understanding how approaches to differentiation and diversity contribute to effective teaching of writing
	15.2 Reading children's writing like a reader – reflective journal/blog to group Reading children's writing as though it were by a published writer can reveal attitudes to correcting, marking and response which will affect successful writing development and approaches to teaching.	**contextual and pedagogical:** awareness of attitudes to children's writing can help in developing a more productive approach to response to writing
	15.3 Approaches to responding and marking – reflective journal/blog to group Observations (including watching a video) of how teachers' supportive and successful management of the demands of responding to writing contribute to effective time-management and lasting improvement in children's writing. Planning to implement some of these ideas in teaching.	**contextual and pedagogical:** noting teachers' effective practice builds knowledge of a repertoire of response techniques which will genuinely support writing development
	15.4 Noting achievements in writing – reflective journal/blog Selecting two or three children and noting their achievements on the Scale of Progression for Writing in order to consider how to move their writing forward.	**contextual:** building on principles used to make decisions about assessment **textual:** noting the different kinds of written texts and behaviours children have at their disposal **linguistic:** developing knowledge of how children use language to express their own intentions in writing **pedagogical:** developing expertise in making assessments

Chapter	Activity	Subject knowledge
Chapter 15 Responding to and assessing writing	**15.5 Writing miscue analysis – reflective journal/blog to group** Selecting a child whose writing is giving concern and carrying out a writing miscue analysis in order to develop a plan of action to support the young writer's development.	**contextual, textual, linguistic and pedagogical:** using principles about writing development and noting how children use language to compose texts as a basis for building expertise in analysing and planning for more effective writing development
Chapter 16 Multimodal, multimedia and digital texts	**16.1 Analysing the role of different modes – pairs/group to class** Using a complex picture book, annotating double page spreads to distinguish between what the images and the words convey and how the two modes interact.	**textual:** noting the different contributions to meaning made by images and words in multimodal texts **pedagogical:** applying insights from analysis of complex picture book text to classroom activity
	16.2 Critical reading: Magazines – reflective journal/blog to pairs/group to class Using favourite magazines, analysing the advertising to see how popular reading is suffused with persuasive texts. Moving to the classroom, asking children to analyse their favourite magazines.	**contextual:** analysing the ideological content of texts **textual and linguistic:** noting the effects of different kinds of text within a popular cultural text **pedagogical:** maintaining a dialogic relationship with a class based on critical reading
	16.3 Surveying digital and multimodal experience – reflective journal blog to pair/group to class Comparing personal experience and expertise in digital technology with an article about two teachers' experiences as digital technology users. Viewing an internet talk about children's internet use to consider the implications for classrooms. Surveying children's use of multimodal texts at home and at school and considering the implications for the classroom. Creating a personal list of 'Digital Texts I Like' as a resource for later classroom use.	**contextual:** identifying personal strengths in digital technology usage and knowledge of digital texts **textual:** investigating children's expertise in multimodal text usage at home and school **pedagogical:** applying information gained about personal and children's use and knowledge of twenty-first-century technology to plan for teaching
	16.4 Analysing film – pairs/group to class Using a short film clip to consider the contributions to meaning made by sound, camera work, lighting and colour. Asking children to analyse films in terms of how they work as multimodal texts.	**textual and linguistic:** analysing the different contributions made by different aspects of film-making to the effects of the film and building a vocabulary of film language **pedagogical:** applying analytical skills learned to working with children on film in the classroom

ACKNOWLEDGEMENTS

Children and teachers in:

Beam County Primary School, Barking and Dagenham

Broadmeadow Infant and Nursery School, Kings Norton, Birmingham

Colmore Infant and Nursery School, Kings Heath, Birmingham

Greenfields Infant School, East London

Green Meadow Primary School, Selly Oak, Birmingham

Kaizen Primary School, Newham, London

Kings Road Primary School, Chelmsford, Essex

Lansdowne Primary School, Cardiff

Longroad Primary School, East London

Marks Gate Infant School, Barking and Dagenham

Marks Gate Junior School, Barking and Dagenham

Northbury Primary School, Barking

Reddings Primary School, Hemel Hempstead, Herts.

Riverhead Infants' School, Sevenoaks, Kent

Rush Green Primary School, Dagenham

St Mary's C of E Primary Academy and Nursery, Handsworth, Birmingham

St Peter's C of E Primary School, Harborne, Birmingham

St Thomas of Canterbury Primary School, Walsall in the West Midlands

Sheringham Nursery School, Newham, London

Claire Begg, Steve Brown, Daisy, Mandy Cook, Charlie Currier, Charlotte Holland, Emily McIver, Emma Ramsden, Carly Walker and Rachel White, students at Sheffield Hallam University Department of Teacher Education, and Karen Daniels, senior tutor.

Kem Akdeniz, Jane Bednall, Jo Bowers, Leigh Broadbent, Rachel Clarke, Jenny Cooper, Niv Culora, John Davies, Della Dixon, Clare Dowdall, Mark Elvin, Sharon Fell, Abigail Field, Seren Freestone, Corinne Goldstein, Gayle Gorman, Bethan Grimshaw, Donna Hazzard, Jade Hopeton, Noelle Hunt, Kamal Khan, Clare Kavannagh, Stephanie Laird, Caroline Luck,

Gemma Miller, Evelyn Murphy, Karl Nightingale, Dana O'Brien, Stevie Oldridge, Terri Onwochei, Tracy Parvin, Nat Prescott, Ben Reave, Alice Reedy, Rhiannon Rees, Dan Richmond, Sunetra Sharma, Eleanor Smith, Sarah Sword, Ann Tebbutt, Sam Thompson, Peter Washford, Jenny Watson, Ruth Wells, Max Whitehead, Ella Wilkinson, David Wilson, Helen Wolstencroft, Shani Young and Michelle Zylstra.

Helen Hancock for material from *The Primary English Magazine*.

Helen Lucas of the English Association for material from *English 4–11*.

Routledge for material from *Use of Language Across the Primary Curriculum*, *Making Progress in Writing* and *Teaching English Creatively*.

Daniel Elvin for the cover picture.

And particular thanks to Rebecca Kennedy, Carolyn Swain, Jacqui Harrett and Lesley Webb.

INTRODUCTION

I.1   Making connections

Teaching English is commonly separated in curriculum statements into spoken language, reading and writing. This book follows that pattern. However, it is important to remember that all the modes are interrelated and that progress in one mode is supported by development in each of the others. Thus, reading comprehension is fundamentally supported by talk: talking about texts. Similarly, writing is deeply connected to reading. Writers learn from the texts they read and the conversations they have about them. One of the important connections in the book is that between the different language modes.

A second connection is between the global and the local. The material in this book acknowledges that even in countries where English is a national language, most people throughout the world speak more than one language. In addition, populations are becoming more fluid and diverse. This is addressed directly through sections devoted to bilingual/multilingual learners and through examples of texts, case studies, video and audio recordings. Similarly, the globalisation of English means being more in touch with twenty-first century texts and being aware of the importance of multimodality and popular culture. This book and its website reflect the importance of these texts through examples of screen-based literacy, complex picture books, graphic novels and magazines, not just in Chapter 16, which is devoted to multimodal texts in classrooms, but also throughout. But the implications of the internet and the world wide web work at both global and individual levels. Worldwide communication means that individual and cultural identity can be reinforced and developed through connecting with others across the globe. The challenge for teachers is how to use new forms of communication to the benefit of young learners.

A third connection is between the requirements of national curricula, often based on individualistic interpretations of learning, and current work on sociocultural aspects of learning. Focusing solely on individual achievements in the classroom risks missing the important evidence of children's experience and expertise drawn from home and community practices. Home and school experience need to connect if a child's language and literacy is to be fully developed. Again this offers a challenge for teachers to make space for the assets children bring from home to be built on in the classroom.

The material in this book and on the website reflect a view of English and its teaching which is underpinned by some strongly held principles. Some of these are detailed at the beginning of each Part but there are other, overarching principles, founded on a theory of teaching and learning which form the earliest years:

- acknowledges children's existing language and literacy experience and consciously builds on those assets
- creates an environment where learners take an active part in negotiating and organising their own learning
- recognises the importance of all partners in the learning process – families, teachers, adults and children
- values diversity and is culturally inclusive
- sees identity (particularly cultural identity) as central to learning
- has high expectations of children's potential
- offers challenges, but provides models, demonstrations, examples and scaffolds to help children tackle them
- allows for some risk-taking
- values and promotes critical enquiry
- provides opportunities for collaboration, refection and evaluation.

In addition, a commitment to diversity means awareness of children's individual learning and social needs. Again, there are sections which specifically address provision for children who experience difficulties with learning, and throughout there is an awareness that planning for diversity is an essential part of a teacher's professional responsibility. If all children, and particularly bilingual children, are to develop their language skills, and particularly their access to academic forms of language, they need learning challenges that are accessible and scaffolded by inclusive teaching and learning approaches (Gibbons, 2015; Garcia, 2009). The Planning Access Key devised by Bednall *et al.*, of the London borough of Newham EMAS team (2007), is based on researched strategies that make learning accessible for bilingual pupils but are inclusive for all children.

The Planning Access Key for minority ethnic learners

In order for all pupils to reach common outcomes the following strategies need to be embedded in planning:

- High-quality, culturally relevant materials
- Peer support through mixed ability grouping
- Collaborative learning in pairs/groups, e.g. talk partners and investigative tasks
- Speaking and listening integral to activities
- Vocabulary/word/phrase banks developed with pupils
- Teacher/peer modelling of tasks and outcomes
- Repetitive process and/or language
- Opportunities to use first language/home language
- Visual support
- Real objects: props, puppets, etc.
- Graphic organisers, e.g. tables and bar charts
- Scaffolding for reading tasks

- Scaffolding for writing tasks, e.g. writing frames
- Drama and role play
- Clearly identified roles for adults
- Opportunity for all pupils to have a voice
- Opportunity for all pupils to show understanding and learning
- Parental involvement
- Homework that is supportive of the classroom curriculum.

(Based on Bednall *et al.*, 2007)

The British Council's INDIE project (Inclusion and Diversity in Education) is aimed at promoting social cohesion and raising educational standards in culturally inclusive schools. Visit: www.thebigidea.co.uk/project-indie-british-council-promote-inclusion/ (accessed 1 May, 2017); www.britishcouncil.org/school-resources/curriculum-resources (accessed 1 May, 2017).

1.2   Subject knowledge in English

English is a complex 'subject' in that it draws on a range of disciplines, amongst them literature, linguistics, child development, psychology, sociology and cultural studies. This makes it tricky to pin down just what subject knowledge in English might be. However, in its barest essentials, English comprises a study of *texts* (both spoken and written), the linguistic elements that make up longer stretches of text (sub-words, words, sentences, paragraphs/sections) and the *contexts* of their production and use; for example, the historical period, geographical location, the perceived status of the authors and of the texts themselves (think of 'classic' texts and popular cultural texts such as comics). Allied to these are the *processes* through which the texts are composed (the ways in which language is put together to make meaning) and the *products* themselves – the texts. When it comes to teaching English, another strand of subject knowledge comes into play: *pedagogical knowledge* – how teaching and learning work and how different elements of English can best be deployed to help children make progress in English.

So there are four main interconnected strands to subject knowledge in English. These all combine to lead to competence in successful English teaching (Figure I.1).

- *Contextual subject knowledge:* a view of the principles underlying English teaching, and knowledge of the historical, cultural, social and ideological aspects of English and how these can be critically evaluated. Contextual subject knowledge is derived from reading (in books, journals, on screen and online), professional development sessions, investigation, discussion and debate.
- *Textual subject knowledge:* knowledge of different kinds of spoken and written texts, including children's literature, films, information, picture books, plays, poetry, popular cultural texts, etc.
- *Linguistic subject knowledge:* knowledge about how language is put together to make meaning in a variety of ways for different purposes and audiences. It includes knowledge at sub-word level, word, sentence and text level.

- *Pedagogical (teaching and learning) subject knowledge:* knowledge of how the environment of the classroom, how children learn and children's individual strengths, weaknesses and needs combine with the other elements of subject knowledge to promote successful teaching and learning in English. This includes planning to integrate spoken language, reading and writing to support wider learning.

In addition, teachers need to keep up to date with knowledge of national curricula and requirements which affect English teaching. As these change from time to time, this knowledge needs to be updated as national policies are revised.

The material in this book is designed to enhance and develop all these strands of subject knowledge.

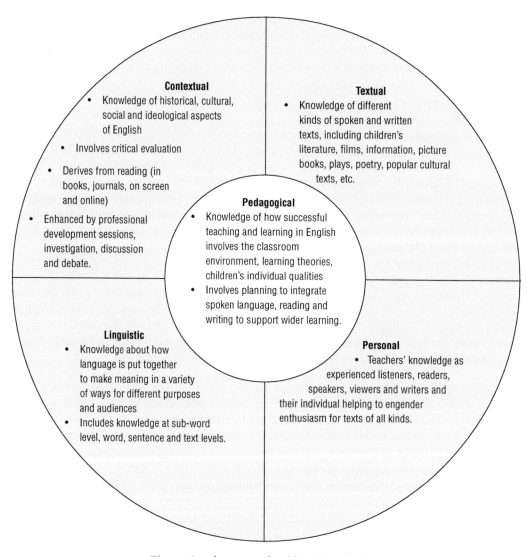

Figure I.1 Aspects of subject knowledge

I.3   Long-term planning for English

A long-term overview ensures that learners are provided with opportunities to develop the stamina and skills to write at length and across a range of text types. Yearly plans for each year group make it easier to check that all text types have been covered in each year. The choice of texts is, of course, up to the teaching team, but it is important to make sure that these are not repeated with any one class, so plans will include indications of which texts (books, films, poetry, information) might be used. However, if the choice of text is just replicated from year to year, the teaching may stagnate, so it is important that staff regularly review the texts they are planning to use and introduce new ones each year. Rachel, a Year 1 teacher, explains:

> Whatever text I use, I've always read it myself and thought, that would be brilliant for my class and so I then *want* to read it to the children. Because I love it, I know the children will and I'm really keen to use it.
>
> (Website resource 4.4 interview transcript, Rachel)

A teacher's own enthusiasm for a text is infectious so that teaching becomes more engaging. It is worth gathering 'Texts I Like' as a resource and talking about them to trainee and teaching colleagues.

    Figure I.2 gives a pared down example of a long-term English plan (see website resource WI.1 for full details of planning in one school).

	Year 1 England and Wales **P2** Scotland and Northern Ireland	**Year 2** England and Wales **P3** Scotland and Northern Ireland	**Year 3** England and Wales **P4** Scotland and Northern Ireland
Narrative	• Traditional fairy tale x 2 • Fantasy • Stories from other cultures • Contemporary x 2 (familiar settings and predictable patterns) • Stories by the same author	• Contemporary • Traditional fairy tale with a twist • Adventure • Fantasy • Stories by the same author	• Traditional (myth/legend/fable) • Adventure • Contemporary • Fantasy • Playscripts • Author study (choice)
Non-fiction	• Instruction x 2 • Non-chronological report x 2 • Recount x 2	• Instruction x 2 • Non-chronological report x 2 • Recount x 2 • Persuasion	• Instruction • Recount • Non-chronological report • Persuasion • Discussion (balanced argument and debate)
Poetry	• Imagery (description) • List poetry • Patterns and rhyme • Poems on a theme	• Imagery (description) • Patterns and repetitive poetry • Poems on a theme • Classic poetry	• Form (haiku, cinquain, limerick, couplets) • Performance poetry • Poems on a theme • Classic poetry

	Year 4 England and Wales P5 Scotland and Northern Ireland	Year 5 England and Wales P6 Scotland and Northern Ireland	Year 6 England and Wales P7 Scotland and Northern Ireland
Narrative	• Traditional (myths/legends) • Adventure • Contemporary • Fantasy • Science fiction • Playscripts	• Adventure (stories from other cultures) • Historical • Contemporary • Science fiction/fantasy • Classic • Author study (including choice and comparison and writing in the style of the author)	• Contemporary/classic • Adventure • Historical • Mystery/horror • Scripts • Author study – contemporary/classic (including choice, comparison and writing in the style of the author)
Non-fiction	• Recount (to include newspapers) • Non-chronological report • Persuasion (including a one-sided argument) • Explanation • Discussion (balanced argument and debate)	• Explanation • Evaluation • Persuasion • Discussion and debate • Recount (including newspapers and biography) • Instruction	• Explanation • Evaluation • Persuasion • Discussion and debate • Recount • Summaries • Non-chronological report
Poetry	• Imagery and description (figurative language, simile, metaphor, onomatopoeia, alliteration) x 2 • Rhythms (patterns, repetitions, structure) • Performance poetry • Classic poetry	• Imagery and description (figurative language, extended metaphor and word choices) • Classic narrative • Form • Free verse • Poems on a theme • Poet study	• Imagery (including extended metaphor) • Classic • Free verse • Poet study

Figure I.2 Long-term English plan

I.4   Planning and teaching sequence: From reading into writing/composition via talk

NB. Although we suggest using the flexible planning format in Figure I.3, the process aligns with any other approach to medium-term planning and teaching.

Figure I.3 (a printable version is available in website resource WI.2) shows the format that will be used throughout the book for medium-term planning. The format shows the flow of any given teaching sequence in English planned for anything between one and four weeks (and sometimes longer). This model of planning and teaching sequences of lessons ensures that:

• reading and writing objectives are linked
• spoken language is planned into the teaching sequence at every stage

- texts are carefully selected to fit the objectives and intended outcomes
- there is a writing/composition outcome(s) which links clearly to the specific objectives identified for each teaching sequence.

This process allows preparation for composition, integrating spoken language, reading comprehension, grammar and the writing process in order to build towards a chosen composition or outcome.

The circles in the diagram indicate three overlapping phases. They are interlinked to emphasise that the process may not be entirely linear, but that certain aspects of the teaching may be revisited; for example, it may be useful to capture more ideas during the shared and supported writing/composition phases, or for more explicit language/grammar teaching and modelling to take place at later stages in the sequence. Similarly, there may be discussion and experimentation whilst capturing ideas.

The planning process

Select the aspect of the range/text type to be taught and the chosen outcomes of the sequence.

Choose texts from a range of traditions and genres which will familiarise the class with text features to be covered. These should include whole texts: novels, short stories, picture books, poetry, DVDs, information texts, etc.

Using the relevant curriculum documents and ongoing assessment of children's achievements:

- identify the key reading objectives to be covered
- select the grammar focus for the work
- link these with key writing/composition objectives
- note the aspects of spoken language that will be covered throughout the sequence.

The teaching process

The teaching process consists of three overlapping phases. The overlap indicates that teaching may not proceed in a straight line, but may revisit certain parts of the process; for example, a teacher may still be capturing ideas well into the final, supported writing phase.

The first phase involves *reading*, *investigating*, teaching comprehension skills, exploring and discussing the characteristics of the chosen text type. This might include viewing and analysing extracts from DVDs, reading novels, picture books or information in digital or book form. The idea is that children should become *familiar* with the features of the text and how to make sense of it; for example, by studying the writer's craft.

Ideas for writing/composition may be *captured* in different ways but in the second phase the class will particularly benefit from responding to the text through spoken language, drama or role-play activities and through writing; for example, through writing in role. The text should be chosen to provide the model for the skills being taught. In exploring the features of the text, the teacher will *explicitly teach* the grammar/language focus, *modelling* its use, *discussing* the effect of the specific grammatical feature on writing/composition, drawing on examples from the chosen text(s) and giving the children chances to *experiment* with its use to enhance their writing.

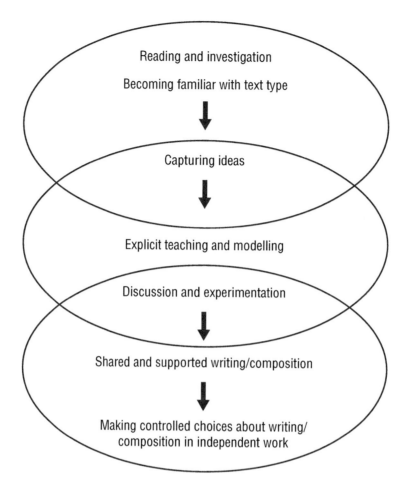

Figure I.3 Planning and Teaching Sequence

Talk, investigation and reflection will be important at this stage, allowing the children the space to explore how to make their writing more effective.

Shared and *supported* writing/composition will then help children in *making controlled choices* as they compose their own texts. Throughout the sequence, but specifically in this phase, the teacher will model different ways to plan; support children as they draft their ideas; teach the skills of editing and proofreading; provide children with real audiences for their writing/composition and opportunities to publish (in the classroom and beyond).

(This planning and teaching sequence builds on Bearne's (2002) Expanded Process for Teaching Writing; Unit planning for literacy, an integrated model by the United Kingdom Literacy Association/PNS (2004) and Reedy and Bearne's (2013) REDM model for teaching grammar in context.)

I.5   Using the material in this book

Although the first three parts of the book focus on the different language modes – spoken language, reading and writing – they are, of course, deeply interrelated. However, we have chosen to keep to the distinctions for the sake of clarity. There are sections of each chapter which deal with background theory and practical applications of that theory. Running throughout the book are the important threads of diversity and inclusion and suggested further reading for those who want to study at a more advanced level.

In each chapter there are activities designed to help you build your subject knowledge. You are asked to keep a journal/blog in which you can jot down reflections, observations and planning tasks. If it is possible, a blog on a protected site would be a very good way to share your thoughts and ideas with others. However, there may be some reflections that you would like to keep to yourself, so you will need to decide whether you keep a handwritten journal/blog, an online journal/blog and/or a shared blog.

References

Bearne, E. (2002) *Making Progress in Writing*. London: Routledge.

Bednall, J., Fell, S., Colura, N., Handscombe, J. and Hewitt, M. (2007) *Developing a Culturally Inclusive Curriculum*. London: Mantra Lingua and Newham EMAS.

Garcia, O. (2009) *Bi-lingual Education in the 21st Century: A Global Perspective*. Oxford: Wiley Blackwell.

Gibbons, P. (2015) *Scaffolding Language Scaffolding Learning: Teaching English Language Learners in the Mainstream Classroom*. Portsmouth, NH: Heinemann.

Reedy, D. and Bearne, E. (2013) *Teaching Grammar Effectively in Primary Schools*. Leicester: United Kingdom Literacy Association.

United Kingdom Literacy Association supported by the Primary National Strategy (2004) *Raising Boys' Achievements in Writing*. Leicester: United Kingdom Literacy Association.

PART 1
SPOKEN LANGUAGE

In every part of this book you will be asked to keep
a journal (or a blog) in which you can jot down reflections,
observations and tasks. There are also recommended
readings to support your learning.

INTRODUCTION TO PART ONE

P1I.1 Principles

The materials in this Part are founded on the following principles:

- Spoken language is the bedrock of children's personal, social, cultural, cognitive, creative and imaginative development. It is a means of thinking through ideas as well as a medium of communication and the most important resource for teaching and learning in and beyond the classroom.
- Spoken language is not only the basis of reading and writing but also has a repertoire of its own which deserves equal attention in teaching.
- The characteristics of effective classroom talk should be understood and deployed by teachers in their own talk as well as planned for pupils to acquire and practise.

The teacher's role is crucial in:

- listening to children and having genuine conversations
- modelling spoken language in all its functions – developing and communicating ideas, analysing, questioning, speculating and hypothesising, reflecting on learning and language
- scaffolding children's use of language and establishing a range of contexts in which children can practise different types and forms of spoken language
- creating opportunities for constructive dialogue between adults and children and between children and children
- planning opportunities for play (particularly in the early years), drama, role play and storytelling
- encouraging active and critical listening
- making opportunities for children to reflect on their own use of spoken language
- developing children's ability to adapt language for different circumstances and listeners
- acknowledging and valuing home language, accent and dialect as legitimate aspects of personal identity and an apt foundation for school-based learning.

Figure 1I.1 Classroom talk

P1I.2   Teaching spoken language

Teaching spoken language has often been seen as more tricky than teaching reading or writing. It seems more of a challenge to describe the different strands of spoken language – the purposes and functions that we use it for; the different audiences for talk; the effects of context on how we speak and listen. Because talk is necessarily transient, it cannot easily be pinned down unless you record it. Then there is the problem of describing progress in spoken language and the question of what the spoken language repertoire includes. Teaching spoken language in school is a complex matter and this part of the book outlines how teachers can help children get better at speaking and listening, and, in improving spoken language, how teachers can respect home language or dialect. It also shows how spoken language is at the heart of good teaching and deep learning.

Even the official terminology about spoken language has shifted and evolved over recent years: *Talk, Oracy, Speaking and Listening* and *Spoken Language. Oracy* (Wilkinson, 1970) is intended to convey something about a range similar to the breadth indicated by the parallel word 'literacy'. *Talk*, used in an educational context, is usually taken to mean the everyday uses of spoken language. It signals, perhaps, some of the less formal elements, and includes listening as a matter of implicit understanding; it has to be there to make spoken discourse work. *Speaking and Listening,* which for some time was the terminology of the national curriculum in England and Wales, refers to a more formalised view of spoken language. Finally, *Spoken Language* denotes the full potential range of oral forms and functions. Since speech is the basis on which literacy is founded, it is clear that spoken language has wide application. It suggests the potential to draw on a wide, diverse and flexible repertoire as well as indicating the social, cultural and individual nature of discourse.

P1I.3   The spoken language curriculum

The following list draws together key ideas from the national curricula of England, Northern Ireland, Scotland and Wales. In planning for teaching, you may want to refer also to a specific national curriculum.

For effective spoken language development, children should be given opportunities to:

- hear good models of spoken language
- speak audibly and fluently
- listen and respond appropriately, adapting spoken language to a wide range of contexts
- explore and discuss features of spoken language; distinguish between formal and informal types of spoken language and know when it is appropriate to use each
- participate actively in collaborative conversations, in groups and class and use the conventions of group discussion
- ask relevant questions to extend understanding to seek information, views and feelings and build a spoken language repertoire
- speculate, hypothesise and explore ideas
- give extended spoken responses to questions, books, poems and visual texts
- articulate and justify answers, arguments and opinions
- give clear descriptions and explanations
- listen and respond to a range of fiction, poetry, drama and media texts through the use of traditional and digital resources
- explore the richness and diversity of language and its personal and creative purposes
- reflect on and explain their literacy and thinking skills, using feedback to refine ideas and sensitively provide useful feedback for others
- engage in a range of imaginative and creative spoken language – for example, drama, role play, storytelling, poetry, presentations, performances and debates.

P1I.4   A note about Standard English

There is no requirement for teaching Standard English in the curricula of Northern Ireland, Scotland or Wales, although formal English is included in some. However, the national curriculum for English in England puts emphasis on this.

Standard English is just one dialect of English. It is the form of English widely accepted as the 'correct' (high status) form and is most usually applied to written forms of language and formal speaking. Standard English should not be confused with variation in dialect or accent according to where someone is born or brought up. Speakers from all over the English-speaking world will be able to speak in Standard English but with variations of accent and vocabulary. All speakers vary the register of their language according to where they are and who they are speaking to – for example, when people talk to friends, they are likely to use a less formal register; when they talk to someone they do not know, they are likely to be more formal.

The National Curriculum for English in England explains Standard English like this:

> Standard English ... is not limited to any particular accent. It is the variety of English which is used, with only minor variation, as a major world language. Some people use Standard English all the time, in all situations from the most casual to the most formal, so it covers most registers. The aim of the national curriculum is that everyone should be able to use Standard English as needed in writing and in relatively formal speaking.

> (DfE, 2017: 95)

Verb forms are important in Standard English, particularly the correct use of the past tense of the verbs 'to do' and 'to be'. The examples given in the English curriculum document are:

> I did it because they were not willing to undertake any more work on those houses. (formal Standard English)

> I did it cos they wouldn't do any more work on those houses. (casual Standard English)

> I done it cos they wouldn't do no more work on them houses. (casual non-Standard English)

> (*ibid.*)

However, there are other sentence variations which are not regarded as Standard English, often in the use of pronouns. For example: *Her's always complaining* (dialect form of *She's always complaining*). In conversation someone might say: *Him and me went shops.* In written Standard English this should be *He and I went to the shops.* But it is easy to notice that this sounds more stilted than the conversational version (see Activity P1I.1).

Ian Eyres (2000) summarises some key points about Standard English:

- Standard English is one of a number of varieties of English, each of which has its own rules and vocabulary
- Variation may be due to social and regional factors (dialect) or governed by context (register)
- Varieties overlap considerably and the differences between Standard and non-Standard varieties can be exaggerated
- There are social and educational advantages resulting from mastery of Standard English
- Learning to read and write is largely a matter of learning to read and write Standard English
- Suppressing non-Standard varieties does not in itself foster the development of Standard varieties (Eyres, 2000: 18).

(For more detail and explanation, see Ian Eyres' book *Primary English* (2000) pages 12–18.)

> **Dialect:** variety of speech differing from the standard or literary language and characterised by local vocabulary, constructions or pronunciations. Dialect forms may differ in syntax from Standard varieties but are internally consistent to that form and perfectly understandable.

Accent: pronunciation specific to a particular person or place.

Register: a variety of a language used for a particular purpose or in a particular social setting; for example, informal or more formal.

Activity P1I.1
Standard English quiz

Try the short quiz WP1 on the website to check out your understanding of what is Standard English and what is dialect/accent/register variation.

References

Department for Education (2017) The National Curriculum in England Framework Document. www.gov.uk/government/publications/national-curriculum-in-england-primary-curriculum (accessed 2 May 2017).

Eyres, I. (2000) *Primary English*. Subject Knowledge Series. London: Paul Chapman/Open University Press.

Wilkinson, A. (1970) The concept of oracy, *The English Journal*, 59 (1) pp. 71–77.

CHAPTER 1
DEVELOPING TALK

This chapter covers:

- Theories of early language acquisition
- The development of bilingual speakers
- Early language in the home
- Language at home and school – supporting the transition
- Language deficit or assets?
  - Case study, middle primary: Finding out about children's home and community language experience
- Supporting language in the early years
- Functions, audiences, purposes and contexts for spoken language
- Children's perceptions about spoken language
  - Case study, early, middle and upper primary: The classroom environment for spoken language
- Spoken language and inclusion

1.1　Theories of early language acquisition

From early in the twentieth century there have been debates about how children acquire their home language, each of which contributes to the more complex view of language development that is held now. The following summary outlines theories of early language acquisition. Chapters 2 and 3 consider language development in school; for example, the use of dialogic teaching to extend language and thought.

Skinner (1957) argued that language is formed by imitation from input provided by the environment and stimulus-response conditioning. So a baby repeats what it sees others doing and, receiving positive feedback in the form of praise, the utterance becomes part of the child's learned repertoire. This view, described as *behaviourist*, sees the learner as an empty vessel to be filled up with language and the process as input–output based on positive reinforcement.

Chomsky (1959, 1968) responded critically to Skinner's views by proposing that human beings have an inbuilt predisposition towards making language. This position, known as *Nativism*, holds that hearing language used triggers a language acquisition device (LAD) which is innate and makes the understanding and production of language possible. A criticism of this position is that it emphasises grammatical construction (syntax) at the expense of recognising the role of making meaning (semantics).

Piaget (1923), *a cognitive theorist*, did not focus exclusively on childhood language acquisition but thought that language and cognitive development proceed in stages, seeing children's early language as egocentric, becoming social later. He argues that children's early physical active interactions put mental schemata in place which provide a framework for language.

In the 1930s, Vygotsky (1962) built on but developed some of Piaget's theories. However, where Piaget argued that the child would have to reach a particular stage to be introduced to the concepts associated with that stage, Vygotsky introduced the idea of a zone of proximal (potential) development (ZPD) where learning triggers a variety of internal developmental processes that can only operate when the children interact with their environment and in cooperation with peers (Vygotsky, 1978). To Vygotsky, language is the tool for such learning (Vygotsky, 1962). In this way, he brings together *cognitive* and *social interactionist perspectives* (before social interactionism was more clearly formulated). Vygotsky's work was not available outside Russia until the 1960s and 1970s when American scholars began to translate and build on his theories and experimental evidence.

Social interactionist theorists stress the importance of the social setting, arguing that children learn to make meaning through conversation with others. Halliday (1975) argues that language has 'meaning potential' and is a cultural resource. The child learns language as part of a community of language users and also learns how to make use of those resources for a variety of purposes in relation to different people and in a range of different contexts.

Bruner (1986) also emphasises the importance of the social and cultural contexts for language but argues (echoing Vygotsky) that most children seem to be able to understand more complex language than they can utter. Bruner developed the idea of a child's language acquisition support system (LASS) in response to Chomsky's LAD. This refers to the support available in the child's social environment which works with the innate mechanisms for language to aid or hold back language development. He emphasises the role of support from more experienced others and the central importance of shared contexts:

> I have come increasingly to recognise that most learning in most settings is a communal activity, a sharing of the culture. It is not just that the child must make his knowledge his own, but that he must make it his own in a community of those who share his sense of belonging to a culture.
>
> (Bruner, 1986: 127)

Wells (1986) carried out extensive analyses of children's and parents' conversations at home, showing how parents expand children's language in authentic conversations which seek to understand what the child is trying to say. In a similar way to Bruner, Wells sees learning a language as about learning the social and cultural values of a language community.

The zone of proximal development (ZPD): a concept developed by the Soviet psychologist Lev Vygotsky in the 1930s. The ZPD indicates the difference between what a learner can do without help and what he or she can do with help. Children follow the example of adults and can be supported until they can work independently, so learning proceeds by working with children at the ZPD. It is closely associated with the concept of scaffolding (see section 2.8).

Language acquisition device (LAD): a theoretical construct developed by Noam Chomsky to explain that the ability to use and develop language is hard-wired into the human brain and enables any child to learn language.

Cognitive: related to conscious mental activities such as thinking, understanding, learning and remembering.

Syntax: the study of the principles and processes by which sentences are constructed in a language.

Semantics: related to meaning.

Language acquisition support system: Bruner's LASS formulation emphasises the importance of the social support network surrounding the child which, together with the child's innate ability to acquire language, helps the development of language.

1.2 The development of bilingual speakers

In global terms, operating in more than one language is normal (Smidt, 2016). Nevertheless, in many Anglophone countries it is more likely that the majority will be monolingual. This has its implications for teaching and learning where teachers may feel stretched in catering for both monolingual and bilingual/multilingual learners. Most theories of language acquisition are based on studies of children who acquire one language, but there are many studies of bilingual children's language acquisition which consider the cognitive and communicative issues related to learning more than one language either simultaneously with or in addition to the home language. Second or additional language acquisition can happen as a result of 'picking up' a language through informal learning. Krashen prefers to use the term 'language learning' as this includes 'conscious knowledge of a second language, knowing the rules, being aware of them, and being able to talk about them' (Krashen, 2009: 10). However, in unfamiliar settings, bilingual learners may spend time in a 'silent period' (*ibid.*) while they are taking in not only the rhythms and cadences of an unfamiliar language but also the behaviours and conventions associated with that language.

Where views on bilingualism some years ago may have been somewhat negative, more recent research, particularly in neuroscience, has clarified the assets brought to learning by bilingual children (Nagy, 2007; Bialystok, 2008). Genesee and Nicoladis emphasise the active resourcefulness of bilingual (or multilingual) children's simultaneous language acquisition, describing it as 'an active creative process that draws on the linguistic, communicative, and cognitive resources of the developing child' (Genesee and Nicoladis, 2007: 339).

In looking at early language acquisition, therefore, it is clear that children developing more than one language do not suffer any cognitive disadvantages compared with mono-lingual children. Whilst urging caution about the comparability of the research methods and samples of children, Cummins and Swain (1998) cite a range of research studies suggesting that bilingual children have greater awareness of linguistic structures than monolingual (Cummins refers to them as 'unilingual') children. Cummins (2001) reminds us that all children who learn additional languages have a common underlying proficiency (CUP) so that skills, ideas and concepts learned in one language will transfer to an additional language.

It is important to remember that, just as with any young language learner, language acquisition cannot be divorced from the culture of the home and community. Cultural identity is a central element in the progress of English language learners (Cummins, 2000, 2016; Smidt, 2016).

> **Anglophone country:** a country where English is the main language used in formal settings.
>
> **Common underlying proficiency:** in learning one language, a child acquires skills and implicit knowledge about how language works (metalinguistic knowledge) that help in learning another language. Such common underlying proficiency forms the basis for learning the first and then additional languages and expansion of the CUP has a beneficial effect on learning other languages. This accounts for why it becomes progressively easier to learn additional languages.

1.3 Early language in the home

The briefest observations of children at home reveal how they take on the language of their community. Even very young babies learn how to 'take turns' in conversations with adults, through gurgles and early 'speech'. Wells (1992) argues that as children develop their spoken language they actively construct their own hypotheses about the way language is patterned and used. If you hear children saying something like 'I runned', they are showing just this search for patterned meaning. They know that in English the regular past tense is made by adding 'ed', so they over-generalise to verbs which later they will notice have irregular forms. They do not think about it in this way, of course, but they do show a predisposition to seek for and follow the patterns (grammar) of language. But children are not just active makers of meaning in terms of acquiring the vocabulary and grammar of their language community. In taking on the forms of language, children also take in the meanings carried by the language – the social and community principles about how life should be lived.

The songs, rhymes, jokes, sayings, advertising jingles and stories encountered by children at home have a profound influence on their facility with spoken and written language as they reach formal education, acting as models for the forms and functions of language children can use for themselves later. Children's play is often a good arena for rehearsals of adult speech. In addition, children learn from popular oral culture – television, films and DVDs, and the internet. It is likely, then, that children will have had a wide range of language experiences before they come to school.

Personal experience is always a good starting point for thinking about language:

> I have always liked talking. I was a very talkative child, I have been told, and did not always stop in school when I supposed to either! I know this talking habit came from having a home where talk was encouraged and a home that had noise. We were a TV watching family; I can remember the very exciting day we had our first one delivered. We would sit down together and watch favourite programmes and then talk about what we saw. The radio was always on in the car or when my Mum was in the kitchen. They were always the music stations that were on in the background. I think this music must have had quite an impact on me because I would then practise them with my cousin – usually Abba songs – and perform them for the family. I also remember being ill from school, curled up with a blanket on the sofa, half sleeping and hearing my Mum and Nan in the same room chatting quietly together so as not to disturb me. To this day I still find it comforting to drift off to sleep or wake up and hear the hum of voices. I still enjoy talking and think my chosen career of teaching has enabled me to use it well.

This teacher's memories draw attention to some of the forgotten aspects of oracy – the social and cultural features. It points to an awareness that talk has an emotional, or affective, function as well as helping structure understanding or add to knowledge.

> I was always a very quiet child, and I'm not very talkative now. It may have been because I was the only child in a big family of uncles, aunts, older cousins and grandparents. When they got together I used to listen avidly and got to know a lot about how the family worked! Because my parents were busy in the shop until quite late in the day and rose early, I spent quite a lot of time reading or watching television. When I look back, it's not surprising that I love soap opera because not only did I watch it on the television, my own family was a bit like a soap opera! I'm still quite reticent in large groups of people, but my friends will tell you I can chat away when there's just two or three of us and I'm perfectly happy to talk with children in the classroom. I'm also quite a good mimic – years of listening to the family, perhaps?

Even this different kind of experience indicates the social and emotional aspects of early language experience. This teacher's reminiscences are a reminder about the value of listening as well as talking.

> **Affective:** related to feelings or attitudes.

Activity 1.1
Early language experience – reflective journal/blog

What can you remember about your own home language experience? Did you hear different languages being spoken? Were there stories, discussions, songs? Jot down as much as you can remember and consider how it might have influenced your language or literacy as an adult. In later activities you will be considering the implications these experiences might have for your teaching. This will help you to support children as they explore the richness and diversity of their own language use. Compare these reflections with the curriculum statements for spoken language on page 53 and identify how home language forms a good basis for developing spoken language in school.

1.4 Language at home and school – supporting the transition

In the 1970s, Basil Bernstein caused some controversy with his theories of elaborated and restricted codes of speaking which he aligned with social class (Bernstein, 1973). He argued that some homes (mostly working class) offer a restricted code of language which is less formal with short phrases, such as 'you know what I mean' interjected to confirm understanding and brief, incomplete utterances. It is suitable for people who share assumptions; it implies rather than explains. Many middle-class homes, on the other hand, present a more elaborated use of language with longer, more complicated sentence structure which does not assume shared knowledge and explains rather than implies. This is more in line with written language and the language of school and has been used to explain educational underachievement by children from lower socioeconomic backgrounds.

Although Bernstein later distanced himself somewhat from a hard and fast distinction between the language of different socioeconomic groups, over the years since his initial research, his ideas have prompted a good deal of discussion and there is still debate today. In 2014, a report by the Office for Standards in Education (Ofsted) in England, commented:

> For too many children, especially those living in the most deprived areas, educational failure starts early. Gaps in achievement between the poorest children and their better-off counterparts are clearly established by the age of five.
>
> (Ofsted, 2014: 4)

Manison Shore (2015) describes how her own classroom research was informed by debates between those who agree with or dispute Bernstein's views:

> I engaged increasingly with the arguments surrounding the impact of poverty and socio-economic status on language presented by Bernstein's critics. With reference to, and in support of Bernstein, Eke and Lee (2009) state that 'in a society organised around social class ... working class pupils,

on the whole, will have access to a more limited range of knowledge than their middle class peers' (Eke and Lee, 2009, p. 9). Meanwhile, arguing against Bernstein's perspective, Tizard and Hughes (2007) make a claim for 'difference in frequency of different types of talk' (Tizard and Hughes, 2007, p. 130) as opposed to the quality of the talk itself. While much of Bernstein's data were collected in a controlled laboratory environment where situations were created as experiments, Tizard and Hughes' research engaged with real life. They observed mothers from both working and middle class families at home interacting with their daughters. The significant difference between the groups was the impact of social class on the sort of conversation that took place between the mothers and their daughters, with Tizard and Hughes claiming that working class children are not speech deficient and working from a restricted code; rather, their subject matter is socially distinct from that of their peers (Tizard and Hughes, 2007).

(Manison Shore, 2015: 99)

Although Tizard and Hughes provide evidence that context and opportunities for genuine conversation make all the difference to children's language use at home and at school, Shore's research indicates significant variance in vocabulary between two groups of children from different socioeconomic backgrounds and she makes the point that the children in the more affluent area had 'the confidence to robustly challenge each other's ideas' (*ibid.*: 103). However, she also notes:

[E]xamining the reactions of the case study children during the interviews, it may be the case that certain resources and choices of activities may favour one social group above another. If so, this has major implications for teachers, raising the question, do children need to be supported to gain access to the vocabulary and the way language is used that is valued in schools?

(*ibid.*: 103)

Cummins (2016) similarly describes some language as 'context embedded' – which includes everyday language – and 'context reduced' – which includes the more academic register of school. He emphasises the need for teachers to help children, particularly those learning English as an additional language, to get to know the difference between the two.

More than sixty years ago, an important educational report was commissioned by the English government. It was wide ranging and drew on the views of many teachers and academics and many of its recommendations were wise and thoughtful. In looking at the home and school experience of bilingual children, the report recommends:

No child should be expected to cast off the language and culture of the home as he [sic] crosses the school threshold, or to live and act as though school and home represent two totally separate and different cultures which have to be kept firmly apart. The curriculum should reflect many elements of that part of his life which a child lives outside school.

(Bullock *et al.*, 1975: para 20.5)

It may be worth considering how far this recommendation of the Bullock Report has been fulfilled in the second decade of the twenty-first century.

> **Ofsted:** the Office for Standards in Education, Children's Services and Skills in England. This is the body which inspects and regulates provision in schools, colleges, universities and children's services.

1.5   Language deficit or assets?

The Ofsted report gives examples of good practice in supporting children's language development in school, significantly, the role of adults in modelling spoken language. But there are dangers associated with views of deprivation. Not all homes which are economically poor are language poor. As with all theories of education, it is important to look at current and relevant research and how it is carried out. Manison Shore's research was conducted in school and Bernstein's in 'neutral' ground. Later, in 1990, when considering teaching and learning, Bernstein argued for teachers having greater understanding of children's home cultures:

> If the culture of the teacher is to become part of the consciousness of the child, then the culture of the child must first be in the consciousness of the teacher.
>
> (Bernstein, 1990: 46)

Such greater understanding often comes from reading, and even better, taking part in, research. Ethnographic researchers, living and working with communities, have offered a window into the home culture of the child (Heath, 1983; Nutbrown *et al.*, 2005). Research carried out in homes and communities offers an alternative to deficit views of children and their home language and literacy (Mottram and Hall, 2009). In the 1980s, Tizard and Hughes (2007) carried out extensive research of children's language in homes and schools. Their book concludes:

> [I]t is time to shift the emphasis away from what parents should learn from professionals, and towards what professionals can learn from studying parents and children at home.
>
> (Tizard and Hughes, 2007: 225)

Moll and his team of researchers (1992) working in Tucson, Arizona developed an approach based on a view of the 'funds of knowledge' which children draw from their homes and communities. In research carried out in England (Cremin *et al.*, 2015), a team of teacher researchers and university researchers explored the 'assets' which children bring from school to home, including their experience of language drawn from digital, television and DVD texts. This more positive view means that teachers can build on what children bring to school if they first take the time to find out what those resources are.

Having an open-minded approach to children's funds of knowledge is perhaps particularly important when considering bilingual children's language assets. Rather than seeing bilingual leaners as a 'problem' in the classroom, Kenner (2000) argues that being bilingual and biliterate is an advantage for learning. Describing one child's potential, she explains:

> Simran reminds me of young bilingual children I have known and worked
> with in primary school. Like their monolingual classmates, they are

fascinated by everyday literacy materials in English, from take-away pizza menus to birthday cards and travel brochures. They also have many literacy experiences at home in other languages, ranging from watching world events on satellite TV in Turkish to reading the Bible with a parent in Spanish. If teachers find out about these experiences and make connections with them in the classroom, they can tap into huge potential for literacy learning in English and other languages.

(Kenner, 2000: ix–x)

Lucas and colleagues (2008) have identified six principles underlying teaching English language learners (ELLs) in mainstream classrooms (Figure 1.1).

---

1   **Conversational language proficiency is fundamentally different from academic language proficiency.**

2   **ELLs must have access to comprehensible input that is slightly beyond their current level of competence and also opportunities to use language for meaningful purposes.**

3   **Active participation in social interaction fosters the development of conversational and academic English.**

4   **ELLs with strong home language (L1) skills are more likely to catch up academically than those with weak L1 skills.**

5   **ELLs will learn more effectively in a safe, welcoming classroom environment that does not generate anxiety about performing in English (L2).**

6   **Explicit attention to linguistic form and function is essential to L2 learning.**

Figure 1.1 Six principles of teaching ELLs in mainstream classrooms

Of course, these principles hold good for monolingual learners, too.

Ethnography: the systematic study of people and cultures.

Deficit view: a view that people from some cultural groups lack the ability to achieve because of their cultural background. It can also suggest that the individual is 'at fault' rather than conditions for learning being unsatisfactory.

Case study, middle primary: Finding out about children's home and community language experience

As part of a research project into the introduction of the *Framework for Languages* (DfE, 2005) carried out in Birmingham and Coventry in 2008–2009 (Bearne and

Kennedy, 2009), Sarah Allen and Emma McGovern, teachers at Clifton School in Sparkbrook, Birmingham, discovered a great deal not only about the children's language but also about their cultural and linguistic identities. Initial language investigations with their middle primary class revealed detailed and important insights and prompted the teachers not only to want to find out more but also to support the children's home languages. They began their research by asking the children to complete (with help if needed) language family trees. They were asked to make notes about the language experience of different members of the family.

From these, the teachers were able to see the diversity and range of the children's language knowledge:

M speaks Somalian and English. He knew some Dutch but has 'lost it' since leaving Holland age 3. His older brother can still speak Dutch. His Mum uses Dutch to communicate with relatives still in Holland. At home, they speak Somalian to adults and English with cousins and siblings. M doesn't have language lessons but he does attend Mosque school, hearing Arabic.

(Teacher, Clifton School)

and

M speaks English and Urdu. Her parents speak English, Urdu and Punjabi. Her two elder sisters speak Punjabi too. M will learn Punjabi soon as she gets older. Her brother (aged 5) only speaks English. There is little literature in Urdu. At home her parents write Urdu to Nan. M speaks Urdu to Nan on the phone. She has lots of fluency in Urdu (want to know more!) and she can speak some phrases in French (taught at this school). I would like to investigate her further in terms of her fluency in reading and writing in Urdu. Would like to involve the TA/Learning Mentor (Urdu, Punjabi and Swahili speaker).

(Teacher, Clifton School)

These discoveries prompted the teachers to reflect on their own understanding of the children's language knowledge:

Our experience from these activities and this knowledge has emphasised the importance of children's home language and rich language knowledge. We are planning to review our curriculum next year, and acknowledging our pupils' backgrounds and home language will be central to this.

(Teacher, Clifton School)

Source: Bearne, E. and Kennedy, R. (2009) *Primary Languages Action Research Group 2008–2009 Evaluation Report.*

This case study shows the importance of the cultural and social aspects of language acquisition, and even if you do not speak a language other than English, you will still have variations in your language use according to where you are and who you are speaking to. Figure 1.2 shows the language experience of Lesley, an early years teacher of considerable experience. Although she comes from a monolingual English background, she has some acquaintance with other European languages. Her family moved around a great deal when she was very young so she had varying language experiences. She is confident in speaking to different groups of people in work contexts and chatty when with friends and in small groups.

Grandparents' generation		
	GM Mother's side GF	'Father's side'
Where were they born? Have they lived anywhere else?	Sheffield, Eyam Birmingham Eastbourne, Pevensey Bay Newbury	North London Grandmother – Dorset
What language(s)/ dialects did they speak?	English (Grandad a bit of Yiddish)	English
What can you remember about them talking to you? Did they tell you stories? Can you remember any family sayings?	Grandmother talked a lot about family history	Grandfather died when I was very small. Didn't see grandmother often. Don't remember any stories
Did they speak differently from you? How?	A few 'old fashioned phrases' e.g. 'She threw her cap over the windmill'	
Parents' generation		
	Mother	Father
Where were they born? Have they lived anywhere else?	Sheffield, Eyam Bakewell, London Aylesbury, Germany Maidstone, Newbury	London, Aylesbury, Margate Germany Maidstone, Newbury
What language(s)/ dialects do they speak?	Learnt German while living there. Spoke French. Slight Yorkshire accent when younger	Smattering of German.
Do your parents/carers tell you stories? Can you remember any family sayings?	Used to tell me Peter Rabbit Stories. Instilled 'responsibility' – Told to stop fighting with my sister.	Reluctantly talked about personal history. Reminisced more as older. Talked about responsibility of being a parent.
Do they speak differently from you?	More cultural references	
Your generation		
Where were you born? Have you lived anywhere else?	Margate, Germany, Maidstone, Newbury, Israel, Bournemouth, Hull, Ormskirk, Sydney, Palmers Green, Newcastle, Wood Green, Tottenham, Wanstead	
What language(s)/ dialects do you speak?	Smattering of school girl French English	
How do you change the way you speak when you talk: • to friends • with someone you don't know?	Yes! Tend to lapse into 'East London' in more informal situations	

Figure 1.2 Language family tree

Activity 1.2
Language family tree – reflective journal/blog

Add to your earlier reflections by completing your own language family tree (download the format from the website resource W1.1). What language assets do you bring from your home to the classroom? For example, have you had experience of hearing a range of different languages/dialects? Have you learned to be a careful listener? Has your family experience led you to be a good storyteller (even of everyday anecdotes)? These can be useful assets in the classroom as you act as a model of spoken language.

1.6 Supporting language in the early years

Language is learned through personally meaningful exchanges, between children and adults and between children and children. Any activities designed to help children develop spoken language should be authentic (see case study 'The classroom environment for spoken language', p. 33) but particularly should involve listening to children and having genuine conversations.

Activity 1.3
Adult intervention in children's language development – discussion

According to Maclure (1992), adults actively, and often spontaneously, induct children into the language patterns and expectations of their communities through:

- **Shaping:** responding to children's attempts at language with more conventional language and phrasing.
- **Sharing:** having conversations about feelings, ideas and experiences.
- **Supporting:** providing children with responses which will sustain conversation but not take over the discourse.
- **Stretching:** asking genuine questions, seeking children's opinions about what they are watching, reading or experiencing.

View the video *Developing Communication* (13 minutes long) on www.tes.com/teaching-resource/teachers-tv-early-language-6085027
(accessed 3 May 2017).

Consider together how the different adults shape, share, support and stretch the children's language. This should help you to understand how authentic conversations, including asking relevant questions, help to extend children's use of language.

1.7 Functions, audiences, purposes and contexts for spoken language

Planning to develop children's spoken language in the classroom will need to take the following into account.

Different functions of language:

- *Social functions of spoken language:* establishing, confirming and changing personal relationships.
- *Communicative functions of spoken language:* helping to shape and share ideas, experiences and feelings.
- *Cultural functions of spoken language:* reflecting home and community language experienced from an early age.
- *Cognitive functions of spoken language:* developing concepts and constructing knowledge.

Different purposes for language:

- *Formative language:* reflective, exploratory and negotiatory talk to help shape and develop ideas – particularly in group work.
- *Informative language:* to explain ideas, knowledge or opinions.
- *Performative, expressive or presentational language:* more 'public' and shaped language to communicate opinions, feelings or what has been learned.
- *Reflective and evaluative language:* 'thinking language' reflecting on learning (and language) and reviewing progress.

Planning will also need to consider how spoken language varies according to audience and context, from informal to more formal uses. For example, you are likely to speak differently in a conversation with the parents of a child in your class from a conversation with your friends or family at home.

1.8 Children's perceptions about spoken language

Children's and teachers' perceptions and expectations can influence teaching and learning spoken language and teachers can sometimes be surprised about children's responses to questions such as: 'Do you think you are a good talker?' and 'Do I like you to talk in the classroom?'

Children aged 6, 7 and 8 years old were asked about their perceptions of themselves as speakers and listeners. A selection of their responses to each of the questions (with spelling and punctuation regularised) shows that they understand a great deal about the social and cultural roots of spoken language as well as knowing about the purposes and functions of talk, the different audiences and the effects of context on how we speak and listen.

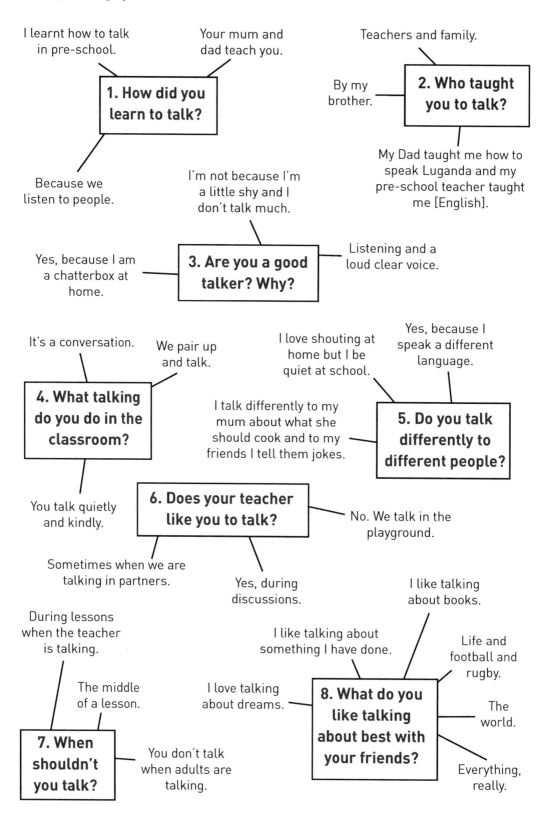

I learnt how to talk in pre-school.

Your mum and dad teach you.

Teachers and family.

By my brother.

1. How did you learn to talk?

2. Who taught you to talk?

Because we listen to people.

I'm not because I'm a little shy and I don't talk much.

My Dad taught me how to speak Luganda and my pre-school teacher taught me [English].

Yes, because I am a chatterbox at home.

3. Are you a good talker? Why?

Listening and a loud clear voice.

It's a conversation.

We pair up and talk.

I love shouting at home but I be quiet at school.

Yes, because I speak a different language.

4. What talking do you do in the classroom?

I talk differently to my mum about what she should cook and to my friends I tell them jokes.

5. Do you talk differently to different people?

You talk quietly and kindly.

6. Does your teacher like you to talk?

No. We talk in the playground.

Sometimes when we are talking in partners.

Yes, during discussions.

I like talking about books.

During lessons when the teacher is talking.

I like talking about something I have done.

Life and football and rugby.

The middle of a lesson.

I love talking about dreams.

8. What do you like talking about best with your friends?

The world.

7. When shouldn't you talk?

You don't talk when adults are talking.

Everything, really.

Even in a very small sample like this, children show that they understand a good deal about purpose, audience and register in talk as well as knowing about some of the behaviours surrounding spoken language. The responses to questions 3, 4, 6 and 7, particularly, might lead the teachers to be more explicit about the kinds of talk they value and the characteristics of 'good' spoken language including the ability, for example, to contribute ideas to a discussion or to explain something clearly.

Activity 1.4
Perceptions survey: Spoken language – reflective journal/blog

Using the perceptions survey format on the website (resource W1.2), ask the class you are working with about their perceptions of spoken language. If the children are young, you may want to scribe for them.

Were there any surprises? Reading through the responses, what ideas do they give you about what you might focus on in teaching spoken language? For example, were there responses which suggest the children think they 'shouldn't talk' in class? Jot down any thoughts so that you can remember them for planning. This will help you to think about how you can allow time for children to have genuine conversations about their learning and to participate actively in collaborative conversations and group discussions. Chapter 2 also gives useful pointers about how to plan for authentic dialogue for learning.

Case study, early, middle and upper primary: The classroom environment for spoken language

Teachers in a suburban primary school decided to make spoken language a focus for their school development plan. They began by taking an audit of their classrooms as hospitable environments for talk. They asked themselves:

- What do I value about the children's talk?
- What are the key features in my classroom that support spoken language (including home languages)?
- How do I provide opportunities for a range of:
  - groupings and audiences for talk
  - different purposes for speaking and listening
  - different kinds of talk
  - levels of formality/informality
  - differences in children's fluency and assurance as speakers?

Their answers to some of these questions led them to take a more deliberate approach to planning for developing spoken language. They decided to tackle classroom provision as well as explicitly including spoken language in their planning across the curriculum.

Figures 1.3, 1.4, 1.5 and 1.6 Role-play area

The teachers of children aged 3–7 agreed to develop their role-play areas so that they could prompt and support specific types of spoken language (Figures 1.3–1.6). They based many of their ideas on books the children were enjoying. In the outdoor area, early years practitioners set up a post office with stamps, a till, envelopes to be addressed and a post box. Drawing on Emily Hughes' book *The Little Gardener* (2015), one class set up a potting shed, with plants and flowers, instructions of how to care for them and how to plant seeds (Figures 1.7 and 1.8).

Figures 1.7 and 1.8 Growing plants

There was paper for observational drawing and website links for the children to look up flowers, herbs and vegetables. Another class set up a pastry shop, based on Mini Grey's *Biscuit Bear* (2005), with bakers' uniforms, table cloths for the café, menus, pads for taking orders, instructions for baking and pretend baking materials and a till with a list of cakes (with pictures) and their prices. Linking with a science topic, where the children had been reading *One Day on Our Blue Planet in the Antarctic* by Ella Bailey (2015) and *Iris and Isaac* by Catherine Rayner (2011), another class set up an Antarctic laboratory/base with white coats, goggles, magnifying glasses and maps. The children made posters of Antarctic animals, observational drawings, maps of where animals have been spotted and tally charts, labelled diagrams, lists of animal facts and logs. In each area the teaching assistant or teacher acted in role, having conversations which extended the children's explanations and in all areas there were notices in the children's home languages.

With the older children, the teachers opted for a range of prompts for a talk corner in each classroom. These included:

● A box for children to make suggestions for topics for group discussion. To avoid the possibility of children posting personal comments, the teacher asked the children to develop their own ground rules. These included a requirement for each discussion group to have a chair and a note-maker, so that over the period of a few weeks everyone in the group had a chance to chair and to summarise. The notes from each group were written up in brief for a 'hot topics' bulletin board which the children could respond to with sticky notes. The teacher modelled making bullet point notes and, occasionally, when a topic was particularly 'hot', the teacher used their preparatory discussions as the basis for persuasive writing.

- A poetry corner with plenty of poetry books and access to the children's poetry archive of recorded poems (www.childrenspoetryarchive.org, accessed 3 May 2017). Each week, one group learned poems for a performance for Friday afternoon.
- An interview corner linked to the school magazine, with iPads, where children could prepare questions and record interviews with each other about their hobbies and interests and with members of the school; for example, the school lunchtime supervisor who ran a five-a-side football team.
- A storytelling area with a big comfortable chair for the teller and beanbags and cushions for the audience. Each week the teacher put a question in the corner and any stories told that week were about that that theme, such as *Can you remember a time when you were very young when you were naughty? What did you do? What happened?*

These activities led to broader discussions of the differences in language used in different settings – at home, work and school.

After trying out these ideas for a term, the teachers evaluated the effects and found that overall the different approaches had been successful in prompting much more spoken language from their classes than before. Inspired by thinking more deeply about variation in spoken language, one teacher of 10 to 11 year olds and the teaching assistant modelled role play of an interview for a job in a bank, demonstrating formal language, then modelled role play of an audition for play where the potential actor could use their dialect to create the character. The children devised similar role plays to explore formal/informal language in relation to audience and purpose.

By celebrating and valuing the children's own language, the staff felt they had a stronger base of knowledge to build on. After this focus on spoken language, the staff felt that they were clearer about the children's achievements in specific types of spoken language and the range of language they wanted to develop in the future.

1.9   Spoken language and inclusion

The diversity of learners

Planning to develop spoken language needs to take account of the different kinds of speakers and listeners in the classroom. They might include those who:

- know when to contribute and when to let others contribute
- are naturally reticent
- help others by explaining things to them

- are bi/multilingual
- are fluent and assured speakers
- can move comfortably from dialect to Standard English reflecting understanding of audience and context
- are not confident about the value of their thoughts and opinions
- find it difficult to process heard information
- are selective listeners
- can listen actively for some time
- find learning generally difficult and do not communicate their ideas with ease
- have intermittent hearing difficulties
- do not seem to be able to control their talk
- have speech impairments
- elect to be silent when upset
- are good storytellers
- have physical or medical conditions which make speech difficult (e.g. cerebral palsy).

It is certainly a challenge to provide for the range but planning and classroom management, particularly organising groups for talk (see p. 85), can help. (For more information and suggestions of how to support children who have additional needs in spoken language, see the Department of Education Northern Ireland booklet *Speech, Language and Communication Difficulties* (2011). See also the Communication Trust at www.thecommunication trust.org.uk/ (accessed 3 May 2017).)

Spoken language and gender

The Raising Boys' Achievement research project (2005) provided evidence of the importance of systematic and clearly planned work on spoken language and identified some specific approaches to speaking and listening which contribute to improvements in boys' literacy. However, the report points out that generalisations about 'boys' and 'girls' 'conceal as much as they reveal' (Younger *et al.*, 2005: 8). Many boys do well at school, both academically and in social and sporting aspects and there are equally some girls who under-achieve academically, socially and in physical activities. They add that 'the 'problem' needs to be carefully contextualised, both in scale and in response' (*ibid.*). One of the main features of successfully balanced classrooms for boys' and girls' achievement was the way teachers included spoken language frequently and systematically in their teaching (Warrington *et al.*, 2006). The teacher's use of language was important:

- *Modelling the language of texts and of learning:* this means not only introducing specific terminology about texts but also consistently modelling ways of approaching texts or ideas. For example, when reading a poem or book, 'I'm wondering why the author chose to use those words'; or in discussing a problem in maths or science, 'What might be a solution?'.
- *Thinking aloud:* teachers sharing their thought processes and giving their own opinions. For example, 'I think this is more effective because...' and 'I can see that working...', 'How might we sort this out?' These more speculative, tentative uses of language are particularly helpful models for group work.

- *Negotiating and collaborating:* the kinds of invitations teacher offer children in open discussion can be very powerful examples for paired or small group exchanges. For example, 'I think it might be helpful if we...', 'Would you like to...?', 'Who might be the best person to do this?'.
- *Asking questions – teachers:* questions from teachers which are work-focused (rather than behaviour-focused) should vary between those requiring a precise response and those inviting reflection or speculation. This can be further supported by the teacher not expecting that everyone will have to answer all the time and providing chances for extended expression of opinion (see p. 49 and p. 53).
- *Asking questions – children:* there are gains in learning when children are encouraged to formulate their own questions about learning and opportunities are created for them to ask questions of each other and the teacher. Teacher questioning acts as a model for children's questions (Warrington *et al.*, 2006, ch. 7).

Activity 1.5
The teacher's role – discussion (pairs or small groups)

Share some of your jottings from the reflective activities in this chapter. After discussion, identify three or four key points to summarise what these reflections suggest for the teacher's role in developing spoken language in the classroom. Compare them with the list below (from page 13) about the teacher's role:

- listening to children and having genuine conversations
- modelling spoken language in different ways
- scaffolding children's use of language
- creating different contexts for children to practise different types and forms of spoken language
- providing opportunities for dialogue between adults and children and between children and children
- planning opportunities for drama, role play and storytelling
- encouraging active and critical listening
- making opportunities for children to reflect on their own use of spoken language
- developing children's ability to adapt language for different circumstances and listeners
- valuing home language, accent and dialect.

Make a note of any areas you feel you still need to concentrate on. Select one or two to develop in your classroom teaching when you plan your next teaching sequence.

Activity 1.6
Observing young children's language: Implications for classroom practice – discussion/reflective journal/blog

Read the background paper on the website (resource W1.3) and the following sections of the Ofsted report *Are You Ready?*: Assessing children's starting points; Working with parents and carers; Adapting provision to children's needs; Developing communication skills (www.gov.uk/government/publications/are-you-ready-good-practice-in-school-readiness, accessed 3 May 2017).

Consider how the views of Tizard and Hughes and Ofsted relate to your own experience of young children's language as you have observed in your classroom or placement school. (If you have not yet been able to observe young children, jot down a few prompts to yourself to focus your observations when you will have the opportunity.) What are the implications for your classroom practice? You may want to refer back to the list of aspects of the teacher's role in Activity 1.5 and your own notes about what you want to focus on.

Summary

This chapter has emphasised that spoken language is social, cultural and communicative and that children bring with them considerable implicit knowledge about language when they come to school. Debates about socioeconomic factors influencing children's spoken language require balance and researched evidence of home and school language experience. It is important that teachers know as much as possible about children's language resources drawn from home, particularly bilingual children's funds of knowledge, and formats offer opportunities for investigation, including surveying children's perceptions about spoken language.

The teacher's role is crucial in planning for effective development of spoken language and for the range of functions, audiences, purposes and contexts for spoken language. Part of this provision is to establish a supportive environment for spoken language in the classroom. In addition, catering for diversity is an essential element in planning for a full spoken language curriculum.

Recommended reading

Cremin, T. and Maybin, J. (2013) Language and creativity: Teachers and students, in K. Hall, T. Cremin, B. Comber and L. Moll (eds) *The Wiley Blackwell International Research Handbook of Children's Literacy, Learning and Culture*. Oxford: Wiley Blackwell, pp. 275–290. A thorough review and discussion of recent research on young children's language drawn from Anglophone countries. **Advanced**

Genesee, F. and Nicoladis, E. (2007) Bilingual first language acquisition, in E. Hoff and M. Shatz (eds) *Blackwell Handbook of Language Development*. Oxford: Blackwell, pp. 324–342. www.psych.mcgill.ca/perpg/fac/genesee/HDBK%20BFLA%20FINAL.pdf (accessed 3 May 2017). Comprehensive analytic review of international research into bilingual children's early language development over the last fifty years. **Advanced**

Maybin, J. (2009) A broader view of language in school: Research from linguistic ethnography, *Children & Society*, 23 pp. 70–78. A challenging read but rewarding because of the scope of the research. **Advanced**

Myhill, D. (2010) Understanding language development, in D. Wyse, R. Andrews and J. Hoffman (eds) *The Routledge International Handbook of English, Language and Literacy Teaching*. Abingdon: Routledge, pp. 216–227. Clear, reflective and based on recent classroom research mostly in the UK.

Richmond, J. (2015) *Talk* in the series *English Language and Literacy 3 to 19: Principles and proposals*. Leicester: Owen Education and United Kingdom Literacy Association. A short booklet which summarises theoretical perspectives, gives case study accounts and outlines implications for the spoken language curriculum in the UK.

Smidt, S. (2016) *Multilingualism in the Early Years: Extending the limits of our world*. Abingdon: Routledge. A highly accessible text that examines the theoretical, ideological and, importantly, the practical issues involved in educating multilingual children.

References

Bearne, E. and Kennedy, R. (2009) *Primary Languages Action Research Group 2008–2009 Evaluation Report* (unpublished report). Birmingham local authority in partnership with Coventry local authority.

Bernstein, B. (1973) *Class, Codes and Control: Volume 1 Theoretical studies towards a sociology of language*. St Albans, UK: Paladin.

Bernstein, B. (1990) *Class, Codes and Control: Volume 4 The structuring of pedagogic discourse*. London: Routledge.

Bialystok, E. (2008) Bilingualism: The good, the bad, and the indifferent, *Bilingualism: Language and Cognition*, 12 (1) pp. 3–11. www.yumingschool.org/wp-content/uploads/2011/07/Bilingualism.-The-good-the-bad-and-the-indifferent.pdf (accessed 3 May 2017).

Bruner, J. (1986) *Actual Minds: Possible worlds*. Cambridge, MA: Harvard Educational Press.

Bullock, A. (chair of panel) (1975) *A Language for Life*. Report of the Committee for Enquiry appointed by the Secretary of State for Education and Science (Bullock Report). London: Her Majesty's Stationery Office.

Chomsky, N. (1959) A review of B.F. Skinner's *Verbal Behavior*, *Language*, 35 (1) pp. 26–58.

Chomsky, N. (1968) *Language and Mind*. San Diego, CA: Harcourt Brace Jovanovich.

Cremin, T., Mottram, M., Collins, F., Powell, S. and Drury, R. (2015) *Researching Literacy Lives: Building communities between home and school*. London: Routledge.

Cummins, J. (2000) *Language, Power and Pedagogy: Bilingual children in the crossfire*. Clevedon: Multilingual Matters.

Cummins, J. (2001) Empowering minority students: A framework for intervention, *Harvard Educational Review*, 71 (4), pp. 649–675.

Cummins, J. (2016) Conference keynote speech 'Individualistic and Social Orientations to Literacy Research: Bringing Voices Together?' at the United Kingdom Literacy Association International Conference *Literacy, Equality and Diversity: Bringing voices together*, 8–10 July 2016.

Cummins, J. and Swain, M. (1998) *Bilingualism in Education: Aspects of theory, research and practice*. London: Longman.

Department for Education and Skills (2005) *Framework for Languages*. http://dera.ioe.ac.uk/5830/13/framework%20for%20languages%20-%20part%202_Redacted.pdf (accessed 3 May 2017)

Department of Education Northern Ireland (2011) *Speech, Language and Communication Difficulties*. www.education-ni.gov.uk/sites/default/files/publications/de/speech-language-and-communication-difficulties.pdf (accessed 3 May 2017)

Eke, R. and Lee, J. (2009) *Using Talk Effectively in the Primary School*. London: Routledge.

Genesee, F. and Nicoladis, E. (2007) Bilingual first language acquisition, in E. Hoff and M. Shatz (eds) *Blackwell Handbook of Language Development*. Oxford: Blackwell, pp. 324–342. www.psych.mcgill.ca/perpg/fac/genesee/HDBK%20BFLA%20FINAL.pdf (accessed 3 May 2017).

Halliday, M. A. K. (1975) *Learning How to Mean: Explorations in the development of language*. London: Edward Arnold.

Heath, S. B. (1983) *Ways with Words: Language, life and work in communities and classrooms*. Cambridge: Cambridge University Press.

Kenner, C. (2000) *Home Pages: Literacy links for bilingual children*. Stoke-on-Trent: Trentham Books.

Krashen, S. (2009) *Principles and Practice in Second Language Acquisition*. www.sdkrashen.com/content/books/principles_and_practice.pdf (accessed 3 May 2017).

Lucas, T., Villegas, A. M. and Freedson-Gonzalez, M. (2008). Linguistically responsive teacher education: Preparing classroom teachers to teach English language learners, *Journal of Teacher Education*, 59 (4) pp. 361–373.

Maclure, M. (1992) The first five years: The development of talk in the pre-school period, in K. Norman (ed.) *Thinking Voices: The work of the National Oracy Project*. London: Hodder and Stoughton, pp. 16–26.

Manison Shore, L. (2015) Talking in class: A study of socio-economic difference in the primary school classroom, *Literacy*, 49 (2) pp. 98–104.

Moll, L., Amanti, C., Neff, D. and González, N. (1992) Funds of knowledge for teaching: Using a qualitative approach to connect homes and classrooms, *Theory into Practice*, 31 pp. 132–141.

Mottram, M. and Hall, C. (2009) Diversions and diversity: Does the personalisation agenda offer real opportunities for taking children's home literacies seriously? *English in Education*, 42 (3) pp. 98–112.

Nagy, B. (2007) The effects of early bilingualism on children's language development. www.academia.edu/10045490/The_Effects_of_Early_Bilingualism_on_Children_s_Language_Development (accessed 3 May 2017).

Nutbrown, C., Hannon, P. and Morgan, A. (2005) *Early Literacy Work with Families: Policy, practice and research*. London: SAGE.

Office for Standards in Education (2014) *Are You Ready? Good practice in school readiness*. London: Office for Standards in Education. www.gov.uk/government/publications/are-you-ready-good-practice-in-school-readiness (accessed 3 May 2017).

Piaget (1923/ 2002) *The Language and Thought of the Child*. London: Routledge.

Skinner, B. F. (1957) *Verbal Behavior*. Acton, MA: Copley.

Smidt, S. (2016) *Multilingualism in the Early Years: Extending the limits of our world*. Abingdon: Routledge.

Tizard, B. and Hughes, M. (2007) *Young Children Learning*. Oxford: Wiley Blackwell.

Vygotsky, L. (trans. 1962) *Thought and Language*. Cambridge, MA: MIT Press.

Vygotsky, L. (1930, trans. 1978) *Mind in Society: The development of higher psychological processes*. Cambridge, MA: Harvard University Press.

Warrington, M. and Younger, M. with Bearne, E. (2006) *Raising Boys' Achievements in Primary Schools: Towards an holistic approach*. Maidenhead: The Open University Press.

Wells, G. (1986) *The Meaning Makers: Children learning language and using language to learn*. London: Hodder and Stoughton.

Wells, G. (1992) The centrality of talk in education, in K. Norman (ed.) *Thinking Voices: The reader of the National Oracy Project*. London: Hodder and Stoughton, pp. 283–310.

Younger, M. and Warrington, M. with Gray, J., Rudduck, J., McLellan, R., Bearne, E., Kershner, R. and Bricheno, P. (2005) *Raising Boys' Achievement: Research report No. 636*. London: Department for Education and Skills. http://webarchive.nationalarchives.gov.uk/20130401151715/www.education.gov.uk/publications/eOrderingDownload/RR636.pdf (accessed 3 May 2017).

Children's books

Mini Grey (2005) *Biscuit Bear*. Red Fox. ISBN 9780099451082
Emily Hughes (2015) *The Little Gardener*. Flying Eye Books. ISBN 9781909263437
Ella Bailey (2015) *One Day on Our Blue Planet in the Antarctic*. Flying Eye Books. ISBN 9781909263673
Catherine Rayner (2011) *Iris and Isaac*. Little Tiger Press. ISBN 9781848950924

Film

BBC Animated Tales. *A Midsummer Night's Dream*. https://vimeo.com/68294795 (accessed 3 May 2017)

CHAPTER 2
SPOKEN LANGUAGE FOR TEACHING AND LEARNING

This chapter covers:

- The essential role of talk in learning
- Teacher/pupil interaction
- The repertoire of teaching talk and its characteristics
- Moving thinking on
  - Case study, early primary: Teachers and children thinking together
  - Case study, middle primary: Maths word problem solving with 8 to 9 year olds
- Constructing productive classroom conversations
- The practical and social context
- The pupils' voices
- Teachers and their responses
- Building vocabulary
- Pupil to pupil talk
  - Case study, upper primary: Exploratory talk
  - Case study, upper primary: Deploying the repertoire of talk
- Children who speak English as an additional language
- A note of caution

2.1   The essential role of talk in learning

> Language is the essential condition of knowing, the process by which
> experience becomes knowledge.

(Halliday, 1993: 94)

At the heart of pedagogy lies oracy. This chapter focuses upon the central role of interaction in learning and the implications for primary classrooms. The chapter goes on to describe the repertoire of teaching and learning talk, including dialogic teaching and the role of spoken language in generating ideas, formulating opinions, and developing and expressing points of view. It argues that, through talk, a teacher builds the ethos of learning in the classroom. Because interaction infuses all areas of teaching in the primary classroom, some of the examples are drawn from subjects beyond English.

Extensive research over half a century has emphasised the importance of talk in and beyond classrooms. As early as the 1960s, the publication *Language, the Learner and the School* (Barnes *et al.*, 1969) was the first serious study to draw attention to the crucial role of talk for learning and the implications for classrooms. Indeed the ability to communicate effectively is fundamental to all aspects of human development; the capacity to think, to learn and, ultimately, to be successful in life depends upon it.

Almost all current thinking about the role of language in learning draws on a social constructive approach. This perspective draws primarily on the social interaction theories of Vygotsky (1978) (see also Chapter 1, p. 20). It suggests that children are competent and capable users of oral and written language. The focus is upon meaning-making and sense-making in the cultural context within which the children operate. This is, in essence, no different from the processes engaged in by adults and there is no set of universal, fixed, developmental stages. What is important is the developing ability to use language intentionally for an increasing range of cultural purposes. The role of the adult/teacher is one of modelling and scaffolding learning. This can be through repeating, rephrasing or demonstrating appropriate language use in different situations. Thus the focus for assessment is based upon purpose and the increasing ability of children to use spoken language effectively in a broadening range of contexts.

Alexander argues that:

> Children construct meaning not only from the interplay of what they newly
> encounter and what they already know, but from interaction with others. In
> turn this interaction is critical not just for children's understanding of the
> kind of knowledge with which schools deal ... but for the development of
> their very identity; their sense of self and worth.

(Alexander, 2008: 11)

As Clay puts it:

> Language ... is a pervasive, persuasive, perpetual fountain of learning – and
> there is no equipment that will give children the interactive experiences that
> will power their progress.

(Clay, 1998: 11)

Clay summarises succinctly the implications for classrooms: language has to be used effectively to promote learning and that this has to be engendered through explicit planning and provision of rich opportunities for groups of people to use talk together. Classrooms and schools are ideal places for learning through focused communication. In addition, Alexander implies, if we do not get it right, we undermine not only development in domains of knowledge but also pupils' own sense of who they are.

The danger is that it is all too easy to assume that if there is a lot of talk going on in classrooms, all is well and effective learning is taking place. However, research is very clear that not any old talk will do. It is not just about encouraging more interaction in classrooms but particular forms. In research into classroom interactions in the period of the National Strategies in England (1997–2011), Smith *et al.* found that:

> Teachers spent the majority of their time either explaining or using highly structured question and answer sequences. Far from encouraging and extending pupil contributions to promote higher levels of interaction and cognitive engagement, most of the questions asked were of low cognitive level designed to funnel pupil's responses towards a required answer. Open questions only made up 10% of the questioning exchanges and 15% of the sample did not ask any such questions ... Only rarely were teachers' questions used to assist pupils to more complex or elaborate ideas. Most of the pupils' exchanges were very short lasting on average 5 seconds and were limited to three words of fewer ... It was rare for pupils to initiate the questioning.
>
> (Smith *et al.*, 2004: 408)

More recently the *Final Report and Recommendations of the Cambridge Primary Review* (CPR) summarises the research on the importance of language in learning:

> The ways in which teachers talk to children can influence learning, memory, understanding and the motivation to learn. Learning and memory benefit when the teacher adopts an elaborative conversational style, amplifying and evaluating what the child says. This elaboration helps children to make sense of temporal and causal aspects of their experiences.
>
> (Alexander, 2010: 289)

The transcript Version 2 of the discussion about *Nothing to be Afraid Of* (see p. 47) shows how the teacher elaborates and extends the children's thinking by suggesting possible effects (causal) of what the characters do, making sure that the children have understood the relationship of events in the narrative (temporal).

The CPR report also points out that:

> Classroom research shows that, in England, teacher-pupil and pupil-pupil talk are under exploited as tools for learning and understanding, and that their potential for much more than transmission is rarely fulfilled ... Talk – at home, in school, among peers – is education at its most potent. It is the aspect of teaching which has arguably the greatest purchase on learning. Yet it is also the most resistant to genuine transformation.
>
> (*ibid.*: 306)

Since the publication of the CPR in 2010 there has been little evidence that the situation described by Smith and the CPR has changed significantly.

What research does indicate, though, is that there are particular kinds of classroom discourse which are more effective in promoting thinking and learning and the features of that discourse can be identified and deployed by skilled teachers.

2.2   Teacher/pupil interaction

Sinclair and Coulthard (1975, 1992) identified the most common type of classroom discourse as following a pattern of Initiation–Response–Feedback (IRF). A typical example of IRF would be a closed question, 'Who is the author of this story, John?', followed by a short response, 'Roald Dahl, Miss', followed by feedback, 'Roald Dahl. Well done John!'. The teacher then moves on to question another child and very little has been achieved by the exchange. Sadly, this limited form of IRF is still a common phenomenon in classrooms.

However, in moving classroom discourse on, there are two key researchers whose insights are worth examining more closely: Robin Alexander and Neil Mercer. Alexander's research provides great insights into the characteristics of effective teacher-to-pupil interaction. Mercer's research is important because it provides significant insight into effective pupil-to-pupil interaction.

Alexander has long argued that the type of talk that goes on in classrooms matters. In his seminal comparative research in five different countries, *Culture and Pedagogy* (2000), and his subsequent booklet *Towards Dialogic Teaching* (2008), Alexander makes a very useful distinction between 'teaching talk' and 'learning talk'. Teaching talk is the interaction between teachers and individual pupils, whilst learning talk is the different kinds of talk (narrating, explaining, justifying, questioning, etc.) that pupils can utilise and develop to extend and deepen learning between themselves (as well as with adults). He identifies five kinds of teaching talk which teachers should have as part of their repertoire:

- *rote* (teacher-class): the drilling of facts, ideas and routines through constant repetition, for example;
- *recitation* (teacher-class or teacher-group): the accumulation of knowledge and understanding through questions designed to test or stimulate recall of what has been previously encountered, or to cue pupils to work out the answer from clues provided in the question;
- *instruction/exposition* (teacher-class, teacher-group or teacher-individual): telling pupils what to do, and/or imparting information, and/or explaining facts, principles or procedures;
- *discussion* (teacher-class, teacher-group or pupil-pupil): the exchange of ideas with a view to sharing information and solving problems;
- *scaffolded dialogue* (teacher-class, teacher-group, teacher-individual or pupil-pupil): achieving common understanding through structured and cumulative questioning and discussion which guide and prompt, reduce choices, minimise risk and error, and expedite 'handover' of concepts and principles. There may, or may not, be a right answer but justification and explanation are sought. Pupils' thinking is challenged and so understanding

is enhanced. The teacher is likely to share several exchanges with a particular child several times in order to move the thinking on.

(Alexander, 2008: 30)

Alexander argues that these forms of teaching talk should be an integral part of a teacher's repertoire but that discussion, and particularly scaffolded dialogue, is the most effective in moving thinking on – the most cognitively challenging. This also gives teachers a good way of assessing whether their interaction has been effective or not: is there evidence that children's thinking has moved on? Alexander's research also found that these latter two forms are less often seen in English classrooms in comparison to central and eastern Europe, and that recitation is the default mode in English classrooms. Therefore the job of teachers is to understand what the different types of teaching talk are, what kind of learning outcomes they lead to and when to deploy them effectively at different times during lessons, including more discussion and, particularly, dialogue.

2.3 The repertoire of teaching talk and its characteristics

Transcripts of classroom interaction offer useful insights into the characteristics of the repertoire of teaching talk. All the transcripts in this chapter were collected by teachers themselves as a way of reflecting on their own teaching talk.

Transcript 1: Nothing To Be Afraid Of by Jan Mark

The following transcript is an excerpt from a Guided Reading session with a group of 8 and 9 year olds. The session objectives were:

To identify the main characteristics of the key characters, drawing on the text to justify views and using the information to predict actions.

Version 1

Teacher: OK. So you think Robin is scared do you? Why do you think that?

Pupil: Cos in the story he's scared

Teacher: Yes. Can you tell me more?

Pupil: Cos he hides under the table and that.

Teacher: Yes, what about when he went to the park?

Pupil: Well, he screams and runs away in the park from the fever pit and his mum said that he was frightened out of his wits because the toilet demons will get him.

Teacher: So that shows he was scared?

Pupil: Yeh.

Version 2

Teacher: OK. So you think Robin is scared do you? Why do you think that?

Pupil: Cos in the story he's scared

Teacher: Yes. Can you tell me more?

Pupil: Cos he hides under the table and that.

Teacher: Yes, what about when he went to the park?

Pupil: Well, he screams and runs away in the park from the fever pit and his mum said that he was frightened out of his wits because the toilet demons will get him.

Teacher: Yes, but right at the end he asks Anthea to go back to the park with him. That means he's not really scared doesn't it?

Pupil: Yes he is really scared because he won't go to the bathroom on his own now and he's chewed his doggy to bits.

Teacher: OK. I'm going to give you some thinking time now to come up with an answer to this problem. If Robin is really scared, why does he ask Anthea to take him back to the park?

(Paired discussion here within the group)

OK, John, what do you think now? Do you think he is really scared, as he still wants to go back to the park?

Pupil: Well, we think that he is scared, but he likes being scared and wants to go back and be scared again. So he is really scared, but it's only Anthea's imagination scaring him.

Teacher: Yes because otherwise why would he want to go back? Anthea might have helped him rather than just scared him. What do other people think?

You will have noticed that both versions start in the same way and that both are unusual as examples of classroom conversations. In each case the pupil says as much if not more than the teacher. Even long after Sinclair and Coulthard's original work, research shows that teachers tend to dominate classroom talk, taking up approximately two-thirds of the time with one-third shared amongst the others present (see Alexander 2008: 14 for a fuller discussion of 'unequal rights to talk'). Additionally, the teacher conducts the conversation with the same child over a number of exchanges: four in the first example and more in the second. This is in contrast with the standard IRF structure of classroom conversations.

However, there is a significant difference between these two versions when considering the learning outcome. In the first example, the teacher's questions are designed to get the child to recall examples from the story that he already knows about. Thus the learning outcome is recalling events in the story. In the second example, the learning outcome is very different and richer. The teacher challenges the child's thinking by citing an event from the story which seems to contradict the child's initial summary of an aspect of one of the main characters. The child sticks to his answer, offering justification. The teacher then gives the child and the rest of the group some thinking time to discuss the conundrum, thus making the problem one which is to be considered and discussed by the whole group. After a short period of paired discussion, the teacher returns to the same child and asks for his thoughts now. The next utterance shows that the child's thinking (and his partner's at the very least) has moved on considerably and has a much more subtle understanding of the situation described in the story; deeper learning is evident, which is not present in the first version even though there is some justification of the initial answer.

The characteristics of this more cognitively challenging teacher talk can be summarised as when the teacher:

- asks a question where there are a range of possible answers
- develops a conversation over two or more exchanges
- asks for justification so that children articulate their thinking
- challenges thinking by making statements as well as asking questions
- gives children thinking and discussion time to consider new or challenging problems/information
- ensures that in conversations children speak more than the teacher and the teacher does not habitually repeat their answers.

The two versions are examples of two of the five kinds of teaching talk identified by Alexander. The first is 'recitation' as it 'stimulates recall of what has previously been encountered' and the second is 'dialogue' as 'pupils' thinking is challenged and so understanding is enhanced'. The key test of dialogue is that there is evidence of changed thinking – that deeper learning has taken place. Thus the second example is an episode of dialogic teaching.

Alexander defines dialogue as having the following principles:

- *collective:* teachers and children address learning tasks together, whether as a group or as a class, rather than in isolation;
- *reciprocal:* teachers and children listen to each other, share ideas and consider alternative viewpoints;
- *supportive:* children articulate their views freely without fear of embarrassment over wrong answers; and they help each other to reach common understandings;
- *cumulative:* teachers and children build on their own and each other's ideas and chain them into coherent lines of thinking and enquiry;
- *purposeful:* teachers plan and facilitate dialogic teaching with particular educational goals in mind.

(Alexander, 2008: 28)

Activity 2.1
Principles of dialogic teaching – reflective journal/blog

Read the second transcript again and note how Alexander's principles are present in the conversation. When you next have a chance to observe in the classroom, make these principles a focus and jot down examples of them in action. Keep these notes as you will be adding to them in later activities.

Another key distinction is the difference between discussion and dialogue. Video 1, section 1 (see website) shows Lloyd, the teacher, orchestrating a discussion where he prompts children to share their ideas and give reasons for their opinions. The different contributions are taken as a basis for later consideration. He then moves to dialogue in section 2 where he guides and prompts the thinking of two of the children.

2.4   Moving thinking on

The following two case studies further demonstrate how the effective deployment of teacher talk can develop thinking and deepen understanding across the curriculum.

Case study, early primary: Teachers and children thinking together

The following transcript was collected from a class of 4 to 5 year olds in the spring term.

    The context was Bath Time. Children are bathing a doll in warm water, after a whole class introduction of the topic when a parent/carer brought in her baby and bathed it in front of the children.

Teacher:	What are we going to do first with this baby?
Child 1:	We're gonna put him in the bath.
Teacher:	Right ok. Shall we put him in face down like that? (*Goes to put baby in bath face down*)
Child 2:	No, no that's bad!
Teacher:	Why, what's wrong, why can't I do that?
Child 1:	He might cry.
Teacher:	I suppose he might cry.
Child 3:	Get water in his eyes.
Teacher:	He could. I wonder if there are any other bits of his face that might get water in them?
Child 2:	His lips.
Teacher:	Ah!
Child 2:	He's gonna open his mouth and then he's gonna get water.
Teacher:	Right ... Do you think he'll be able to breathe with water in his mouth?
Child 2:	No.
Teacher:	Do you know what it is called when you go in water and you can't breathe? (*children look blank*) ... It's called drowning.
Child 3:	My dad done that, went under water.
Teacher:	He went under the water did he?
Child 3:	But he ain't dead.
Teacher:	I'm glad he's not dead!

Child 3:	He was sick.
Teacher:	He was very lucky then, wasn't he?
Child 3:	(*Nods*)
Teacher:	Right shall we put this baby in the bath then?
Child 2:	Put him in face up. So he don't get ... what was that word miss?
Teacher:	Drowned.
Child 2:	Yeah, so he doesn't get drowned.

Case study, middle primary: Maths word problem solving with 8 to 9 year olds

Teacher:	I need 150g of butter, to make one cake. How much butter will I need to make four cakes?
Child 1:	First, you have to, you have to multiply 150 by 4 ...
Teacher:	How do you know it's multiply'?
Child 2:	Because you have to make four cakes,
Child 3:	Yeah, and you need 150g to make each cake
Child 1:	And if you don't know that one, you could use column addition.
Teacher:	Ok, let's see ...
Child 1:	Ok, so if you had 150,150,150,150 ... (*demonstrates using column addition*). Units; zero. Tens; 20 and you put the 2 under there (pointing to the hundreds).
Child 3:	But, you need to put the 2 down there (under the hundreds) so you can add that to the hundreds as well. So then, 1 + 1+ 1+ 1 + 2 is 6. So 600.
Teacher:	OK, which method have you used there?
All:	Column addition.
Teacher:	Good. Can we find an alternative method?
Child 2:	Yes, yes I know ... THE GRID!
Teacher:	(*Teacher repeats the question*).
Child 2:	(*partitions numbers and places into grid*). 4 times 100 – easy 400 ... but wait – I can't do 50 times 4 because that will take ages.
Child 1:	Yes you can use your cheat card – if we know what 4 times 5 is ... 20. Then we can do 4 times 5. Make 20 tens times bigger.
Child 2:	Ah yeah, so now add the two totals together. 600 (*using columns once again*).
Teacher:	Do we agree or does anyone want to challenge?
All:	Yes – all happy.
Child 2:	I reckon there is another calculation we could have used to get to the answer!?

| **Child 1:** | Yeah, I can find out what 2 lots are by doubling. So 150 times 2 is 300, because I know that 15 times 2 is 30. Then I double again, to get four lots. Look so ... I still get to 600. |
| **Child 3:** | Ah, that's well good! Just another way to do it. That's well clever! |

In both these short transcripts the children are actively engaged in working together to make meaning: clarifying and adding to each other's and the teacher's contributions so that the eventual understanding displayed by Child 2 in the first transcript and Child 3 in the second is collectively owned and developed. In both cases the children at their different ages are individually and collectively striving for and clarifying meaning. There is evidence of changes in thinking thus making both effective examples of learning classroom discourse. In the first case study the change of thinking is clear from the last two contributions of Child 2, drawing directly on the clarification that Child 3 has offered: that drowning means going underwater and losing one's life by being unable to breath in water – which is far worse that simply getting lips wet! However, the conversation comes to life when Child 3 enters the conversation and links the classroom discussion to his own life experience. In the second transcript the children come to an understanding that there are different ways of calculating the answer to the problem and are delighted by the discovery.

2.5   Constructing productive classroom conversations

In the transcripts, the way the teacher initiates and shapes the discourse is of crucial importance. The teachers skilfully build the conversations with the pupils and avoid the classic IRF pattern of classroom interaction. Although the teachers are instigating the conversations and directing them, there are some key features that make them more likely to lead to deeper learning:

- The teachers open the conversations with an authentic question which allows for various answers, including those not anticipated by the teacher.
- The conversation is built with individual children over more than one exchange.
- The pupils ask questions and make contributions that add to and clarify their own thinking and that of other children in the group. The thinking is thus collective.
- The teachers vary their responses to the pupils' utterances, asking questions, making statements and inviting the pupils to help develop the collective understanding.
- The teachers respond directly to the content of what the pupil has just said.
- The teachers use tentativeness to invite pupils into the conversation ('I suppose he might...', 'I wonder if...', 'Let's see...'). They are supportive, inviting the pupils to say more ('He went under the water did he?', 'Do we agree...?').
- Both teachers use the pronoun 'we' rather than 'you' when talking to the children. This invites the children to see that they are partners in their learning with the teacher; they are all in this together, including the teacher, not simply there to take note of what the teacher tells them.

Alexander (2008) defines the type of teacher talk most likely to lead to learning as 'conversation with cognitive challenge'. In the above there are proper conversations going on between the pupils and the teachers; they are reciprocal with each building on the content of what went before. In addition, the teachers are skilful in ensuring 'cognitive challenge' ('Do you think he'll be able to breathe with water in his mouth?', 'Do you know what it's called?', 'Can we find an alternative method?'), moving pupils towards new understanding.

2.6 The practical and social context

In the case studies above the talk arises out of a practical context where teachers and pupils are engaged in an interesting shared enterprise and the talk is integral. Both the teacher and the pupils have experience and thoughts to contribute to the collective meaning-making. But the classroom context is more than the activity and the physical space where participants are located. The ethos is also a crucial part of the context. The ethos is created, sustained and encapsulated in the way that the teacher shapes the ongoing conversation with the pupils. As Barnes puts it:

> [T]he communication system that a teacher sets up in a lesson shapes the roles that pupils can play and goes some distance in determining the kinds of learning they engage in.
>
> (Barnes, 2008: 2)

As mentioned above, the teachers use language to include inviting the pupils into the conversation so that they can add to the understanding from their own experience, ask questions of the teacher and each other and articulate their own tentative thoughts without fear of ridicule. In addition there is evidence here of the children initiating new phases in the conversations ('I reckon there is another way...', 'My dad done that, went under water') not simply waiting for the teacher to ask them a question. This shows that the children know that learning in these classrooms is a shared enterprise; they are partners in their learning. This ethos is essential if it is to be a classroom where discussion and dialogue and sustained shared thinking and collaboration are likely to happen.

2.7 The pupils' voices

The Bath Time and mathematics transcripts exhibit the features of what is known as 'sustained shared thinking' (Siraj-Blatchford *et al.*, 2002) where all those involved in the conversation contribute to the thinking and develop and extend that thinking. Neil Mercer (Mercer, 2000; Mercer and Dawes, 2007) termed this 'interthinking'. Interthinking is essentially the joint engagement with one another's ideas to think aloud together, solve problems or make mutual meaning (Mercer, 2000). Pupils are directly involved in adding information and comments to the collective understanding and teachers need to ensure that pupils' voices are heard, listened to and central to the ongoing discourse of the classroom so that thinking is taken forward in the most productive and powerful ways. Video 1, sections 3 and 5 (see website) give examples of children having the space to make extended contributions and ask their own questions.

2.8   Teachers and their responses

Pupils are not simply passive recipients but they do need to interact with experienced adults who know how to scaffold learning. Thus the teacher is:

> [S]omeone who can use dialogue to orchestrate and foster a community of enquiry in the classroom in which individual students can take a shared, active and reflective role in building their own understanding. Seen in these terms, the students are apprentices in collective thinking, under the guidance of their teacher.
>
> (Mercer and Dawes, 2007: 70)

As the transcripts show, effective teachers vary their responses to what children say: asking another question, making a statement, suggesting that others might have some thoughts to contribute, drawing attention to a challenging piece of information and so on. What they do not do is habitually repeat what has just been said, which is common in many classroom conversations.

Scaffolding as a term in education first appeared when Wood *et al.* described how adults interacted with pre-school children to help them solve a problem with building blocks (Wood *et al.*, 1976). Similar to Vygotsky's ZPD (see p. 13), *scaffolding* involves supportive, planned interaction by adults to help children achieve specific goals.

Activity 2.2
Talk moves – discussion pairs/small groups

There has been some very useful research in science regarding responding effectively. The Inquiry project published the Talk Science Primer (2012) identifies four Goals for Productive Discussion and nine associated Talk Moves which teachers and others, including children, can use to achieve those goals when responding to pupils. Visit http://inquiryproject.terc.edu/shared/pd/TalkScience_Primer.pdf and read pages 10 and 11. Think of times when you have observed any of these Talk Moves. Add to your list of observation focuses for when you are next in the classroom. You may need to observe several sessions to identify them.

2.9   Building vocabulary

In the two transcripts, Bath Time and mathematics, both teachers deliberately pay attention to vocabulary building and its use in context. In the first case study the teacher introduces the word 'drowning', which the children then explore and incorporate into their spoken language. In the second case study the participants ensure that the mathematical vocabulary is used accurately in context and ensure that all are clear about which process is being described.

In their summary of research regarding the importance of vocabulary, Lane and Allen (2010) note the strong evidence that vocabulary knowledge is one of the best predictors of reading performance and overall school achievement, and that among students from different socioeconomic groups or with different learning abilities, there is a marked difference in vocabulary knowledge. They conclude that vocabulary must become an integral part of everyday literacy instruction otherwise the gap among groups will continue to widen.

Activity 2.3
Observing dialogic teaching – reflective journal/blog

This activity is in two parts.

1. Read part 2 of Robin Alexander's Dialogic Teaching Essentials here: www.serwis. wsjo.pl/lektor/1316/FINAL%20Dialogic%20Teaching%20Essentials.pdf (accessed 3 May 2017)

How do these practical indicators relate to what you have observed in your classroom or placement school? What are the implications for your own classsroom practice?
    Note one or two ways that you might plan to try out the different kinds of teaching and learning talk to extend your own repertoire.

2. Alexander's article lists the following elements of scaffolded dialogue:

    - interactions which encourage children to think, and to think in different ways
    - questions which require much more than simple recall
    - answers which are followed up and built on rather than merely received
    - feedback which informs and leads thinking forward as well as encourages
    - contributions which are extended rather than fragmented
    - exchanges which chain together into coherent and deepening lines of enquiry
    - classroom organisation, climate and relationships which make all this possible.

Watch Video 1 (Lloyd's lesson) (see website) and notice how Lloyd includes many of these elements, for example, encouraging extended contributions from the children and questions which require more than simple recall.
    Watch the video again, this time without the sound, and notice how the children's body language and general behaviours suggest a positive classroom climate which makes scaffolded dialogue possible. Remember, however, that building this kind of environment in primary classrooms may take some time.

2.10 Pupil to pupil talk

Neil Mercer is the key researcher for identifying the cognitive benefits of talking in groups and the practicalities which should be addressed. Mercer identifies productive talk in groups as 'exploratory talk':

> Exploratory talk is that in which partners engage critically but constructively with each other's ideas. Relevant information is offered for joint consideration. Proposals may be challenged and counter challenged but if so reasons are given and alternatives offered. Agreement is sought on a basis for joint progress. Knowledge is made publicly accountable and reasoning is visible within the talk.

> (Mercer, 2000: 153)

Exploratory talk can operate equally in a whole class setting or in small groups or pairs (Figures 2.1 and 2.2). Mercer forcefully argues (Mercer and Hodgkinson, 2008) that pupils must be explicitly provided with the skills they will need to generate high-quality exploratory talk which is likely to be educationally effective. To do this the first step is to create with each class a set of ground rules for talk which will provide a basis for all their discussions.

Figures 2.1 and 2.2 Pupil to pupil talk

Mercer and Dawes suggest that ground rules which enable exploratory talk should include:

- Partners engage critically but constructively with each other's ideas.
- Everyone participates.
- Tentative ideas are treated with respect.
- Ideas offered for joint consideration may be challenged.
- Challenges are justified and alternative ideas or understandings are offered.
- Opinions are sought and considered before a decision is taken.
- Knowledge is made publicly accountable (and so reasoning is visible in the talk).

(Mercer and Dawes, 2007: 66)

Case study, upper primary: Exploratory talk

The context is an inner-city, multi-ethnic and multilingual classroom of 9 to 10 year olds. In a mathematics lesson the learning objective was to understand the term 'mode' and use it in relation to given sets of data. A group of four pupils are discussing the following word problem:

> Ali's mum wants Ali to stock more lines in his shop. Ali though has only limited spaces on his shelves. This means he can't stock all the pack sizes he had previously. He decides to find the modal size for sales for the last month. Should Ali only stock the modal pack size and why or why not?

Moshin: If the stock runs out he should make more money selling off the pack sizes.

Charlie: I disagree, he should buy the modal packs to get more money because lots of people want that size.

Alisha: Buy what the people want to get, you'll get satisfied customers.

Moshin: I think that because he'll make a lot of money if he sells not just the modal size but the ones that he had.

Charlie: He should sell only the modal pack size and one other size that sells well because then he'll get the most money.

Nene: I don't agree. It's not only the modal pack size that sells. Customers need to be satisfied and buy what they want – other pack sizes too.

Charlie: He should only sell the ones that most people want – otherwise he's only wasting packs if they go out of date.

Alisha: But I still think that some of the customers will come to the shop and won't get what they want.

Nene: Maybe they could decide to get a bigger size pack.

Alisha: But what if they don't have enough money to buy the bigger size?

Nene: Then they could wait and come back with the money they need.

This transcript demonstrates some of the key features of exploratory talk. Pupils engage critically with each other's ideas. They have been shown how the polite use of the sentence starters 'I agree and...' and 'I disagree because...' are very useful in signalling their view of the preceding utterance(s) and then add to the thinking through additional information or justification when putting an alternative view. At the beginning of the year the teacher and class had discussed and agreed their own class version of ground rules for talk and explored words and sentences which would help them implement the ground rules.

In this extract the pupils have not yet come to a collective conclusion; in the end they did not fully agree and thus had to report back that some of them thought that Ali should simply stock the modal pack whilst the others thought he would lose sales if he did not stock some of the other pack sizes. The group had considered critically all the individual opinions and come to a conclusion that they could report back to the whole class in the plenary session. Everyone in the group participated and contributions were respected and built on.

Activity 2.4
Thinking together – discussion pairs/group

Mercer and Dawes have developed excellent teaching resources to support primary age children in developing their own ground rules through the Thinking Together Project. Visit http://thinkingtogether.educ.cam.ac.uk/resources/ (accessed 3 May 2017) and look at the Ground Rules for Talk and Talk Cue Cards and plan how you might use these in a forthcoming teaching sequence.

Case study, upper primary: Deploying the repertoire of talk

In David's class of 10 and 11 year olds the focus text was the narrative poem 'The Malfeasance' by Alan Bold. Two of the learning intentions were to:

- develop an understanding of the poem, both literal and beyond, using inference
- justify inferences and opinions using evidence from the text.

The focus for the development of the use of talk was for the pupils to work effectively in small and large groups, giving reasons for what was said and responding directly to the content of other people's comments. The class had already begun to compile a list of phrases and sentences that they thought were 'useful talk'.

The lesson started with the whole class. The teacher used *recitation* teaching talk to ask the children to recall what they knew about narrative poems and then their agreed ground rules for talk. This then made explicit the knowledge and understanding they would be building on during the session.

The whole class element then continued with the teacher using *exposition* to introduce the children to some possible new ways of expressing themselves when they responded to each other when working independently in their groups which would help their discussions be more productive, particularly when dealing with disagreement; for example, 'Why do you think that?', 'I don't understand what you mean', 'Could you say a bit more?', 'I agree and/because...', 'I think I disagree because...', 'Those are good reasons but I'm not sure about that idea because...'. The pupils then briefly had some thinking time and, in pairs, discussed if they could come up with any more examples.

The teacher explained that the children would be working in groups of four to read and explore the meaning of the poem helped by the following authentic questions:

- What is happening in the poem?
- What is the Malfeasance?
- What lesson is the poet trying to teach us in this poem?

The pupils engaged in *exploratory* talk as they discussed their response to the poem and annotated their A4 copies of the poem with their thoughts about each stanza and/or the conclusions they had come to about the framing questions. The teacher joined some of the groups during this time and deployed *discussion* teaching talk to share her ideas about the poem with the children, but in a way that showed that her ideas were not the 'right' interpretation but a contribution to the developing understanding.

Towards the end of the session the class were brought back together to share their thinking about the poem and their responses to the framing questions. The teacher asked each group in turn for their conclusions and then engaged in *dialogic* teaching talk to challenge their thinking through posing alternative views, returning to the same child to press them to justify their thinking, pointing out contradictions, bringing in other members of the class and asking the children to reconsider their views as a result of what they had heard. Finally, the class and the teacher reflected upon their use of language in their exploratory talk and *discussed* whether they could add further words, phrases or sentences to their list of *useful talk.*

2.11 Children who speak English as an additional language

All the examples in this chapter come from schools where the majority of children are bi- or multilingual. Their teachers have provided opportunities for them to build their confidence and competence in English through carefully managed classroom pairings and groupings and through explicit modelling of the vocabulary and grammar of English. These interventions contribute towards children learning effective ways of communicating.

2.12 A note of caution

The above examples of effective learning conversations between children and between teachers and children should not give the impression that it is straightforward to move away from the traditional 'teacher question/pupil answer' approach. As Alexander noted (see pp. 46–7) (2010: 306) patterns of classroom discourse are very resistant to genuine transformation. One of the key reasons for this resistance is that effective conversations are about the quality of classroom relationships, not a simple strategy for adults to pick up and use immediately:

> The struggle for a dialogic pedagogy is not reducible to a formulaic set of techniques; rather it is concerned with the quality of the human relationship established between a teacher and his or her students, and the limits placed on this by prevailing social circumstances.
>
> (Skidmore and Gallagher, 2005)

But the struggle to transform classroom talk is worth the effort:

> Lessons that encourage and organise pupils to talk about their learning are not easy to teach but, if successful, they are highly stimulating for pupils and teachers alike. Teachers require courage, expertise about how pupils learn and determination to engage in this type of pedagogy, particularly in the most challenging classrooms.
>
> (Coultas, 2007: 1)

Summary

Through looking at the work of significant researchers in classroom talk, and reading a variety of transcripts, this chapter has outlined that effective classroom talk occurs when teachers:

- know what they want pupils to learn (but are flexible!)
- plan contexts that support productive uses of talk – they must encourage participation, building on current learning and be engaging
- ask genuine questions which do not merely require children to guess what they are thinking or recall simple and predictable facts
- expect pupils to provide extended, thoughtful answers
- give pupils time to formulate ideas, views and questions through small and large group discussion
- expect pupils to speak clearly and audibly and do not repeat the pupils' answers.

The language that teachers plan for pupils to use needs careful thought, both about vocabulary and about genre. Teachers need to be clear what language modes are important and how to model and embed them. The language that teachers use when conversing with pupils in classrooms has particular features that lead to teaching and teachers need to understand and deploy the repertoire of teaching talk in different contexts. Listening carefully to pupils' voices and responding to what those voices reveal, lies at the heart of effective teaching and learning. Teachers must encourage those pupil voices to flourish and incorporate them into the ongoing teaching and learning in their classrooms.

Recommended reading

Alexander, R. (2008) *Towards Dialogic Teaching: Rethinking classroom talk*, 4th edn. Cambridge: Dialogos. A short booklet outlining the key components of a dialogic approach to teaching and learning. It includes an overview of international research and practical applications. **Advanced**

Lane, H. and Allen, S. (2010) *The Vocabulary-Rich Classroom: Modelling sophisticated word use to promote word consciousness and vocabulary growth.* www.readingrockets.org/article/vocabulary-rich-classroom-modeling-sophisticated-word-use-promote-word-consciousness-and (accessed 3 May 2017). Drawn from UK classrooms, this is an accessible and practical guide to language use and vocabulary building with young children.

Mercer, N. and Littleton, K. (2007) *Dialogue and the Development of Children's Thinking.* Abingdon: Routledge. The focus in this book is on classroom talk but it is particularly useful about pupil-to-pupil learning conversations. UK based. **Advanced**

References

Alexander, R. (2000) *Culture and Pedagogy.* Oxford: Blackwell.
Alexander, R. (2008) *Towards Dialogic Teaching: Rethinking classroom talk*, 4th edn. Cambridge: Dialogos.

Alexander, R. (ed.) (2010) *Children, Their World, Their Education. Final report and recommendations of the Cambridge Primary Review.* Abingdon: Routledge.

Barnes, D. (2008) Exploring talk for learning, in N. Mercer and S. Hodgkinson (eds) *Exploring Talk in School.* London: SAGE, pp. 1–12.

Barnes, D., Britton, J. and Rosen, H. (1969) *Language, the Learner and the School.* London: Penguin.

Clay, M. M. (1998) *By Different Paths to Different Outcomes.* York, ME: Stenhouse.

Coultas, V. (2007) *Constructive Talk in Challenging Classrooms.* Abingdon: Routledge.

Halliday, M. A. K. (1993) Towards a language based theory of learning, *Linguistics and Education*, 5 pp. 93–116.

Lane, H. and Allen, S. (2010) *The Vocabulary-Rich Classroom: Modelling sophisticated word use to promote word consciousness and vocabulary growth.* www.readingrockets.org/article/vocabulary-rich-classroom-modeling-sophisticated-word-use-promote-word-consciousness-and (accessed 3 May 2017)

Mercer, N. (2000) *Words and Minds.* London: Routledge.

Mercer, N. and Dawes, L. (2007) The value of exploratory talk, in N. Mercer and K. Littleton (eds) *Dialogue and the Development of Children's Thinking.* Abingdon: Routledge, pp. 55–71.

Mercer, N. and Hodgkinson, S. (2008) *Exploring Talk in School.* London: SAGE.

Sinclair, J. and Coulthard, M. (1975) *Toward an Analysis of Discourse: The English used by teachers and pupils.* Oxford: Oxford University Press.

Sinclair, J. and Coulthard, M. (1992) Toward an analysis of discourse, in M. Coulthard (ed.) *Advances in Spoken Discourse Analysis.* London: Routledge, pp. 1–34.

Siraj-Blatchford, I., Sylva, K., Muttock, S., Gilden, R. and Bell, D. (2002) *Researching Effective Pedagogy in the Early Years. Research Report 356.* REPEY Technical Paper. London: DfES.

Skidmore, D. and Gallagher, D. J. (2005) A dialogic pedagogy for inclusive education, *Inclusive and Supportive Education Congress* (Section: Dialogic Teaching). Glasgow, 1–4 August. www.isec 2005.org.uk/isec/abstracts/papers_s/skidmore_d.shtml (accessed 3 May 2017)

Smith, F., Hardman, F., Wall, K. and Mroz, M. (2004) Interactive whole class teaching in the national literacy and numeracy strategies, *British Education Research Journal*, 30 (3) pp. 395–411.

Vygotsky, L. (1930, trans. 1978) *Mind in Society: The development of higher psychological processes.* Cambridge, MA: Harvard University Press.

Wood, D. J., Bruner, J. S. and Ross, G. (1976) The role of tutoring in problem solving, *Journal of Child Psychiatry and Psychology*, 17 (2) pp. 89–100.

Children's books

Alan Bold (1990) The malfeasance, in M. Harrison and C. Stuart-Clark (eds) *The Oxford Book of Story Poems.* Oxford: Oxford University Press. ISBN 9780192760876

Jan Mark (1982) *Nothing to be Afraid Of.* Harmondsworth: Puffin. ISBN 9780140313925

CHAPTER 3

STORYTELLING, DRAMA AND ROLE PLAY

This chapter covers:

- The uses of story
- Stories in the home
- Personal stories
  - Case study, middle primary: Storytelling in the classroom
- Prompts for remembering story structures
- Children telling stories
- Drama and role play
- The teacher's role in improvisational classroom drama
  - Case study, upper primary: Using books as a basis for classroom improvisations
- A note about diversity

If teachers are to contribute imaginatively to the construction of confident and curious individuals, their ability to interest and inspire, tell stories and take up roles in drama, using words flexibly and creatively, deserves development.

(Cremin and Reedy, 2015: 15)

Storytelling and drama share some features but are distinct art forms. Both kinds of narrative experience allow children (and adults) to bring the known world and the world of the imagination together and both can be informal or more formally performed. For both to flourish in classrooms, they need teachers who are ready to be adventurous and who will occasionally tolerate uncertainty. This can be daunting, so it is best to develop storytelling and drama steadily in planned activities.

3.1   The uses of story

We listen to them endlessly, tell them as easily as we grasp them – true or false ones, real ones or make-believe, accusations and excuses, we take them all in our stride. We are so adept at narrative that it seems almost as natural as language itself. We know how to tailor our stories quite effortlessly to further our own ends (beginning with those sly twists that shift the blame for the spilt milk to a younger sibling) and know when others are doing the same.

(Bruner, 2003: 3)

Stories permeate everyday life – to explain, persuade, argue or entertain. These daily narratives often warn, encourage and pass on ideas of 'what we do in *our* family' or in *our* community. Narrative not only plays a part in social and cultural development, but also has an essential role in affective or emotional development, helping to organise feelings and make sense of experience. Hopes, aspirations, disappointments, fears and pleasures are rehearsed and replayed through stories. In their play and reading/viewing, young children use story to wonder about the world, to make hypotheses as they explore the possible worlds of 'what if'. Narrative is central to learning. It occurs in anecdote, gossip and every-day conversation but even these forms pre-suppose a certain ordering and selection of experience to fulfil specific intentions. Telling anecdotes about any incident is not just a re-running of events like an unedited video recording, it is necessarily selective. In these selections, experience is categorised: a cognitive operation which sets mental frameworks for more complex forms of categorising, selecting and generalising experience or facts – the basis for constructing more formal kinds of learning (Cremin *et al.*, 2017).

Cognitive: related to conscious mental activities such as thinking, understanding, learning, and remembering.

Affective: related to feelings or attitudes.

3.2 Stories in the home

For young learners, being able to explore and express narrative meaning comes from experience of hearing and watching stories, playing in role and becoming familiar with particular stories or kinds of stories. These might be shared with family members, watched on video, listened to as story tapes, enjoyed as puppet plays, danced or acted out in drama.

This is one teacher's reminiscences of stories at home:

My Dad was a policeman and, as a very young child, my home was the police house, which was attached to the local police station. Here I would swing on the garden gate and chat with all of the neighbours, passers-by and those who were visiting the police station for one reason or another: I was known for my ability to chat. This skill, I believe, I learned from my Grandmother.

In fact, my most significant early memories are of the weekends I spent with Gran and Grampy. Gran was not only the most phenomenal cook, but her hand-knitted garments were a delight to behold, and I loved wearing her intricately crafted designs. My weekends spent with her were when I learned the most valuable lessons: how to cook, how (not) to knit and, possibly most importantly, how to 'gossip' and interact with people and how to turn the most ordinary events of our everyday lives and family histories into fascinating stories.

While teaching me to weigh out the ingredients for Welsh cakes, or Victoria sponges, Gran would be telling me stories about the people in my family: about my Grampy and how she met him when he was a guard on the railway and she was off on holiday to Fishguard; about the time Aunty Ethel (her sister) and she argued over the swapping over of their faux fur coats; how her brother, Uncle James, became a butcher, opening the first butcher's shop in Bridgend (it is still there!); about my mum when she was a little girl. All of these stories would be told while I would be at the table measuring and she sat by the kitchen fire, knitting: the air would be filled with the crackling of the fire, the rapid ricocheting clickety clack of her needles and the warm tones of my Gran's lilting stories. This wasn't a one sided activity: Gran would want to know about my friends and, when I was old enough, about my school days. Through her questions, she would encourage me to elaborate on the details: to describe the weather, or someone's facial expression, or the tone of voice that was used during a conversation, or how I felt at crucial points, or how someone else might have felt. What Gran taught me was that we all, even the smallest of children, can be storytellers when encouraged and allowed.

Recent research into young children's storytelling and story acting (Faulkner, 2017) shows how early years practitioners and children as young as 3 and 4 co-constructed stories through guided participation (Rogoff *et al.*, 2003) which was accompanied by collective story-making between the children through play. As Vygotsky points out:

Play creates a zone of proximal development of the child. In play a child always behaves beyond his [sic] average age, above his daily behaviour; in play it is as though he were a head taller than himself.

(Vygotsky, 1978: 102)

(See p. 21 for a definition of the zone of proximal development.)

Storytelling, story acting, imaginative play and drama are essential to secure early language and literacy development. However, Wohlwend and Peppler (2015) warn that play is losing out to the demands of standardised measures, particularly in early years class-rooms. Similarly, creativity is in danger of being squeezed out of the primary curriculum because of high-stakes testing (Moss, 2017). Since these activities are not only necessary to children's language and literacy development, but also very enjoyable activities for children and adults, it is important to foster story and imaginative play in all its forms.

3.3   Personal stories

Personal oral stories are as important as fictional oral stories. Storytelling and imaginative play are highly significant to cognitive and affective development during early childhood (Engel, 2005) and personal stories help forge a sense of identity within a social community (Mardell and Kucirkova, 2017).

> Through affording space for children to share their personal stories, teachers demonstrate their respect for individuals and offer them the chance to make connections, reflect upon their lives and enhance their confidence and narrative fluency. As children retell chosen anecdotes and incidents from their lives, they make spontaneous choices about vocabulary, style and language.
>
> (Cremin and Reedy, 2015: 17)

Telling stories in the classroom can be a challenge, so it is worth starting with personal stories before moving on to more rehearsed stories. It is always best to start with something familiar that can be told with gusto, and this is where personal experience is really helpful – memories evoke emotions which can fuel the telling. It is also worth remembering that everyone has experience of telling stories:

> speakers have at their disposal a rich repertoire of resources ... with which to deliver ideas and feelings, which are not available to a writer – rate of speech, pauses, pitch, volume, intonation, forms of articulation (throatiness etc.) and a body language with its repertoire of gesture and facial expressiveness. Even that does not exhaust the possibilities; consider humming and hawing, kinds of laughter and the range of sounds which we call exclamations.
>
> (Rosen, 1998: 156)

Activity 3.1
Anecdote from childhood – pairs/small groups

Think of a time when you were naughty as a child – it might have been eating biscuits when you had been told not to, or playing with an ornament that was delicate. Tell each other about it, but while you're telling it, ask your partner to remember the exact words of your final sentence. Retell your story and ask your partner to notice any differences on the second telling.

Often when people tell these personal anecdotes, they take on some of the features of a more formed story. For example, what was the last sentence you said? It might have been something like: 'and I never did *that* again!' or 'she never trusted me after that.' A tag like that is called a 'coda' (Bruner, 2003: 20) – an evaluation of the significance of the story – which can be found very explicitly in Aesop's fables, but commonly in many traditional stories which often have oral roots.

What about the second version of your anecdote? How did it vary? (If it did.) Often, people find that the second telling has more descriptive detail because the teller does not have to track through the thought process at the same time as telling the story and, anyway, might feel more at ease the second time.

Did your anecdotes involve people other than yourselves as characters in the story? What was the 'critical moment' of the story? It might have been the moment when you stretched out to get the biscuit tin off the shelf, or when the ornament began to topple and, in slow motion, to fall to the ground.

It is clear, then, that even the most everyday anecdote has many of the ingredients of a fully formed story: a beginning, middle and end; characters; a critical moment or story climax; a coda or moral.

You might like to visit www.michaelrosen.co.uk/myfamily_cake.html (accessed 3 May 2017) to see Michael Rosen telling his chocolate cake story/poem. You could use your story and Rosen's poem as a starting point for asking the children to tell their own 'naughty' stories. It doesn't matter whether you work with year upper primary or lower primary, as you have found, telling such stories is not restricted to young children!

Case study, middle primary: Storytelling in the classroom

Telling stories that have been told before can be a feat of memory, but the difference between reading a story and telling one is so powerful that it is worth developing expertise as a classroom storyteller. Ty van Brown and Matthew Friday began storytelling with their class of 7 and 8 year olds which led to them setting up a school storytelling club:

> Before we started teaching, neither of us were (or even dreamed of becoming) storytellers. As for becoming a storyteller, you probably already are one; and you have been for years. You are likely to be amongst the vast majority of human beings who love stories in one form or another (probably predominantly in the form of television or a book), and you have fond memories of stories from your childhood. You may have experienced oral storytelling as delivered by 'professional' storytellers who have mastered the tricks of memory, confidence, and who have the time to develop their storytelling skills. But these skills are innate within you, and as a teacher, you are perfectly placed to harness them within the structure of your everyday teaching role.

How to start 'being' a storyteller

Confidence is the key to starting storytelling, and the main reason many people dare not try. The best way to gain confidence, in the absence of anyone in your school who can share their skills with you, is to take a step-by-step approach. Throughout your own development process, try to observe professional story-tellers at work, especially in museums and libraries.

Start gaining storytelling skills by reading your favourite picture book and elaborating and embellishing the story. Stop every now and again to ask the children to respond to what's just happened, what they would do if they were the character, etc. This will help you to gain confidence in breaking away from prescribed narratives (i.e. what the book tells you should say), and allows your own imagination to work with the children's. It also indicates to the children that storytelling is a 'shared creative process' that they are also involved in.

The inevitable question is: Where do I get stories from? We have collected and adapted some classic tried and tested fables and legends that you can download and use for free from www.matthewfriday.com/storytelling. These have already been re-written for use by those new to storytelling, reduced to their bare structure to aid memory retention. There are also many cheap volumes of worldwide myths and folktales which can be easily found online.

Internalising and remembering stories

If, like us, you have a poor memory, then the key to remembering stories may be to internalise the key events visually. Regardless of what your memory is like, you do not have to remember all the words in the story. Retain the skeleton plot only, and flesh out and embellish the rest with your own words, focusing on the vocabulary and phrases that you would naturally be trying to promote through your teaching.

- At first, pick short stories, until you've built up your technique and confidence.
- Select stories with a plot progression that is logical to you.
- Often, the best stories to tell are the stories you love best (from your own childhood).
- The easiest stories to remember have a small number of characters and a repeating structure. For example, in the West African folktale *The Leopard's Drum* a series of animals (elephant, snake and monkey) try and take a drum from a leopard in order to gain a reward from the sky god. The stages of the story for each character repeat a basic form. Once that form is memorised, the rest is easy!
- Don't worry about remembering description or the dialogue. Just retain the main events and characters; the dialogue can be improvised, and the description pared down or embellished depending on the age of your audience.
- Don't worry about making mistakes, repeating words, getting the wrong character name – all of this can be easily fixed without breaking the 'spell' of storytelling. Children can cope with whole interruptions to a story. And you can always use the children to recap what's happened, through questioning, while you find your place again.

This is an edited version of a longer article 'The Storytelling Club: Bringing literacy to life', from *English 4–11*, Summer 2011.

Recent research into children's storytelling and story acting (Faulkner, 2017) shows how early years practitioners and children as young as 3 and 4 co-constructed stories through guided participation (Rogoff *et al.*, 2003). Collaborations between adults and children in the classroom can support the move towards children's independent story-making.

3.4   Prompts for remembering story structures

Jacqui Harrett gives this advice about prompts for storytelling:

> Ways to remember a story vary from person to person. One of the best ways of remembering a story is to tell it over and over again until it is part of the subconscious memory. Some storytellers depend on keeping a kind of cinematic viewpoint in their minds, while others like to map the main points out or draw pictures and diagrams ... Some storytellers like to use props to help them remember the sequence of events in a story. Props can range from a puppet to the storytelling apron, bag or coat from which various objects connected to the story are produced during the telling. Prompt cards with drawings of the main events may be turned over at appropriate times during the telling of the story ... Although all these items have their uses it must be remembered that the main attributes of a storyteller are voice, eye contact and gesture. Props can be useful but can also detract from the main purpose of the exercise, which is to involve the audience to become *participatory* or *reflective* listeners. Children who are lost in story sit quietly with eyes, and mouths, open when actively listening to the tale unfold.
>
> (Harrett, 2009: 9)

Sometimes, prompts such as story mountains, story hands, story maps, storyboards or flow charts can help keep hold of key events. Objects and artefacts, pieces of fabric, puppets, toys, items of clothing or hats can also act as memory nudges.

Many traditional tales (and modern superhero stories) have a common structure:

- opening (setting the scene)
- build-up (introducing the characters)
- problem (the critical point of the story/the central character is in difficulties)
- resolution (how the central character gets out of trouble)
- ending (and coda).

Of course, there may be events in between the build-up and the critical point of the story and indeed the central character may go through several adventures before getting 'home' but the basic structure helps recall stories based on traditional type tales.

However, one of the main lessons to learn from experience of heard and read stories, is that there is no straightforward formula to telling a story – and no fixed pattern or structure. There are 'linear' stories, problem-resolution stories, circular stories and chain-of-events stories. Figures 3.1 and 3.2 show a how a 5 year old, using a familiar book, and two 10 year olds, making a narrative with the ingredients of a fairy story, drew maps to help them retell them.

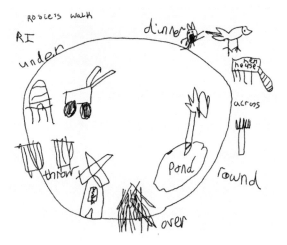

Figure 3.1 Joe's story map of *Rosie's Walk* by Pat Hutchins (2009)

Figure 3.2 Andri's and Louise's map for a fairy story

Knowledge of traditional stories can lead to transformations where, for example, the children might be invited to consider:

- What if Jack's Giant ate something that made him shrink?
- What if Sleeping Beauty didn't like the Prince?
- What would the story of Snow White be like as an episode of a soap such as *Coronation Street* or *Eastenders*?
- What would have happened if the Big Bad Wolf had met Aladdin and wanted the lamp?

Activity 3.2
What is the story? – pairs/small group

Sometimes very short stories can be a vehicle for creating the back story and the resolution and ending. Try this one:

He thought of all the different ways to make it look like an accident.

(hitRECord, 2012)

What questions do you need to ask? Is this a personal story or crime fiction? Between you, using a storyhand (Figure 3.3), create the story that led to this point. Retell the story to the middle point. Individually, decide on how the story will be resolved and how it will end (will all be revealed or will he get away with it?) and tell each other your own versions.

How easy was it to retell the story using the storyhand? What other structures might you have used to help recall the main events?

Figure 3.3 Storyhand

Activity 3.3
Making a story frame – individual/pairs

Listen to the story 'The Fairy Tree' told by Jacqui Harrett (website resource W3.1) adapted from 'Rathlin Fairy Tale' in Liz Weir's book *Boom Chicka Boom* (1995) and draw a map or other frame to help you retell the story. Using your frame, try telling the story. You may be able to tell it to the class you are working with, or at home. If you have the chance to tell the story in the classroom, ask the children to envisage a part of the story that was particularly vivid to them. Ask for volunteers to tell about what they can see. Encourage them to describe it like a photograph or picture beginning 'I can see...'. After several volunteers have offered their pictures, you can organise them into a living narrative sequence and see if the class can fill in the gaps of the story. They might then tell the story themselves in order of their 'mind pictures', each one contributing their own part of the narrative with you prompting and adding details. (This is something you can do with any story.)

How was that experience? Jot down your feelings about telling the story and, if you had a chance to tell it in the classroom, the children's responses. Is there anything you would change if you did it again?

Alternatively (or additionally!) read *The Button Story* (website resource W3.2) which has a different – and, because it is repetitive, easily memorised – structure.

Try telling this, getting the audience to join in with the repeated parts of the narrative and make suggestions about what the tailor might make next.

Again reflect on your experience of telling this story. How might you change it when you tell it again?

3.5   Children telling stories

Carol Fox (1993) collected two hundred invented oral stories told by five children between ages 3 and a half and 5. She notes:

> The children in my study took enormous pleasure in their storytelling. They laugh, mock, make strange sound effects, invent silly or grotesque characters, sing, coin words, relate the bits they like, and play around with story structures. Yet at the same time they work hard to sustain the narrative, to remember what they have already said, to keep up an uninterrupted flow of talk.
>
> (Fox, 1993: 19)

Activity 3.4
What children know about telling stories – individual/pairs

Watch website resource W3.3 where Ben (aged 5) from Lansdowne Primary School in Cardiff tells a story about meeting a stegosaurus on the way to school. What do you notice about how he structures the story? How much of the 'opening, build-up, problem, resolution, ending' structure does he use? Think about how you would respond to Ben's story. What would you praise about it and what would you suggest he might improve for his next story?

In the classroom, children may be able to use the story frames and prompts mentioned in section 3.5, but storyboxes are also a powerful way to support and extend storytelling – and learning – in the classroom. The most usual are boxes which might themselves be attractive and intriguing, with four or five unrelated objects – a key, a magnifying glass, a miniature book, a strange egg (Figure 3.4). Or you can use doll's house furniture packed in a box to create a setting that will have to be peopled with characters who have a story to tell (Figure 3.5).

Figure 3.4 Mystery storybox

Figure 3.5 Doll's house setting storybox

Boxes like these challenge the tellers to construct (often collaboratively) a story using all the objects. However, Bromley (2002) took the idea a step further. She pioneered the idea of designed storyboxes. Her storyboxes contain different objects specifically to encourage children to tell stories which draw on their knowledge in different curriculum areas offering a range of possibilities for learning: cognitive, affective, experiential and textual (see website resource W3.4 for her account of using storyboxes across the curriculum).

Bromley's early work on storyboxes has had wide influence, as a recent project in Medway carried out by Carolyn Swain and Ruth Wells shows. They worked with student teachers to create storyboxes as models for pupils to develop their own (Figures 3.6 and 3.7).

Figure 3.6 Secret garden storybox

You might want to use iPads to capture children's storytelling, or invite the children to use Skype to tell stories for people at home.

There are masses of suggestions for storytelling in *StoryQuest: 28 Ways to Turn Children into Storytellers*, produced by The Prince of Wales Arts & Kids Foundation (find the pdf on www.crickcrackclub.com/MAIN/28WAYS.PDF (accessed 3 May 2017).

Figure 3.7 Fridge storybox

3.6 Drama and role play

Activity 3.5
Personal memories of drama/role play – reflective journal/blog/pairs/group

Jot down any memories you have of drama or role play activities in your own school experience – formal or informal. Note how you felt about participating in these. Discuss your reflections with someone else. Did your experiences or feelings differ?

Between you, add to the list any drama experiences you have observed in the classroom.

As a whole group, make a composite list of these experiences, placing them on a continuum from informal to formal (see Figure 3.8). This continuum represents the range of practices and opportunities that drama offers the learner to make connections between real-life experiences and the world of the imagination and emotions.

This continuum could be copied and added to as you extend your experience of classroom drama and role play.

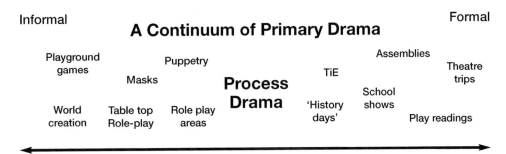

Figure 3.8 The primary drama continuum (Cremin, 2015: 26)

Drama is recognised both as a creative activity in its own right and as a vehicle for learning subject content in different curriculum areas. It has been differently defined:

- 'the art form of social encounters' (Cremin, 2015: 25)
- 'the active and integrated engagement of mind and body, involving imagination, intellect, emotion and physical action' (Franks, 2010: 242)
- 'creative learning' (Neelands, 2011: 168)
- and a multimodal art form which 'makes meanings through the languages of movement, visual images, sound and music as well as thought the spoken word' (Nicholson, 2000: 113).

Wyse *et al.* summarise the value of drama:

- Drama helps children understand their worlds more deeply and allows them an opportunity to find ways to explore and share that understanding.
- Drama promotes an awareness of the self.
- Drama encourages self-expression and focuses the child on the art of communication.
- Although not exclusive to speaking and listening, drama includes a large oral element which allows children to use, practise and develop their language skills, sometimes broadening their vocabulary.
- Drama offers the early years and primary teacher a route into language study that is not covered by any other form of teaching.
- Drama helps children to cooperate and collaborate with their peers. It encourages them also to see themselves in a wider social context and should help them become more sensitive to others.
- Drama allows children to explore and experience familiar and not so familiar situations.
- Drama can help bring a story and its characters alive.
- Drama can invigorate children's writing (Cremin *et al.*, 2006).
- Drama can raise the self-esteem of even the most disaffected of pupils (Woolland, 2010).
- Relationships between the teacher and the child through their shared language are different in drama sessions. Expectations change, negotiated progress is a more prominent feature and there is a greater sense of active participation for the child.
- Drama creates direct links across the curriculum into other areas of study.
- Drama can be highly motivating for children and highly productive for teachers as learning becomes a more dynamic process.
- Drama offers an element of negotiation and unpredictability within the curriculum.
- Drama is an art form which has played a central part in our cultural heritage.

(Wyse *et al.*, 2013: 102–103)

At the heart of drama lies imaginative play but 'play' can be both a noun and a verb; it can refer to a finished scripted object – a play – or to the process of imaginatively exploring situations and ideas – playing. This duality extends to educational drama and the matter of whether it should be seen as a product or as a process (Richmond, 2015). As the continuum in Figure 3.8 suggests, however, process and product need not be seen as opposing ideas, with scripted work and theatre arts at odds with process drama. All forms of drama have their value and creative potential.

Perhaps the most familiar form of classroom drama is improvisational, where children in role, often alongside a teacher in role, imaginatively explore ideas and themes from what they have read, heard or viewed, whether in a designated role-play setting or as a whole class. This is variously referred to as active storytelling (Hendy, 2015), structured improvisation (Greenwood, 2009), process drama (Taylor and Warner, 2006) and classroom drama (Grainger and Cremin, 2001). Whatever the terminology, the sense is similar: that the teacher will structure and support the explorations of children as they enter imaginary worlds and relate those worlds to their own living experience.

3.7 The teacher's role in improvisational classroom drama

Improvisational classroom drama, where children and teacher together explore ideas and issues, can be a challenge for some teachers and a great pleasure to others, but it has a key role in helping children enter into imaginative empathy and explore wider words and understandings. However, the teacher has a key role to play, not only in setting up the possibilities of the drama by creating imaginative and interactive role-play areas and situations but also as Teacher in Role (TIR), improvising and exploring issues alongside the children. Improvisational drama, aided by TIR helps children to dig deeper into the book, film or information text they are working with. TIR allows for posing problems in an imaginative way, inviting children to discuss and attempt to solve the dilemma. The teacher can adopt a low-status role as well as a high-status one and contribute to the drama in different ways (Cremin and Pickard, 2009: 7).

Setting up possibilities for role play and TIR is equally important for the upper primary age range as for younger children.

Conventions for classroom improvisational drama include:

Decision alley
Forum theatre
Group sculpture
Improvisation: Small group
Mantle of the expert
Role on the wall
Thought tracking

Drawing
Freeze frame
Hot seating
Improvisation: Whole class
Overheard conversations
Teacher in Role
Writing in role

See website resource W3.5 for fuller explanations of these but to see some of them in action, watch www.youtube.com/watch?v=qkaCtuJBD5A (accessed 3 May 2017) which shows how Louise Blakemore, a Year 6 teacher, probes the deeper meanings of *The Green Children* by Kevin Crossley Holland (1997) using some of these conventions.

Activity 3.6
Opportunities for role play – pairs

Jot down the different role-play areas/scenarios you have seen in classrooms you have visited or worked in. Add to this list by noting books you have read with the class or have seen teachers using and identifying the possibilities they offer for role play. Teresa Cremin (2015) suggests that role-play settings can be real-world settings, imaginary or fantasy settings or fictional settings.

Using the chart in website resource W3.6, note your ideas and begin to list the kinds of resources: objects, artefacts or clothes that might be used in the setting. Leave the third column blank for the moment.

Case study, upper primary: Using books as a basis for classroom improvisations

Tension, uncertainty and ambiguity trigger the 'electricity' of drama, and demand the children's involvement, prompting them to respond to the situation in which they find themselves without knowing where it will take them.

(Grainger, 2003: 114)

Roger McDonald used a complex picture book *The Watertower* by Gary Crew (1999) to take steps into uncertainty and ambiguity. This extract describes the beginning of a longer teaching sequence using the book:

The children were aged 10–11. It was the afternoon; the class had just come in from lunch. The blinds were pulled down and the front lights in the classroom turned off. So from the outset there was an air of mystery in the classroom. I introduced the complex picture book *The Watertower* and read the first few pages to the class. The children took part in freeze frames and role-play all designed to immerse the children in the story and leave questions in their minds. The front matter of the book suggests a mystery about the tower, describing it as 'casting a long, dark shadow across the valley'. The first two double page spreads set the scene for the boys' adventure, with Spike saying, 'My mother says it's dangerous up there.' The class role played the conversation Spike had with his mother who was adamant that he should never venture up towards the watertower. Through the role play children were involved in creating many suggestions for why the tower was out of bounds. The barbed wire fence which had once stood forcefully around the tower is now lying twisted and broken on the ground. The children's freeze frames explored the moment that the fence came down. Some children imagined people trying to break in, such as vandals, police or the water board. Others imagined that the wreckage was caused by someone or something trying to get out. The foundations of intrigue and mystery had been laid in the children's minds which drove them forward to wanting and needing to solve the problem.

Adapted from Roger McDonald 'Windows to the imagination: The power of drama in developing children's imagination', *English 4–11*, Autumn 2006.

Activity 3.7
Scenarios and problems for role play – pairs/group

Return to your list of possible scenarios for role play (website resource W3.6) and add possible characters and problems that might be introduced into the role-play setting. Any of these might offer possibilities for TIR; for example, a worried dog owner who says the medicine isn't working, an explorer who wants to steal the dragon's eggs, or a town councillor who fears that soldiers will arrest anyone who opposes them.

   When you have completed your charts, share them with the group and arrange for them to be copied as a future resource.

In website resource W3.7 Roger McDonald suggests ways of using another picture book, this time with a younger age range.

Activity 3.8
Finding resources for storytelling and drama – individual to group

Many picture books (for all ages) are good starting points for both storytelling and drama; for example, *The Arrival* by Shaun Tan (2014), a wordless, but very detailed story about emigration, is suitable for upper primary. Similarly, the beautifully illustrated and poignant book *The Journey* by Francesca Sanna (2016) allows discussion of identity and removal from one's home. *Mirror*, by Jeannie Baker (2010), a beautiful picture book with two narratives, one starting from the front of the book and the other from the back, each from the point of view of a young boy, one in Australia, the other in Morocco – for middle-upper primary. For the early years:

- *So Much!* by Trish Cooke and Helen Oxenbury (2008)
- *The Great Big Book of Families* by Mary Hoffman and Ros Asquith (2010)
- *Just Imagine* by Pippa Goodheart and Nick Sharratt (2013)
- *Last Stop on Market Street* by Matt de la Peña and Christian Robinson (2017).

These all provide excellent springboards for story or drama and also provide plenty of stimulus for drama and role play.

   Website resource W5.4 suggests beginning a list of 'Texts I Like' that you might want to use with your classes. You might start by noting some books you think would be suitable for storytelling and drama.

Drama can also enhance understanding of poetry. See Video 2 section 4 (see website) where Lee uses freeze framing to help the class identify the different parts of a narrative poem.

Spend some time at a local bookshop (find an independent one if you can because they often have a wider range of books) or library and select two picture books that you think would be useful starting points for storytelling or drama. Bring them back to the group and start a group list. Add to this whenever you can.

Search the web for storytelling videos. You might already have some favourite authors/poets to guide your search but the more you look, the more you find. Share what you've found to build up a group resource.

Jan Blake is a compelling storyteller. Find her on the web or see her telling *The Leopard Woman* on www.youtube.com/watch?v=ZfOVnfGpjWM (accessed 3 May 2017).

There are also some splendid CDROM resources *Story Spinner* and *Stories from Around the World* plus an app *The Traditional Storyteller*. These have the advantage of being played several times so that children can really focus on details of the way the story is told, the language, the gestures and facial expressions (for details visit http://thestoryspinner.co.uk/ (accessed 3 May 2017)).

Search the internet for local groups that offer theatre and Theatre in Education for young people; for example, Big Brum based in Birmingham (www.bigbrum. org.uk/ (accessed 3 May 2017)) or Replay Theatre in Belfast (www.replaytheatre-company.org/ (accessed 3 May 2017)).

Look up local library services. Many of them offer storytelling/drama sessions for children.

Trawl local charity shops for books.

Gather stories from all round the world.

Share as much as you can with colleagues.

3.8   A note about diversity

Teachers wanting to plan for children with a variety of needs and differing language and literacy experiences can find storytelling and drama ideal supports for learning. Children with learning difficulties can benefit from the opportunities offered by storytelling and drama for the development of social skills and oral expression as well as improving peer relationships (de la Cruz *et al.*, 1998). Drama strengthens children cognitive and language development (Mages, 2006), which is particularly important for bilingual children who can benefit from the opportunities inherent in stepping into other people's shoes and situations. While the multimodality of both forms allows for diversity in children's approaches to learning, and certainly for the exploration of the emotions in a supportive environment, it has to be remembered that storytelling and drama require individuals to be publicly visible. Sensitivity is needed, and this is where TIR can be helpful in allowing the focus to be shifted from individuals to the teacher or to groups. (See www.ncca.ie/uploadedfiles/P_Mod_Drama.pdf (The Republic of Ireland) (accessed 3 May 2017) for many excellent examples of classroom approaches for children with moderate general learning difficulties.)

Activity 3.9
Planning for storytelling, role play and drama – individual to pairs and group

Using a picture book as a starting point, and referring back to your notes for all the activities in this chapter, use the planning and teaching sequence format (website resource WI.2) to jot down some ideas for including some aspects of storytelling, role play and drama *in the first phase of the sequence only*: reading and investigation, familiarising with the text and capturing ideas. Check that you have included some of these:

- Storytelling – anecdote and more developed stories using puppets, storyboxes or bags of props, toys, objects, pictures.
- Drama conventions (see section 3.6 and website resource W3.5).
- Performance outcomes: poetry; scripted plays and stories using language and actions; sound broadcasts/podcasts; debates.
- Response and evaluation.

Summary

Narrative, both as story and drama, helps individuals to understand themselves and others, bringing together the worlds of reality and imagination in order to make sense of the world. In the classroom, narrative has both an affective and a cognitive dimension, helping to express emotions and empathise with others and to learn more about the world. When teachers become storytellers, they can take children with them on voyages of discovery and encourage the children, too, to become storytellers, enlivening their learning through imaginative and more extensive use of language. Being able to tell stories means using a variety of prompts and frames to help recall the basic structure of the story so that it can be embellished in the telling.

Drama and role play equally offer imaginative possibilities and the potential for measuring life as it is lived against fantasy or imaginary worlds. In the classroom, drama has many strengths in terms of individual emotional and creative development, collaborative learning and social and cultural significance. Classroom drama is diverse, however, and may be seen as spontaneous improvisation in the role-play area to the development of more scripted and rehearsed plays. The teacher's role is central in being the catalyst for action and the creator of problematic scenarios that lead children to dig into the deeper meanings of the texts and situations they meet. Both drama and storytelling offer sound supports for children who experience difficulties with learning and bilingual learners.

Recommended reading

Cremin, T. and Maybin, J. (2013) Language and creativity: Teachers' and students, in K. Hall, T. Cremin, B. Comber and L. Moll (eds) *The Wiley Blackwell International Research Handbook of Children's Literacy, Learning and Culture*. Oxford: Wiley Blackwell, pp. 275–290. This chapter looks at international studies that focus on the relatively untapped potential for creativity within the official language and literacy curriculum and reviews empirical work that connects to teachers' creativity in and through language in the classroom, noting the limited research-base in this area. **Advanced**

Cremin, T., Flewitt, R., Mardell, B. and Swann, J. (eds) (2017) *Storytelling in Early Childhood: Enriching language, literacy and classroom culture*. Abingdon: Routledge. A collection of research studies carried out in the USA and the UK into storytelling and story acting in young children. **Advanced**

de la Cruz, R. E., Lian, M. J. and Morreau, L. E. (1998) The effects of creative drama on social and oral language skills of children with learning disabilities, *Youth Theatre Journal*, 12 (1) pp. 89–95. This article describes research carried out in Illinois, USA, that demonstrates the value of drama for children with learning difficulties. **Advanced**

Franks, A. (2010) Drama in teaching and learning language and literacy, in D. Wyse, R. Andrews and J. Hoffman (eds) *The Routledge International Handbook of English, Language and Literacy Teaching*. Abingdon: Routledge, pp. 242–253. A comprehensive account of the recent history of approaches to educational drama in the UK and the USA with useful sections on research and references to research projects in drama. **Advanced**

Grainger, T. (1997) *Traditional Storytelling in the Primary Classroom*. Leamington Spa: Scholastic. This is an absolute treasure trove of traditional stories from around the world that you can learn to tell, with suggestions for activities, including drama, based on traditional stories.

Harrett, J. (2009) *Tell Me Another... Speaking, Listening and Learning through Storytelling*, 2nd edn. Leicester: United Kingdom Literacy Association. A wonderfully practical book with examples of story structures and ways of telling throughout the primary age range in the UK, including examples of how to move children from telling into writing.

Mages, W. K. (2006) Drama and imagination: A cognitive theory of drama's effect on narrative comprehension and narrative production, *Research in Drama Education: The Journal of Applied Theatre and Performance*, 11 (3) pp. 329–340. Written in the USA, this article proposes a cognitive theory of how drama affects two aspects of language development: narrative comprehension and narrative production. **Advanced**

Medlicott, M. (2004) Story-telling, in P. Hunt (ed.) *International Companion Encyclopaedia of Childrens' Literature*, Vol. 1, 2nd edn. Abingdon: Routledge, pp. 532–538. A practical, helpful account of a storyteller's art.

Richmond, J. (2015) *Drama*, in the series *English, Language and Literacy 3 to 19*. Leicester: Owen Education and United Kingdom Literacy Association. This short and punchy booklet gives the historical background to educational drama and outlines the value and role of drama in learning, suggesting a curriculum for drama teaching drawing on work in Australia.

References

Bromley, H. (2002) *50 Exciting Ideas for Storyboxes*. Birmingham: Lawrence Educational Publications

Bruner, J. (2003) *Making Stories: Law, literature, life*. Cambridge, MA: Harvard University Press.

Cremin, T. (2015) Developing creativity in drama, in T. Cremin, D. Reedy, E. Bearne and H. Dombey (eds) *Teaching English Creatively*. Abingdon: Routledge, pp. 25–40.

Cremin, T. and Pickard, A. (2009) *Drama: Reading, writing and speaking our way forward*. Leicester: United Kingdom Literacy Association.

Cremin, T. and Reedy, D. (2015) Developing creativity through talk, in T. Cremin with D. Reedy, E. Bearne and H. Dombey (eds) *Teaching English Creatively*. Abingdon: Routledge, pp. 11–24.

Cremin, T., Goouch, K., Blakemore. L., Goff, E. and McDonald, R. (2006) Connecting drama and writing: Seizing the moment to write, *Research in Drama Education*, 11 (3) pp. 273–291.

Cremin, T., Flewitt, R., Mardell, B. and Swann, J. (eds) (2017) *Storytelling in Early Childhood: Enriching language, literacy and classroom culture*. Abingdon: Routledge.

de la Cruz, R. E. , Lian, M. J. and Morreau, L. E. (1998) The effects of creative drama on social and oral language skills of children with learning disabilities, *Youth Theatre Journal*, 12 (1) pp. 89–95.

Engel, S. (2005) The narrative worlds of *what is* and *what if*, *Cognitive Development*, 20 (4) pp. 514–525.

Faulkner, D. (2017) Young children as storytellers: Collective meaning-making and sociocultural transmission, in T. Cremin, R. Flewitt, B. Mardell and J. Swann (eds) *Storytelling in Early Childhood: Enriching language, literacy and classroom culture*. Abingdon: Routledge, pp. 85–100.

Fox, C. (1993) Tellings and retellings: Educational implications of children's oral stories, *Reading*, 27 (1) pp. 14–20.

Franks, A. (2010) Drama in teaching and learning language and literacy, in D. Wyse, R. Andrews, and J. Hoffman (eds) *The Routledge International Handbook of English, Language and Literacy Teaching*. Abingdon: Routledge, pp. 242–253.

Grainger, T. (2003) Exploring the unknown: Ambiguity, interaction and meaning-making in classroom drama, in E. Bearne, H. Dombey and T. Grainger (eds) *Classroom Interactions in Literacy*. Maidenhead: Open University Press, pp. 105–114.

Grainger, T. and Cremin, M. (2001) *Resourcing Classroom Drama 5–8*. Sheffield: NATE.

Greenwood, J. (2009) Drama education in New Zealand: A coming of age? A conceptualisation of the development and practice of drama in the curriculum as a structured improvisation, with New Zealand's experience as a case study, *Research in Drama Education: The Journal of Applied Theatre and Performance* (Special issue: *Drama for School Education: Global Perspectives*), 14 (2) pp. 245–260.

Harrett, J. (2009) *Tell Me Another... Speaking, Listening and Learning through Storytelling*, 2nd edn. Leicester: United Kingdom Literacy Association.

Hendy, L. (2015) It's only a story isn't it? Interactive story-making in the early years classroom, in D. Whitebread and P. Coltman (eds) *Teaching and Learning in the Early Years*, 4th edn. Abingdon: Routledge, pp. 136–153.

hitRECord.org. (Gordon-Levitt, J. and wirrow) (2012) *The Tiny Book of Tiny Stories 2*. New York: HarperCollins.

Mages, W. K. (2006) Drama and imagination: A cognitive theory of drama's effect on narrative comprehension and narrative production, *Research in Drama Education: The Journal of Applied Theatre and Performance*, 11 (3) pp. 329–340.

Mardell, B. and Kucirkova, N. (2017) Promoting democratic classroom communities through storytelling and story acting, in T. Cremin, R. Flewitt, B. Mardell and J. Swann (eds) *Storytelling in Early Childhood: Enriching language, literacy and classroom culture*. Abingdon: Routledge, pp. 169–185.

Moss, G. (2017) Assessment, accountability and the literacy curriculum: Reimagining the future in the light of the past, *Literacy*, 51 (2) pp. 56–64

Neelands, J. (2011) Drama as creative learning, in J. Sefton-Green, P. Thomson, K. Jones and L. Breslar (eds) *The Routledge International Handbook of Creative Learning*. Abingdon and New York: Routledge, pp. 168–176.

Nicholson, H. (2000) Drama, literacies and difference, in E. Bearne and V. Watson (eds) *Where Texts and Children Meet*. London: Routledge, pp. 113–122.

Richmond, J. (2015) *Drama* in the series *English, Language and Literacy 3 to 19*. Leicester: Owen Education and United Kingdom Literacy Association.

Rogoff, B., Paradise, R., Arauiz, R. M., Correa-Chavez, M. and Angellilo, C. (2003) Firsthand learning through intent participation. *Annual Review of Psychology*, 54 pp. 175–203.

Rosen, H. (1998) *Speaking from Memory: The study of autobiographical discourse*. Stoke-on-Trent: Trentham Books.

Taylor, P. and Warner, C. D. (2006) *Structure and Spontaneity: The process drama of Cecily O'Neill*. Stoke-on-Trent: Trentham Books.

Vygotsky, L. (1930, trans. 1978) *Mind in Society: The development of higher psychological processes*. Cambridge, MA: Harvard University Press.

Wohlwend, K. and Peppler, K. (2015) All rigor and no play is no way to improve learning. *Phi Delta Kappan*, 96 (8) pp. 22–26.

Woolland, B. (2010) *Teaching Primary Drama*. Harlow: Pearson Education.

Wyse, D., Jones, R., Bradford, H. and Wolpert M. A. (2013) *Teaching English, Language and Literacy*, 3rd edn. Abingdon: Routledge.

Children's books

Jeannie Baker (2010) *Mirror*. Walker. ISBN 9781406309140

Trish Cooke, illustrated Helen Oxenbury (2008) *So Much!* Walker. ISBN 9781406306651

Gary Crew, illustrated Steven Woolman (1999) *The Watertower*. Crocodile Books USA. ISBN 9781566563314

Kevin Crossley Holland, illustrated Alan Marks (1997) *The Green Children*. Oxford University Press. ISBN 9780192723239

Pippa Goodheart, illustrated Nick Sharrat (2013) *Just Imagine*. Picture Corgi. ISBN 9780552563567

Mary Hoffman, illustrated Ros Asquith (2010) *The Great Big Book of Families*. Dial Books. ISBN 9781845079994

Pat Hutchins (2009) *Rosie's Walk*. Random House. ISBN 9781862308060

Matt de la Peña, illustrated Christian Robinson (2017) *Last Stop on Market Street*. Puffin. ISBN 9780141374185

Francesca Sanna (2016) *The Journey*. Flying Eye Books. ISBN 9781909263994

Shaun Tan (2014) *The Arrival*. Hodder Children's Books. ISBN 9780734415868

Liz Weir (1995) *Boom Chicka Boom*. O'Brien Press. ISBN 9780862784171

CHAPTER 4

PLANNING FOR, DEVELOPING AND ASSESSING SPOKEN LANGUAGE

This chapter covers:

- Capturing spoken language achievement
- Talk behaviours
- Organising groups for spoken language
- The purposes of assessment
- Finding the evidence
- Managing assessment of spoken language
- Observing spoken language
- Involving children in assessment
- Planning for spoken language throughout a teaching sequence
  - Case study, early primary: Using the planning and teaching sequence: phase one – focus on spoken language
  - Case study, middle primary: Planning for and assessing spoken language in history
- Describing progress in spoken language
- Bilingual or multilingual learners
- Children with language and communication difficulties

4.1   Capturing spoken language achievement

As earlier chapters have shown, developing spoken language includes provision for different purposes for talk:

- to formulate and generate ideas
- to think through language and hypothesise
- to explain, describe, justify opinions
- to present ideas and imaginary situations through drama and role play, tell stories, perform poetry
- to reflect on and evaluate what is learned and experienced.

In addition, the audiences, contexts and forms of talk have to be taken into account (see pp. 13–15 for a reminder of the spoken language curriculum).

The purpose of assessing spoken language is to help children improve their skills and the language choices they can make but planning for and assessing spoken language can be a challenge. It may be difficult to see how to help children make progress in spoken language, partly because talk is the natural medium of the classroom and it is transient, tricky to pin down. Spoken language (unlike writing) cannot be taken away to be appraised later, unless it is recorded – and this can be difficult to organise. Nevertheless, it is important to help children develop and extend their spoken language repertoire: to help them improve their use of spoken language by offering a range of contexts and opportunities for different kinds of talk. Assessment then becomes part of the planning–teaching–evaluating cycle.

The upside is that spoken language is the vehicle for learning throughout the curriculum so there are many opportunities for extending and enhancing children's spoken language and for keeping an eye on their progress, both in learning the content of different curriculum areas and in becoming more adept in using spoken language.

4.2   Talk behaviours

As talk is necessarily social and cultural in its origins, any classroom agenda for spoken language needs to take talk behaviours into account. Being able to present or perform ideas will be influenced by factors such as personality, gender, interests, culture, fluency and assurance in whatever language is used. In addition, responses from other participants can influence the flow and the content of a conversation. These factors can affect turn-taking, fluency of explanation or the extent of contribution made.

Previous experience of activities can also affect the successful development of spoken language. When a new strategy, such as 'talk partners', is introduced, sometimes even fluent speakers might be temporarily quiet while they learn to negotiate new ways of collaborating. When practices such as 'time to reply' or 'think, pair, share' (see section 4.3) become part of regular classroom experience, previously reticent contributors can find their voices. Positive or supportive response from others can be significant in helping to unlock tongues.

Talk partners: an arrangement designed to help children develop ideas through conversation. The teacher might choose the pairs, or children might be asked to find someone they work well with. Talk partners (sometimes called response partners) can be used in any area of the curriculum and for spoken language, reading or writing activities.

Time to reply: (sometimes known as 'wait time' or 'think time') when teachers ask children to take a few seconds before they reply to a question. This can help children formulate more coherent responses.

4.3   Organising groups for spoken language

A good deal of children's learning takes place in groups as this is an efficient way of allowing children the space to develop their ideas and a chance to learn how to work in a collaborative setting. Some groups will be based on the children's achievements (e.g. groups in maths or reading); others can be organised according to a range of different decisions (e.g. selecting children who work well together or balancing groups so that less forthcoming children can be paired with supportive others). Also, throughout the year, groups should be assessed and changed so that children have greater experience of working with different partners/groups. It is often a good idea for children to take on roles within groups (chair, scribe, listener/reporter, observer) and to rotate these roles over a period of time so that all children have the experience of managing, reporting or recalling what has been said or commenting on how the group has been working.

Other grouping strategies include:

Pair building: children very often work with a partner, so it is useful to build on the children's experience of established ways of working together. But pairs can be the basis for mixing and varying groups. According to the kind of work in hand, pairs might join into fours or sixes to discuss a specific part of what they have been learning in history or science, for example. They might be asked either to compare findings or contrast ideas. The teacher can manage the content of the discussions for a specific purpose; for example, to build confidence or bring together children who will stimulate each other to further learning.

'Think, pair, share': children are encouraged to take time to think (sometimes covering their eyes to help concentration), to outline their ideas with a partner, then share with another pair. This moves the process of exploratory talk to more explicit articulation of ideas. By reformulating ideas, all four children clarify their thinking and the thinking becomes 'interthinking' (see Chapter 3).

Jigsawing: a cooperative learning strategy where learners are arranged in 'home' groups with each member assigned a different piece of information or investigative task to carry out. Group members then join with members of other groups assigned the same task or information and discuss ideas. After a fixed period of time, these 'experts' return to their original home groups and put together a broader view of the topic.

Envoying: allows any member of the group to become a consultant researcher. One member of the group is given the task of finding out more information, from the library, the internet, another teacher or resources in the classroom. It may be simply to check out a detail or fact, or it might be to find out something more complex. The information is then brought back to the group. Envoys can also be used to explain the findings of one group to another group.

Activity 4.1
Decisions about groupings – reflective journal/blog/group discussion

In the classroom you are working in, or on your next placement, ask the teacher how he or she makes decisions about grouping the children. For example, are the groups based on reading groups/writing fluency/maths ability? Do the children always work in the same groups? When you have the chance to discuss this with others, compare the ways different teachers make decisions about grouping. Jot down a few ideas that you think will help you in deciding how best to group children for learning.

4.4 The purposes of assessment

Assessment enters at every stage of the planning–teaching–evaluating cycle. In more or less formal ways, assessment helps to make decisions about how best to move individuals or the whole group forward. In making decisions about how to ensure progress, teachers constantly assess, appraise and evaluate learning. They keep an eye both on curriculum coverage – *Has the class as a whole learned what I wanted them to learn?* – and individual progress – *How far has each child grasped the ideas, concepts, facts, experiences offered in this sequence of lessons?* Knowing where the children are in any teaching sequence means that through whole class teaching, supported group work or individual attention, a teacher can, as far as possible, keep all the children in the class on track, although, of course, there will be individual variation in the rate of getting hold of ideas and levels of fluency and assurance in expressing them.

There are three main types of assessment of children's progress: summative, formative (or continuous) and diagnostic assessment:

- *Summative assessments* can be defined as assessment *of* learning. Summative assessment is often carried out by testing at the end of a period of teaching. This could be termly, half termly or more frequently. Although some summative assessments can be used formatively, they are generally used to monitor the progress of individuals and groups of children and to identify attainment at ages 7 and 11.
- *Formative/continuous assessments* – assessments *for* learning. These ongoing assessments are designed to monitor children's learning at any stage in the teaching sequence. They give teachers the chance to address gaps in understanding. They also offer opportunities to identify children's strengths and weaknesses and provide

feedback that can move learning forward. Formative assessment can also be diagnostic, helping to identify groups of children who may require extra support.

- *Diagnostic assessments* are specifically designed to identify any problems a child might be experiencing or address any causes for concern (see sections 9.10 and 15.9).

4.5   Finding the evidence

Any assessment means collating evidence and weighing it up in the light of the teaching objectives. Hall and Sheehy put it like this:

> Assessing learning is about collecting information or evidence about learners and making judgements about it. The evidence may be based on one or more of the following:
>
> - what learners say
> - what learners do
> - what learners produce
> - what learners feel or think.
>
> The information or evidence may come from learners' responses to a test, such as a spelling test; a classroom activity such as a science investigation; a game or a puzzle; or a standard assessment task or test such as the SATs. It may come from a task or activity that is collaborative, that is, one where several pupils work together on the same problem. It may come from a task that pupils do on their own, without interacting with other children.
>
> (Hall and Sheehy, 2015: 325)

With spoken language, collecting evidence is a little more demanding as it depends on on-the-spot observations or digitally recorded examples of spoken language in group or drama work. However, it is well worth collecting evidence because observing, recording and assessing spoken language can:

- reveal children's thinking
- provide information about learning across the curriculum
- help in decisions about groupings
- give insights about what children understand about a topic/concept
- paint a more informative picture of a child's achievement or potential than assessments based only on reading or writing
- open a teacher's eyes to the quality and sensitivity of thinking from children who might otherwise be considered to be failing
- identify progress and inform future planning
- give evidence for reporting to parents and for summary reports.

4.6   Managing assessment of spoken language

Incorporating spoken language opportunities into plans means considering from the outset the kinds of talk that will fit with the objectives of the teaching sequence. In any programme of work it is possible to cover quite a range of spoken language purposes, forms and audiences. Since it is impossible to assess all children all the time, it is important to decide on how best to manage assessments. Over the course of a term or half term, a teacher will want to observe and assess the progress of all the children in the class for spoken language, so it is more practicable to make assessments of just a few children each week. This can be done during guided group work on a rotational basis, where teaching assistants may be on hand to give the teacher more time and space to focus on individuals. It is likely that a teacher will have a file recording termly or half termly assessments of each child in reading and writing, so a section including spoken language is easy to incorporate. Some teachers favour a tick- or tally-sheet approach to recording children's achievements, but although this may be a manageable procedure for busy teachers, it cannot provide the kind of detail and context necessary for proper judgements of successful use of spoken language. It is always worth jotting down precise examples of what the observations reveal, as in the website resource W4.1 used in the case study on pages 90–94.

4.7   Observing spoken language

Observations will need to focus on specific children and specific elements of the spoken language curriculum. Broadly, over a year or perhaps even a term, observations will be made of:

- how children work in groups
- how children use:
  - formative language – *generating ideas, questioning*
  - informative language – *informing, describing, narrating, explaining, reporting, justifying*
  - responsive and reflective language – *reasoning, speculating, hypothesising, responding, talking about language*
  - performative and expressive language – *presenting, performing.*
  - clarity and fluency of expression, language versatility – *vocabulary, intonation*
  - development of a repertoire of registers – *formal/informal.*

Focusing on specific aspects will help in providing useful information: for example, a story-telling session might focus on fluency, narrative organisation and vocabulary whilst a group discussion may be analysed in terms of the language used to generate ideas and pose questions as well as how the individual contributes to the collaborative enterprise of group work. In observing group work in order to assess spoken language, it is important to decide on which aspects of talk are being assessed – asking and responding to questions, for example, or giving clear explanations.

Occasionally it may be useful to record and listen to (even transcribe) children's spoken language in group discussions. This is helpful particularly if the school language development focus is on spoken language. Teachers may make notes and jottings which they later enter into individual children's English record files and the frequency of observations will vary. More often, teachers opt to record talk digitally and keep it on file. A short video clip of a group discussion taken on a tablet or phone can be very useful evidence. And, of course, it has the advantage of being able to be revisited to share or check evidence.

4.8   Involving children in assessment

It is useful to develop regular procedures for self- and peer assessment and to discuss them frequently with the children, since the success of these strategies depends on having a supportive classroom environment where the children feel safe to offer – and appropriately challenge – opinions. At the end of a sequence on storytelling, they might be asked to tell their talk partner about the part of their story that was most enjoyable. If the children are used to working in pairs and evaluating their work, they might make a suggestion for improvement. After group work, the whole group might be asked to comment on how well they think the group worked together; what they think their own best contribution to the discussion was; how the collaboration might be improved next time, using ground rules that they have developed (see Activity 2.4, p. 58).

Deciding on success criteria is a regular feature of some teachers' practice. At the beginning of a teaching sequence, the teacher outlines the objectives of the work of the next few weeks and together the class and teacher reach a list of features that would show success in learning. At the end of the teaching sequence, this is sometimes expressed in a series of 'I can...' statements; for example: 'I can listen carefully to my partner', 'I can give reasons for my ideas'.

Effective feedback from the teacher will support self-assessment. Feedback should refer back to the original learning objectives set at the beginning of the teaching sequence and make precise comments and suggestions for next steps. For example: 'Well done, Sameet, you have successfully told a story with a clear beginning, middle and end. I liked the way you described how you felt when you saw the giant, so it would be good to include more detail like that next time you tell a story.'

Activity 4.2
Evidence about spoken language – reflective journal/blog/group discussion

On your placement or the classroom you are working in, ask the teacher how he or she observes and keeps evidence of children's spoken language, including involving the children in assessments. Make a note of the ideas you think are most helpful and focus on one or two children over the course of a week, making your own observations using website resource W4.1. Were there any difficulties? Discuss these and note how they might be overcome.

4.9 Planning for spoken language throughout a teaching sequence

Figure 4.1 shows notes for a teaching sequence using the book *Three by the Sea* by Mini Grey (2011) where the teacher has indicated where she will introduce particular spoken language activities (see website resource W4.2 for a brief account of the sequence).

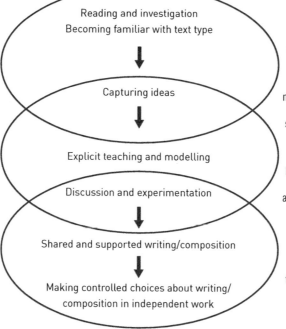

Planning for spoken language *Three by the Sea*

Modelled talk: teacher retelling the original narrative and new adventure

Oral rehearsal: retelling and rehearsing the narrative to engage the audience

Drawing new episodes and acting them out

Talk for writing: drafting through oral rehearsal

Planning using story maps to plot the narrative and retell in preparation for writing

Planning: using story maps to plot new narratives

Editing and redrafting with others

Reading and investigation
Becoming familiar with text type

Capturing ideas

Explicit teaching and modelling

Discussion and experimentation

Shared and supported writing/composition

Making controlled choices about writing/ composition in independent work

Three by the Sea – shared reading and re-reading

Book talk: explorations of multimodal aspects of the text (e.g. typography)

Book talk: discussion around aspects of the text (e.g. characters, events)

Modelled talk: teacher modelling (different writing across the teaching sequence, e.g. lists of jobs to be done, for packing, writing in role, narrative)

Modelled talk: undertaking discussion, constructing answers and responding to the text in sentences and using Standard English

Hot seating characters

Exploration of the text through practical activities and talk (e.g. role play, freeze framing)

Drafting the narrative through modelled and independent writing

Giving opinions: creating a podcast about the book

Figure 4.1 Teaching sequence planning indicating spoken language opportunities

---

Case study, early primary: Using the planning and teaching sequence: Phase one – focus on spoken language

Planning

Rachel, teaching 5 to 6 year olds, planned to use *The First Slodge* by Jeanne Willis and Jenni Desmond (2015) as the stimulus to teach a three-week teaching sequence

---

using contemporary fiction. She identified the following objectives drawn from the national curriculum for English in England.

Spoken language

- Articulate and justify answers and opinions.
- Give well-structured descriptions and narratives.
- Use spoken language to develop understanding through speculating, hypothesising, imagining and exploring ideas.
- Speak audibly and fluently with an increasing command of Standard English.
- Participate in discussions, role play. (Links to phonics, spelling and handwriting would be modelled as part of the writing process as well as through discrete teaching.)

Word reading and spelling

These would be taught during explicit phonics sessions as the teaching sequence was early in the year.

Reading comprehension

Develop pleasure in reading, motivation to read, vocabulary and understanding by:

- listening to and discussing stories at a level beyond that at which children can read independently
- discussing word meanings
- discussing the significance of the title and events
- making inferences on the basis of what is being said and done
- predicting what might happen on the basis of what has been read so far
- participating in discussion about what is read to them.

Handwriting

This would be taught during explicit handwriting sessions.

Writing composition

Write sentences by:

- saying out loud what they are going to write about
- composing a sentence orally before writing it
- sequencing sentences to form short narratives
- re-reading what they have written to check that it makes sense.

Grammar and punctuation

- Understand what makes a sentence: verb, noun/subject and punctuation.
- Leave spaces between words.
- Begin to punctuate sentences using a capital letter and a full stop.
- Use a capital letter for names of people, places, the days of the week and the personal pronoun 'I'.

Across the sequence of lessons, she planned the following opportunities for children to respond to the text in writing (pupil outcomes):

- thought bubbles (writing in role)
- predictions
- notes from one character to another (writing in role)
- character description: creating a character – design, draw, describe
- retelling a familiar tale (with a new character) – plan through mapping (drawing); story structure (setting, character, problem, beginning and ending); sequencing sentences in order to tell a new story.

During the first phase of this teaching sequence, there is a greater focus on spoken language so this case study provides more detail of this phase with some examples of the teacher's questioning.

Phase one: Reading and investigation; becoming familiar with the text type

During the first week of the sequence, Rachel focused on reading comprehension (reading for meaning), including inference and prediction, as well as spoken language. Initially, the children looked at the title double-page spread and the front matter which shows the Slodge emerging from the green slime. Rachel read the opening sentences of the first double page spread:

> *Once upon a slime there was a Slodge.*
> *The first Slodge in the Universe.*

In order to encourage speculating and hypothesising, she asked the children, 'What is a Slodge?' and as they gave answers:

- *a green monster*
- *a strange creature*

She encouraged them to articulate their ideas in full sentences:

> *A Slodge is a green monster.*
> *The Slodge is a strange creature.*

She then read the next double-page spread from 'She saw the first sunrise' to '"My star; my moon," she said.' And to allow for imaginative ideas, she asked the children to make up more sentences about the Slodge, 'What is she like? Where does she live? How do you know?' Some of the children suggested:

> *The Slodge lives by a lake.*
> *The Slodge likes the moon.*
> *She is lonely.*

Rachel selected sentences offered by the children which had easily identifiable nouns and verbs and wrote them on flipchart paper. First of all she chose sentences that began 'The Slodge is...' so that the class could talk about nouns before going on to talk about pronouns. She reminded the children that the verb 'is' tells you something about the person, using some of the children as examples: 'Minna is a girl'; 'Scott is a boy.' They identified the names as nouns and 'is' as the verb.

Returning to the sentences they had composed about the Slodge, Rachel asked the class to talk in their pairs and decide on the nouns and verbs:

A Slodge is a green blob.
The Slodge is a lonely creature.
The Slodge lives by a lake.
The Slodge likes the moon.

They were quickly able to identify 'Slodge' as a noun and 'is', 'lives' and 'likes' as verbs. Then Rachel asked, 'Can you see any more things – nouns – in the sentences?' and together the class found 'blob', 'creature', 'lake' and 'moon'. While they had been discussing these, the teaching assistant, Nita Widemore, had cut up the sentences noted on the flipchart paper into separate words plus the full stop. In small groups, the children were asked to reassemble the sentences, making sure they used every piece of the jigsaw, and when they were sure they had used them all, to make 'human sentences' where each child held up their word (or full stop) in the right order. To check that they made grammatical sense and were accurately demarcated, Rachel asked the class to read each group's sentence aloud in turn.

In the following session, they recapped the story and read on to where somebody had taken a second bite of the fruit. Rachel asked the children, 'Who might have taken that second bite? Why do you think that?' and after some suggestions they read on to where the Slodge meets another Slodge and the words say 'It was a terrible shock.' The children realised that the Slodge had thought she was all alone and to meet another Slodge would have been a surprise. Rachel presented the children with four adjectives and asked, 'How would you feel – angry, surprised, scared, happy...?' The children worked with a partner to choose the most appropriate one and explain why. In role as the Slodge, Rachel demonstrated wondering to herself 'Who is this? Did she eat MY fruit?' and the children then worked in pairs in role as the two Slodges, each wondering aloud about the other Slodge. Rachel took children's ideas and modelled writing thought bubbles, in first person, present tense, one by the first Slodge, and another by the second and the children wrote their own thought bubbles.

To start the next session, Rachel re-read the story to the page where the Slodges were fighting, inviting the children to speculate and infer by asking, 'Why are they fighting?' After some discussion, she read on to the end of the following double-page spread where the fruit fell into the sea and the first Slodge jumped in after it. Rachel asked the children to predict what might happen next, using a sentence prompt 'I think that...' to support their sentence construction and to model possibilities and the children articulated, drew and wrote what they thought would happen next. They continued reading to where the Slodges escape from the Snawk, share the fruit and become friends, and asked the children how they felt, offering some words on a continuum: *angry*, *hot*, *worried*, *relaxed*, *contented*, *happy*. As she pointed to them, the children had to say whether she was 'hot' or 'cold' according to how accurately they thought the words described the way the Slodges were feeling. She then wondered aloud, 'How will they let each other know what they're thinking? I think they'll write each other a note.' Asking for suggestions about what the Slodge might say to her friend, Rachel modelled writing a note from the first Slodge to the second, and in groups the children wrote their own notes on special paper, choosing which Slodge they were going to write to.

At the end of this phase of the sequence, Rachel invited the children to identify what they had learned, offering sentences that began with 'I...':

- I understand what a sentence is.
- I can understand a character's feelings.
- I can write in sentences to describe a character.
- I can predict what might happen.
- I can give reasons for my ideas.

Reviewing her own plans, Rachel was able to note that the children had been exposed to the planned reading comprehension objectives and most of the spoken language objectives.

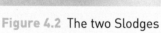

Figure 4.2 The two Slodges

Figure 4.3 The Snawk

See website resource W4.3 for an account of the full teaching sequence.

Activity 4.3
Planning a teaching sequence focusing on spoken language – individual/pairs

Read website resource W4.4 where Rachel explains how she goes about planning, then using the planning and teaching format in website resource WI.2, choose a book or film that you would like to use with your class. Identify reading, writing, grammar and spoken language objectives and the planned writing outcomes. Notice how Rachel plans 'backwards', making sure she has allowed enough time for phase three – written composition – before allocating time for phases one and two. Highlight the opportunities for spoken language that you could provide throughout the sequence. Check that you have covered:

- whole class discussion and dialogue
- modelling speaking and listening including 'thinking aloud'
- paired and small group discussion
- sharing a wide range of texts, including multimodal texts
- exploring ideas through the imagination, in storytelling, role play and drama
- involving children in reviewing and evaluating their own spoken language.

Share your planning with a colleague who works with the same age range as you and add any further opportunities you might spot as you discuss your plans. As soon as possible, put these plans into action and note on the planning format any changes you will make when you teach a similar sequence again.

Multimodal text: a text that combines elements of:

- performance – gesture, movement, posture, facial expression
- images – moving and still, photographic, drawn, painted, computer-generated, etc.
- sound – spoken words, sound effects, music and silence
- writing – including font, graphics and layout
- duration – shot length, sequence, rhythm and transitions (Bearne and Bazalgette, 2010).

Case study, middle primary: Planning for and assessing spoken language in history

Caroline, class teacher of 8 to 9 year olds, and Noelle Hunt, the language support teacher, planned a history project lasting several weeks aiming to develop the children's spoken language. They were keen that the children should be able to formulate useful questions, feel safe to offer opinions, to be adventurous with ideas and be confident to question others. Near the beginning of the project they planned a visit to a Tudor house not far from the school.

Session one: Generating ideas and forming ideas and questions

The aim was to give children the opportunity to look at historical evidence at first hand. Noelle and Caroline asked the children to bring something old from home as a basis for considering the kinds of questions that would help find out about the past. About two-thirds of the class brought in examples of old books, photographs and coins, explaining:

> My grandma kept this to remind her of...
> My friend found this Tudor coin in London Colney...

This led to a session where the children asked each other questions about the things they had brought in. The teachers modelled the kinds of questions that might be asked during the upcoming visit so that each child had at least one genuine question to pursue on the visit.

Session two: Using language to inform, explain and speculate

In the session following the visit, Noelle and Caroline adopted roles, one as a rich Tudor woman and the other as a poor servant, and hot-seated themselves. With the background knowledge from the visit and from some of their own research, the children asked the teachers about their life experiences. After the teacher modelling, the children played a game 'Rich and Poor' that provided opportunities for speculation and explanation.

Session three: Using language to research

Moving into the wider context of explorers of the Tudor era, each group had an information sheet about different explorers, including Christopher Columbus and the less well-known Estevanico, a North African adventurer. Members of the group had to find out six key facts to pass on to another group who generated questions fitting the facts and returned the questions to the original group for confirmation.

Session four: Using language to plan, hypothesise and design

Each group devised a game incorporating all the questions and answers developed in the previous session. The groups decided on roles (to draw out the board, design and write out the questions, etc.) and drew up mini-contracts signed by each member of the group. All this generated discussion, debate about how best to proceed, and negotiation of roles. The games were completed and played by the other groups in turn, evaluated (language of reflection) and revised if necessary.

Session five: Using language to present and perform

In this session, Noelle and Caroline introduced the children to Shakespeare. They watched the BBC Animated Tales version of *A Midsummer Night's Dream* and, led by the teachers, analysed and discussed the style of language used. Drawing on the transformation of Bottom with the ass's head, the children worked in groups of four to devise a short play of about two minutes to include some kind of magic or transformation scene which were performed to the whole class.

Session six: Using language to question/research/report

The final session allowed the teachers to assess the language skills they had been trying to develop with the children. Using the 'jigsaw' technique, children were organised into 'Home' groups and 'Expert' groups, each set up to examine an aspect of life at the time of Henry VIII; for example, life in rural England during his reign. The Expert groups had a set of statements to consider and decide whether they were true or false. Experts then returned to Home groups to help compile a summary sheet of Henry VIII's reign.

There were, of course, history outcomes for this work, but in terms of language, Noelle and Caroline were pleased to see the development of a wider range of spoken language. They were also satisfied to note that individual children had made progress: the reticent children were generally less so and the dominant talkers more often gave way to others.

Assessing individual children's spoken language

The teachers had planned to assess the spoken language of seven children, repre-senting a range of achievement and levels of bilingual language fluency, over the course of the project:

- *Michael* – a clever, capable boy who finds it difficult to concentrate and is challenged by working individually or in groups, but with a carefully chosen partner he has achieved some excellent work.
- *Darryl* – a keen learner who is quite sensitive but can have quite fixed ideas of what he wants to do and finds it hard to go along with the views of others if they do not agree with him.
- *Sadia* – speaks Punjabi as her first language. When spoken to she seems to understand but if questioned more persistently she closes down and will not answer at all.
- *Rachel* – is supportive in group work. She can be assertive in discussion, but is also receptive to other people's ideas. She can hold thoughtful conversations.
- *Susan* – seems a quiet girl who, unless prompted, will sit back in the classroom. Her first language is Cantonese.
- *Rosheen* – a moderately fluent bilingual girl who has recently joined the class having attended three other schools in a relatively short period. She is keen to try but can misunderstand what is expected. She has specific learning difficulties and receives learning and language support.
- *Mustapha* – a fluently bilingual, capable boy with a good vocabulary in English. Very articulate but will opt out if he can.

In considering their planned objectives, Caroline and Noelle were satisfied that all the children had become more adept at questioning and generating ideas and that all had benefitted from the experience of working collaboratively over an extended project. Figure 4.4 shows their notes about each of the children's spoken language achievements during the course of the project. Further focused assessments later in the term will fill in the gaps in the chart.

Observation of spoken language   **Class 4 CL**   **Half term:** Summer 1

Context: Project on Tudor England

Objectives:

Pupils to develop the ability to:

- ask appropriate questions, open or closed according to the learning context in order to gain maximum information
- follow a line of questioning, i.e. predicting responses and phrasing a series of questions to solve a problem
- articulate clear and appropriate responses to questions and, in writing, construct answers in well punctuated sentences
- using the information gained from question and answer activities, represent information in a variety of ways
- gain confidence in giving opinions, taking risks with ideas and challenging the views of others confidently and courteously.

Name	Working in groups collaborating cooperating	Formative language generating ideas questioning	Informative language informing describing explaining narrating reporting justifying	Responsive reflective language speculating hypothesising responding talking about language	Performative/ expressive language presenting performing	Fluency and clarity/ versatility in expression
Rachel		Realised that *Is it...?* questions lead to *yes/no/ don't know* answers whereas *Why is it...?* yield a more satisfying response.	Entered into lively debate with Martin over where to put START in the board game. Was able to give good reasons for opinions			Fluent and assured in group and whole-class discussion. Speaks clearly with good expression and intonation.
Sadia	Quiet and unobtrusive in group. Gave bilingual support to Asmaa (beginner bilingual girl).	Stubbornly resistant to asking a question until given time to formulate one when she asked some sensible questions.				

98

Susan	Often quiet but surprised us by taking the lead in work with Peach group, firmly and competently organising the others.	Needed some prompting but given support was able to phrase a useful question.			
Rosheen	Quiet and unobtrusive in group.	At first, she misunderstood task, probably because of her level of fluency in English. She thought she had to answer, not ask questions but when explained, she volunteered a good question.			
Mustapha	Quiet in the group; did not enter into the discussion but always listened carefully.	Reticent but contributed a question when his turn came.	Surprised us with his profound comments, e.g. *The poor had considerable difficulties in getting food because of their masters holding all the power.*	Described Shakespeare's writing as 'very describable'.	Extensive vocabulary, e.g. *considerable, piracy, intricate*
Darryl	Had some problems with the game making activity – very set ideas and would only collaborate with others who agreed with him. Later, managed to settle when he explained the use of compasses.	Contributed thoughtful questions.		Particularly interested in the language of Shakespeare. Attempted a snippet of his own in the improvisations: 'And behold....'	
Michael	Inspired by the thought of making the game. Excellent ideas. Stayed on task and supported Paul, who was less confident.		Identified the statement 'Henry VIII was tall and handsome when he was young' as a matter of opinion, not a fact.		

Figure 4.4 Record sheet for spoken language observations

4.10   Describing progress in spoken language

At the transition from year to year or from early primary to upper primary, it is important to be able to inform colleagues (and parents and governors) about children's progress in a specific area of learning. As mentioned earlier, spoken language can be particularly tricky to pin down but all teachers need to have a means of describing children's current achievements which go beyond tick sheets of national curriculum objectives. The Scale of Progression for Spoken Language in Figure 4.5 offers a means of recording and reporting on children's spoken language in a descriptive way. It reflects what teachers might expect to see as children develop assurance and versatility in spoken language and was originally derived from discussion with teachers who wanted to establish record keeping systems which would supplement national curriculum programmes of study (Bearne, 1998). Since its inception it has been further developed by teacher discussion and has been aligned with the national curricula of England, Northern Ireland, Scotland and Wales. The scale is best seen as a basis for discussion with colleagues and open to adaptation, as the descriptors may not always reflect particular school circumstances. The statements are not arranged in any order of importance but are grouped according to the following categories:

- spoken clarity
- adapting language to purpose/context
- working in groups
- formative language
- informative language
- responsive/reflective language
- performative/expressive language.

The statements are not intended to be all-inclusive, or exclusive, and might form the basis for school discussion of how best to describe progress in spoken language and communicate that progress to others.

One way to use the Scale is to track individual progress. As each termly observation is made, it can be checked against a matching statement on the Scale. Used in discussions with parents or colleagues, the descriptors can be a useful basis for talking about specific elements of the spoken language curriculum; for example, Sameet's ability to tell a story with a clear beginning, middle and end. If certain statements are not covered, that may suggest that the teacher needs to plan to teach those aspects or that a particular child is experiencing difficulties. Identifying statements which genuinely reflect what children can do in spoken language can provide a very clear idea of the areas they need help with. For example, if several children are at the stage of 'a fluent but less experience speaker/ listener' in group work, indicated by:

- discusses familiar issues (e.g. classroom rules) with a known group
- asks own questions in response to other people's ideas

the teacher would want to set up opportunities, for example, for group discussion based on the children's own interests and experience to give them further opportunities for talking from a base of knowledge and assurance. Drama and role play might also be used to put children into the position of learning how to negotiate relationships with others. Both these kinds of experiences would move them towards becoming a moderately experienced speaker/listener who:

- begins to use more specific language/vocabulary relating to personal interests/activities
- in group work, copes (verbally) with peers who present awkward behaviour
- listens to and is tolerant of others' points of view.

Children who are achieving highly in speaking and listening would be encouraged to use their skills in developing a wider repertoire of spoken texts and extending their experience of using different media – for example, podcasts or vidcasts – to challenge them further.

At the end of the year, the scale might be used to evaluate whole class progress and indicate areas for future planning.

4.11 Bilingual or multilingual learners

It is important to note that any of the descriptive statements in the Scale can be applied to a child's home or preferred language. This is particularly relevant in the early years or for children who enter school later with little or no experience of English. It is possible for speakers of a language other than English to be assessed by another adult who speaks the same language. This is particularly important when remembering that assessing spoken language is often bound up with assessing what children show they know about other curriculum areas *through* talk. Language support teachers, parents and community leaders, even older siblings, can play an important part here. The descriptors allow anyone, including the children themselves at times, to consider how the statements describe what an individual can do in spoken language.

In their very helpful book, *Practical Bilingual Strategies for Multilingual Classrooms*, Tözun Issa and Alayne Öztürk explain:

> Assessment will help teachers develop strategies to facilitate learning, and will also inform planning, enabling high expectations and the selection of language content specific to the task. It is important to take into consideration the knowledge and skills that bilingual children bring to the classroom, and to plan for the incorporation of these in the curriculum. Effective, targeted questioning will be an essential assessment tool, but it is worth bearing in mind that some children will understand the questions but lack the confidence to respond in front of larger groups.
>
> (Issa and Öztürk, 2007: 30)

4.12 Children with language and communication difficulties

Children's difficulties in speech and communication may be *phonological* (delayed or disordered sound system), *articulatory* (problems with the mechanics of speech), *receptive* (difficulties in understanding spoken language), *expressive* (problems with formulating words into sentences) or *pragmatic* (difficulties in the social use of language). In their booklet *Speech, Language and Communication Difficulties* (2011), the Department of Education Northern Ireland estimates that as many as three children in a class of thirty may have speech and language difficulties. However, they point out:

> Many pupils with speech, language and communication needs (SLCN) can succeed in mainstream education, particularly where schools embrace collaborative working arrangements and teachers have access to the specialist training and resources they need.
>
> ... It is of interest that the strategies suggested [in the booklet] are not unique to pupils with speech and language difficulties. The same strategies go a long way to encouraging better classroom practice and teaching that are of benefit to all children's learning.

(DENI, 2011: 403)

General guidance for supporting children who have language and communication difficulties (which is also good advice for general classroom practice) include:

- encourage active listening
- use multisensory teaching methods, visual strategies and non-verbal cues to support what is being said
- emphasise key words with slight stress
- think about the length and complexity of instructions
- check understanding, observe responses and clarify any misunderstandings
- encourage children to use self-help strategies; for example, rehearsal or visualisation
- ask children to let you know when they have not understood
- allow children time to process information
- avoid asking a child to repeat a sentence again after you
- avoid finishing a child's sentences or saying the words they cannot find as this can be frustrating for the speaker.

For more detailed suggestions and explanations of speech and language disorder, see www.education-ni.gov.uk/sites/default/files/publications/de/speech-language-and-comm unication-difficulties.pdf (accessed 3 May 2017).

As the Scale of Progression in Spoken Language (Figure 4.5) is not tied to any age or year group, the statements can be used as they fit the level of development of the individual.

Inexperienced speaker/listener:

- asks for things or gets friends to ask
- listens to teacher instructions when asked to
- responds to adults with short, simple utterances
- talks with others spontaneously (during play, for example) but does not necessarily respond as 'conversation'
- joins in a whole class group story led by the teacher
- begins to ask other people questions (based on teacher modelling)
- conveys a simple or familiar message and repeating a straightforward verbal answer (with a friend)
- answers questions about an area of personal knowledge or experience
- talks about parts of books/DVDs read and enjoyed
- comments on characters they like from their reading/viewing
- tells a story from given pictures and picture books in a simple sequence
- plays in role for lengthy periods
- uses rhythmic/rhymed patterns to help read aloud
- remembers parts of poems and songs they are familiar with
- tells members of the group/class about preferences and interests
- knows that language is made up of words

Fluent but less experienced speaker/listener:

- shows a sense of audience – waiting for quiet and speaking to be heard
- listens and responds in conversations with a friend
- listens to instructions without being reminded
- joins in a whole class/group story without adult prompting
- discusses familiar issues (e.g. classroom rules) with a known group
- asks own questions in response to other people's ideas
- conveys a verbal message and bring a verbal reply independently
- remembers, and tells in sequence, an event of personal significance
- explains own work to another adult or child
- uses reasons in discussion
- talks with enthusiasm/conviction about books read or films seen
- describes characters from fiction
- tells a story with a beginning, middle and end from own pictures or story maps
- structures situations in role-play activities, taking on character roles from fiction
- creates a rhythm and notice rhyme when reading aloud
- recites (with support) short poems/songs learned by heart
- knows that language is different according to who is talking

Moderately experienced speaker/listener:

- retells events giving relevant detail for group/class audience
- uses different forms of talk for different people (e.g. friend, teacher, visitor) and different situations (including using Standard English)
- begins to use more specific language/vocabulary relating to personal interests/activities
- in group work, copes (verbally) with peers who present awkward behaviour
- listens to and is tolerant of others' points of view
- has an established concept of turn-taking (even if not always doing it!)
- organises a group activity and delegates tasks
- formulates questions about classroom work
- begins to hypothesise about things known or learned about
- with support/collaboration, presents and explains work/ideas to a large audience (e.g. assembly)

Figure 4.5 Scale of Progression for Spoken Language

- explains personal preferences for books/films
- discusses motivation of characters in fiction giving reasons for holding particular views of characters
- creates and sustains roles in response to fiction
- narrates an extended storyboard sequence
- gives attention to rhythm, rhyme and intonation in discussion and performance
- recites poems learned by heart, with some attention to expression and intonation
- can talk about informal and formal language

Experienced speaker/listener:

- explains ideas/opinions clearly using standard English
- indicates awareness of others' conversational needs
- uses specific language register and/or vocabulary relating to activities or topics learned
- acts as enabler as well as contributor in group discussion
- makes appropriate and relevant (succinct) comments in group/class discussion
- shows empathy with others' points of view
- gives opinions about things known or learned about
- analyses and discusses ideas found in research/information materials
- talks about their own and a partner's collaborative work, using specific vocabulary and giving adequate explanation and reasons
- discusses books (films, television, poetry) giving reasons for choice, enjoyment or satisfaction
- analyses character development and motivation
- talks about language, vocabulary and dialect
- explains ideas/tells story in a clear sequence
- uses role play to create different characters, genres, situations
- gives a sustained talk to the class/group (using presentational software if appropriate)
- performs texts learned by heart (poetry or plays), creating effects with intonation and vocal range
- can talk about reasons for using formal and informal language

Very experienced speaker/listener:

- varies tone and formality according to context and subject (including use of Standard English)
- confidently (or apparently so!) initiates questions and make contributions or offer opinions in a range of contexts
- empathises with the points of view of others and articulate them in a range of settings (familiar/unfamiliar; pairs/groups/class; with peers/adults; known/unknown)
- makes sustained (or brief, as appropriate) contributions to group/class discussion
- listens actively and attentively, responding perceptively to ideas
- initiates and leads discussion, extending and elaborating on others' ideas where necessary
- engages in discussion as a contributor and listens attentively without reminders about turn-taking
- understands complex ideas presented orally (e.g. when read aloud or in a talk) and shows understanding in responses made
- gives a sustained talk/presentation, taking questions and responding thoughtfully
- discusses literature, music, ideas with balance and conviction
- analyses character and comments on the role of character in conveying the theme of a book/film
- takes on character, sustains suspense in drama/role play
- describes, presents and evaluates a piece of work or activity to a group
- debates an issue, giving evidence for opinions held
- as part of a planned performance, engages in lengthy expressive work using intonation and vocal range for dramatic effects
- can identify differences vocabulary and sentence structure according to formal/informal register

Figure 4.5 continued

Figure 4.5 is also available to be downloaded as website resource W4.5.

Activity 4.4
Observing two children and noting their achievements in spoken language – reflective journal/blog

In the classroom where you are working, or on your next placement, in discussion with the class teacher, select two children to observe for two or three weeks. With the teacher, note their achievements on the Scale of Progression for Spoken Language.

If you share these observations with anyone outside the school, make sure you use only initials or pseudonyms.

Having noted the children's achievements, make a few notes about how you might move their spoken language forward.

Summary

This chapter has considered the difficulties of capturing spoken language achievement since classroom talk is everyday and everywhere and permeates the whole curriculum. Assessing spoken language includes not only the types of talk that might be expected – formative, informative, performative and reflective – but also the importance of taking account of talk behaviours and how these might affect children's oral fluency and assurance in the classroom. An outline of the value of group work includes suggestions for managing flexible classroom groupings. Assessments can be made for different purposes and choices made about how, what, when and why to assess – and who does the assessments – will have an influence on the kinds of evidence that may be sought to show progress. Assessments should be staged and systematic, using observations and video recording where appropriate and including the children in self- and peer assessment. Two case studies show how spoken language can be planned throughout a teaching sequence and provide evidence for assessments. Catering for a range of learners, including bilingual children and those who experience difficulty, may be less problematic than anticipated, since good practice for those groups is equally effective for mainstream learners. The Scale of Progression in Spoken Language concludes the chapter, offering a means of describing progress and achievement which goes beyond basic curriculum coverage.

Recommended reading

Corden, R. (2002) *Literacy and Learning Through Talk: Strategies for the primary classroom.* Buckingham: Open University Press, esp. pp. 81–108 'Group work: Learning through talk'. Very thorough and comprehensive book with plenty of practical examples of classroom talk drawn from the UK.

Hargreaves, E., Gipps, C. and Pickering, A. (2014) Assessment for learning: Formative approaches, in T. Cremin and J. Arthur (eds) *Learning to Teach in the Primary School.* Abingdon: Routledge, pp. 313–323. Highly recommended chapter which covers the whole area of formative assessment, including involving children in assessments. **Advanced**

Northcote, A. (2014) Responding to linguistic diversity, in T. Cremin and J. Arthur (eds) *Learning to Teach in the Primary School*. Abingdon: Routledge, pp. 420–433. This chapter is worth reading to give background to the whole Spoken Language part of the book, not just assessment. **Advanced**

O'Sullivan, O. (2007) Children with special educational needs, in T. Cremin and H. Dombey (eds) *Handbook of Primary English in Initial Teacher Education*. Cambridge: Short Run Press, pp. 190–209. This chapter was originally written for tutors on ITE courses in the UK, but its coverage of different kinds of special educational needs in literacy is clear and comprehensive.

References

Bearne, E. (1998) *Making Progress in English*. London: Routledge.

Bearne, E. and Bazalgette, C. (eds) (2010) *Beyond Words*. Leicester: United Kingdom Literacy Association.

Department of Education Northern Ireland (2011) *Speech, Language and Communication Difficulties*. www.education-ni.gov.uk/sites/default/files/publications/de/speech-language-and-comm unication-difficulties.pdf (accessed 3 May 2017)

Hall, K. and Sheehy, K. (2015) Assessment for learning: Summative approaches, in T. Cremin and J. Arthur (eds) *Learning to Teach in the Primary School*. Abingdon: Routledge, pp. 324–338.

Issa, T. and Öztürk, A. (2007) *Practical Bilingual Strategies for Multilingual Classrooms*. Leicester: United Kingdom Literacy Association.

Children's books

Mini Grey (2011) *Three by the Sea*. Red Fox. ISBN 9781862308091

Jeanne Willis, illustrated J. Desmond (2015) *The First Slodge*. Little Tiger Press. ISBN 9781848690394

PART 2
READING

In every part of this book you will be asked to keep
a journal (or a blog) in which you can jot down reflections,
observations and tasks. There are also recommended
readings to support your learning.

INTRODUCTION TO PART TWO

P2I.1   A history of debate about reading

> Controversy about the teaching of reading has a long history, and throughout it there has been the assumption, at least the hope, that a panacea can be found that will make everything right ... there is no one method, medium, approach device or philosophy that holds the key to the process of reading. We believe that the knowledge does exist to improve the teaching of reading, but that it does not lie in the triumphant discovery, or re-discovery, of a particular formula ... a glance at the past reveals the truth of this.
>
> (DES, 1975: 77)

The informed words of the Bullock Report, written almost fifty years ago, are a reminder that current concerns about reading are part of a long history of debate. It is difficult to see just what it is that makes teaching reading such a contentious issue. Partly, it may be because satisfying or satisfactory reading does not just depend on the range of available texts but on readers, contexts and communities. Contexts for reading (e.g. reading on screen as well as on paper), the experience of readers and the communities in which reading takes place are not static. Perhaps, as Manguel (1996) points out in his wide-ranging book *The History of Reading,* it is not so surprising that issues of what will be the best ways to develop and sustain reading engagement and commitment are likely to be the focus of continuing debate.

    One of the enduring difficulties of discussing how best to teach reading is that it is an inner process – a receptive language mode, like listening – and whilst writing and talking involve inner processes, they are heard and seen (expressed or produced) in speech and written text. It is not possible to 'see' reading or hearing so that judging how effectively children are becoming readers means doing something to check it out – hearing them read or asking them questions about what they have read.

> **Receptive and expressive/productive modes:** there are four language modes – hearing/listening, reading, speaking, writing. Two of them – hearing/listening and reading – are receptive, that is, information and ideas are taken in by the ears and eyes and understood within the mind. The other two – speaking and writing – involve taking in information and ideas from a range of sources, but then transforming that information and expressing it through speech or writing.

P21.2   What does 'reading' imply?

Reading is, for many people, an almost automatic process. Road signs, messages on computer screens or smartphones, books, magazines, newspapers, recipes, instructions, etc. all contribute to the range of reading that anyone may expect in the course of any day or week. Reading helps people get through their everyday lives, both at home and at work. But reading is more than just dealing with communications or instructions; it is the means by which many people explore the other worlds of imaginative fiction or add to their knowledge through factual information. Reading gives us access to life beyond the here and now, adding to our experience of life through reading what others have to say about what it is to be human. Reading is not only life-affirming, it can also be life-saving, which is why teaching reading is so important.

Becoming a teacher of reading is more than simply instructing children how to decode marks on a page. It is a matter of sharing personal experience of the satisfactions of reading, even if those satisfactions have sometimes involved a lot of effort and persistence. It means talking about choices of reading material and different ways of reading – the range and repertoire of an experienced reader. It means reflecting on childhood reading and the pleasures of meeting familiar and new 'friends' through reading or the excitement of finding out about new things and sharing those experiences with young readers.

Learning to read and becoming a reader

Much of the academic research about reading had been about the most effective way to teach reading and the preferred approach will determine what 'learning to read' means. For some, the emphasis is on getting the words off the page – decoding – before going on to think about meaning. For others, meaning is key and the process of decoding is assisted by wanting to find out what the words mean. But beyond this difference in approach there is the matter of how to introduce young readers to the range of texts available, on screen and on paper and, importantly, how to develop a repertoire of reading behaviours that will lead towards independent and committed readership. That is, how to encourage children to become readers. There is a difference between 'learning to read' and 'becoming a reader'; the second is a matter of laying the foundations for a life where print can enhance and expand experience. And teachers, as well as families and communities, have a key role to play in encouraging a lifelong commitment to being a reader.

Individual and social aspects of reading

At first sight, reading seems to be a profoundly individual and personal experience. Of course it is. Two people reading the same book will have different experiences of it according to their own life experiences, preferences for particular genres or authors and state of mind at the time of reading. But when those two people begin to talk about their different perceptions of the book, then reading becomes a social act, prompting communication between individuals. At times, too, reading will be collaborative with two or more people enjoying a reading experience together. Or someone (or an audiobook) might read to another. At home, sometimes someone reads aloud from the newspaper, a letter or email. Any complete view of reading has to be able to take into account the social and cultural aspects of reading as well as remembering the deeply personal importance of reading.

Talk and reading

Spoken language underpins all learning and social interaction and so is an essential component of learning to be a reader. Being able to decode the words is greatly enhanced by experience of rhymes, wordplay and songs. Recognising the differences between sounds is the basis of beginning to recognise how these sounds are represented on the page. Reading poetry remains a key reading experience as readers grow in fluency and competence. In addition to that, talking about reading helps readers to identify their preferences as well as key aspects of the content of reading. Ideas take on a clearer shape when they are articulated and discussed. Then there are the performative aspects of reading – the enjoyment derived by reader and listener from reading aloud (given that the reader has had a chance to prepare for reading) and the joys of sharing reading books or texts on iPads with children. Reading and talk are interdependent (see *Talk for Reading* by Warner (2013) for a full exploration of the significance of talk in all its forms in promoting reading and readers).

P21.3 Principles about teaching reading

The best reading teachers:

- encourage and model reading for pleasure and establish an appreciation and love of reading
- have expert knowledge about how children learn to read words and create a language rich environment to support word reading
- value the knowledge and experience of reading all kinds of texts that children bring from home.

Children learn best when they develop the habit of reading widely in and out-of-school.

Links with home over reading are essential if children are to make progress in reading and gain satisfaction from it. It is important to recognise that homes, families and communities offer good models of what it is to be a reader.

Talk is essential throughout the reading process. Discussion, questioning, drama and role play support pupils' understanding and appreciation of texts.

Successful reading is taught through a balance between word recognition and reading for meaning.

Children should have extensive experience of listening to, sharing and discussing a wide range of high-quality books to engender a love of reading at the same time as they are reading independently.

Exploring texts and encouraging children to ask questions is essential in their development as critical readers.

Children become even more engaged and committed readers if their school has a library or strong links to library services.

Reading does not just involve books: film, television and reading online contribute to children becoming more engaged and critical readers.

The teacher's role is crucial in:

- providing a role model of an enthusiastic and committed reader through sharing their own reading lives
- creating a supporting and challenging reading environment
- planning for shared, guided and independent reading
- making opportunities for talk before, during and after reading
- engaging in genuine dialogue about the texts being read in class
- offering a range of strategies to help children get to grips with decoding
- balancing decoding and reading for meaning and satisfaction
- teaching a range of types of text, explicitly discussing why they are effective.

All these principles are explored in Chapters 5, 6, 7, 8 and 9.

P2I.4 The reading curriculum

The following list draws together key ideas from the national curricula of England, Northern Ireland, Scotland and Wales. In planning for teaching, you may want to refer also to a specific national curriculum.

For effective reading development, children should be given opportunities to:

- *develop range and repertoire*
  - Read and be read to from a wide range of poems, stories and non-fiction.
  - Read with some independence for enjoyment and information.
  - Read, explore, understand and make use of a range of traditional and digital texts.
  - Read for different purposes – for example, for personal pleasure; to retrieve, summarise and synthesise key information; to find, interpret and verify information.
  - Research, select and use information relevant to specific purposes, using traditional and digital sources.
  - Use a range of comprehension skills, both oral and written, to interpret and discuss texts and use evidence to support their views and explain opinions.
  - Explore and begin to understand how texts are structured in a range of genres.

Figure 21.1 Reading class anthology   **Figure 21.2** Reading area

- Read analytically and critically, compare and contrast texts, distinguish between fact and opinion, recognise persuasive language and evaluate the reliability and relevance of sources.
- Transfer reading skills across all areas of the curriculum.

- *develop reading behaviours and reflecting on reading*
  - Read individually and collaboratively.
  - Sustain reading and make discriminating choices.
  - Relate what they have read to their own experience.
  - Retell, re-read and act out a range of texts, representing ideas through drama, pictures, diagrams and digital technology.
  - Explain preferences for certain texts and authors.
  - Share ideas about events, characters, setting, structure and theme, supporting their views with evidence from the text.
  - Develop appropriate vocabulary and terminology to discuss, consider and evaluate texts.

- *develop reading/language skills and strategies*
  - Phonic skills.
  - Build up a sight vocabulary.

- Use knowledge of sight vocabulary, analogy, phonics, context clues, punctuation and grammar to read with understanding, expression and increasing fluency and independence.
- Identify phrases, words, patterns or letters, punctuation, sentence structure and grammar.
- Link new meanings to those already known.

Teachers need to be able to evaluate how effectively they have taught the relevant parts of the curriculum in any one year judged by how far individual children have been able to develop engagement and response to texts, their understanding/comprehension of increasingly complex texts and the skills of getting the words off the page (see Chapter 9).

References

Department of Education and Science (1975) *A Language for Life. Report of the Committee of Inquiry appointed by the Secretary of State for Education and Science* (The Bullock Report). London: HMSO.

Manguel, R. (1996) *The History of Reading*. London: HarperCollins.

Warner, C. (2013) *Talk for Reading*. Leicester: United Kingdom Literacy Association.

CHAPTER 5
PERSPECTIVES ON READING

This chapter covers:

- Perspectives on reading development
- Teachers as readers
- What can a developed reader do?
- Reading on screens
  - Case study, upper primary: Reading a short film with 9 and 10 year olds
- The components of a rich and balanced reading curriculum
- Reading by children: Independent reading

5.1   Perspectives on reading development

There have long been debates about the best ways to teach reading, some referred to as 'bottom-up' and 'top-down' models or theories. Essentially, any teacher of reading wants to encourage competence and performance as well as individual response and satisfaction and enjoyment of reading. The debates are about what is the best way to achieve these aims.

Skills and drills

Until about the 1970s the main approaches to teaching reading were skills-based. For many years, teaching reading was regarded as the same as teaching spelling but in the mid-nineteenth century the alphabetic method gave way to greater attention to phonics, the difference being that phonics is about decoding using letter *sounds* rather than the *names* of letters. However, teaching simply by phonics was seen to have its difficulties, particularly in English-speaking countries where there is not a direct sound-symbol correspondence. The Initial Teaching Alphabet (ITA) was developed by Pitman (1961) in an attempt to match sound-symbol correspondence in English. Twenty extra symbols were added to the twenty-six letters of the alphabet but this initiative was soon abandoned, since there were no real-life examples of texts written in ITA and children who experienced difficulties with reading were baffled by having to transfer back to the standard alphabetic system.

> **Phonics:** a method of teaching reading by matching sounds with symbols in the writing system (see Chapter 7).

'Look and say', another approach to reading, focused on whole words, or even sentences, often accompanied by pictures. In the early 1800s, supporters of this approach argued that it was better for a child to learn twenty-six known words rather than twenty-six unknown letters of the alphabet (Diack, 1965). In the same way as phonics instruction, which intro-duced children to sounds in a staged and controlled way, in 'look and say' key words were also graded and restricted. The teaching methods for both approaches were based on learning by memory and drills.

Cognitive-psychological view

The cognitive psychological approach to teaching reading sees language as made up of segments so that the reading process is a matter of perception of letters, spelling patterns and words to sentences. Cognitive theorists regard learning to read as a matter of decoding print in terms of phoneme/grapheme correspondence. They also see reading as acquired in stages (Gough and Hillinger, 1980) and explain reading difficulties as lack of progression through these stages (Chall, 1983). In order to progress through the stages, children need to use phonetic knowledge when they come to unfamiliar words. However, some cognitive theorists (Spiro *et al.*, 1994) have argued for a more flexible approach once the basic concepts have been learned. A cognitively flexible learner needs to understand complex concepts in order to apply existing knowledge to different situations, which means a break away from a linear approach. This more complex view of learning, however, does not translate easily into policy for teaching, where policy makers tend to opt for simple solutions.

Currently, in England at least, there is a great deal of emphasis on teaching phonics (or more precisely, phonological awareness) as a necessary pre-requisite to reading for understanding (DfE, 2015) (see Chapter 7 for a fuller exploration of phonics teaching). A great deal of research indicates a strong relationship between phonological awareness and literacy development (Ehri *et al.*, 2001; Goswami, 2003; Shaywitz, 2005). Recent neuroscientific research across the languages of the world indicates that the syllable rather than the phoneme is the primary phonological processing unit (Port, 2006; Goswami, 2008) and the most recent research (see Goswami, 2015) raises questions about separating phonics teaching (decoding) from understanding meaning.

One problem with a cognitive-psychological perspective lies in the idea of stages of development as fundamental (Chall, 1983; Ehri, 2005). Children who do not conform to the prescribed stages are likely to be seen as in some way 'deficient' (see p. 27 about deficit theories). This raises questions about children who are learning English as an additional language who experience difficulties with reading. They may have developed competent reading strategies in their first language which are not yet evident in their English reading (Cummins, 2000; Kenner and Gregory, 2003). It does not seem productive to judge successful reading solely through a lens of 'stages' since a linear approach risks ignoring a whole range of other attributes that children bring to reading.

Onset and rime: a syllable can normally be divided into two parts – the *onset*, which consists of the initial consonant or consonant blend, and the *rime*, which consists of the vowel and any final consonants (see Chapter 7).

Phoneme: the smallest unit of sound in a word.

Phonological awareness: the ability to hear and discriminate sounds. Phonological awareness is not about recognising letters in print, but about the inner process of making sense of sounds. Developing phonological awareness means recognising that words are made up of small sound units (phonemes), that words can be segmented into larger sound units known as syllables and that each syllable begins with a sound (onset) and ends with another sound (rime).

Psycholinguistic view

Where a cognitive-psychological view may be described as 'bottom-up', building from small components towards meaning, the psycholinguistic view is often seen as a 'top-down' model. One of the major psycholinguistic theorists was Goodman, who described a 'whole language' approach where the focus is on making sense of a piece of language as a whole, rather than concentrating on the details of decoding print (Goodman, 1986; Goodman *et al.*, 2016). His close observations of many children reading led to his description of reading as a 'psycho-linguistic guessing game' (Goodman, 1967) where he suggested that readers draw simultaneously on three cueing systems to make sense of text: graphophonic, syntactic and semantic. Goodman's research led to the development of miscue analysis as a means of diagnosing children's strengths and stumbling blocks as readers (see Chapter 9).

> **Semantic cues:** related to meaning.
>
> **Syntactic cues:** related to sentence structure (syntax).

Goodman (1992) sees language and literacy development as closely bound up with whole, real, functional language which would include the use of literature and other authentic texts in reading (as distinct from commercial reading schemes), using whole texts rather than isolated skills and drills, integration of listening, speaking, reading and writing, and building on the language, culture and experience of learners. He sees prediction as a key to successful reading (Goodman *et al.*, 2016) (see Chapter 7 for more on prediction).

The psycholinguistic view assumes a non-staged reading process: older readers simply have better knowledge of language and of the world than less experienced readers. Frank Smith (1971) argued that reading is a matter of making informed predictions about texts based on what the reader already knows about language and the world:

> Children learn to read only by reading. Therefore, the only way to facilitate their learning to read is to make reading easy for them. This means continuously making critical and insightful decisions – not forcing children to read for words when they are, or should be, reading for meaning; not forcing them to slow down when they should speed up; not requiring caution when they should be taking chances; not worrying about speech when the topic is reading; not discouraging errors.
>
> (Smith, undated, www.arvindguptatoys.com/arvindgupta
> /essaysintoliteracy.pdf (accessed 1 May 2017))

The psycholinguistic perspective was an attempt to move away from the idea that 'reading is a linear process of letter-by-letter deciphering, sounding out, word recognition and finally text comprehension' (Hall, 2003: 42–43) towards a view of reading as a constructive, problem-solving process of making meaning.

The Simple View of Reading

The Simple View of Reading (SVR) was first proposed by Gough and Tunmer (1986) as a way of bringing the two sides of the great reading debate together – the 'top-down' (whole language) approach and the 'bottom-up' (phonics) view. Gough and Tunmer presented the Simple View of Reading as a formula:

Decoding (D) x Language Comprehension (LC) = Reading Comprehension (RC)

They emphasised that both sides of the equation must be present in reading for meaning to occur. The Rose Report (2006) for the English government about teaching early reading translated the formula into a diagram (see Figure 5.1).

Gough and Tunmer argued that SVR brings together comprehension and decoding but it was not seen as satisfactory either by the whole language or the phonics theorists (for a detailed explanation and critique of the Simple View of Reading, see www.teachingtimes. om/news/the-simple.htm (accessed 1 May 2017)).

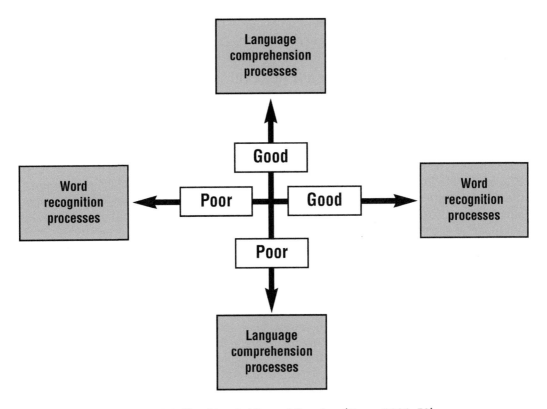

Figure 5.1 The Simple View of Reading (Rose, 2006: 53)

In this diagram, word recognition processes include using phonic cues and information to decode words and learning high-frequency words in order to read words quickly and fluently. These aspects of reading should be acquired quickly. Language comprehension processes, on the other hand, are expected to develop cumulatively with more experiences of reading – and life. The diagram indicates that successful acquisition of reading is indicated by the upper right-hand quadrant and that if a child's reading is becalmed in the lower left-hand quadrant, some action needs to be taken.

However, although the diagram looks appealing in its clarity, reading is not a 'simple' matter. Reading words is not only a matter of decoding but may also include compre-hension; for example, when understanding words that carry different meanings. Take the word 'read': in order to recognise whether this is present or past tense, and so know how to pronounce the word, the reader needs to have some understanding of the context (Goswami, 2008). As Goswami argues:

> Reading is one of the most complex cognitive skills that humans can learn.
> It is supported by multi-modal networks uniting motor systems, language
> systems, semantic systems and reasoning systems. It seems inherently
> unlikely that a 'simple view' of reading can provide a framework for teaching
> that is sufficiently rich to capture this complexity.
>
> (Goswami, 2008: 73)

To many researchers, a 'simple' view of language is not sufficient to capture the richness and complexity of what readers do when they read.

Sociocultural theories of reading development

A sociocultural view sees reading as socially and culturally embedded, shifting the emphasis from the individual learner to the cultural context for reading. According to this perspective, meaning develops from social interactions. It draws on the work of Vygotsky (1978) about socially mediated learning. A central Vygotskian view is that children learn through the support of others, moving gradually from assisted to independent performance. Bruner (1996) similarly emphasised the importance of the cultural context for learning and the role of communities in constructing learning (socioconstructivism). In terms of reading, people bring their cultural experiences of text (and of the world) as well as knowledge of language to their interpretation of the written word. Snow (2002) in the United States presented a report on reading based on a model of the relationship between reader, text, activity and the sociocultural context for reading (see www.rand.org/pubs/research_briefs/RB8024/index1.html (accessed 1 May 2017)).

Researchers such as Heath (1983) and Street (1993) have for some time argued for a greater awareness of how texts are used in different cultural settings, laying emphasis on the effects of learners' different language and literacy experiences on their school-based learning. For example, in some cultures, singling out a child in front of peers is not only unfamiliar but undesirable (Au, 2000) so that asking a child to read to the class might meet with a reluctant or negative response, not because the child cannot read but because the practice of standing out before others is culturally discouraged. Collaboration and cooperation may be valued more than competition and these details of diversity, when a teacher is aware of them, can feed productively into classroom work; for example, paired reading. Becoming literate is not only a matter of learning the skills and concepts associated with print but also learning particular ways of thinking, using and valuing texts so that learning to read is likely to be more successful if teachers are alert to cultural differences in ways of using and responding to texts.

> **Socioconstructivism:** emphasises the importance of collaboration and negotiation in learning, using the notion of proximal learning where a learner moves from being assisted with learning towards independence through, for example, scaffolding (see section 2.8).

Sociocultural views have fed into many explorations of the cultural and social relationships between home literacy experiences and school-based reading practices (Minns, 1997; Compton-Lilly, 2006; Pahl and Rowsell, 2012). Chapter 11 outlines theories of situated practice and researchers who set out to identify, value and use the 'funds of knowledge' (Moll, 1992) or 'language assets' (Cremin et al., 2014). This perspective has been key in studies of the rich language and literacy resources and experiences in bi-/multilingual homes and communities (Gregory et al., 2004; Kenner, 2004; Gregory, 2007; Gregory, 2008; Smidt, 2016). Gregory gives examples showing that children's reading experiences outside school are complex, cultural and personal and also that home, family and community practices vary widely. It is equally true that home language practices in apparently monolingual homes and communities vary greatly. Despite great diversity, the home language and literacy experiences of bi- and multilingual children can combine successfully with the official reading practices of the school. However, such 'syncretism' of home and school language and literacy experience is more likely to bear fruit if teachers first find out about children's home and community learning in order to build on this in the classroom (Cremin *et al.*, 2015).

> **Syncretism/syncretic literacy:** describes how different cultural literacy practices and traditions can merge to enrich, inform and organise literacy activities. All children, but notably bi- and multilingual children, mix and blend practices from home and school into new ways of understanding and expressing ideas.

Sociopolitical perspective

Sociopolitical studies highlight differences in the experience of literacy for different groups of learners; for example, boys/girls, children who are learning English as an additional language and children from lower socioeconomic groups (Hall, 2003). Based on research from US schools, Duke (2000) found that not only were there fewer resources made available to pupils in lower socioeconomic status schools, but also that restricted teaching approaches may play a part in underachievement. The sociopolitical perspective, closely allied to a sociocultural view, sees literacy as fundamentally related to issues of power (Baker and Luke, 1991). Freebody and Luke (1990) developed a 'four resources model' (sometimes referred to as 'four roles' or 'families of practice'): to be fully literate, readers must learn to make meaning from texts through 'breaking the code', using texts functionally and analysing texts critically. None of these roles precedes another; all must be activated simultaneously:

- Code Breaker: How do I crack this code?
- Meaning Maker/Text Participant: What does this mean to me?
- Text User: What do I do with this text?
- Text Analyst: What does this text do to me?

This model integrates a focus on phonemic awareness (code breaker), what the reader brings to the text and context (meaning maker), genre theory (text user) and critical literacy (text analyst).

The sociopolitical approach extends the sociocultural view of constructivism to consider how discourses of power influence learning to read (or learning literacy more generally). Most particularly, a sociopolitical perspective sees critical literacy, inclusion and social justice as central (Comber, 2007; Janks, 2013). The child is viewed as having agency and the reading curriculum seen as including all kinds of texts: popular cultural and media texts as well as school-approved reading (Marsh and Millard, 2005; Marsh *et al.*, 2015). A sociopolitical stance takes the view that no knowledge is neutral but is always based on some group's perspective on what counts as valuable or valued. It follows that texts themselves are not neutral or 'innocent' and so need to be seen in the light of critical enquiry about the underlying assumptions and values that they carry. As Hall explains:

> Taking a critical stance requires that issues of equity come to the fore, so questions like the following become prominent in classrooms that foster critical literacy:
>
> - What images of and ideas about, say, race, gender, ethnicity, socioeconomic class, disability are on offer in the text?

- Whose interests are being served by the text?
- Whose voices are included and excluded?

(Hall, 2003: 176)

This approach helps young readers see that texts have power and to consider how a text might represent particular beliefs, attitudes and values, thus marginalising others.

A critical literacy perspective goes further than examining texts for their power dimensions and raising awareness of issues of equity and social justice. It proposes an agenda for social action to create citizens who can analyse texts for their underlying assumptions, challenge any unfair representations of people and use their literacy to make a difference in their world. The challenge for schools is to find ways of valuing the knowledge and experience of literacy all children bring to school while introducing them to new and enjoyable text experiences and providing them with the tools to become critical, responsive and active readers.

Finding a balance

When it comes to teaching, there is often overlap between different perspectives on reading development. Research describing classrooms where children are taught to read most effectively and maintain consistently high standards (Pressley *et al.*, 2001; Taylor and Pearson, 2002; HMIE, 2006) indicates that they all have certain things in common:

- a balanced approach which attention to word recognition skills is matched by attention to comprehension
- attention to individual children's literacy skills, experiences and interests through high quality interaction and close monitoring of individual progress
- high levels of engagement in reading (Dombey *et al.*, 2010: 5).

In New Zealand, for many years, early reading instruction was based on 'Balanced Reading Programmes' which were:

> highly complex programmes, including environmental design, assessment, modelling, guidance, interactivity, independence, practice, oral language acquisition, writing and reading processes, community building and motivation.
>
> (Reutzel, 1999: 322)

These offered a far more nuanced view of balance than the 'simplistic and undisciplined expressions of eclectic thinking and rhetoric' (*ibid.*) surrounding the phonics versus whole language debate. In attempting to maintain a sense of the necessary complexity of the debate, a position of 'principled eclecticism' (Stahl, 1997; Larsen-Freeman, 2000) seems to be a sensible way forward when considering different perspectives on reading development and acquisition.

Principled eclecticism: begins by considering the learners' needs and ways of learning and develops coherent but flexible teaching approaches to cater for the variety of learners.

5.2   Teachers as readers

Commeyras *et al.* (2003) argue that all teachers should be reading teachers – teachers who read and readers who teach (see also Chapter 7), so it is worth reflecting on personal experience as a touchstone for teaching reading.

Stevie recalls her first memories of reading print:

> *I don't remember not being able to read. I could read when I went to infant school, but we did have to go through those awful repetitive reading scheme books before I was allowed to read on my own – 'independent reading' we'd call it now. Most of my reading memories are about reading at home. I can't recall my parents reading to my sister and me at bedtime but my Mum used to read to me during the day, especially after my sister had started school. I remember snuggling on my Mum's lap while she read fairy stories (we had a great one with lovely illustrations and an embossed cover), poems, rhymes and picture books. We didn't have lots of books in the house but we did have magazines and newspapers. My Mum was a great newspaper reader and my Dad had motorcar magazines. I enjoyed browsing the pictures with him explaining all about engines, etc. I think it fair to say that I was (and still am) a bookworm and if I couldn't get enough to read at home there was always the local library. I still remember the smell as you went in ... floor polish, dust and paper ...*
>
> *At school I loved it when the teacher read to us. I remember Mr Davies reading* Wind in the Willows *... I still like listening to audiobooks now.*

It is interesting that Stevie's memories of reading are mostly about reading at home – and reading different kinds of texts: books, poems, pictures. She associates reading with particular sensations – the feel of a book's cover, being warm and cosy, the smell of the library – and sees reading as a social act – with her parents and her sister. Being read to was important, too. Her experiences emphasise the social and cultural nature of reading as well as the way she had managed to 'crack the code' before she had formal instruction. A River of Reading (Cliff Hodges, 2016) shows key moments in Stevie's personal reading experience (Figure 5.2).

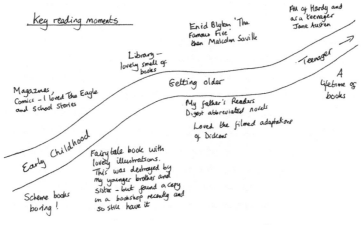

Figure 5.2 Stevie's River of Reading

After discussion about her own reading preferences, Della asked her 5 and 6 year olds to complete their own Rivers of Reading (see website resource 5.1 for her account of the project). Here, Jessica, Shifah and Aaron show the variety of their reading as well as the ways their families are involved in reading (Figures 5.3, 5.4 and 5.5). Examples like this emphasise that reading is more than simply decoding and that children bring a wealth of reading experience to school, which it is worth first of all finding out about and then building on.

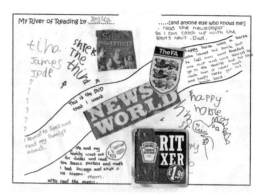

Figure 5.3 Jessica's River of Reading

Figure 5.4 Shifah's River of Reading

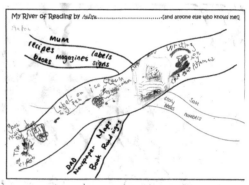

Figure 5.5 Aaron's River of Reading

Activity 5.1
Reading autobiographies – reflective journal/blog/pairs/group

Using website resource W5.2, make your own River of Reading. Jot down memories of reading from as early as you can remember. What were some of the key reading experiences at home and at school? Share your memories with others in the group. What differences were there in your experiences of reading? What similarities? For example, are there any gender differences in preferences for particular kinds of reading? Did any of the group find reading at school more difficult than reading at home – or vice versa?

Look back at the principles about teaching reading outlined in the Introduction to this Part. How do the insights you have gained from reflecting on your reading histories relate to these principles? For example, did any of your teachers discuss their own reading for pleasure, or were you encouraged to ask questions about what you were reading?

Note down one or two key points arising from your discussions that could act as your personal principles about teaching reading.

5.3   What can a developed reader do?

Reading is not a single act. People read differently according to the reasons for reading and the type of text. Meek puts it like this:

> The reading experts, for all their understanding about 'the reading process' treat all text as the neutral substance on which the process works as if the reader did the same thing with a poem, a timetable, a warning notice.
>
> (Meek, 1987: 7)

Stevie filled in a Personal Reading Profile with questions about reading behaviours (Figure 5.6). She has ticked some items twice – indicating that at some times she feels comfortable with a particular type of reading and sometimes she doesn't. She explains:

> *I love doing my accounts – I've got all sorts of spreadsheets, but when I see a column of figures in a book, my mind closes up. I really like to look at maps, particularly historical ones but when the satnav can't help to get round a traffic holdup and I have to read the road map, I panic! I like information books if they have pictures but I don't read much factual material for pleasure ... I find it quite difficult to process instructions as well.*

Looking at the array of ticks on the chart, it seems that Stevie is quite a versatile reader and there is definitely a tendency towards the visual. One interesting feature is that she finds it easier to write/produce numerical information than to read it. Notice, too, that she mentions twice that she gets flustered with having to read certain types of text. In terms of reading behaviour, she seems to have developed particular routines and strategies, some of them individual, but others as a shared experience. Although she is clearly an experienced reader, the fact that she finds certain kinds of reading difficult means that she will have a sense of how some of the children in her class might struggle with particular kinds of text. Personal struggles are often a good starting point for understanding children's difficulties.

Type of reading	Very comfortable	Quite comfortable	OK	Quite uncomfortable	Very uncomfortable
Letter/cards/emails from friends/family	✓				
Diagrams		✓			
Columns of figures	✓	*I find it hard to read them but like to do my monthly accounts*			✓
Magazines	✓				
Newspapers				✓	
Internet information		✓			
Novels	✓				
Maps	✓	*Like reading historical maps but find it hard to read the A-Z*			✓
Notices (e.g in museums/staff rooms)			✓		
Information books		✓ *If these have pictures*		✓	
Pictures/photographs	✓				
Films	✓				
Other, for example, material in another language than English					

Where do you like to be in order to read happily?
Depends – I like to read novels on the train. I don't often read novels at home. For work or academic reading I like to be at a table. I read magazines or browse through recipe books on the sofa.

Is there any particular time of day when you find you can read more easily?
'Serious' reading – early in the day.

How long can you comfortably read for?
If I'm absorbed I can read for more than 4 hours, (not always very easy to find the time to do that though!)

What strategies have you developed to help you read more easily?
Academic/professional texts – I find these harder than reading novels so I read them several times – (fast, slow, then fast again) and sometimes out loud.

What makes reading difficult for you?
Narrow columns (like in newspapers)
Long, complicated sentences in academic/professional texts.

How do you choose what you want to read?
Friends' recommendations or presents from friends (so I don't have to choose those!) Favourite authors or genres
Favourite bookshops or the internet.
Audio programmes recommending books or magazine recommendations.

When do you read aloud?
In class.
Reading out Facebook/emails to my husband.
If I need to understand a difficult text.

Does anyone ever read aloud to you?
My husband reads snippets from newspaper/internet news.
We like listening to audiobooks in the car.

Figure 5.6 Stevie's Personal Reading Profile

Activity 5.2
Personal Reading Profiles – reflective journal/blog/pairs/group

Complete the Personal Reading Profile and the questions about reading behaviours in website resource W5.3. Before you share these with someone else, see if you can detect any patterns in your reading preferences. Do you, like Stevie, have a tendency towards the visual? Or do you prefer reading factual material? Share your profiles and responses with a colleague – what differences/similarities can you find? What about when, where and how you like to read? Are they the same for both of you? If not, what might the implications be for the classroom? And what about the things that make reading difficult for you? Again, are these the same or different? When you compare a group of reading profiles and responses about reading behaviours, it becomes very clear that even with a group of experienced readers, there are significant differences in preferences, approaches and difficulties. This will be very much the same with any class of children so that it will be important to bear in mind the diversity of your class and their reading preferences.

After looking at a range of reading profiles and responses about behaviours, make a few notes about the implications these have for teaching reading. Keep these notes and add to them for Activity 6.1.

5.4   Reading on screens

The increase in home and school use of screens has implications for teaching reading. The amount of material is one challenge: there is far more online information available, made up of words and images and including movement and animation, sound and colour. On-screen texts are designed to be navigated differently from the usual direction of reading of a printed page of continuous text (top to bottom and left to right). Also, screen texts often invite interaction, moving between screens reached by hyperlinks. Not only does reading on the internet offer different navigational pathways, the reader also has to make decisions about what to read and which options to follow in internet reading (Kress, 2003).

Such possibilities for reading mean different approaches to teaching reading, yet little research has been carried out about how children can be helped to make on-screen reading decisions. A study by researchers from Canada, the United States and Australia, following pairs of readers using iPads (Simpson *et al.*, 2013), reveals the complexities of multidirectional reading paths and how children work across and between screens. Heath (2000) draws attention to the growing evidence that the interaction between verbal and visual information has become more complex:

> The line between word and image is getting harder to draw; the visual, through colour, line and form, enables understanding of metaphor – our ability to map interactions, experiences and cognitive operations across concepts to form images. In other words, the visual and the verbal reinforce one another in the sustained and adaptive learning necessary to increase learning.
>
> (Heath, 2000: 124)

For young (and older) readers, she explains, the task of gathering information from internet texts calls on multiple kinds of literacy which go beyond reading print in a linear way to knowing how to interpret colour, different icons and images, and blocks of text. In addition, the reader has to organise in their minds disparate items of information which are not presented according to any necessary logic and may be put together just to make a screen look appealing.

However, although previous research has focused on eye movements across visual texts (Heath, 2000; Holsanova and Holmqvist, 2006) Simpson *et al.* (2013) identify the importance of haptic (touch) practices. Touching or tapping the screen or a key indicates a cognitive choice – to follow a particular line of thought:

> This has challenged our traditional notions of the reading process to take account not only the cognitive demands of the design of a text but also the physical interaction of the reader with the text.
>
> (Simpson *et al.*, 2013: 129)

Mackey (2002) considers the role of hands in both paper-based and on-screen reading, suggesting the need to research more about whether using hands when reading is a matter of usual interaction of a reader with a text or whether 'the use of the hands engages the brain in ways that play a constitutive role in the reading process' (Mackey, 2002: 12).

Haptic: relates to the sense of touch.

Figure 5.7 Reading on screen   **Figure 5.8** Reading on screen

Mangen and van der Weel (2016) have responded to the plethora of different perspectives on reading, particularly those that deal with on-screen reading, by proposing a multidimensional framework that can take into account elements of embodied experience of reading (reading involves eyes, hands and posture), perceptions, cognitive processing, emotional and personal responses and cultural aspects. It also takes account of the different ways in which texts are presented (on screens, on paper), text types, levels of comprehension and reader motivation and experience. The complexity and integration of the framework recognises the complexity and integration of the process of reading itself (see Chapter 8 for in-depth discussion of comprehension).

In addition to trying to find logical pathways through texts presented multimodally with many different possible pathways, there are problems of authorship and validity with many internet texts. Screen-based texts do not have to go through an editorial process. Blogs, websites and social media sites are not susceptible to any critical scrutiny so that 'information' which is little more than unconfirmed assertion can appear on any site. This 'post-truth' landscape, perhaps particularly in respect of social media, makes it even more important to help young readers develop discernment and responsibility for the information flows they access (Burnett and Merchant, 2011; Facer, 2011).

However, there are potential dangers in bringing learners' cultural practices under scrutiny in the classroom. It is all too easy to view children as 'passive' consumers of different media, or for teachers to think that some of children's preferred screen watching is in some way inferior to reading books. In fact, children are sharp critics even of the texts they enjoy the most; for example, research by Marsh and Bishop (2014) shows children appropriating, changing, subverting and critiquing popular reality television shows (see Euromedia (2004) for a fuller examination of issues about critical media literacy).

Reading film

Most children have experience of watching films at home, and reading film in the classroom has often been seen as a starting point for some other activity – usually writing. Whilst this is a perfectly valid classroom practice, it can direct attention away from the fact that film is a particular kind of constructed text with its own conventions and language which children have to learn how to read. Parry and Hill Bulman (2017) argue for film being studied in its own right. They suggest a range of ways to help children become attentive and analytical readers of film, starting with Chambers' (2011) 'Tell Me' approach which establishes a dialogue between children and teachers not only about what they might have liked about a film but also more probing questions such as:

- What did you notice?
- What puzzled you?
- What would you like to look at or listen to again?

Discussion like this is more like negotiating meaning and developing the ability to justify a particular reading of a text, rather than moving children towards a predetermined 'teach-erly' reading (Parry and Hill Bulman, 2017: 14) (see Chapter 8 for examples of using film to support comprehension).

Case study, upper primary: Reading a short film with 9 and 10 year olds

Keen that her class should learn to read film analytically, Ella, who teaches 9 and 10 year olds chose the British Film Institute (BFI) (2001) animation *El Caminante* (the walker/traveller), directed by Debra Smith as the basis for an extended teaching sequence. This is a wordless film with poignant guitar music about a visit by a mysterious stranger to a village and the effect he had on the people there. The learning objectives for the three-week unit were to develop the children's engagement, understanding and response through talk and to look at the structure and organisation of texts with a view to writing a mystery story as a first person narrative

---

(viewer's perspective). As a starting point, Ella covered the screen and just played the soundtrack, asking the children to make predictions about the story from the sound alone.

The class watched the film several times, discussing the children's predictions and how they compared with what they could now tell from the images. They identified different 'episodes' of the story, and for the third viewing, Ella gave pairs an A3 sheet with the episodes down the left side and three columns headed *camera*, *colour* and *character*, planning to explore each of these elements in turn. She began with *camera*, looking at the different effects of long, medium and close-up shots but also considering who might be 'looking' through the eye of the camera. For the first minute or so of the action, she modelled discussing how camera angles and 'point of view' make a difference to how viewers respond to the film and asked the class to continue making notes about the use of the camera in the film.

Re-watching the film, Ella modelled discussing the director's use of colour. To complete this part of the film reading, the class looked at the characters. As this is a wordless film, there are no names, but the children knew that the central character was the traveller and several of the children and villagers were easily identifiable. Ella asked pairs to identify a child for themselves and follow her/him through the film, making notes about their contribution to the story. They wrote short diary entries by their chosen child, commenting on the events of the day the traveller arrived. They read them to each other and made a collage on the wall of 'The Day the Traveller Arrived'. Finally, Ella asked them to follow El Caminante throughout the film, noting how he influenced events. To end this week's work the traveller (Jamie, the teaching assistant) was hot-seated to try to determine where he had come from, why he chose to visit this village, where he learned his tightrope walking skills and where he was heading.

The second week began with drama where the villagers discussed the traveller's visit the day after he had left. The class added to the collage their views on 'The Day After the Traveller Left'. This week focused on *setting*, *sound* and *story*, so that the class could discuss how these three elements combined to make a compelling narrative. They already had the basic episodes of the story but needed to look at how the director created tension. Keeping their A3 sheets from the previous week, the children started a new A3 sheet, again with the episodes down the left-hand side and this time *setting*, *sound* and *story* at the top of the columns. Ella modelled commenting on setting, then sound, just for a few minutes of the film, and asked the class to make their own comments on how these elements contributed to the flow and narrative tension of the film. They drew 'temperature charts' of the narrative, indicating where the director created tension and where there was a more relaxed atmosphere. In the final session of this week, they put the two A3 sheets together and each pair wrote a brief comment on how the director had created such a compelling narrative.

The final week was devoted to drafting and writing a first person narrative about the visit of the traveller and how it had affected the villagers. The children used their diary entries and A3 sheets to help prompt ideas and worked in pairs to respond to each other's work. Ella was particularly pleased with the work of some boys who were not avid writers. Jaden wrote:

> *It's a mystery. When I look back at it now I'm older, I don't really know what happened on that magical day in the hot, dusty summer. I better start from the beginning. Manuel and me were playing when we heard a buzz of sound from the village centre.*

Simran wrote:

> *I was heartbroken when he went. I wanted to be him. A hero who could do dangerous things without showing any fear. The rest of the boys always teased me but if I could just be like him they wouldn't bully me anymore. As the day grew darker, I watched him leave. I stayed there until he was just a dot.*

(To view the film, go to: www.youtube.com/watch?v=p0zoTc-_5oE (accessed 1 May 2017); see Chapter 3 for definitions of hot seating and other drama strategies.)

5.5 The components of a rich and balanced reading curriculum

Any balanced reading curriculum needs to encompass three key elements:

- reading *to* children
- reading *with* children
- and reading *by* children.

Reading to children

Many adults remember with pleasure being read to either at home or at school. Reading aloud not only helps children understand how different text types work – for example, the difference between reading narrative and instructions – but also shows them how to read fluently with intonation and phrasing suitable to the piece of text. Being able to read fluently supports reading for meaning and the ability to sustain reading – both of which aid comprehension, interpretation and response. Above all, reading to children allows them to experience texts beyond their level of fluency and introduces them to more varied and complex language and ideas. In a research project with adults in a London borough, Duncan (2015) identified a range of gains from reading aloud including: memorisation, understanding, reviewing writing and creating a sense of fellowship. In Chapter 6, Chambers (2011) gives advice about preparing for reading by reading the story several times and suggests that it is important to read from a variety of different text types, all of which should be available in the classroom for the children to experience for themselves once they have been enthused by hearing part of the text.

Texts used in classrooms should include:

- extracts and complete texts – information and reference texts
- traditional and contemporary poetry and prose
- classic children's fiction and poetry
- graphic novels and picture books
- drama, including drama in performance
- texts written by authors from the four countries of the UK as well as texts from other cultures
- texts that have challenging subject matter, which broaden perspectives and extend thinking
- texts on audio and screen
- texts with a variety of structures, forms, purposes, intended audiences and presentational devices
- texts that demonstrate quality and variety in language use
- texts that reflect individual choice of reading matter
- texts that reflect the diversity of 21st century classrooms
- texts that extend learners' intellectual, moral and emotional understanding
- texts with a variety of tone, such as humour, parody, word play
- texts that demonstrate the impact of technology on language use
- texts that present challenge.

Reading picture books

Not simply for young readers, picture books offer a wealth of possibilities in fiction and information. Classics such as Anthony Browne's *Zoo* (1994), Chris Van Allsburg's *The Mysteries of Harris Burdick* (2011) and Neil Gaiman's *The Wolves in the Walls* (2007) as well as the more recent, such as *Greenling* by Levi Pinfold (2016), Jeannie Baker's *Circle* (2016) and Shaun Tan's *The Singing Bones* (2016), have challenged older readers. Quirky picture books for younger readers such as *Triangle* by Mac Barnett and Jon Klassen (2017) and *The Big Book of Bugs* by Yuval Zommer and Barbara Wilson (2016) enrich reading across the curriculum for the youngest readers. Beautiful design as in *It Starts with a Seed* by Laura Knowles and Jennie Webber (2016) or *The Promise* by Nicola Davies and Laura Carlin (2014) leads to thoughtful consideration of the environment.

The best picture books (as the best print books) are those that can be read and re-read by adults and children alike, and offer layers of meaning both in the words and the images and in the interrelationships between the two (Evans, 2015; Arizpe and Styles, 2016). Design, typeface and colour all add to the reading experience. Picture books encourage reading fluency and prediction, reading for inference, questioning and comparison. The images do not simply 'illustrate' the words but add to the whole meaning of the text.

There is a wealth of writing about picture books – their origins, range and variety (Lewis, 2001; Graham, 2008; Arizpe and Styles, 2016) but the following extracts focus on the role of picture books in promoting reading and readers. Mills and Webb propose three general questions that help in selecting books (including picture books) for young readers:

> *Does this book give the young reader access to ideas, themes and possibilities, while keeping 'the surface' accessible?*
>
> ... the 'look' of the page, and the interplay between text and pictures, has to be appropriate. Yet within this frame of accessibility, there has to be a challenge in terms of ideas and themes ...
>
> *Does this book give young readers possibilities for growing as thinkers and imaginers, while keeping the pleasure of reading at the forefront?*
>
> ... is there scope within this book for extending children's power to think, empathise, imagine and create new ideas and patterns of thought? Is there enough in the story to take readers in and along through the patterning of language, pictures (often), character and action? ...
>
> *Does this book help children in their growth as readers?*
>
> Good books for the young give valuable lessons in reading and literacy: teacher, librarians, parents and others involved should take note of the ways in which texts 'work' for young children. Being aware of some of these ideas and looking and listening to what young readers make of the books we give them, help us to be more attuned to the powerful reading lessons that good books give to the young. In books such as Eric Hill's *Where's Spot?* and Pat Hutchins' *Rosie's Walk*, the very young are encouraged to read, anticipate, predict, make sense of what is implicit and have their 'guesses' confirmed or changed during the course of their reading. Stories with clear patterns such as John Burningham's *Mr Gumpy's Outing*, teach young readers the value of repetition, the role of dialogue in moving action on, the strong sense of anticipation that will be crucial when they come to read longer texts.
>
> (Mills and Webb, 2004: 771–772)

Watson and Styles suggest that:

> A picture book welcomes and provides for young readers' detailed observation of image and, as a bonus, supports their developing vocabulary and growing phonic confidence. Who in their right mind could ever have believed that picture books somehow worked against a proper and necessary development of these capacities? Yet it is true that a reader cannot simply decode or decipher a picture book. We have come in recent years to understand that central to the picture book is the notion of the readerly gap – that imaginative space that lies hidden somewhere between the words and the pictures, or in the mysterious syntax of the pictures themselves, or between the shifting perspectives and untrustworthy voices of the narratives. And we have come to acknowledge young readers' extraordinary ability to allow their growing wisdom and knowledge of their own lives to inform and shape those gaps of meaning – except this ability is not extraordinary at all; it is *ordinary*, the ordinary curiosity of young minds weaving together the strands of their lives in search of patterns and meaning.
>
> (Watson and Styles, 1996: 2)

Bromley (1996) writes about how picture books can support the developing reading of bilingual children. In her classroom, the practice of sharing picture books on an individual basis with the children was already well established:

> It was during one of these sessions that I began to realise how good Momahl was at reading pictures. I had the opportunity to share reading *Each, Peach, Pear, Plum* with Momahl ... It soon became clear, from Momahl's reaction to the book, that she was able to understand many of the Ahlberg's literary jokes. Her favourite page was that of 'Bo Peep up the hill, I spy Jack and Jill'. When she saw this page, Momahl immediately sang the nursery rhyme, Jack and Jill, in its entirety. This was before she had heard the page read to her. This meant that she was able to identify the essential clues to their identity from the picture. She also used the opportunity to sing other rhymes to us, some in English, some in Urdu ...
>
> *Each Peach, Pear, Plum* was to become Momahl's first known text ... It is a text that places heavy reliance on rhyme and rhythm. These factors supported Momahl's reading, providing her with a strong tune on the page to follow. Momahl also spent a long time looking at the pictures, spotting the characters, singing the rhymes that she knew and guessing those that she did not ... It is important to note that Momahl was by no means fluent in English, though she could recite the alphabet, count to twenty and label many objects. It was in the art of discourse that she was not so skilled. However, picture books were to help her go some way towards overcoming this problem.
>
> (Bromley, 1996: 137–138)

Coulthard (2016) reports on research with young bilingual learners responding to visual texts, indicating the importance of picture books for developing readers of all ages.

There are suggestions in Chapter 6 for bookshops which specialise in quality picture books as well as suggestions throughout this book for classic and new picture books and review sites such as *Books for Keeps* (http://booksforkeeps.co.uk/reviews) and the English Association's Primary English site (www2.le.ac.uk/offices/english-association/primary/ww1/book-reviews) offer many suggestions for choosing good picture books for all ages. Padlet has suggestions for high-quality picture books that can be used across the curriculum: https://padlet.com/p0077346/Picture bookPlan (all accessed 15 May 2017).

Activity 5.3
'Texts I Like' – individual to group

Read website resource W5.4 'Texts I Like' which has a list of suggestions of books for use with children of all ages including ideas of activities. Start a list of texts you think would be good to read with classes but which you have not yet had a chance to try and add to it as you come across new texts.

Share your list with other members of the group and build a fuller list.

It is important to know a range of texts well in order to select for specific curriculum and learning objectives, including magazines, for example:

Aquila magazine which is a fun educational magazine which offers challenges to children in maths, science and English. www.aquila.co.uk/ (accessed 1 May 2017)

First News is a national (UK based) newspaper for young people. It is also the world's first online news channel for children and teenagers. www.firstnews.co.uk/ (accessed 1 May 2017)

The Phoenix comic magazine is designed for 6 to 12 year old boys and girls with fiction, non-fiction, comic strips and short stories, jokes and puzzles. www.the phoenixcomic.co.uk/ (accessed 1 May 2017)

Scoop, a magazine for 8 year olds and over which includes short stories, poetry, graphic fiction, biography and non-fiction and features comic strips, activities, puzzles and jokes. www.scoopthemag.co.uk/ (accessed 1 May 2017)

National Geographic Kids contains varied and beautifully photographed features about the natural world. www.ngkids.co.uk/ (accessed 1 May 2017)

With middle and upper primary classes it is always useful to have a good knowledge of short stories and short novels, for example:

The Stone Mouse by Jenny Nimmo (2007) and *Dinner Ladies Don't Count* by Bernard Ashley (1984) (both suitable for 7 to 9 year olds)

The Runner by Keith Gray (2005) and *The Kites are Flying* by Michael Morpurgo (2016) (both suitable for 10 to 11 year olds)

In website resource W5.5, Mallett makes a range of recommendations for short stories suitable for children aged 6–11.

Information books, poetry and complex picture books are equally good for guided reading (see Chapter 7 for more suggestions).

The Centre for Literacy in Primary Education has a free website to help choose the very best children's literature for primary classrooms. www.clpe.org.uk/ corebooks (accessed 1 May 2017)

The Just Imagine Story Centre also offers free online reviews and recommendations. http://justimaginestorycentre.co.uk/blogs/resources (accessed 1 May 2017)

COMPANION @ WEBSITE

Activity 5.4
Reading aloud – individual to small group

In Activity 5.2 you noted when you last read something aloud. Reading aloud in a more public place like a classroom can be a daunting prospect, but when you feel that you know the text and have practised, it can be a very pleasurable experience – not just for the listeners but for you, too. One participant in a reading aloud project commented:

It feels as if you are being given a bit of a gift, I think, when somebody reads to you. They are giving you time, they're acknowledging you and giving you something quite special really.

(Duncan, 2015: 87)

Find a text you really like (it may be one on your 'Texts I Like' list) and prepare a section to read aloud to a small group of colleagues. You might like to do this with a friend – sharing the reading. After each of the group has read aloud, talk to each other about how it felt – both to read aloud and to be read to.

Plan to read aloud to your class as soon as you can, and try to make it a regular practice.

Reading with children: Shared reading

Shared reading is a key area where the reading teacher can act as a model for reading, and in line with Vygotskian theories of collaborative and supported learning, can demonstrate not only the skills of reading but the pleasures and satisfactions of reading, the questions prompted by reading and engagement with text. Shared reading is when a teacher uses a Big Book or an enlarged text on the visualiser or interactive white board, or perhaps multiple copies of a normal size book, and reads in a sustained way with the whole class, not only modelling the rhythms and cadences of the particular kind of text but also using intonation and different speech effects to bring the text to life. It is important for the children to hear the whole of a text (a whole picture book or poem, for example) or a complete chapter before discussion so that they have the experience of hearing a full story, episode or section of an information book. Shared reading can be planned into any area of the curriculum and gives the teacher a chance to introduce children to texts that, if read independently, might stretch their current capabilities but which, when read to them, will extend their thinking – whether about information, themes, character or the style of writing. The teacher may have a specific focus in terms of skills, but shared reading also shows children how to speculate (not so often that it harms the flow of meaning) as the teacher voices thoughts aloud, for example:

> I'm not sure I trust this wolf.
> I wonder why the author isn't telling us what Maya saw.
> I'd like to know more about what the lizards feed on.
> I can't imagine what it must have been like to be imprisoned for so long.

Not only does this signal that the children can also speculate, inviting similar comments, but it gives them examples of tentative, exploratory language. Similarly, discussion after reading a section of a text can allow for reflection on the information, action and characters as well as the themes and the author's intentions. Planning shared reading over a term or a year gives the teacher a chance to introduce children to a range of different authors and types of text, particularly non-fiction, and to create a sense of the classroom as a community of readers.

Shared reading often takes place at the beginning of an extended teaching sequence (see, for example, website resource W4.3 and W12.4) where specific elements of the text are the focus for the teaching, such as narrative structure, characterisation or a particular grammatical feature.

Reading with children: Guided reading

Guided reading originated in the 1960s in New Zealand (Tennent *et al.*, 2016) and has become regularly used in Anglophone countries to describe teaching reading in small groups. Guided reading allows the teacher explicitly to teach reading strategies to support comprehension and response (including interpretation skills, critical reading and inference). In Australia in the 1970s the approach was advocated for early reading instruction (Holdaway, 1979; Clay, 2005a, 2005b). Later, in the United States of America, Fountas and Pinnell (1998) developed guided reading with older readers. In England, the National Literacy Strategy (DfEE, 1998) cemented the role of guided reading as part of teaching English from ages 4–11 (and beyond). The aims were to help overcome barriers to learning so that children become confident in using a range of strategies to get meaning out of a text and, importantly, to encourage children's enjoyment of being readers.

The purpose of every guided reading session is to encourage and extend independence. In planning guided reading, there are two sets of objectives:

- *Curriculum objectives*: the kinds of texts the teacher wants the children to experience drawn from the relevant national curriculum
- *Learning objectives*: the progress the teacher wants the whole group – and individuals within the group – to make during the course of the guided reading sessions. When deciding on objectives, the teacher will bear in mind strategies which needs practice and consolidation and those which will need to be introduced and modelled.

Texts are selected to match the reading ability of the group but also to present some challenge. Groups of children work together on the same text so that support is drawn not only from the teacher but also from other members of the group, through a combination of discussion, thinking out loud and reading. Each session focuses on a particular reading strategy/strategies and when the teacher has identified the objectives for the group and selected a text, a guided reading session often follows the sequence:

- Introducing/reintroducing the book
- Strategy check
- Independent reading
- Returning to the text
- Responding to the text (see website resource W5.6).

As children become more fluent readers, this sequence may be altered to fit the curriculum and learning objectives; for example, if comprehension is the focus of a session, independent reading could precede the guided element. While working with the group, the teacher (or teaching assistant) gives focused attention to individuals as they read. Children's thinking is challenged through careful questioning and assessments are made of the children's reading from observations of their reading behaviours and analysis of their oral responses.

While the class teacher works with the guided group, the remainder of the class work independently of the teacher (this may be individually, in pairs or as a group). Groups may work with other adults and the class teacher ensures that they are clear about their roles and expectations in supporting other children and in gathering evidence of progress in reading. The teacher will listen to each child read to a given point independently. Because it is carried out in small groups, guided reading makes it possible for teachers to focus on the specific learning needs of each child, improving children's reading fluency, understanding (comprehension), response to texts and reflection on what has been read on the road to independence as readers. Iaquinta sees guided reading as means of helping the young reader discover more about the process of reading while re-reading:

> As children develop these understandings they self-monitor, search for cues, discover new things about the text, check one source of information against another, confirm their reading, self-correct and solve new words using multiple sources of information.
>
> (Iaquinta, 2006: 414)

Pearson and Gallagher (1983) developed a model of reading instruction (Gradual Release of Responsibility Model – GRoR) based on Vygotskian ideas of a move from collaboration to independence in learning. Reading instruction moves from explicit modelling and instruction to guided practice and then to activities which will gradually lead to independent reading. This process may take a short or longer time but overall, the principle is to develop self-reliance in reading. Fisher (2008) describes GroR as having four interrelated components:

- Teacher's focus lesson – 'I do it'
- Guided instruction – 'We do it'
- Collaboration – 'You do it together'
- Independent – 'You do it alone'.

These need not necessarily be carried out in this order, but a lesson should contain all four interactive elements (see Chapter 8 for more about guided reading and comprehension).

For older, fluent readers, guided reading offers the opportunity to engage in longer, sustained reading and so reach deeper understanding. When children are more assured readers, the teacher may organise for much of the reading of the text to be carried out between the guided reading sessions so that time can be given in the sessions to discussion and analysis of key points in the text and the exchange of opinions.

Over a year, teachers will need to provide a wide range of reading experiences drawn from a variety of text types. They will also know their year's objectives for teaching reading and the age-related expectations for their class. Effective ongoing teacher assessment is essential to identify what the children need next in order to progress (see Chapter 9). Fountas and Pinnell (2016) emphasise the role of the teacher in being responsive, making moment-to-moment decisions based on observation and analysis of children's reading and reading behaviours. These observations indicate the next teaching moves. However, the age of the children will make a difference to the content of the guided reading sessions. With early readers, it is necessary to include the cueing strategies needed for decoding print (see Chapter 7) but decoding skills alone are not the only guides to reading progress; where there is a need to develop fluency or certain aspects of comprehension, the teacher may decide to create groups that are not based on common levels of reading fluency but perhaps on interests. As reading abilities change, so groups will need to be adjusted to ensure that the guided reading session addresses the particular needs of each child.

Activity 5.5
Reflective journal/blog/pairs/group

Read the guided reading case study in website resource W5.6 and, first of all individually, or in pairs, consider:

- Which questions were intended to provide evidence of the children's use of inference? Highlight any responses that give evidence of their ability to infer.
- Which questions focused on response and interpretation? Highlight any sections of the case study that give evidence of their responses to the meaning of the story and their interpretation of events.

The next opportunity you have, discuss with the class teacher how he or she plans for guided reading (deciding on groupings, deciding on texts, deciding next steps) and ask to observe a group session, paying specific attention to the kinds of questions asked to elicit different kinds of evidence of reading for accuracy, fluency, understanding.

5.6 Reading by children: Independent reading

Children read independently from the moment they can lay hands on a book or open a screen. In terms of reading in school, however, even independent reading will be monitored to ensure that children are developing the ability to make discriminating choices about what they read, to extend their repertoires and to respond thoughtfully to what they read. It is important that teachers know what the children are choosing to read independently, both at home and at school, in books and on screens so that they can better advise about and extend the children's reading experience. In order to do this, there needs to be a clear understanding that *all* reading counts and that the life of a reader will include reading sports programmes, magazines, internet information, fiction and information (and more). Familiar ways of encouraging reflection on reading are literature circles and reading journals or blogs (see Chapter 6). Modelling keeping a reading log/blog or journal and drawing can support young readers who are growing in independence to keep their own records of reading.

Working reading journals might be used as part of classroom activities, for example, they might involve drawings about books currently being read or annotations of picture book double-page spreads (Figure 5.9). However, one of the dangers of creating any routine way of responding to reading is if the response becomes a chore. The main aim of a blog, reading group or

Figure 5.9 Drawing of Matilda in journal

reflective journal is to capture the kinds of emotions and questions a reader has when reading independently. These can then become the basis for pleasurable conversations and discussions about reading because the main aim of any of these activities is to develop lifelong, engaged and committed readers.

Summary

The chapter begins by outlining a range of perspectives on reading, including 'bottom-up' and 'top-down' theories, the so-called 'simple' view of reading and the broader sociocultural and sociopolitical approaches, concluding that a balanced approach to teaching reading needs a sense of the complexity of what is involved in becoming a reader. A central part of this chapter is the role of a teacher's personal experience and expertise. Since reading on screens is now an everyday feature of children's reading experience, the chapter discusses the different features of reading on paper and on screen including reading e-books and the internet with a case study example of teaching children to read film. Finally, the chapter describes the three key reading experiences for a balanced and rich reading curriculum.

Recommended reading

Cremin, T. (2014) Reading teachers: Teachers who read and readers who teach, in T. Cremin, M. Mottram, F. M. Collins, S. Powell and K. Safford (eds) *Building Communities of Engaged Readers: Reading for pleasure*. London: Routledge, pp. 67–88. In this chapter, Teresa Cremin describes the experiences of teachers involved in a year-long research project exploring the challenges offered by sharing reading experiences, satisfactions and difficulties with their pupils. **Advanced**

Goswami, U. (2008) Reading, complexity and the brain, *Literacy*, 42 (2) pp. 67–74. In this article, Usha Goswami gives a brief overview of recent studies in brain imaging analysing them within a cognitive framework of reading development. **Advanced**

Gregory, Eve (2008) *Learning to Read in a New Language: Making sense of words and worlds*. London and New York: SAGE. Combining research with teaching approaches, this book is a useful guide for teachers of bilingual learners.

Hall, K. (2003) *Listening to Stephen Read: Multiple perspectives on literacy*. Buckingham: Open University Press. In this balanced, wide-ranging and scholarly review of four main perspectives on reading, Kathy Hall uses the example of one child reading, inviting different theorists to comment on how to help him improve, drawing on their views to examine different views on reading development and pedagogy. **Advanced**

Meek, M. (1987) *How Texts Teach What Readers Learn*. Stroud: Thimble Press. Old but gold, this slim book is a must for any teacher of reading. Margaret Meek explores some of the key issues about teaching reading in an erudite, but accessible way.

References

Arizpe, E. and Styles, M. (2016) *Children Reading Picturebooks: Interpreting visual texts*, 2nd edn. Abingdon: Routledge.

Au, K. H. (2000) A multicultural perspective on policies for improving literacy achievement: Equity and excellence, in M. L. Kamil, P. B. Mosenthal, P. D. Pearson and R. Barr (eds) *Handbook of Reading Research*. Englewood Cliffs, NJ: Erlbaum, pp. 835–851.

Baker, C. and Luke, A. (eds) (1991) *Towards a Critical Sociology of Reading Pedagogy*. Amsterdam: John Benjamins.

British Film Institute Education (2001) *Story Shorts: Short films for seven to eleven year olds*. London: British Film Institute.

Bromley, H. (1996) 'Madam, read the scary book, Madam': Momahl and her picture books – the emergent bilingual reader, in V. Watson and M. Styles (eds) *Talking Pictures: Pictorial texts and young readers*. London: Hodder and Stoughton, pp. 137–138.

Bruner, J. (1996) *The Culture of Education*. Cambridge, MA: Harvard University Press.

Burnett, C. and Merchant, G. (2011) Is there space for critical literacy in the context of social media? *English Teaching, Practice and Critique*, 10 (1) pp. 41–57. http://education.waikato.ac.nz/research/files/etpc/files/2011v10n1art3.pdf (accessed 1 May 2017)

Chall, J. (1983) *Stages of Reading Development*. New York: McGraw Hill.

Chambers, A. (2011) *Tell Me (Children, Reading and Talk) with the Reading Environment*. Stroud: Thimble Press.

Clay, M. M. (2005a) *Literacy Lessons Designed for Individuals: Part one: When, why and how?* Auckland: Heinemann.

Clay, M. M. (2005b) *Literacy Lessons Designed for Individuals: Part two: Teaching procedures*. Auckland: Heinemann.

Cliff Hodges, G. (2016) *Researching and Teaching Reading: Developing pedagogy through critical enquiry*. London: Routledge/NATE.

Comber, B. (2007) Assembling dynamic repertoires of literate practices: Teaching that makes a difference, in E. Bearne and J. Marsh (eds) *Literacy and Social Inclusion: Closing the gap*. Stoke-on-Trent: Trentham Books, pp. 115–132.

Commeyras, M. Bisplinghoff, B. S. and Olson, J. (2003) *Teachers as Readers: Perspectives on the importance of reading in teachers' classrooms and lives*. Newark: International Reading Association.

Compton-Lilly, C. (2006) Identity, childhood culture and literacy learning: A case study, *Journal of Early Childhood Literacy*, 6 (10) pp. 57–76.

Coulthard, K. (2016) The words to say it: Young bilingual learners responding to visual texts, in E. Arizpe and M. Styles (eds) *Children Reading Picturebooks: Interpreting visual texts*. Abingdon: Routledge, pp. 75–88.

Cremin, T., Mottram, M., Collins, F., Powell, S. and Safford, K. (2014) *Building Communities of Engaged Readers: Reading for pleasure*. London and New York: Routledge.

Cremin, T., Mottram, M., Collins, F., Powell, S. and Drury, R. (2015) *Researching Literacy Lives: Building communities between home and school*. London: Routledge.

Cummins, J. (2000) *Language, Power, and Pedagogy: Bilingual children in the crossfire*. Clevedon: Multilingual Matters.

Department for Education (2015) *Statutory Guidance: National curriculum in England: Primary curriculum*. www.gov.uk/government/publications/national-curriculum-in-england-primary-curriculum (accessed 1 May 2017)

Department for Education and Employment (DfEE) (1998) *National Literacy Strategy: Framework for teaching*. London: Department for Education and Employment.

Diack, H. (1965) *In Spite of the Alphabet: A study of the teaching of reading*. London: Chatto and Windus.

Dombey, H. with Bearne, E., Cremin, T., Ellis, S., Mottram, M., O'Sullivan, O. Öztürk, A., Reedy, D. (UKLA) and Raphael, T. and Allington, R. (International Reading Association) (2010) *Teaching Reading: What the evidence says*. Leicester: United Kingdom Literacy Association.

Duke, N.K. (2000) For the rich it's richer: Print experiences and environments offered to children in very low and very high socioeconomic status first grade classrooms, *American Educational Research Journal*, 37 (20) pp. 441–478.

Duncan, S. (2015) Reading aloud in Lewisham: An exploration of adult reading-aloud practices, *Literacy*, 49 (2) pp. 84–90.

Ehri, L. C. (2005) Development of sight word reading: Phases and findings, in M. J. Snowling and C. Hulme (eds) *The Science of Reading: A handbook*. Malden, MA: Blackwell, pp. 135–154.

Ehri, L. C., Nunes, S. R., Willows, D. M., Schuster, B. V., Yaghoub-Zadeh, Z. and Shanahan, T. (2001) Phonemic awareness instruction helps children to read: Evidence from the National Reading Panel's meta-analysis, *Reading Research Quarterly*, 36 pp. 250–287.

Euromedia (2004) *The European Charter for Media Literacy*. www.euromedialiteracy.eu/charter. php (accessed 1 May 2017).

Evans, J. (ed.) (2015) *Challenging and Controversial Picturebooks: Creative and critical responses to visual texts*. Abingdon: Routledge.

Facer, K. (2011) *Learning Futures: Education, Technology and Social Change*. Abingdon: Routledge.

Fisher, D. (2008) Effective Use of the Gradual Release of Responsibility Model. www.mheonline. com/_treasures/pdf/douglas_fisher.pdf (accessed 1 May 2017)

Fountas, I. C. and Pinnell, G. S. (1998) *Guided Reading: Good first teaching for all children*. Portsmouth, NH: Heinemann.

Fountas, I. C. and Pinnell, G. S. (2016) *Guided Reading: Responsive teaching across the grades*, 2nd edn. Portsmouth, NH: Heinemann.

Freebody, P. and Luke, A. (1990) Literacies programmes: Debates and demands in cultural contexts, *Prospect: A Journal of Australian TESOL*, 11 pp. 7–16.

Goodman, K. S. (1967) Reading: A psycholinguistic guessing game, *Journal of the Reading Specialist*, 4 pp. 126–135.

Goodman, K. (1986) *What's Whole in Whole Language?* London: Scholastic.

Goodman, K. (1992) Why whole language is today's agenda in education, *Language Arts*, 69 pp. 354–363.

Goodman, K., Fries, P. H. and Strauss, S. L. (2016) *Reading – The Grand Illusion: How and why people make sense of print*. Abingdon: Routledge.

Gough, P. B. and Hillinger, M. L. (1980) Learning to read: An unusual act, in *Bulletin of the Orton Society*, 30, pp. 179–196.

Gough, P. B. and Tunmer, W. E. (1986) Decoding, reading and reading disability, *Remedial and Special Education*, 7, pp. 6–10.

Goswami, U. (2003) Early phonological development and the acquisition of literacy, in S. B. Neuman and D. K. Dickinson (eds) *Handbook of Early Literacy Research*. New York: Guilford Press, pp. 111–125.

Goswami, U. (2008) Reading, complexity and the brain, *Literacy*, 42 (2) pp. 67–74.

Goswami, U. (2015) Children's cognitive development and learning. A report for the Cambridge Primary Review Trust. http://cprtrust.org.uk/wp-content/uploads/2015/02/COMPLETE-REPORT-Goswami-Childrens-Cognitive-Development-and-Learning.pdf (accessed 1 May 2017).

Graham, J. (2008) Picturebooks, looking closely, in P. Goodwin (ed.) *Understanding Children's Books: A guide for professionals*. London: SAGE, pp. 95–108.

Gregory, E. (2007) What counts as reading and learning outside school? And with whom? How? and Where?, in E. Bearne and J. Marsh (eds) *Literacy and Social Inclusion: Closing the gap*. Stoke-on-Trent: Trentham Books, pp. 41–72.

Gregory, E. (2008) *Learning to Read in a New Language: Making sense of words and worlds*. London and New York: SAGE.

Gregory, E., Long, S. and Volk, D. (eds) (2004) *Many Pathways to Literacy: Young children learning with siblings, grandparents, peers and communities*. London: Routledge.

Hall, K. (2003) *Listening to Stephen Read: Multiple perspectives on literacy*. Buckingham: Open University Press.

Heath, S. B. (1983) *Ways with Words: Language, life and work in communities and classrooms*. Cambridge: Cambridge University Press.

Heath, S. B. (2000) Seeing our way into learning, *Cambridge Journal of Education*, 30 (1) pp. 121–132.

Her Majesty's Inspectorate for Education (HMIE) (2006) *Pilot Inspection of the Education Functions of Clackmannanshire Council in October 2005*. Edinburgh: SEED.

Holdaway, D. (1979) *The Foundations of Literacy*. Gossford, Australia: Ashton-Scholastic.

Holsanova, J. and Holmqvist, K. (2006) Entry points and reading paths on newspaper spreads: Comparing a semiotic analysis with eye-tracking measurements, *Visual Communication*, 5 (1) pp. 65–93.

Iaquinta, A. (2006) Guided reading: A research-based response to the challenges of early reading instruction, *Early Childhood Education Journal*, 33 (6) pp. 413–418.

Janks, H. (2013) Critical literacy in teaching and research, *Education Enquiry*, 4 (2) pp. 225–242. www.lh.umu.se/digitalAssets/122/122861_critical_literacy_in_teaching_eduinq_vol4_no2_june13_225-242.pdf (accessed 1 May 2017).

Kenner, C. (2004) *Becoming Biliterate, Young Children Learning Different Writing Systems*. Stoke-on-Trent: Trentham Books.

Kenner, C. and Gregory, E. (2003) Becoming biliterate, in N. Hall, J. Larsen and J. Marsh (eds) *Handbook of Early Childhood Literacy*. London: SAGE, pp. 178–188.

Kress, G. (2003) Interpretation or design: From the world told to the world shown, in M. Styles and E. Bearne (eds) *Art, Narrative and Childhood*. Stoke-on-Tent: Trentham Books, pp. 137–153.

Larsen-Freeman, D. (2000) *Techniques and Principles in Language Teaching*, 2nd edn. Oxford: Oxford University Press.

Lewis, D. (2001) *Reading Contemporary Picturebooks*. Abingdon: Routledge.

Mackey, M. (2002) *Literacies Across Media: Playing the text*. London: Routledge.

Mangen, A. and van der Weel, A. (2016) The evolution of reading in the age of digitisation: An integrative framework for reading research, *Literacy*, 50 (3) pp. 116–124.

Marsh, J. and Bishop, J. C. (2014) 'We're playing *Jeremy Kyle*'! Television talk shows in the playground, *Discourse: Studies in the Cultural Politics of Education*, 35 (1) pp. 16–30.

Marsh, J. and Millard, E. (eds) (2005) *Popular Literacies, Childhood and Schooling*. London: Routledge/Falmer.

Marsh, J., Hannon, P., Lewis, M. and Ritchie, L. (2015) Young children's initiation into family literacy practices in the digital age, *Journal of Early Childhood Research*, 15 (1) pp. 47–60.

Meek, M. (1987) *How Texts Teach What Readers Learn*. Stroud: Thimble Press.

Mills, C. and Webb, J. (2004) Selecting books for younger readers, in P. Hunt (ed.) *International Companion Encyclopaedia of Children's Literature*. Vol. 1, 2nd edn. London and New York: Routledge, pp. 771–772.

Minns, H. (1997) *Read It to Me Now!: Learning at home and at school*. Buckingham: Open University Press.

Moll, L. (1992) Literacy research in community and classrooms: A sociocultural approach, in R. Beach, J. Green, M. Kamil and T. Shanahan (eds) *Multidisciplinary Perspectives on Literacy Research*. Urbana, IL: National Council of Teachers of English, pp. 211–244.

Pahl, K. and Rowsell, J. (2012) *Literacy and Education: Understanding the new literacy studies in the classroom*, 2nd edn. London: SAGE.

Parry. B. and Hill Bulman, J. (2017) *Film Education, Literacy and Learning*. Leicester: United Kingdom Literacy Association.

Pearson, P. D. and Gallagher, M. C. (1983) The instruction of reading comprehension, *Contemporary Educational Psychology*, 8, pp. 317–344.

Pitman, J. (1961) *The Pitman Initial Teaching Alphabet*. www.omniglot.com/writing/ita.htm (accessed 1 May 2017)

Port, R. (2006) The graphical basis of phones and phonemes, in M. Munro and O. Schwen-Bohn (eds) *Second Language Speech Learning: The role of language experience in speech perception and production*. Amsterdam: John Benjamins, pp. 349–365.

Pressley, M., Wharton-McDonald, R., Allington, R., Block, C. C., Morrow, L., Tracey, D., Baker, K., Brooks, G., Cronin, J., Nelson, E. and Woo, D. (2001) A study of effective first grade literacy instruction, *Scientific Studies of Reading*, 5 (1) pp. 35–58.

Reutzel, D. R. (1999) Commentary: On balanced reading, *The Reading Teacher*, 52 (4) pp. 322–324.

Rose, J. (2006) *Independent Review of the Teaching of Early Reading* (Rose Report). London: DfES.

Shaywitz, S. (2005) *Overcoming Dyslexia*. New York: Vintage Books.

Simpson, A., Walsh, M. and Rowsell, J. (2013) The digital reading path: Researching modes and multidirectionality with iPads, *Literacy*, 47 (3) pp. 123–130.

Smidt, S. (2016) *Multilingualism in the Early Years: Extending the limits of our world*. Abingdon: Routledge.

Smith, F. (1971) *Understanding Reading: A psycholinguistic analysis of reading*. New York: Holt, Rinehart and Wilson.

Smith, F. (undated) *Essays into Literacy: Selected Papers and Some Afterthoughts.* www.arvindgupta toys.com/arvindgupta/essaysintoliteracy.pdf (accessed 1 May 2017)

Snow, C. (2002) *Reading for Understanding: Toward an R&D program in reading comprehension.* Santa Monica, CA: RAND. www.rand.org/content/dam/rand/pubs/monograph_reports/2005/ MR1465.pdf (accessed 4 May 2017)

Spiro, R. J., Coulson, R. L., Feltovich, P. J. and Anderson, D. K. (1994) Cognitive flexibility theory: Advanced knowledge in ill-structured domains, in R. B. Ruddell, M. R. Ruddell and H. Singer (eds) *Theoretical Models and Processes of Reading*, 4th edn. Newark, DE: International Reading Association, pp. 602–615.

Stahl, S. A. (1997) Instructional models in reading: An introduction, in S. A. Stahl, *Instructional Models in Reading.* Hillsdale, NJ: Erlbaum, pp. 1–29.

Street, B. V. (ed.) (1993) *Cross-Cultural Approaches to Literacy.* Cambridge: Cambridge University Press.

Taylor, B. M. and Pearson, P. D. (2002) (eds) *Teaching Reading: Effective schools, accomplished teachers.* Mahwah, NJ: Lawrence Erlbaum Associates

Tennent, W., Reedy, D., Gamble, N. and Hobsbaum, A. (2016) *Guiding Readers: Layers of meaning.* London: University College London, Institute of Education.

Vygotsky, L. (1978) *Mind in Society the Development of Higher Psychological Processes.* Cambridge, MA: Harvard University Press.

Watson, V. and Styles, M. (1996) (eds) *Talking Pictures: Pictorial texts and young readers.* London: Hodder and Stoughton.

Children's books

Alan and Janet Ahlberg (1999) *Each, Peach, Pear, Plum.* Kestrel Picture Books. ISBN 9780670882786

Bernard Ashley, illustrated Janet Duchesne (1984) *Dinner Ladies Don't Count.* Puffin Books. ISBN 9780140315936

Jeannie Baker (2016) *Circle.* Walker Books. ISBN 9781406338010

Mac Barnett, illustrated Jon Klassen (2017) *Triangle.* Walker Books. ISBN 9781406376678

Anthony Browne (1994) *Zoo.* Red Fox. ISBN 9780099219019

John Burningham (2001) *Mr Gumpy's Outing.* Red Fox Picture Books. ISBN 9780099408796

Nicola Davies, illustrated Laura Carlin (2014) *The Promise.* Walker Books. ISBN 9781406355598

Neil Gaiman, illustrated Dave McKean (2007) *The Wolves in the Walls.* Bloomsbury Publishing PLC. ISBN 9780747591627

Keith Gray (2005) *The Runner.* Yearling, New Ed. edition. ISBN 9780440866565

Eric Hill (2009) *Where's Spot.* Warne. ISBN 9780723263661

Pat Hutchins (2009) *Rosie's Walk.* Red Fox Picture Books. ISBN 9781862308060

Laura Knowles, illustrated Jennie Webber (2016) *It Starts with a Seed.* Words & Pictures. ISBN 9781910277171

Michael Morpurgo, illustrated Laura Carlin (2016) *The Kites Are Flying.* ISBN 9781406367317

Jenny Nimmo (2007) *The Stone Mouse.* Walker Books. ISBN 9781406306057

Levi Pinfold (2016) *Greenling.* Templar. ISBN 9781783701872

Shaun Tan (2016) *The Singing Bones.* Walker Books. ISBN 9781406370669

Chris Van Allsburg (2011) *The Mysteries of Harris Burdick.* Andersen Press. ISBN 9781849392792

Yuval Zommer and Barbara Wilson (2016) *The Big Book of Bugs.* Thames and Hudson. ISBN 9780500650677

CHAPTER 6
READING FOR PLEASURE

This chapter covers:

- Defining reading for pleasure
  - Case study, middle primary: Reading information for pleasure
- Why is reading for pleasure important?
- Children's attitudes to reading
- Reading for pleasure in the reading curriculum
- Strategies for promoting engagement and enjoyment
  - Case study, early primary: Incorporating children's reading interests into curriculum planning
  - Case study, early, middle and upper primary: Planning opportunities for children to read independently
- Apps to support reading for pleasure
- Creating diverse, comfortable, supportive and social reading environments
- Engaging children with challenging texts
  - Case study, upper primary: Chaucer in the original Middle English – a challenging text

6.1   Defining reading for pleasure

Reading for pleasure and engagement needs to be distinguished from reading skills. The two are linked, of course; getting to grips with the skills of reading enables fluency so that young readers can focus on the content of what they are reading. But, as the Introduction to this Part points out, 'learning to read' is different from 'becoming a reader' and fostering engagement in reading is part of the teacher's role in helping children become lifelong committed readers:

> The active encouragement of reading for pleasure should be a core part of every child's curriculum entitlement because extensive reading and exposure to a wide range of texts make a huge contribution to students' educational achievement.
>
> (UK APPG, 2011: 6)

Engagement in reading is fundamental to the progressive development of readers:

> Engagement is increasingly seen by researchers as central to progress in reading ... Children who are engaged learn more from their classroom lessons. They also read more, inside and outside school. As they read more, they become better readers – better at recognising words and better at making sense of the world.
>
> (Dombey *et al.*, 2010: 7)

However, although these quotations reflect some of the key aims of teachers who want to encourage children to read for pleasure, they may seem a little instrumental: reading is (quite rightly) seen as the pathway to educational achievement and an increase in the frequency of reading, but what about the pleasures many adults feel when settling down to indulge themselves in a book? Raleigh extends these quotations to include:

1. Pleasure: the pleasure of reading easy and entertaining material effortlessly, as well as the more strenuous pleasure which comes from understanding difficult material.
2. Personal enrichment: as a source of experience and of knowledge, reading extends your horizons, broadens your vision, enlarges your perspective.
3. Practical value: being able to put reading to use maximises your chances of benefiting from schooling and enables you to find out things from print, now and in the future.
4. Power: reading means access and enables you find out things about your history and the society you live in which it's harder to discover in other ways; you can also discover things about other histories and societies which may surprise you.

> (Raleigh, 1996: 118)

However, reading for pleasure is a term that is not used consistently in the literature. The terms 'reading for pleasure', 'reading for enjoyment' and other similar terms are often used interchangeably (Clark and Rumbold, 2006). Reading for pleasure is also frequently referred to, especially in the USA, as independent reading (Cullinan, 2000), voluntary reading (Krashen, 2004), leisure reading (Greaney, 1980), recreational reading (Manzo and Manzo, 1995) or ludic reading (Nell, 1988) (all cited in Clark and Rumbold, 2006). This variety of definitions incorporates the idea that all such reading is underpinned by the free will of the reader, and sustained.

Drawing on these insights Clark and Rumbold define reading for pleasure as:

> reading that we do of our own free will, anticipating the satisfaction that we will get from the act of reading. It also refers to reading that having begun at someone else's request, we continue because we are interested in it.
>
> (Clark and Rumbold, 2006: 5)

Such reading can involve any kind of text: fiction, comics, poetry, information, both on screen and on paper, and can happen anywhere it is possible to read.

The varied definitions seem to overlap so that the distinction between reading for pleasure and the satisfaction the reader obtains for what Raleigh terms 'personal enrichment' is unclear. Perhaps a better way of describing this area would be 'personal motivation and engagement in reading which leads to sustained voluntary reading'. It may be best to see reading for pleasure as interrelated with ideas about engagement, motivation, fulfilment and purpose – all of which underpin pleasure and satisfaction in reading.

Lockwood (2012) refers to the concept of 'flow' – complete absorption in an activity and pleasure and enjoyment as its own reward (Csikszentmihalyi, 2008). In his research, Lockwood found that children who reported intensive absorption in reading tended to have positive attitudes towards reading whilst negative views came from pupils who had not personally experienced such engagement. However, Lockwood also points out that 'This order of motivated experience is not readily available within the situation of formal schooling' (Lockwood, 2012: 231). Guthrie *et al.* (1996) argue that classroom contexts which promote pleasure and engagement are:

- self-directing, featuring student autonomy in choice of topics, books, peers
- metacognitive, containing explicit teaching of reading strategies, problem solving, composing
- collaborative, involving the social construction of meaning.

Activity 6.1
Reflecting on personal reading for pleasure – reflective journal/blog

Make a quick list of what you have read voluntarily over the last few days. It might have been any kind of text: sports programme, novel, internet material, magazine, recipe, etc. Consider how long it took to read it and the purpose for reading. Were some texts harder to read than others, or were they all fairly easy? How many were read on screen or on paper? Was some of what you read recommended to you? What do you think the balance is between texts you read voluntarily and those you had to read for work, study or business?

Much of what we read for our own enjoyment is chosen because someone else has recommended it to us, through conversation, book reviews on internet sites and newspapers and magazines, for example. You may also have found that although someone else has asked you to read a particular text for work or study purposes, you carried on reading it, or parts of it, for your own interest.

You probably found there were two strands in what motivated you to read. First, *intrinsic motivation*. This refers to reading for personal interest which can be self-initiated or based on social interaction and encompasses a wide variety of texts: genre fiction, poetry, online information, communities of interest, Facebook and so on. Readers who are intrinsically motivated are more likely to develop an accompanying sense of pleasure (Hidi, 2000; McGeown, 2013).

Second, *extrinsic motivation*. This refers to reading in response to external requirements. For example, reading to meet teachers' or lecturers' requests. In extrinsically motivated reading the desire to read is controlled externally. Although extrinsic motivation may not lead to pleasure as such, it still is in the pursuit of certain outcomes, such as pleasing the teacher or preparing for a presentation. It can sometimes result in the development of intrinsic motivation (see section 6.7).

Some of the texts you read were probably not easy reads. You had to work hard at them. Perhaps they were full of technical vocabulary, or you read some poetry that was full of literary allusions that needed concentrated attention and re-reading a few times, or you have been reading a novel that plays with conventional structures. However, you did have a purpose for reading these more challenging texts and no doubt felt some kind of satisfaction and fulfilment, including pleasure, once you had finished them. These texts were hard but worth it. Engagement with reading, or reading for pleasure, is not therefore just about 'having fun'.

Reading challenging texts can be hard but ultimately satisfying, both in the sense of achievement as well as fulfilling the reader's purpose. Thus a definition of reading for pleasure should perhaps include reading for purpose and fulfilment.

Case study, middle primary: Reading information for pleasure

This case study illustrates how Kamal uses a short film to introduce 7- and 8-year-old children to a new topic. Kamal engages the children through extrinsic means, but by careful structuring and the encouragement of children's own interest in the topic they become intrinsically motivated to read further themselves. Kamal planned to develop children's reading for purpose and pleasure by introducing them to the topic of blue whales through a short film clip from the BBC series 'The Blue Planet': www.youtube.com/watch?v=44NXXmMCdj8 (accessed 3 May 2017).

Kamal had collected a number of books about whales in the class library and identified three reasonably easy to access websites with relevant information. First the class watched the clip together all the way through without comment or interruption. Then Kamal asked the children to watch the film again but to note down two or three facts that they found particularly interesting. The children shared the facts that they had found and Kamal wrote them up on the white board under the headings *size*, *food* and *other*. In this way the class created a shared understanding of what they had seen.

Kamal then asked the children whether anything had puzzled them and whether they had any questions they would like to ask. The children enthusiastically contributed questions such as:

What do krill look like?
Do blue whales eat anything else?
Why do whales blow air out of the tops of them?
How do blue whales breathe under water if they are mammals?
Why do humans know so little about the blue whales?
Why have humans killed such beautiful creatures?

Kamal said that he could not answer their questions so they would need to find out for themselves from resources he could provide and from what they could find themselves. This led to highly motivated research by the children who then shared their findings through short paragraphs and illustrations displayed on the classroom wall. This display remained for some time and was constantly added to as children independently researched and read by going online, visiting the school and class library.

Unexpectedly, the children began to discover that there were stories and other texts about whales they could read and began to bring them in to show the class. This led to a large collection of books that children brought in, both story and non-fiction, which the children chose to borrow and read when they could.

6.2 Why is reading for pleasure important?

A survey of reading habits in the UK, commissioned by Booktrust (Gleed, 2013), suggests there are substantial personal and practical benefits of regular reading for pleasure:

Overall, the research highlights four justifications for initiatives to encourage reading for pleasure from an early age, particularly among disadvantaged groups.

- People who read books are significantly more likely to be happy and content with their life.
- Most people who read books feel this improves their life. It also makes them feel good.
- People who were read to and encouraged to read as children are significantly more likely to read as adults, both to themselves and to their own children.
- Those who never read books live in areas of greater deprivation and with more children in poverty.

(Gleed, 2013: 4)

Further research evidence (OECD, 2002; Clark and de Zoysa, 2011; ESARD, 2012) shows that reading for pleasure leads to increased attainment. OECD (2002) found that regularly reading for enjoyment is more important for children's educational success than their family's socioeconomic status, that being a frequent reader 'is more of an advantage than having well educated parents' (OECD, 2002: 3) and that 'finding ways to engage children in reading may be one of the most effective ways to leverage social change' (*ibid.*). The OECD research found that 'Cognitive skills and reading motivation are mutually reinforcing ... Rather than being alternatives, schools need to address both simultaneously' (*ibid.*: 19).

Echoing the sense that reading for pleasure is an essential part of reading instruction, Lockwood points out that:

> Strategies that promote positive attitudes to reading need to be used alongside the teaching of reading skills in any effort to raise attainment.
>
> (Lockwood, 2012: 228)

Clark and de Zoysa (2011) also found a significant positive relationship between enjoyment and attainment, indicating that pupils who read more are also better readers. However, they are careful to point out that there is no evidence of a causal link between enjoyment of reading and higher attainment and that higher attainment may lead to more enjoyment of reading or greater enjoyment may lead to higher attainment. Similarly Clark and Douglas (2011), in a large-scale survey of over 18,000 young people, found that those who reported enjoying reading very much were six times more likely than those who did not enjoy reading to read above the expected level for their age. Young people who reported not enjoying reading at all were eleven times more likely than those who enjoyed reading very much to read below the level expected for their age. In a meta-analysis of international studies linking young readers' attitudes to reading and reading attainment, Petscher (2010) reports findings which support the view that there is a relationship between attitudes and achievement which is stronger in schools with 5 to 11 year olds.

In their review of the research literature, Clark and Rumbold (2006) indicate that promoting pleasure and independence in reading can have a significant impact not only on children's reading attainment but also on their writing ability. Gains are found in the areas of:

- text comprehension and understanding of grammar
- breadth of vocabulary
- positive reading attitudes
- greater self-confidence as readers
- pleasure in reading in later life
- general knowledge
- understanding of other cultures
- community participation
- insight into human nature and decision-making (Clark and Rumbold, 2006).

6.3   Children's attitudes to reading

International comparisons of attitudes to reading form part of the PIRLS reports (Twist *et al.*, 2012), which compares attitudes to reading in the many countries that take part in the survey. The report had this to say about attitudes to reading of 10 year olds in England:

In common with a number of other high achieving countries, pupils' attitudes to reading were less positive in England than the average internationally. The more able readers were more likely to enjoy reading and be motivated to read than the weaker readers. Compared to 2006, fewer pupils in 2011 reported never or almost never reading for fun out of school. Over half of pupils in PIRLS 2011 reported reading for half an hour or more every day out of school.

(Twist *et al.*, 2012: 2)

The trend in England seems to be positive, albeit from a low base, but if engagement in reading is so important, then schools in countries where engagement is lower need to consider what can be done to improve the situation.

Generally, different groups have varying attitudes to enjoyment of reading. The Booktrust survey (Gleed, 2013) indicates that there is a substantial gap in reading habits between the economically advantaged and disadvantaged groups in the UK. Moss and Washbrook (2016) report that irrespective of early language skills, girls at age 7 report much more positive attitudes to school and read more for pleasure than boys (Moss and Washbrook, 2016: 4). These differences between groups have implications for how teachers might foster engaged and committed reading regardless of socioeconomic status or gender. It is simply not enough just to focus on teaching word reading skills and comprehension strategies. Schools must also develop approaches to motivation and engagement in reading. They must also consider whether their current approach is encouraging all the differing groups within their schools to develop engagement in reading. The Simple View of Reading (see Chapters 5 and 7), which is largely promoted in schools in the UK and the USA, is not an adequate approach to fostering a lifelong love of reading.

6.4 Reading for pleasure in the reading curriculum

Cremin *et al.* (2014) argue that although reading instruction is critically important in developing successful readers, it is also crucial for schools to focus on both 'the skill *and* the will' to read. Currently, in both England and internationally, policy seems to have emphasised the skills of reading rather than engagement, motivation and the commitment to reading. Although national policies do acknowledge reading for pleasure (see, e.g., England's National Curriculum, DfE, 2015), the emphasis through high-stakes national tests and school inspections concentrates almost exclusively upon skills.

> **High-stakes testing:** when tests have significant consequences for the pupil, for example, passing the test has important benefits and failing has equally important consequences. High-stakes tests are carried out as single, specifically timed assessments, have a clear pass/fail boundary and have distinct consequences for passing or failing; in other words, something important is 'at stake'. Results of high-stakes test are often used to judge the effectiveness of the teacher, school or institution.

In Figure 6.1, Cremin *et al.* (2014) represent the distinctions between 'the skill and the will' – between reading instruction and reading for pleasure.

Reading instruction is oriented towards:	Reading for pleasure is oriented towards:
Learning to read	Choosing to read
The skill	The will
Decoding and comprehension	Engagement and response
Reading for the system	Reading for oneself
Teacher direction	Child direction
Teacher ownership	Child ownership
Attainment	Achievement
Solitary reading	Social and collaborative reading
The minimum entitlement (A set reading level)	The maximum entitlement (A reader for life)

Figure 6.1 Distinctions between reading instruction and reading for pleasure (from Cremin *et al.* 2014: 157)

What is clear from Figure 6.1 is that if schools want to develop children as lifelong readers, they have to incorporate strategies for both 'the skill and the will' into their ongoing teaching. Equally, if reading for pleasure strategies are to be successful, children's agency, and desire to read, must be central. Cremin *et al.* (2014) argue that their research, which investigated reading instruction in a number of English schools, identified:

> a multi-layered Reading for Pleasure Pedagogy, and subtle, but significant distinctions between reading instruction and reading for pleasure. These distinctions and the interplay between children's desire to read and their capacity as readers – the skill and the will – were central to the project.
>
> (Cremin *et al.*, 2014: 3)

The research summarised the following important findings:

- that reading and talk are mutually supportive
- that reading urgently needs reconceptualising in the twenty-first century to take into account new forms of text
- that reading for pleasure is strongly influenced by relationships between teachers, teachers and children, children and families, and schools, families and communities.

The research also found that a reading for pleasure agenda can be developed effectively through the creation of supportive classroom reading communities. Such communities are most effectively led by 'Reading Teachers – Teachers who Read and Readers who Teach' (Commeyras *et al.*, 2003: 4). Cremin *et al.* conclude that 'Reading Teachers recognise the significance of reader identity in reader development and frame their practice in responsive ways, encouraging interaction, choice, autonomy and increased reading for pleasure' (Cremin *et al.*, 2014: 3).

The last point is worth emphasising. Teachers who are increasingly aware of their own reading lives, their preferences, habits, behaviours and strategies and reflect upon the implications for teaching are able not only to set up sound reading communities in schools but also to recognise that children have rights as readers and develop their own identities as readers.

Activity 6.2
Rights of a reader – reflective journal/blog/pairs/group

Individually at first, read website resource W6.1 Pennac's 'Rights of a Reader'. You may not agree with all his ideas. When you have read all of them, choose one that you disagree with or would want to add to. Talk to a colleague about your opinions and amend Pennac's list of rights to suit your own ideas.

Are there any rights you would want to add? This would be a good topic for group discussion and the compilation of a new list of reading rights.

Thinking about your personal reflections on reading, are there any of the rights that you identify with strongly? If so, what implications might this have for your role as a Reading Teacher in Commeyras' terms?

You might like to download the poster and display it in the classroom as a basis for discussion. It is available on: www2.curriculum.edu.au/verve/_resources/Connections_72_poster.pdf (accessed 1 May 2017).

6.5   Strategies for promoting engagement and enjoyment

Researchers and teaching organisations (Clark and Rumbold, 2006; Lockwood, 2008; Cremin *et al.*, 2009; CLPE, 2014; Traves, 2015; NUT, 2016) have identified a range of factors as crucial for promoting reading for pleasure in schools:

- Incorporating children's own reading interests into curriculum planning.
- Creating diverse, supportive and social reading environments that promote children's agency as readers and are based on a view of the classroom as a community of readers.
- Teachers who are knowledgeable about texts and share their own reading lives with children, talk about books and make recommendations to individuals and the whole class.
- Reading aloud to the class for pleasure rather than for instrumental literacy teaching purposes.
- Creating frequent opportunities for children to read independently for pleasure, and giving them choices about what to read.
- Providing creative opportunities, such as drama and role play, to help children explore and understand texts, including those with challenging content and theme.

Case study, early primary: Incorporating children's reading interests into curriculum planning

Teachers of 5 and 6 year olds in Greenfields Infant School in East London decided that to develop their reading curriculum they needed to know much more about the children's literacy experiences outside school: what they were interested in reading about, and thus what could be built in school in a variety of ways. Greenfields serves a diverse and economically challenged community where thirty-six languages are spoken.

The teachers asked the children to:

● research their own literacy lives by taking photographs of when they engaged in literacy experiences with members of their families and to bring in texts that they read together at home into school to share
● bring into school, or talk to the teachers about, texts they liked to read because the contents were interesting to them and that they would like to see more of in school.

Literacy activities were defined widely, including print and screen texts – on small or larger screens. When the children brought in texts and talked about their literacy experiences, the teachers were surprised by the richness of the children's home literacy lives and how they shared these with their families, both in print and on screen, sometimes going on simultaneously.

To illustrate the variety of home reading experiences, one 6-year-old boy, who had four older sisters, reported that he:

● enjoyed stories about football, rabbits and pirates
● was very interested in wildlife and nature
● enjoyed family outdoor activities – for example, hunting, ferreting and fishing with his father
● regularly read information texts, mainly magazines, about hunting and wild life with his father
● liked to watch television programmes about Ben 10, Power Rangers and Wrestling, and looking at their respective websites
● played the Wii with the family in their living room most days.

This was typical of the range of literacy activities children engaged with in their homes. Religion also played a central role in many families, with daily reading of the holy book as well as regular trips to the local place of worship. The teachers also found that children engaged intensely with a constellation of texts around current popular cultural interests. Children watched television programmes about the characters, visited dedicated websites, collected magazines, played associated computer games, read books and magazines, role played the characters in playground games and watched their popular cultural favourites at the cinema.

It was also particularly noticeable that many boys and their fathers shared the same keen interests and liked to read texts together, which extended their information and understanding. For example, two of the boys had lorry-driving fathers and so shared an interest in texts about trucks. Aaron brought one of his books about trucks into the classroom and talked knowledgeably to a rapt class about the different trucks and their characteristics. Immediately he finished there was intense interest amongst other members of the class to look at the book and to share the information it contained.

The classroom as a community of readers

As a result of what they found out, the teachers made some far-reaching changes to their practice including:

- Regular focused 'show and tell' sessions where children brought in texts and objects of interest. Teacher's noted what was brought in and considered how they could incorporate into their planning for future teaching and learning.
- Introducing an 'interest tree' in the classes. Children wrote down what they were particularly interested in reading about on a 'leaf' and put it on the tree. Teachers again used these as a prompt for including in planning.
- Making time for 'text talk'. Children were encouraged to bring in texts they engaged with at home and talked about them to other children. The books and other texts were put on display in the book area.
- Reviewing the reading resources in the classroom/school and incorporating texts about areas that children reported interest in. This led to significantly more interest and engagement from the children.
- Teachers now feeling they could talk knowledgeably with parents about their children's interests outside school so that relationships became stronger.
- Teachers shared their literacy lives with the children and together developed a community of readers in the classroom, undermining preconceptions (and deficit views – see Chapter 1) of children's and families' literacy lives.
- Teachers became more knowledgeable about popular cultural and media influences on the children, could refer to them and make lessons more relevant to the experiences of the children.

The teachers reported that engagement in reading at school had significantly improved as a result of the changes that they had made. Their initiative had ensured that many of the recommended strategies for developing reading for pleasure had become part of the warp and weft of everyday classroom life. Children's agency was supported. Talk about texts became central and children's' literacy practices, interests and knowledge of the world were celebrated and built on within the curriculum.

Teachers who are knowledgeable about texts

The case study illustrates how teachers can became knowledgeable about the texts children like to engage with out of school, particularly ones associated with current popular culture. There were some gender differences in the content of the texts that boys and girls liked to read but it was clear that there was little that reflected both boys' and girls' out-of-school interests in the reading materials in school. Magazines which found their way into the classrooms and were avidly read and shared, were mainly donated by the children themselves. This study and others in the research (Cremin *et al.*, 2014) strongly indicated that teachers need to develop knowledge of children's out-of-school reading preferences and a wide knowledge of literature for children. Teachers who have a good knowledge of children's literature are much more able to make well-judged recommendations to children about what they may like to read next and are also more able to develop a community of readers in their classrooms (Younger *et al.*, 2005; Kwek *et al.*, 2007).

Activity 6.3
Keeping up with books for children – pairs/group/reflective journal/blog

It is difficult for a busy teacher to keep up with the large number of texts published. Some schools organise at least one staff meeting a term for teachers to simply read from the school's stock of children's literature and share their own favourite texts with colleagues.

There are many websites which draw attention to and review children's books.

Visit http://justimaginestorycentre.co.uk/blogs/resources (accessed 1 May 2017) and/or http://booksforkeeps.co.uk/ (accessed 1 May 2017) and spend ten minutes looking through the resources, reviews and interviews, noting on your 'Texts I Like' record (website resource W5.4) any books you would like to use with your class.

The Centre for Literacy in Primary Education (CLPE)

This has an extensive and useful list of 'core books' to help schools choose good books for children. This is available to browse at www.clpe.org.uk/corebooks (accessed 29 April 2017).

Reviews, features and interviews

These can also be found at:

Booktrust: www.booktrust.org.uk/books/children/
Love Reading: www.lovereading.co.uk/
Write Away: www.writeaway.org.uk/
National Literacy Trust: www.literacytrust.org.uk/
Reading Zone: www.readingzone.com/home.php
Carousel: www.carouselguide.co.uk/

(All accessed 1 May 2017)

Awards

The CILIP Carnegie and Kate Greenaway Children's Book Awards:

www.carnegiegreenaway.org.uk/ (accessed 1 May 2017)

UKLA's Children's Book Awards are judged by class teachers:

https://ukla.org/awards/ukla-book-award (accessed 1 May 2017)

The English 4–11 Picture Book Award is awarded for the best children's fiction and non-fiction picture books for ages 4–7 and 7–11: www2.le.ac.uk/offices/english-association/primary/english-4–11-book-awards (accessed 1 May 2017)

Reading aloud

Reading aloud conditions a child's brain to associate reading with pleasure, creates background knowledge and provides a reading role model; when children are read aloud to, they are 'enveloped' in a risk free learning environment that 'removes the pressure of achievement and the fear of failure, allowing the freedom to wonder, question and enjoy material beyond their reading abilities'.

(Wadsworth, 2008, cited in Safford, 2014: 94)

Chambers provides this advice to teachers to make reading aloud more effective:

- Prepare: read the story several times, think about the key things you want to bring out, what the mood of the story is at different points and how you will convey this.
- Read picture books, non-fiction and poems as well as longer fiction.
- Some children may like to follow the text, either in their own copies of the book or perhaps, if the text is relatively simple, on-screen. This will also help them to read it for themselves in due course.
- Encourage children to read aloud themselves – not as a task but for fun.
- Read aloud all through school years – and every day.

(Chambers, 2011: 89)

Reading aloud by an adult is a very important strategy for supporting children in their development as readers all through their primary years. Research (Taylor *et al.*, 2003; Parkhill *et al.*, 2005) clearly suggests that this should be a daily activity. This is also a good opportunity to introduce young readers to less familiar authors as they are likely to access well-known authors such as Roald Dahl, Jacqueline Wilson and Jeff Kinney by themselves (see also Chapter 5, particularly Activity 5.4).

Creating opportunities for children to read independently for pleasure, and giving them choices about what to read

Children get better at reading by reading, so it is important to provide frequent opportunities for them to read during and beyond the school day. Just 15 minutes a day of independent recreational reading significantly improves children's reading abilities (Block and Mangieri, 2002). Children's choices are critical here (Gambrell, 2011). Children should choose what they want to read in these planned times and browsing time also needs to be planned for. Short but regular independent reading sessions are better than one long one each week and it is important that there are no interruptions. The key issue here is how to make a regular time in busy school days for independent reading.

Case study, early, middle and upper primary: Planning opportunities for children to read independently

Longroad Primary School decided to develop a systematic approach to planning regular opportunities for children to read, to browse the school library or class reading area, to choose at leisure and to read independently. Immediately after lunchtime, for 15 minutes, ERIC (*Everybody Reading In Class*) took place. This meant that everyone read at the same time, including the adults who acted as positive role models. Occasionally the adults talked about what they were reading and why they had chosen that particular text. The school also suggested to some children who found reading individually every day problematic that they could choose to read quietly to each other if they wanted to.

In addition, the school created other opportunities such as reading assemblies where every so often, different classes or different adults in the school, shared their reading enthusiasms. This ranged from fairy tales to manuals about motorbikes. There are also reading clubs held at lunchtime where reading monitors/mentors (often older pupils in the school) supervised while children read independently in the school library. Sometimes the mentors read with younger children and share recommendations for books they might like to read. Book swap clubs – 'bring one, take one' – were organised after school once a week and the school set up a book-shop where books that were being read aloud in class could be bought. The school also organised occasional 'reading sleepovers' where older children could come in the evening and read before going to bed. Adults other than teachers – for example, the site supervisor and lunchtime staff – visited classrooms from time to time and talked to the children about what they liked to read.

One of the key initiatives was the Reading Gladiators scheme run by Just Imagine (http://justimagine.co.uk/project/reading-gladiators/ (accessed 1 May 2017)), designed to provide a challenging reading experience that motivates children to read for pleasure. Children are encouraged to read widely and to make adventurous reading choices. They collaborate with others in the class and carry out individual challenges.

Parents and families are also invited to be part of the reading community of the school with book evenings and quizzes where family members and children enjoy activities about reading together. One of the parents has set up a dedicated part of the website for sharing book recommendations and this became a popular social site for adults and for children and special places for reading were set up in the school garden. As a result of these initiatives, the school became a very obvious 'reading school' with a community of engaged and enthusiastic readers.

Paired reading, where older children and younger children read collaboratively chosen texts to each other, is also an effective strategy to promote reading engagement and confidence. The younger children benefit from hearing a role model, and older readers benefit by building their confidence even if they are not themselves particularly fluent.

6.6   Apps to support reading for pleasure

There is an ever-growing number of sites which are intended to support reading for pleasure but it is difficult to assess the reliability of the recommendations. Kucirkova and Cremin (2016) list key features of digital books that support reading for pleasure: that they need to have the potential to engage the emotions (affective), offer opportunities for shared and sustained reading and creative, personalised and interactive engagement. They stress the importance of reading for pleasure being child-chosen, child-directed and intrinsically motivating. These factors involve young readers in making meaning and offer enough reading satisfaction to prompt them to return for more.

Some useful apps

http://literacyapps.literacytrust.org.uk/ (accessed 1 May 2017). An online guide for teachers and parents looking for the best children's apps that support reading for pleasure. The guide is for children aged 0–5 years and is the only online guide in the UK that is research-based.

www.commonsensemedia.org/app-reviews (accessed 1 May 2017)

http://reviews.childrenstech.com/ctr/home.php (accessed 1 May 2017)

These are two US-based curation sites.

http://blog.momswithapps.com/ (accessed 1 May 2017)

www.teacherswithapps.com/ (accessed 1 May 2017)

These provide guides based on parents' and teachers' recommendations.

Publishers

Nosy Crow http://nosycrow.com/ (accessed 1 May 2017). A small, award-winning, independent company whose books for 0–14 year olds are published simultaneously in print and e-book form. All paperback picture books come with a free digital audio reading using an innovation called Stories Aloud.

Barefoot Books www.barefootbooks.com/ (accessed 1 May 2017). Produces books for children with beautiful artwork with engaging stories which are designed to inspire creativity and encourage respect for cultural, social and ecological diversity.

Mantra Lingua books http://uk.mantralingua.com/ (accessed 1 May 2017). An award-winning publisher producing books and resources for multi-ethnic, multilingual classrooms in UK, Sweden, Norway, USA/Canada in about seventy languages. Its dual language e-book library has 450+ e-books with audio in both languages for school and home.

Tiny Owl publishers http://tinyowl.co.uk/ (accessed 1 May 2017). An independent publishing company, producing quality, culturally diverse books for children.

Useful resources

www.pearsonschoolsandfecolleges.co.uk/AssetsLibrary/SECTORS/PRIMARYASSETSNEW/Reading-forPleasure/Documents/S046PracticalGuideRFP.pdf (accessed 3 May 2017). Pearson have produced a useful guide to developing reading for pleasure in the primary school, including Michael Rosen's twenty-point plan for reading.

www.outstandingreading.org/ (accessed 3 May 2017). The Oxford University Press offer guidance on developing an outstanding reading school, with a section devoted to engaging parents.

https://ukla.org/resources/details/promoting-reading-for-pleasure (accessed 3 May 2017). UKLA has produced this resource for parents about reading for pleasure.

Website resource W6.2 'Selecting books for teaching reading' gives guidance about how to choose books for specific readers and reasons.

6.7 Creating diverse, comfortable, supportive and social reading environments

As you may have found when you completed Activity 5.2, not many adults read in uncomfortable places. They choose to find a comfortable chair and many enjoy reading in the comfort of bed. It is clear that being comfortable makes a great difference to the pleasure gained from reading, so schools should ensure that children are physically comfortable when they read independently. Classrooms and the school library should have inviting and stimulating book corners which all children are encouraged to spend time in every day and borrow texts from the library on a regular basis (Figures 6.2, 6.3 and 6.4).

Figure 6.2 Reading environment early primary

Figure 6.3 Reading environment middle primary

Figure 6.4 Reading environment upper primary

Figure 6.5 Pleasurable reading

Creating a supportive environment for reading for pleasure

- Make spaces relaxing and cosy – think about providing cushions, chairs, sofas, tents, etc.
- Make them engaging and attractive – they could be decorated with posters children have made that relate to favourite books or with photos of children, their families and teachers reading at school, at home and elsewhere. This helps to promote reading as a shared, social experience.
- Ensure they are well stocked with books that are well displayed and easy to browse with a selection of new titles, favourite authors, picture books, graphic novels, poetry and non-fiction.
- Displays should be easy to navigate and changed regularly. Help children to browse for books and find what they want.
- Try grouping books by theme (change these regularly) and encourage children to recommend books for display.
- Encourage children to bring in their own books to read (as well as manuals, catalogues, magazines, etc.).
- Think about creating spaces where children can talk about books but also where they can be quiet if they want to.
- Make sure the space is kept tidy (NUT, 2016: 8–9).

Readers will note the references to 'books' in the above. As children (and adults) increasingly read on screen, access to screen-based texts via tablets and e-readers will be important to organise, as well as the storage of both the hardware and the software.

Because reading for pleasure is included in some curricula, teachers may create 'routines' rather than reading opportunities which are more related to children's own interests. Cremin sounds a note of caution to schools that they should not just superficially 'perform' reading for pleasure:

> Physically attractive reading environments can be enticing to children and are part of a reading for pleasure pedagogy ... alongside reading aloud, own reading time, and informal book talk. However their ability to influence the dispositions and engagement of young readers cannot be guaranteed. Much will depend on the quality and diversity of the texts available, the degree of choice and agency offered, and the time set aside for informal talk and interaction.

> In order to avoid reading for pleasure becoming little more than a colourful visual laid across the landscape of schools, we must ensure the social environment receives more attention ... Talking about texts, their possible meanings and interpretations, and informal conversations about reading and oneself as a reader deserve to be placed at the very heart of the reading curriculum. Such talk brings the landscape to life and helps to build communities of engaged readers.

> (Cremin, 2016)

6.8   Engaging children with challenging texts

Developing engagement in reading is not just about reading 'easy' texts. Engagement and pleasure can also come from the struggle with challenging texts, 'strenuous pleasure' as Raleigh (1996) terms it. Reedy and Lister (2007) describe a project with 9–11-year-old children who engaged with an oral retelling of Homer's *Iliad*. They found that grappling collectively with this extensive, complex and emotionally powerful text, with its unfamiliar language, complex characters and moral issues, promoted high levels of engagement and inclusion. In addition 'the oral text provided the stimulus and motivation to explore printed texts. Familiarity with the storyline gave children the confidence to tackle the story in print' (Reedy and Lister, 2007: 5). Books of Greek myths became the most popular books in the class library, and boys in particular went out of the way to find out more about gods and goddesses.

Nicholson (2006) reported similar findings from a project on literature and writing, carried out in Inner London, in which 7–11-year-old children encountered challenging literature through strategies such as reading aloud and drama. This approach proved highly motivational:

> [Teachers] spoke of children desperate to write, of loving books and reading again. In all the teachers' evaluations of the project it was the attitudes of

the children as readers and writers that they were most struck by and most pleased about.

(Nicholson, 2006: 19)

The choice of texts in these projects was just as important as the strategies used to explore them. Some of the books the teachers chose were: *The Winter Sleepwalker* by Joan Aiken (1994), *Fire, Bed and Bone* by Henrietta Branford (2002), *The Green Children* by Kevin Crossley Holland (1997) and *Tennyson's The Lady of Shalott* (1986). These were chosen *as* texts that have an impact on the emotions:

> Books that dealt with important issues and strong themes were more likely to engage and involve children emotionally as readers. These texts enable children to make connections to their own experiences and feelings.
>
> (Nicholson, 2006: 12)

The success of this project indicates that it is important that if teachers wish to promote engagement and further reading, it is worth avoiding class texts that are simplistic or underestimate children's capacities for taking on a challenge.

Case study, upper primary: Chaucer in the original Middle English – a challenging text

As part of an extended teaching sequence using classic fiction as a basis for narrative writing, Corinne decided to tackle a really challenging text with her 10 and 11 year olds. This case study describes phase one, particularly 'reading and investigation' and 'capturing ideas'. The writing was to be a story about a dilemma, written from the point of view of two characters, and the text she chose was Chaucer's *Pardoner's Tale* – a story about the effects of greed. Before she started the first session, Corinne pinned up part of the Middle English version of the story, but made no comment about it. The section begins:

> Thise ryotors three, of whiche I telle,
> Long erste er pryme rong of any belle,
> Were set hem in a taverne for to drinke;
> And as they satte, they herde a belle clinke
> Biforn a cors, was carried to his grave;

(Roughly translated: These three ruffians that I'm talking about, early in the day were sitting drinking in a tavern. And as they sat there they heard a bell being rung before a corpse that was being taken to be buried.)

Corinne began the session by asking the class what they knew about pilgrimages and there was some discussion about Mecca and the Kumbh Mela of 2013. She explained that *The Canterbury Tales* was a collection of stories told to while away the time while pilgrims were travelling by foot and horseback to Canterbury over 700 years ago. She told the children the story of *The Pardoner's Tale*, using artefacts such as drinking vessels, a phial of 'poison' and gold coins as hooks for memory. After telling the story, Corinne asked the children if they had any pictures in their minds of any parts of the story. Encouraging them to explain what they visualised as still images or illustrations in a book, she used these as the basis for groups to freeze frame a chosen episode from the tale and produce a caption to describe the events depicted. The class took photographs of the freeze frames and uploaded them onto the smartboard to use in a later session.

The following session began with a recap of the story followed by watching an animated version of the tale available on YouTube (see reference below). On re-watching, Corinne asked them to notice how the filmmakers emphasised themes in the tale, such as the greed of the different characters and after discussion of camera angle and close-ups, the class watched again with the task of noticing the setting. They did a quick-write describing the village and the tavern and kept these as notes for their later writing.

For the third session, Corinne asked the class to watch the video again but to choose to follow one of the ruffians and note anything about his emotions and reactions to events. Volunteers were hot-seated and asked about their feelings and motivations as a basis for the final point of view writing. To end this session, Corinne finally turned to the original Middle English text. She had noticed that several children had been browsing the passage on display but had not commented. She read the first part of the tale and gave the children copies in their groups, inviting them to ask questions about anything that interested or puzzled them. The questions were written on paper strips and put on the wall for others to think about ready to answer in the next session.

The invitation to become text interpreters engaged even the least assured readers and in the fourth session Corinne asked volunteers to give answers to the questions. There were plenty of people wanting to elucidate, so after a few whole class answers, the children moved into groups to make sure that all their queries had been answered. This session ended with Corinne reading the middle section of the tale and asking the children to discuss what had happened in that section.

In the final session of the week, Corinne read the end of the tale and giving the groups copies of this section in the original language, asked them to make group summaries. There was plenty of talk and excitement when it came to sharing each group's version of the ending of the tale. In the following week the class re-read the Middle English text, relishing reading it aloud and began their own versions in modern English. Corinne had also bought several versions of Marcia Williams' graphic/comic book version *Chaucer's Canterbury Tales* (2008), which encouraged the class to read more of Chaucer's tales.

Find *The Pardoner's Tale* animation on www.bing.com/videos/search?q=you tube+pardoners+tale&view=detail&mid=9F893E0CC357B0FB19F39F893E0CC357B0 FB19F3&FORM=VIRE (accessed 1 May 2017).

(See Chapter 3 for definitions and examples of hot seating and other drama strategies which can be used to support reading.)

Activity 6.4
Children's views on reading – pairs/group/reflective journal/blog

In pairs or a group, view one of Video 3 (6 to 7 year olds talking about reading: left to right on the screen: Emmanuel and Elliot), Video 4 (7 to 8 year olds: left to right on the screen: Harvesh, Jesse and Raya), or Video 5 (9 to 10 year olds: Alex, Gabrielle, Emma, Beatriz and Abigail) (see website) where children are talking about reading for pleasure.

As you hear what the children have to say, consider what they say about:

- why they read
- reading at home
- being a persistent reader.

What are the implications for classroom practice? For example, in terms of opportunities for children to talk to each other about their reading. How might you build on their home experiences of reading?

Summary

This chapter has demonstrated that pleasure in reading is crucial in developing fully rounded readers. Reading for pleasure is a slippery concept, involving engagement, motivation, satisfaction, fulfilment and purpose. Schools and teachers have an important role in promoting pleasure in reading and this chapter has described strategies that will support children's developing sense of what it is to be a successful and satisfied reader. As important as the strategies are the resources schools provide, which should reflect children's interests and expand their reading horizons through working together to make sense of challenging texts. In establishing an environment to support reading for pleasure and purpose, teachers' knowledge of children's literature and the promotion of children's agency as readers are central.

Recommended reading

Clark, C. and Rumbold, K. (2006) *Reading for Pleasure: A research overview.* London: The National Literacy Trust. A comprehensive review of recent research into international studies of reading for pleasure.

Cremin, T., Mottram, M., Collins, F., Powell, S. and Safford, K. (2014) *Building Communities of Readers: Reading for pleasure.* London: Routledge. This groundbreaking text reports on research into the home literacy experiences of children in different locations in England and the implications these findings have for teaching reading in schools. **Advanced**

National Union of Teachers (2016) *Getting Everyone Reading For Pleasure.* London: NUT. www.teachers.org.uk/sites/default/files2014/reading-4-pleasure-10561.pdf (accessed 1 May 2017). A very useful, practical resource covering topics including: developing and sustaining reading for pleasure, reading aloud, reading environments, talking about and recommending books, making time for independent reading, teachers as reflective and knowledgeable readers, developing communities of readers.

Pennac, D. (2006) *The Rights of the Reader*. London: Walker Books. A quirky, different, insightful view of what is important about becoming a reader.

References

Block, C. and Mangieri, J. (2002) Recreational Reading: 20 years later, *The Reading Teacher*, 55 (6) pp. 576–580.

Centre for Literacy in Primary Education (2014) *Reading for Pleasure: What we know works: Research from the Power of Reading Project*. London: CLPE.

Chambers, A. (2011) *Tell Me (Children, Reading and Talk) with the Reading Environment*. Stroud: Thimble Press.

Clark, C. and de Zoysa, S. (2011) *Mapping the Interrelationships of Reading Enjoyment, Attitudes, Behaviour and Attainment: An exploratory investigation*. London: The National Literacy Trust.

Clark, C. and Douglas, J. (2011) *Young People's Reading and Writing: An in-depth study focusing on enjoyment, behaviour, attitudes and attainment*. London: National Literacy Trust. www.literacy trust.org.uk/assets/0001/0177/Attitudes_towards_Reading_Writing_Final_2011.pdf (accessed 1 May 2017)

Clark, C. and Rumbold, K. (2006) *Reading for Pleasure: A research overview*. London: The National Literacy Trust.

Commeyras, M. Bisplinghoff, B. S. and Olson, J. (2003) *Teachers as Readers: Perspectives on the importance of reading in teachers' classrooms and lives*. Newark: International Reading Association.

Cremin, T. (2016) Reading for pleasure: Just window dressing? Cambridge Primary Review Trust blog. http://cprtrust.org.uk/cprt-blog/reading-for-pleasure-just-window-dressing/ (accessed 1 May 2017)

Cremin, T., Mottram, M., Collins, F., Powell, S. and Safford, K. (2009) *Teachers as Readers: Building communities of readers 2007–08 executive summary*. Leicester: United Kingdom Literacy Association.

Cremin, T., Mottram, M., Collins, F., Powell, S. and Safford, K. (2014) *Building Communities of Readers: Reading for pleasure*. London: Routledge.

Csikszentmihalyi, M. (2008) *Flow: The psychology of optimal experience*. New York: Harper Perennial Modern Classics.

Cullinan, B. (2000) Independent Reading and School Achievement, *School Library Media Research* (SLMR) Volume 3. www.ala.org/aasl/sites/ala.org.aasl/files/content/aaslpubsandjournals/slr/vol3/SLMR_IndependentReading_V3.pdf (accessed 1 May 2017)

Department for Education (2015) *Statutory Guidance: National curriculum in England: Primary curriculum*. www.gov.uk/government/publications/national-curriculum-in-england-primary-curriculum (accessed 1 May 2017)

Dombey, H. with Bearne, E., Cremin, T., Ellis, S., Mottram, M., O'Sullivan, O., Öztürk, A., Reedy, D. (UKLA) and Raphael, T. and Allington, R. (International Reading Association) (2010) *Teaching Reading: What the evidence says*. Leicester: United Kingdom Literacy Association.

Education Standards Analysis and Research Division (ESARD) Education Standards Research Team (2012) *Research Evidence on Reading for Pleasure*. London: DfE. www.gov.uk/government/uploads/system/uploads/attachment_data/file/284286/reading_for_pleasure.pdf (accessed 1 May 2017)

Gambrell, L. (2011) Seven Rules of Engagement: What's most important to know about motivation to read, *The Reading Teacher* 65 (3) pp. 172–178.

Gleed, A. (2013) *Booktrust Reading Habits Survey 2013: A national survey of reading habits and attitudes to books amongst adults in England*. London: Booktrust. www.booktrust.org.uk/usr/library/documents/main/1576-booktrust-reading-habits-report-final.pdf (accessed 1 May 2017)

Greaney, V. (1980) Factors related to amount and type of leisure time reading, *Reading Research Quarterly*, 15 (3) pp. 337–357.

Guthrie, J., Van Meter, P. and McCann, A. (1996) Growth of literacy engagement: Changes in motivations and strategies during concept oriented reading instruction, *Reading Research Quarterly*, 31 (3) pp. 306–331.

Hidi, S. (2000) An interested researcher's perspective: The effects of extrinsic and intrinsic factors on motivation, in C. Sansome and J. M. Harackiewicz (eds) *Intrinsic and Extrinsic Motivation: The search for optimal motivation and performance*. New York: Academic Press.

Krashen, S. D. (2004) *The Power of Reading: Insights from the research*, 2nd edn. Portsmouth, NH: Heinemann.

Kucirkova, N. and Cremin, T. (2016) *Digital Books Supporting Reading for Pleasure*. https://digilitey.wordpress.com/2016/07/28/digital-books-supporting-reading-for-pleasure/ (accessed 1 May 2017)

Kwek, D., Albright, J. and Kramer-Dahl, A. (2007) Building teachers' creative capabilities in Singapore's English classrooms: A way of contesting pedagogical instrumentality. *Literacy*, 41 (2) pp. 71–78.

Lockwood, M. (2008) *Promoting Reading for Pleasure in the Primary School*. London: SAGE.

Lockwood, M. (2012) Attitudes to reading in English primary schools. *English in Education*, 46 (3) pp. 228–246.

McGeown, S. (2013) *Reading Motivation and Engagement*. Leicester: United Kingdom Literacy Association.

Manzo, C. V. and Manzo, U. C. (1995) *Teaching Children to be Literate: A reflective approach*. New York: Harcourt Brace.

Moss, G. and Washbrook, L. (2016) *Understanding the Gender Gap in Literacy and Language Development*. Bristol: University of Bristol. www.bristol.ac.uk/media-library/sites/education/documents/bristol-working-papers-in-education/Understanding%20the%20Gender%20Gap%20working%20paper.pdf (accessed 1 May 2017)

National Union of Teachers (2016) *Getting Everyone Reading For Pleasure*. London: NUT. www.teachers.org.uk/sites/default/files2014/reading-4-pleasure-10561.pdf (accessed 1 May 2017)

Nell, V. (1988) *Lost in a Book: The psychology of reading for pleasure*. New Haven, CT: Yale University Press.

Nicholson, D. (2006) Putting literature at the heart of the literacy curriculum, *Literacy*, 40 (1) pp. 11–21.

OECD (2002) *Reading for Change Performance and Engagement Across Countries – Results from PISA 2000*. www.oecd.org/dataoecd/43/54/33690904.pdf (accessed 1 May 2017)

Parkhill, F., Fletcher, J. and Fa'afoi, A. (2005) What makes for success? Current literacy practices and the impact of family and community on Pasifika students' literacy learning, *New Zealand Journal of Educational Studies*, 40 (1 and 2) pp. 61–84.

Pennac, D. (2006) *The Rights of the Reader*. London: Walker Books.

Petscher, Y. (2010) A meta-analysis of the relationship between student attitudes towards reading and achievement in reading, *Journal of Research in Reading*, 33 (4) pp. 335–355.

Raleigh, M. (1996) Independent reading, in M. Simons (ed.) *Where We've Been: Articles from The English & Media Magazine*. London: English and Media Centre.

Reedy, D. and Lister, B. (2007) Busting with blood and gore and full of passion: The impact of an oral retelling of the *Iliad* in the primary classroom, *Literacy*, 41 (1) pp. 3–9.

Safford, K. (2014) A reading for pleasure pedagogy, in T. Cremin, M. Mottram, F. Collins, S. Powell, and K. Safford (eds) *Building Communities of Readers: Reading for pleasure*. London: Routledge, pp. 89–107.

Taylor, B., Pearson, P. D., Peterson, D. and Rodriguez, M. (2003) Reading growth in high-poverty classrooms: The influence of teacher practices that encourage cognitive engagement in literacy learning, *The Elementary School Journal*, 104 (1) pp. 3–29.

Traves, P. (2015) *Reading 7 to 11*. Leicester: United Kingdom Literacy Association.

Twist, L., Sizmur, J., Bartlett, S. and Lynn, L. (2012) *PIRLS 2011: Reading achievement in England*. Slough: National Foundation for Educational Research. www.nfer.ac.uk/pirls (accessed 1 May 2017)

United Kingdom All-Party Parliamentary Group for Education (2011) *Report of the Inquiry into Overcoming the Barriers to Literacy.* London: HMSO.

Younger, M. and Warrington, M., Gray, J., Rudduck, J., McLellan, R., Bearne, E., Kershner, R. and Bricheno, P. (2005) *Raising Boys' Achievement.* www.education.gov.uk/publications/eOrdering Download/RR636.pdf (accessed 1 May 2017)

Children's books

Joan Aiken (1994) *The Winter Sleepwalker.* Red Fox. ISBN 9780224036757

Henrietta Branford (2002) *Fire, Bed and Bone.* Walker Books. ISBN 9780744590494

Kevin Crossley Holland (1997) *The Green Children.* Oxford University Press. ISBN 9780192723239

Alfred, Lord Tennyson (1986) *The Lady of Shalott.* Oxford University Press. ISBN 9781553378747

Marcia Williams (2008) *Chaucer's Canterbury Tales.* Walker. ISBN 9781406305623

CHAPTER 7

EARLY READING INCLUDING PHONICS

This chapter covers:

- Early reading development
- The reading process
  - Case study, early primary: Teaching print concepts
- Reading strategies
- Reading behaviours
  - Case study, early primary: Reading fluently with expression and intonation
- Barriers to early progress in reading
- Reading in homes and communities
- Defining reading comprehension

7.1   Early reading development

Frith (1985) proposed that in languages with alphabetic systems there are three stages in reading acquisition:

- *Logographic:* at first, children process words in the same way as any other visual material and recognise them instantly, for example, the names/logos of favourite shops or treats; road signs; advertising hoardings. At this stage, children are not aware that letters represent specific sounds although they are beginning to understand that a symbol has meaning.

- *Alphabetic:* this is related to children wanting to write, very often their own name. Learning to write helps children begin to understand the principles of sound/letter relationships and see that letters can be used to represent words, ideas and messages. At this stage, children gain explicit knowledge of phonemes, their correspondences with letters, and how to merge those sounds into words.

- *Orthographic:* by now, readers can recognise a large number of words or parts of words automatically, instantly accessing their meaning. Reading the same words frequently allows children to store whole words in an internal dictionary. This is a much faster process than phonological analysis ('sounding out') and proficient readers only need to 'sound out' unfamiliar words.

> **Logographic:** relates to a symbol, sign, character or logo representing a word or phrase.
>
> **Orthographic:** relates to the conventional spelling system of a language.

Chall (1983) similarly describes early reading as consisting of stages from *pre-reading*, including children's spoken language development, listening to stories, some knowledge of letter names, phonological awareness and concepts about print. This is followed by an *initial reading and decoding* stage where children are formally instructed in letter-sound relations, develop phonemic awareness and apply these foundational skills as they learn to read words, followed by the stage of *confirmation and fluency* where practice in reading consolidates mental processes to create greater reading fluency.

In many linear models of reading development, the combination of early high levels of phonemic awareness (the ability to distinguish the smallest units of sound) and letter knowledge are seen to lead to better word reading and, in turn, better word reading is seen to result in more effective comprehension (Stainthorp, 2003). However, learning to read is by no means a straightforward matter of an individual progressing through stages to fluent and competent reading.

Figure 7.1 Thomas reading

Arrow and Tunmer (2012) argue that a staged 'one-size-fits-all' approach is unhelpful as each child enters pre-school or school with different literacy experiences. They describe cognitive entry skills that are gained before formal literacy learning, including alphabet knowledge (names of letters); spoken language gained through experience of conversation at home; phonological awareness, for example, awareness of rhyming words; print knowledge, for example, directionality or words and pages in a book; and emergent writing using letters in invented spellings. Arrow and Tunmer argue that these cognitive entry skills may be evident in different degrees according to the child's previous experience so they propose that 'reading instruction requires early assessment of the critical cognitive entry skills, and that beginning literacy instruction should be differentiated to meet the needs of the children' (Arrow and Tunmer, 2012: 247).

Phonemic awareness: the ability to hear/identify the smallest units of sound known as phonemes; for example, recognising and using the individual sounds in words as in b/a/t – the individual sounds that make up the word 'bat'. Phonemic awareness is part of phonological awareness.

Phonological awareness: includes the ability to identify phonemes but also includes the ability to hear/identify and use larger units of sound such as rimes and onsets. This is absolutely essential for children to become successful readers.

Cognitive entry skills: reading-related knowledge and experiences that a child brings to the process of learning to read.

7.2   The reading process

Despite varying versions of developmental stages, it is clear that the process of reading involves the orchestration (Bussis *et al.*, 1985) of different kinds of knowledge in order to make meaning of text (see Chapter 5) and that these may not follow sequential 'stages'. Goodman (1973) identifies three cueing systems, described by Clay (1991) as 'sources of information' which help a reader identify words:

- semantic: meaning (drawn from pictures and context)
- syntactic: structure (knowledge of sentence grammar and punctuation)
- graphophonic: visual (knowledge of phonics and graphic representation).

Alongside this, children need to develop a range of reading strategies for processing text (see p. 179) and reading behaviours (see pp. 180–181).

Before formal and explicit teaching can take place, children need to develop concepts about print and understand something about reading behaviours; for example, the cognitive entry skills of recognising some words in context, understanding some 'book language' and where to start reading a book printed in English. They also need to know some terminology about language; for example, 'letter', 'word'. However, as all children's literacy experiences are different (Arrow and Tunmer, 2012), it is important to find out what they know before spending time teaching things that they may already be familiar with. Observation while children are playing at reading and during reading activities (shared, guided or independent) will help identify what children know.

Drawing on the work of Clay, Elborn (2015) offers teacher prompts to help identify children's awareness of print concepts:

- Recognising one or two words in different contexts: *Can you find your name? Is that a word you know?*
- Understanding and using simple terminology such as 'book', 'right way up', 'front', 'back', 'upside down': *Put the book on the stand. Show me the front of the book. Bring us a book from the table.*
- Understanding that print goes from left to right in English, including the return sweep to the next line; that the left page comes before the right; that print (not the picture) tells the story: *Where do I start to read? Show me where to start reading. Where do I go after that?*
- Knowing that there are letters, clusters of letters called words, and first letters and last letters in words: *Show me the first letter. Show me the last letter. Show me a capital letter. Show me a word.*
- Matching one to one: *Point to the words as I read them* (adapted from Elborn, 2015: 38).

Figure 7.2 Early reading

Figure 7.3 Early reading

Activity 7.1
A 3 year old reading – reflective journal/blog/pairs/group

Look at website resource W7.1 Isaac reading a Mr Men story. What cognitive entry skills does this 3 year old show that will support later reading? For example, getting meaning out of texts, directionality, expression and intonation, sustaining reading?

How might he have acquired this knowledge?

Having identified what Isaac knows, drawing on the list above about print concepts and prompts, what other print concepts will he need to be taught?

COMPANION @ WEBSITE

If you have access to children aged between 3 and 5, observe them interacting with books and identify what they know about print. If the parents are in agreement, make a short video and share it with the group. In discussion, decide what might be the next steps.

Case study, early primary: Teaching print concepts

Sunetra decided to use *Oi Frog!* by Kes Gray and Jim Field (2014) with her 4 and 5 year olds as a basis for making a class book. The story follows an attempt by a cat to persuade a frog to sit on a log and the rest of the book lists what different animals sit on. There is much word play and the children found the story very funny. Using a visualiser so that all the children could see the pages, Sunetra read through the whole book. As the story goes on, the kinds of animals and what they sit on become more and more outlandish:

"What about puffins?" asked the frog.
"Puffins sit on muffins," said the cat.
"Snakes sit on cakes,
owls sit on towels,
gibbons sit on ribbons,
lambs sit on jams, bees sit on keys, and
pumas sit on satsumas."

Each double-page spread provided Sunetra with plenty of opportunity to talk about the picture and the word that represents it and to look at initial letters and last letters. She later used the rhymes (and the fact that they do not match visually) for teaching about different sounds.

In the following session, Sunetra read the book again, but this time she decided the children would construct sentences based on the story to show the connection between the animal and how its name was written. She chose the picture of the gorilla sitting on a pillar (looking very disgruntled), emphasising that the words tell you what is happening. She showed the children a sentence strip saying *Snakes sit on cakes* and cut the sentence into words, asking the children to tell her how to reassemble it by referring to the book and pointing to the particular words in the sentence. She then repeated this with sentences: *Rats sit on hats. Weasels sit on easels. Moles sit on poles.* The children were soon able to identify 'sit on' and by the time they got to moles and poles, most were confident in reassembling the sentences.

In the third session, Sunetra shared the story again and showed the children the pages for the Big Book she had prepared with names of the animals on each page (there are, conveniently, twenty-nine in the book itself so she was able to choose a variety of animal names to suit those who needed more of a challenge as well as those whose print concepts were less secure). She returned to the final double-page spread where, after frog asks 'What do dogs sit on?' there is a large image of a dog sitting on the frog – but no sentence. So Sunetra asked the children to help her make the sentence: *Dogs sit on frogs.* As part of this process, Sunetra had decided to demonstrate some letter sounds so she used a phoneme frame for the word the children were perhaps most familiar with: *sit.*

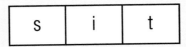

The children were able to process the word and Sunetra added *on* so that the children had two words they recognised:

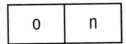

In the fourth and last session, Sunetra read the story once more, revisited the work about *sit* and *on* and gave the children their pages to draw the animal and complete the sentence. As *Oi Frog!* was available on the visualiser, the children could consult it if they wanted to check something. When they had finished, Sunetra put the whole class book together and after they had read it together, put it in the reading area for the children to choose to read independently. It became a firm favourite and shortly afterwards Sunetra read *Oi Dog!* (2016) and *Quick Quack Quentin* (2016) by the same author and illustrator.

Teaching for meaning (semantic cues)

Meaning is, of course, absolutely essential for reading. Children quickly come to understand that reading has meaning. This may be from their knowledge of environmental print – that the sign for 'Ella Road' shows where they live – or from hearing stories or other kinds of text in the home. It is very common for young children to 'read' a favourite book, using the pictures and their memories to help them make sense of it. Isaac, in website resource W7.1, knows that stories have meaning as he 'reads', but it is clear than he leans heavily on the pictures – and his memory of hearing the story – to keep his narrative going.

Although there is a high focus on teaching phonics in the early stages of learning to read, it is important that teachers also emphasise the importance of meaning and that they model using meaning cues to help with unfamiliar words: *I don't know this word. What shall I do? I know, I'll look at the picture to see if that will help.* Or: *I know, I'll read the sentence again to see if I can sort out what it means.*

Teaching about structure (sentence grammar and punctuation)

It is important that grammar is taught in the context of meaning (Reedy and Bearne, 2013; Bearne *et al.*, 2016). Although grammar will often be taught through early writing, grammatical structures can be highlighted through reading and used to help tackle unfamiliar words. As Sunetra showed in the case study above, repeating parts of a sentence can help children see how other sentences can be constructed. It is not a great distance from 'Dogs *sit on* frogs' to 'We *sit on* the mat'. It is important to introduce children gradually to different kinds of sentence structure and, of course, children's picture books are a cornucopia for teaching about sentence structure and punctuation. Some of the 'old and gold' books are ideal: *Where's Spot?* by Eric Hill (2009), for example, with its repeated structure and question marks, or *Shh! We Have a Plan* (2015) and *Oh, No, George!* (2014) by Chris Haughton with repeated phrases and exclamation marks.

Teaching graphophonic knowledge (see also Chapter 5)

In addition to visual recognition of symbols, children's phonic knowledge generally develops through phases, starting with the ability to discriminate sounds in the environment (phonological awareness). This is not about recognising letters in print, but about the inner process of making sense of sounds, a necessary foundation for listening for discrete letter sounds. Children must be able to hear and say sounds in words (phonemes) before they are expected to read and write them (see Figure 7.4). In addition, they need to be able to distinguish individual sounds from the background noise of a classroom or playground. Developing phonological awareness means recognising that words are made up of small sound units (phonemes), that words can be segmented into larger sound units known as syllables and that each syllable begins with a sound (onset) and ends with another sound (rime). Explicit teaching usually starts from children being introduced to the sounds (phonemes) represented by the letters in the alphabet. Phonological awareness continues to be an essential part of becoming a reader, from the early years through to children becoming very experienced with texts. Poetry, for example, which supports the development of phonological awareness (the bedrock for developing graphophonic knowledge), is performed by having an ear for the rhythms and rhymes of the words and the interpretation of poetry is built on the ability to grasp the nuances of sound that the poet uses for particular effects.

> **Graphophonic knowledge:** knowledge of the relationship between sound and print (phonics and graphic representation).

Synthetic, analytic and systematic phonics teaching

There are two main ways of teaching phonics: synthetic and analytic. Each takes a different approach to decoding unfamiliar words:

- *Synthetic phonics:* (part to whole) where the sounds associated with letters are learned separately and blended together (synthesised), for example, reading 'sit' would require decoding the word phoneme by phoneme: 's-i-t'.
- *Analytic phonics:* (whole to part) where the sounds associated with letters are not pronounced separately, but children identify (internally analyse) syllables which begin with a sound (onset) and end with another sound (rime), as in 's-it', 's-ing' , 's-ip' (identifying onset) or 'p-in', 'b-in', 'w-in' (identifying rime).

Although synthetic phonics is the preferred approach in some Anglophone countries, there is no established body of evidence that this is a more effective way to teach early reading (Wyse and Goswami, 2008; Hall *et al.*, 2012). Nevertheless, some governments (notably in England) specify synthetic phonics as the best way to teach early reading.[1] However,

Consonant phonemes		Vowel phonemes	
Sound	**Examples**	**Sound**	**Examples**
/b/	bat	/a/	ant
/k/ (c)	cat	/e/	egg
/d/	dog	/i/	in
/f/	fan	/o/	on
/g/	go	/u/	up
/h/	hen	/ai/	rain
/j/	jet	/ar/	farm
/l/	leg	/ee/	feet
/m/	map	/er/	kerb
/n/	net	/igh/	night
/p/	pen	/oa/	boat
/kw/ (qu)	queen	/oi/	coin
/r/	rat	**/oo/**	boot
/s/	sun	/oo/	look
/t/	tap	/or/	for
/v/	van	/ou/	out
/w/	wig	/ow/	cow
/y/	yes	/ur/	hurt
/z/	zip	/air/	fair
/sh/	shop	/ear/	dear
/ch/	chip		
/th/	thin		
/th/	then		
/ng/	ring		
/zh/	vision		

Figure 7.4 Consonant and vowel phonemes (adapted from DfES, 2007)

amongst all the debates there are sometimes confusions that it is worth clarifying here. One of the main confusions has been over the word 'systematic'. Systematic phonics simply means that teachers teach phonics in a progressively staged way; it describes the planning and organisation of teaching phonics. Teaching is, after all, a systematic activity since all teaching (even the most spontaneous and inspiring) is based on some sense of planning and organisation. However, difficulties arise when 'systematic' is used interchangeably with 'synthetic' because 'synthetic' refers to a theoretical position about the best way to teach phonics in contrast to an 'analytic' approach. So while it seems sensible to agree that phonics should be taught systematically, there are still debates about teaching synthetic or analytic phonics. Whatever the debates about the relative merits of each method, research strongly indicates that using both approaches in combination is more effective than using either on its own (Juel and Minden-Cupp, 2001) and as children's reading vocabulary increases and becomes more varied and complex, they are likely to use both synthetic and analytic approaches anyway.

In fact, a research review by the National Reading Panel (NICHHD, 2000) in the US concludes that there is no evidence that teaching from phonemes (as in synthetic phonics) is more effective than teaching from syllables (onset-rime). More recently, neuroscientific research indicates that the syllable rather than the phoneme is the primary phonological processing unit across the languages of the world (Port, 2006). Goswami points out that: 'Developmental research reveals an apparently language-universal sequence in the development of phonological awareness, from syllable awareness, through "onset-rime" awareness, to "phoneme' awareness"' (Goswami, 2008: 68). Further, the Centre for Economic Performance (Machin *et al.*, 2016), reviewing research into the longer-term effects of teaching synthetic phonics, concludes that although there are immediate gains in reading in the early years of education, by the age of 11 other children who were not taught by synthetic phonics have caught up and there are no average effects, except for children with a higher initial propensity to struggle with reading.

Discrete phonics teaching

Daily discrete phonics sessions should link segmenting and blending skills to what is being read in class or in guided reading. Children are gradually taught phoneme/grapheme correspondences, including the different ways of making the same vowel sounds, such as 'ea' (as in *eat*), 'ee' (as in *feet*). They will begin to learn a range of digraphs (two letters making one sound), trigraphs (three letters making one sound) and be taught to notice phonic irregularities.

A shorthand way of describing a discrete phonics session is: *revisit+review*, *teach*, *practice*, *apply*. After identifying the specific phonics focus for the day/week, a typical discrete phonics session would include:

- A brief warm-up to prepare children to make the connection between sound and print.
- Introduction/review of sound/spelling(s) to make explicit the connection between phonemes and graphemes.
- Blending – providing an activity(ies) to help children accurately decode and recode using the chosen phonic focus.
- Word work – practising and expanding children's knowledge of high frequency words, compound words and/or affixes (adding 's' or 'ed' to the end of words or 'un' or 'pre' to the front of words to change their meaning) through different activities.
- Using specifically prepared decodable text to apply the newly learned phonics focus as well as encountering high frequency words.
- After decoding words according to the chosen focus of the session, a word, phrase or sentence dictation helps to consolidate graphophonic understanding.

Phonics teaching also requires the teacher to articulate sounds clearly and precisely but it is important for teachers to be sensitive to regional accents. Teachers should avoid suggesting that there is one 'received' way of pronouncing words. Alex, in Video 6 (see website), is an excellent example of an effective teacher of phonics who has a particular accent but who works well with children in London, England.

After a discrete phonics session there should be planned opportunities for children to apply their phonic knowledge. This is best developed through daily games and activities, selecting books to share that consolidate phonic learning, and ensuring that children use their phonic knowledge in writing. Multisensory learning opportunities – finger puppets, toys, cut-outs, textures and games – greatly aid phonics teaching. Motivating contexts such as this enable children to apply new knowledge several times so that it moves from working memory to long-term memory and becomes effortless and automatic (Apthorp, 2006).

Activity 7.2
Teaching phonics – reflective journal/blog/pairs/group

Watch Video 6 (see website) in which Alex, a Year 1 teacher at Beam County Primary School, Dagenham, teaches a phonics session. She explains her approach to phonics teaching:

> At Beam County Primary School our phonics groups follow the synthetic phonics programme 'Letters and Sounds' alongside the actions and the songs of 'Jolly Phonics' [a commercially available programme]. Today the learning objective was to segment and to blend words with the new phoneme. We started by revising some of the graphemes that we've been practising since September. Some of them we need to still consolidate. Then we sang the ABC song, doing the actions for ascenders (tall letters) and for descenders (the letters with a tail that goes below the line). I enjoy, and the children enjoy, being detectives and I try to encourage them to listen, to form their listening skills by finding out which sound is common in the words with a new phoneme.
>
> Sometimes I start by giving them words with a grapheme that we have been practising or by giving them a sentence strip or sometimes I give them magnetic letters to make a word.
>
> The children enjoy playing 'Buried Treasure' [a game with cards and prompts], so we have a combination of Phase 2 and Phase 3 [of 'Letters and Sounds'] as the children are working towards Phase 3 and we are consolidating Phases 2 and 3. They enjoy sounding out to segment and blend real words or to find out the nonsense words, so they need to choose a card and they need to think if it is a real word or a nonsense word. And if it's a real word we try to clarify the word to really understand the sense. I focus a lot of work on listening – listening skills and the order of the graphemes within a word.

Watch the video clip again, noting how Alex covers some of the different elements of a phonics session: warm-up, introduction/review, blending, word work, using prepared decodable text, dictation and consolidation of learned words.

Arrange to watch a phonics session at your school with children older than early Year 1 to see how progress is made in teaching phonics.

Letters and Sounds (DfES, 2007) gives a progressive programme of phonics teaching.

Figure 7.5 Environment for phonics teaching

Figure 7.6 Teaching phonics

Phoneme: the smallest sound unit in a word.

Grapheme: letter(s) representing a phoneme.

Digraph: two letters that represent one phoneme. For example, a consonant digraph contains two consonants – *ck, ll, sh*; a vowel digraph contains at least one vowel but usually two – *ee, oo, ar, oi.*

Split digraph: a digraph in which the two letters are not adjacent; for example, take.

Trigraph: three letters that represent one phoneme; for example, igh dge

Blending: identifying the letter sounds in a written word; for example, p-i-g and merging or synthesising them to pronounce the word 'pig'.

Segmenting: distinguishing individual phonemes in a spoken word (e.g., p-a-t) and writing or using plastic/magnetic letters to make the word 'pat'.

Words which are not graphophonically regular

In a language such as English, many of the words which children meet from their earliest years will not be graphophonically regular – including words in texts which are in books intended for phonic instruction. In English many words are not phonically decodable, so there are limitations on what can be taught through phonics alone. Some children find sight recognition a more useful strategy for reading than phonic decoding, which can cause some problems if phonics is the only approach to teaching early reading (see section 9.9). This means that it is important to build children's sight vocabulary at the same time as instructing them in phonics. Ehri explains that children's minds need to make connections:

> Children might apply various strategies to read unfamiliar words: decoding letters to form recognizable words, analogizing from known words to new words, and predicting words based on partial letters and context.
>
> (Ehri, 2012: 175)

This might include drawing on knowledge of simple prefixes such as *un-* or *pre-* and inflectional endings such as *-ing, -ed* or recognition of other words or parts of words (onset and rime) to read unfamiliar words such as *aught* in 'caught' or 'taught' or *ame* in 'came', 'frame', 'shame'.

However, according to Ehri, learning sight words is not just a matter of visual recognition but, involves linking together:

> how letters or graphemes in specific words systematically represent sounds or phonemes in their pronunciations ... Written words are stored in memory when readers form connections between graphemes seen in spellings of words and phonemes detected in their pronunciations along with meanings.
>
> (*ibid.*)

It is important that children learn high frequency words – for example, *the, was, once* – so that they do not put a brake on fluency by stopping to blend them. In addition, explicit attention needs to be given to words which can be pronounced differently according to context; for example, *read* (present or past tense of the verb), *sow* (scattering seed or a female pig), *close* (end or near), *lead* (guide or a metal). All of this indicates the importance not only of building sight vocabulary but also of making sure that words are learned in the context of meaning.

Teaching graphophonically irregular words is developed by sight recognition and familiarity. However, they are best learned in context so using familiar and well-loved books are a good starting point. Teachers can ask children to point to words which they recognise by sight and to find that word on the word wall. Games such as matching words, word bingo, word detectives (finding the same word in another book), or practices such as word of the day/week can support children's development of a repertoire of graphophonically irregular words.

Activity 7.3
Onset and rime – reflective journal/blog/pairs/group

Look at website resource W7.2 Onset and rime and, working individually at first, see how many you can make in one minute. Compare your list with a colleague's and add up how many you have managed between you. Now join with another pair and see what the score is.

This demonstrates just how powerful it is for children to get to know how onset and rime can work to help them understand and generate more vocabulary.

7.3   Reading strategies

Proficient readers use a range of reading strategies (processing and comprehension) in order to read independently which need to be taught systematically and explicitly. Shared and guided reading sessions are the usual means of securing the use of a range of strategies to help children. Processing strategies include: attending and searching; predicting; self-monitoring, cross-checking and confirming and self-correcting; re-reading and reading on; searching for more information. Comprehension strategies include: making connections between prior knowledge and the text; forming and testing hypotheses about texts; asking questions (children's own questions); visualising; identifying the author's point of view; inferring; summarising; analysing, synthesising and evaluating ideas and information.

Elborn (2015) draws on the work of Clay's (2005) teacher prompts to support children's grasp of a range of reading strategies:

- Self-monitoring: *Listen to your reading. Does it make sense? If your reading doesn't make sense, then stop.*
- Cross-checking: *How else can you check? If it was xxx what letter would you see at the beginning? What would make sense and look right?*
- Self-correcting: *You made a mistake. Can you find it? Try that again.*
- Re-reading: *Go back and read it again. Read that part and find what would fit.*
- Reading on: *Leave that word and read to the end. Read the sentence then go back and check.*
- Searching for more information: *Do you know another word like that? What do you know that might help?*

(adapted from Elborn, 2015: 55)

7.4   Reading behaviours

Alongside sources of information and strategies, children need to develop reading behaviours. Some of these are:

- directionality (where to start reading a book printed in English; where to start reading a page – in English, reading from left to right)
- reading fluently without finger pointing
- reading longer phrases and more complex sentences with expression
- reading silently most of the time.

Figure 7.7 Reading together

Figure 7.8 Choosing books

As children develop as readers, one of the essential reading behaviours is how to read fluently with intonation and phrasing suitable to the piece of text. Being able to read fluently is linked to reading for meaning and to the ability to sustain reading – both of which support comprehension. Like strategies, these behaviours have to be systematically taught. Children are more likely to learn how to read aloud with fluency and expression if they are provided with a range of stimulating texts in books and on screens, including information, film, narrative, picture books and poetry and a teacher who reads aloud regularly. Reading aloud as performance needs to be developed as a skill in its own right, not simply as a checking strategy for teachers. Of course, fluency is not just a matter of being able to read aloud with expression and intonation. As readers develop, these processes become internalised so that fluent reading becomes a silent activity.

In the following case study, the teacher carries out deliberate acts of teaching to support children's reading: modelling; prompting; questioning; giving feedback, explaining and directing children towards showing what they have learned. Such strategic instruction provides scaffolding for children's learning and works best when the teacher is aware of what the next steps in the children's learning should be.

Case study, early primary: Reading fluently with expression and intonation

Max began a three-week teaching sequence about friendship with his 5 and 6 year olds with a book which is all about sharing: *We're Going on a Picnic!* by Pat Hutchins (2013). The reading focuses for the first few sessions were on reading fluently with expression and intonation and consolidating what Max had taught about sentence structure and punctuation. This book provides plenty of scope for joining in with repeated phrases like 'We're going on a picnic', but also other patterns and structures – for example 'Let's go...', 'All right, said xxx' and 'I can't wait to eat some of those ...'.

"It's a bit shady," said Duck.
"Let's go up the hill.
We might find an even nicer place."
"All right," said Hen.
"but it's your turn to carry the basket."
"This looks like a nice place
for a picnic," said Hen,
and set the basket down.
"I can't wait to eat
some of those berries!"

Max began the first session by reading the whole book, modelling expression and different voices for the different characters, then re-reading it, inviting the children to join in with any parts they could remember, prompting when they needed it. They soon latched on to 'We're going on a picnic' and 'This looks like a nice place' and the session ended with a third reading where groups of children read these two sentences in chorus each time they appeared in the book.

In the second session, after a quick re-cap, Max took the page beginning 'It's a bit shady', that he had enlarged on the digital board and asked the children to tell him which words Duck and Hen were saying. Inviting children to come and point to words (and punctuation) on the screen, through questioning, feedback and explanation, he soon established the idea of speech marks indicating words that people say. He asked the children to practise reading the page in pairs – one child saying what Duck said and one saying what Hen said – and after some examples, the reading moved on to the later pages where the animals were getting hot. In threes (Hen, Goose and Duck) the children role played their conversation as they got back home after walking a long way and realised that they had lost their picnic as they walked.

The third session began with Max showing the class some sentence frames based on the book:

"It's a bit _____," said Duck.

"I can't wait to eat some of those_____."

"Did you eat the _____?"

They discussed the possibilities for replacing 'shady', 'windy' and 'hot' in the first sentence, and Max noted ideas on the board as well as other kinds of food they couldn't wait to eat and the food that had been lost on the way. He asked the children to work in pairs to complete one of the frames and when they had finished, volunteers read their sentences, which were then stuck on the working wall.

The fourth (and last) session was planned as a performance of the whole book using the variations to sentences from the work of the previous day. Max reminded the children that the aim was to read with fluency and expression and they practised their pages. For the group reading, the whole class read the first two pages aloud together, then different pairs of children read pages incorporating their own sentences. Finally, the whole class read the last three pages together. Max recorded the performance and posted it as a podcast in the reading area.

7.5   Barriers to early progress in reading

Good teachers will try to ensure that there are no barriers to children's progress but there will always be children who find the getting to grips with early reading difficult. There is, however, no single answer to supporting children who have different needs or language and literacy experience. Bowtell and Holding identify some common barriers as:

Ineffective word level reading skills: Children need the skills to decode and recognise unfamiliar and tricky words in a print-rich environment (Rose, 2006). Through careful observation of children's decoding abilities, and an understanding of the beginner reader, the teacher will be able to plan steps to enable children to progress through the phonic phases.

Limited oral language skills: Communication is the engine of a young child's learning. Children need to be talking and actively listening in order to drive their understanding of their world. An abundance of first-hand experiences with the opportunities for meaningful discussion are key.

Lack of print experience: Teachers who flood their classrooms with a broad and varied diet of fiction, non-fiction and poetry are most successful in promoting successful reading development. Teachers and children need to seek out, show and interact with print in the environment, in books and on the world wide web.

Negative attitudes to reading: Reading is the key to lifelong learning and requires a positive attitude. It is a teacher's job to hand over the key to the children by enthusiastically promoting the written word, maintaining resilience and the EYFS (DfE, 2012) 'have a go' disposition.

Low self-esteem: Young readers must be encouraged and praised for their beginning efforts at reading. Every detail of the reading process must be noticed by the teacher and celebrated.

(Bowtell and Holding, 2014)

These barriers suggest that there are ways for teachers to offset some initial difficulties by observation of individual differences and the establishment of a rich and supportive reading environment. It is important to provide texts which reflect cultural diversity and to acknowledge and build on the language and text experiences children bring to school. Balanced teaching, which places phonics instruction within a context of inclusion, reading for enjoyment and meaning can help to move children into more positive attitudes to reading and increase their self-esteem. Alex, whose phonics session is on Video 6 (see website), emphasises the importance of developing a love of reading:

At Beam County Primary school we create a lifelong love of reading. At the end of the day I always try to find even two or three minutes to read and last week we investigated poetry and we found a lot of rhyming words so I have the books 'Oi Frog!' and 'Oi Dog!' that the boys and the girls love so they were so excited. And the children enjoy using the iPad and reading our Bug Club e-books where there is a fantastic variety of genres of fiction, non-fiction, comics that apply again for both boys and girls. Today my class came to look around the library and to understand the fiction and non-fiction in each compartment and they have chosen a book and they read and they wrote a book review. I think recommending books again is a great way to capture the children and to hook them into being enthusiastic readers and read more.

After a session, if they've finished their activity, we do encourage them to go and choose a book that they are interested in and if they would like to share it with a friend they can sit down and read a story and also if they really want to take it home we are more than happy to give them the book.

Every week the children are given a book. First they read with a teacher or they read a new book with a teaching assistant and we encourage them at home to talk about the book. Take the book home. Read it and as I said during my session, if it's still 'bumpy' [not smoothly and fluently read] please don't bring it back. We say to the parents try to re-read it again for their understanding of the story and talk about the stories.

See Chapter 9 for more information about supporting children who experience difficulties with reading.

Bug Club is a whole school reading programme using e-books and activities designed to provide children with reading experiences that will lead to lifelong love of reading. It is available at www.pearsonschoolsandfecolleges.co.uk/Primary/Literacy/AllLiteracyre-sources/BugClub/BugClubOverview.aspx (accessed 1 May 2017).

7.6   Reading in homes and communities

When siblings and families share reading, there are significant gains for building on children's language and literacy experience. This need not only be reading books, although sharing a book with a child can be a most enjoyable experience; newspapers, magazines, holy texts, newspapers, recipes, the internet, all give children a sense of what reading can do for them. In Videos 3 (sections 3 and 4), 4 (section 5) and 3 (section 4) (see website) children from 6 to 10 talk about reading at home and with family members, indicating the pleasure of shared experiences as well as some of the difficulties of managing to read with other family members. The home and community are potentially rich environments for supporting reading yet teachers do not often know much about what happens at home in terms of literacy and language experience (Cremin *et al.*, 2014; Cremin *et al.*, 2015). Reading is not simply set of processes, skills or strategies to be learned by an individual, but part of a complicated series of experiences embedded in the home community. Even involving parents in the school's reading practices may not fully acknowledge or use the literacy strengths which readers bring with them (Cremin *et al.*, 2015).

The value and effectiveness of children sharing books with their parents (or siblings) is a matter of some debate, with some researchers seeing it as 'part of responsible parenting' (McBride-Chang, 2012: 56) arguing that shared book reading provides both cognitive and emotional gains for children, particularly if the reading is dialogic (Whitehurst and Lonigan, 1998) – a planned strategy where children are prompted to interact with the adult reading with them through a series of questions which are then deliberately extended by the adult. Others put greater emphasis on the natural conversations, not necessarily related to reading, which adults have with children, arguing that it is this language exchange that develops robust language and literacy rather than solely shared book reading (Leyva *et al.*, 2012; Reese, 2012). In a study specifically designed to examine the pre-school language and literacy experience of linguistically diverse children from low-income families in the United States, Sparks and Reese (2013) found that when mothers engaged in elaborative forms of talk while they were reminiscing about behaviour-related incidents, children's semantic and print knowledge increased (*ibid.*). However, mothers' elaborative talk in the context of book reading was not a predictor of children's language and literacy development:

> Overall, the results from these studies highlight the importance of parent–child conversation not just for children's language and memory but also for emerging literacy skills; and they illustrate the Vygotskian notion that daily participation in specific kinds of social interactions is linked to both social and psychological benefits for the child. In this case, by

partaking in reminiscing with their mothers, children may be acquiring the complex rules of participation in personal story telling conversations as they develop the psycholinguistic tools needed for literacy learning.

(*ibid.*: 15)

Dialogic reading technique deliberately focuses on scaffolding children's shared book reading experiences. Children are prompted to interact with the adult in relation to the content of the storybook, for example, predicting what may be about to happen, commenting on their favourite character, relating their own emotions to the events in the story. The adult then extends the child's contributions, asking for clarification, or for more comment. The difference between this and every day shared book reading between an adult and a child is the deliberate planning to prompt and extend the child's response.

Reese argues that:

it is vitally important for educators and practitioners working with low-income parents to avoid the suggestion that shared book-reading with children is the only way, or even the best way, to help advance children's language skill ... once we have escaped the tyranny of shared book-reading, new avenues for extended conversation with low-income and middle-income children alike may open up to us ... In other words, keep sharing books with young children, but be creative about it.

(Reese, 2012: 65–66)

The emphasis on parents may also not fully identify the value of siblings and other family or community members to developing readers. Working particularly with bi- and multilingual children, their homes and communities, Gregory (2001) identifies a range of ways in which siblings contributed to literacy development including: reading for pleasure and or school work, direct teaching of the alphabet, playing games like 'school' or word games, singing songs and rhymes together and going to the library or bookshops together. Researching the life histories of people who were the first to go to university in their families, Knoester and Plikuhn identify the role of older siblings as influential in their younger siblings' literacy development through 'sharing reading materials, modelling reading, talking about literature, recommending reading resources and ... as teachers' (Knoester and Plikuhn, 2016: 482).

In researching out-of-school literacy experiences, Gregory and Kenner identify the range of ways in which community classes such as religious instruction, mother tongue classes and Saturday classes covering different subjects contribute to the 'cognitive, linguistic and social benefits accruing to young children in their early years at school' (Gregory and Kenner, 2003: 75). They conclude that community classes may provide children with different cultural and linguistic experiences which help them to develop 'cognitive, cultural and linguistic flexibility with which to tackle the world' (*ibid.*:. 82).

In Video 3, 6-year-old Emmanuel explains:

I have a little brother called Samuel and he's only four years old because his birthday was on Saturday and there was this day when I was in my other house and me and my mum were teaching him sounds so when he's five he can get ready and be quite good at reading.

In this video extract, both boys describe the influences on their choices of reading material. For Emmanuel, television is a great motivator to seek out books related to what he has enjoyed watching while Elliot uses his out-of-school interests, in this case, trains, to help him choose books he might like.

It may, then, be worth expanding views of 'home reading' which move away from a school-focused emphasis on learning the skills of reading books towards a more holistic view which sees developing reading as a matter of becoming a lifelong reader who draws on home and community sources to strengthen motivation and commitment to reading. The implications for teachers are profound, prompting them to discover more about the literacy knowledge and experiences of the children in their classes.

7.7 Reading digital texts

Research (Levy, 2011; Plowman *et al.*, 2012; Rowe and Miller, 2016) suggests that children have much greater exposure to on-screen reading at home than at school and that they are engaged in a variety of multimodal, multimedia practices from a young age (Marsh *et al.*, 2005). This has implications for reading instruction in schools and for perceptions of what reading at home might mean. The move into a digitised world means that sharing reading is becoming more often a matter of sharing a screen. This might be seen as a less satisfying way for an adult to share a reading experience with a child, but in a detailed study of children reading the same book in the form of a picture book and as an e-book, Mackey (2016) argues that the relationship between the child, the adult and the book and the quality of the content are more important than the medium in which the book is presented. Mackey points out that an inferior e-book may result in an inferior reading experience but that 'where a text makes intelligent use of the digital affordances and an adult co-reader is on hand' (Mackey, 2016: 170) sharing an e-book should be equally enjoyable as sharing a print book.

Kindle readers, smartphone, digital cameras and iPad apps mean that children's stories are brought to innovative platforms which offer different possibilities for reader interaction and, indeed, for children to contribute to story-making (Kucirkova, 2014; Kucirkova and Cremin, 2016; Rowe and Miller, 2016). For children whose home language is not English, the potential to record stories in home languages contributes to the syncretic uses of reading mentioned by Gregory (2007) (see p. 000). However, Plowman *et al.* (2012) identify a gap in opportunities for children to see older readers using screens in schools and nurseries; at home screens are often part of the shared environment but in pre-school settings and classrooms, adults access screens in offices/areas separate from communal areas so that although modelling reading behaviours and practices using screens is a familiar home experience for young readers, such modelling is rarely seen in formal educational settings.

Working on community outreach programs in Canada, Burke and Maddigan note the importance of harnessing children's home experience of digital technology:

> The inclusion of digital media in the classroom, and in out-of-school community programs, is an obvious evolution necessary to mirror social conventions and to give students authentic, valuable interactions that will promote responsible, intentional uses of technology.
>
> (Burke and Maddigan, 2014: 21)

The idea of 'intentional' uses of technology reflects back to the discussion in Chapter 5 about critical media reading. To Burke and Maddigan, developing 'healthy digital literacy' is a key aim which can be approached through community digital reading projects bringing homes and schools together.

Reviewing the research into home and school digital literacy practices, Marsh (2010) points out that there is very little research about the home literacy experiences of children who come from fractured backgrounds – children who are cared for, live in refuges, hostels or refugee camps. There are still assumptions that the formal setting of school is the starting point for children learning to read but it is clear that digital technology means that children have access to a world of texts which provide them with knowledge and experience that is often ignored in the classroom. For vulnerable groups of children, such exclusion of experience is even more potentially damaging to children's literacy futures.

Summary

Before formal instruction can begin, children need to have certain concepts in place drawn from their experience of texts in the environment, home and community. The orchestration of reading combines semantic cues (searching for meaning), syntactic cues (sentence grammar and punctuation) and graphophonic cues (the relationship between phonics and graphic representation). Debates about the most effective – or 'right' – way to teach phonics are examined. A video of a discrete phonics teaching session is placed in the context of wider processes of teaching early reading including teaching reading strategies and behaviours. Case studies give examples of teaching early reading and some attention is given to possible barriers to children taking on reading, suggesting the importance of establishing a rich reading environment and a balanced approach in the early years. Finally, the role of homes and communities are considered in relation to school-based reading practices, particularly those related to on-screen reading.

Note

1   In England, teachers are required to carry out a phonics check on 6 year olds. Children have to recognise words and non-words as means of checking their ability to decode phonically. This is used as a way of describing levels of reading (see Darnell *et al.*, 2017 for a critique of the purpose and validity of the phonics screening check and the role of synthetic phonics for teaching early reading).

Recommended reading

Elborn, S. (2015) *The Handbook of Teaching Early Reading: More than phonics.* Leicester: United Kingdom Literacy Association. Based on the work of Marie Clay, this handbook is comprehensive in its coverage and founded on reliable classroom experience.

Hall, K., Goswami, U., Harrison, C., Ellis, S. and Soler, J. (eds) (2010) *Interdisciplinary Perspectives on Learning to Read: Culture, cognition and pedagogy.* London: Routledge. Based on research evidence, this collection of perspectives fully explores the theories, arguments and processes associated with learning to read. **Advanced**

Levy, R. (2011) *Young Children Reading at Home and at School*. London: SAGE. Drawing on research into home and school settings, this book shows how some approaches to teaching reading can be counter-productive, causing some children to lose confidence in themselves as readers. Becoming literate in a digital world is a strong thread throughout the book. **Advanced**

National Institute of Child Health and Human Development (2000) *Report of the National Reading Panel. Teaching Children to read: An evidence-based assessment of the scientific research literature on reading and its implications for reading instruction: Reports of the subgroups.* www.nichd.nih.gov/publications/pubs/nrp/Pages/findings.aspx (accessed 1 May 2017). A significant large-scale enquiry into research about reading from the USA. **Advanced**

References

Apthorp, H. (2006) Effects of a supplemental vocabulary programme in third grade reading/language arts, *Journal of Educational Research*, 100 (2) pp. 67–79.

Arrow, A. W. and Tunmer, W. E. (2012) Contemporary reading acquisition theory: The conceptual basis for differentiated reading instruction, in S. Suggate and E. Reese (eds) *Contemporary Debates in Childhood Education and Development*. Abingdon: Routledge, pp. 241–249.

Bearne, E., Kennedy, R. and Reedy, D. (2016) *Teaching Grammar Effectively at Key Stage One*. Leicester: United Kingdom Literacy Association.

Bowtell, J. and Holding, S. (2014) Early reading, in T. Cremin and J. Arthur (eds) *Learning to Teach in the Primary School*. London: Routledge, pp. 527–540.

Burke, A. and Maddigan, B. (2014) *Using Community Outreach to Build Children's Resiliency and Critical Literacy through Digital Tools*. Newfoundland and Labrador: Faculty of Education, Memorial University of Newfoundland St John's.

Bussis, A. M., Chittenden, E. A., Amarel, M. and Klausner, E. (1985) *Inquiry into Meaning: An investigation of learning to read*. Hillsdale, NJ: Lawrence Erlbaum Associates.

Chall, J. (1983) *Stages of Reading Development*. New York: McGraw Hill.

Clay, M. M. (1991) *Becoming Literate: The construction of inner control*. Portsmouth, NH: Heinemann.

Clay, M. M. (2005) *Literacy Lessons Designed for Individuals: Part two: Teaching procedures*. Auckland, NZ: Heinemann.

Cremin, T., Mottram, M., Collins, F., Powell, S. and Safford, K. (2014) *Building Communities of Engaged Readers: Reading for pleasure*. London and New York: Routledge.

Cremin, T., Mottram, M., Collins, F., Powell, S. and Drury, R. (2015) *Researching Literacy Lives: Building communities between home and school*. London: Routledge.

Darnell, C., Solity, J. and Wall, H. (2017) Decoding the phonics screening check, *British Educational Research Journal*, 43 (3) pp. 505–527.

Department for Education (DfE) (2012) *Statutory Framework for the Early Years Foundation Stage*. Now replaced by: www.gov.uk/government/publications/early-years-foundation-stage-frame work--2 (accessed 1 May 2017)

Department for Education and Skills (DfES) (2007) *Letters and Sounds: Notes of Guidance for Practitioners and Teachers*. www.gov.uk/government/uploads/system/uploads/attachment_data/ file/190599/Letters_and_Sounds_-_DFES-00281-2007.pdf (accessed 1 May 2017)

Ehri, L. C. (2012) Why is it important for children to begin learning to read in kindergarten?, in S. Suggate and E. Reese (eds) *Contemporary Debates in Childhood Education and Development*. Abingdon: Routledge, pp. 171–180.

Elborn, S. (2015) *The Handbook of Teaching Early Reading: More than phonics*. Leicester: United Kingdom Literacy Association.

Frith, U. (1985) Beneath the surface of developmental dyslexia, in K. Patterson, J. Marshall and M. Coltheart (eds) *Surface Dyslexia, Neuropsychological and Cognitive Studies of Phonological Reading*. London: Erlbaum, pp. 301–330.

Goodman, K. (1973) (ed.) *Miscue Analysis: Applications to reading instruction*. Urbana, IL: National Council of Teachers of English.

Goswami, U. (2008) Reading, complexity and the brain, *Literacy*, 42 (2) pp. 67–74.

Gregory, E. (2001) Sisters and brothers as language and literacy teachers, *Journal of Early Childhood Literacy*, 1 (3) pp. 301–322.

Gregory, E. (2007) What counts as reading and learning outside school? And with whom? How? and Where?, in E. Bearne and J. Marsh (eds) *Literacy and Social Inclusion: Closing the gap.* Stoke-on-Trent: Trentham Books, pp. 41–72.

Gregory, E. and Kenner, C. (2003) The out-of-school schooling of literacy, in N. Hall, J. Larson and J. Marsh (eds) *Handbook of Early Childhood Literacy.* London: SAGE, pp. 75–84.

Hall, K., Cremin, T., Comber, B. and Moll, L. (eds) (2012) *International Handbook of Research in Children's Literacy, Learning and Culture.* Oxford: Blackwell.

Juel, C. and Minden-Cupp, C. (2001) Learning to read words: Linguistic units and instructional strategies, *Reading Research Quarterly*, 35 (4) pp. 458–493.

Knoester, M. and Plikuhn, M. (2016) Influence of siblings on out-of-school reading practices, *Journal of Research in Reading*, 39(4) pp. 469–485.

Kucirkova, N. (2014) *iPads and Tablets in the Classroom: Personalising children's stories.* Leicester: United Kingdom Literacy Association.

Kucirkova, N. and Cremin, T. (2016) *Digital Books Supporting Reading for Pleasure.* https://digilitey. wordpress.com/2016/07/28/digital-books-supporting-reading-for-pleasure/ (accessed 1 May 2017)

Levy, R. (2011) *Young Children Reading at Home and at School.* London: SAGE.

Leyva, D., Reese, E. and Wiser, M. (2012) Early understanding of the functions of print: Parent-child interaction and pre-schoolers' notating skills. *First Language*, 32 (3) pp. 301–323.

Machin, S., McNally, S. and Viarengo, M. (2016) *'Teaching to Teach' Literacy: Discussion Paper No 1425.* London: The Centre for Economic Performance.

Mackey, M. (2016) Digital picture books, in E. Arizpe and M. Styles (eds) *Children Reading Picturebooks: Interpreting visual texts*, 2nd edn. Abingdon: Routledge, pp. 169–179.

Marsh, J. (2010) The relationship between home and school literacy practices, in D. Wyse, R. Andrews and J. Hoffman (eds) *The Routledge International Handbook of English, Language and Literacy Teaching.* London: Routledge, pp. 305–316.

Marsh, J., Brooks, G., Hughes, J., Richie, L. and Roberts, S. (2005) *Digital Beginnings: Young children's use of popular culture, media and new technologies.* Sheffield: University of Sheffield. www.digitalbeginnings.shef.ac.uk/DigitalBeginningsReport.pdf (accessed 1 May 2017)

McBride-Chang, C. (2012) Shared book reading: There is no downside for parents, in S. Suggate and E. Reese (eds) *Contemporary Debates in Childhood Education and Development.* Abingdon: Routledge, pp. 51–58.

National Institute of Child Health and Human Development (2000) *Report of the National Reading Panel. Teaching Children to Read: An evidence-based assessment of the scientific research literature on reading and its implications for reading instruction: Reports of the subgroups.* www.nichd.nih.gov/publications/pubs/nrp/Pages/findings.aspx (accessed 1 May 2017)

Plowman, L., McPake, J. and Stephen, C. (2012) Extending opportunities for learning: The role of digital media in early education, in S. Suggate and E. Reese (eds) *Contemporary Debates in Childhood Education and Development.* Abingdon: Routledge, pp. 95–104.

Port, R. (2006) The graphical basis of phones and phonemes, in M. Munro and O. Schwen-Bohn (eds) *Second Language Speech Learning: The role of language experience in speech perception and production.* Amsterdam: John Benjamins, pp. 349–365.

Reedy, D. and Bearne, E. (2013) *Teaching Grammar Effectively in Primary Schools.* Leicester: United Kingdom Literacy Association.

Reese, E, (2012) The tyranny of shared book-reading, in S. Suggate and E. Reese (eds) *Contemporary Debates in Childhood Education and Development.* Abingdon: Routledge, pp. 59–68.

Rowe, D. W. and Miller, M. E. (2016) Designing for diverse classrooms: Using iPads and digital cameras to compose books with emergent bilingual/biliterate four-year-olds, *Journal of Early Childhood Literacy*, 16 (4) pp. 425–472.

Sparks, A. and Reese, E. (2013) From reminiscing to reading: Home contributions to children's developing language and literacy in low-income families, *First Language*, 23 (1) pp. 89–109.

Stainthorp, R. (2003) Phonology and Learning to Read, in N. Hall, J. Larson and J. Marsh (eds) *Handbook of Early Childhood Literacy*. London: SAGE, pp. 207–221.

Whitehurst, G. J. and Lonigan, C. J. (1998) Child development and emergent literacy, *Child Development*, 69 pp. 848–872.

Wyse, D. and Goswami, U. (2008) Synthetic phonics and the teaching of reading, *British Educational Research Journal*, 34 (6) pp. 691–710.

Children's books

Kes Gray, illustrated Jim Field (2014) *Oi Frog!* Hodder Children's Books. ISBN 9781444910865

Kes Gray and Clare Gray, illustrated Jim Field (2016) *Oi Dog!* Hodder Children's Books. ISBN 9781444919592

Kes Gray, illustrated Jim Field (2016) *Quick Quack Quentin*. Hodder Children's Books. ISBN 9781444919578

Chris Haughton (2014) *Oh, No, George!* Walker Books. ISBN 9781406357912

Chris Haughton (2015) *Shh! We have a Plan*. Walker Books. ISBN 9781406360035

Eric Hill (2009) *Where's Spot?* Frederick Warne/Penguin. ISBN 9780723263661

Pat Hutchins (2013) *We're Going on a Picnic!* Red Fox. ISBN 9781782950226

CHAPTER 8

COMPREHENSION

This chapter includes:

- Defining reading comprehension
- The components of comprehension
- Teaching comprehension
- Inference
- The complexity of comprehension
- Comprehension strategies
- Case study, middle primary: Visualising Cyclops
- Reciprocal teaching
- Case study, middle primary: A small group reading session using reciprocal teaching
- Fluency and comprehension
- Using film to support reading comprehension
- Directed activities related to texts
- Skimming and scanning

Learning to read means learning to make sense of text. Reading is not just about the accurate pronunciation of written words (Dombey *et al.*, 2010). Nor is making sense, or comprehension, of texts just about answering questions about the words on the page. The Latin root of the word 'comprehend' means 'to seize' or 'grasp' (monkeys' prehensile tails do just that!) so, although there are definitions based on careful research, at the heart of comprehension lies the ability to grasp ideas. However, just as word reading is no straight-forward matter, reading comprehension involves a complex set of processes. This chapter begins with definitions of reading comprehension, the strategies that support the develop-ment of reading comprehension and how recent research concerning Reciprocal teaching (RT) shows how this approach powerfully supports teaching these strategies and the development of comprehension. Reciprocal teaching is founded on a socioconstructivist theory of learning (see p. 44) developed by Vygotsky (1978) and Bruner (1996), for example, which holds that meaning derives from social interaction. Young readers learn through the support of others, moving from assisted learning towards independence (Van Keer and Verhaeghe, 2005). As Dombey *et al.* explain:

> Children who become avid and accomplished readers focus on making sense from the start: they develop a habit of mind that expects the words they decode to make sense. This allows them to monitor their own performance from an early stage, and to make corrections when they misread.

> (Dombey *et al.*, 2010: 4)

The comprehension strategies outlined in this chapter help readers to glean meaning from any kind of text: narrative, poetic, non-fiction, visual, pictorial, moving image or digital.

Activity 8.1
Making sense of texts – individual/pairs/group

Read the following short text:

> Tuatara live in holes in the ground called burrows. They are nocturnal – they emerge from their burrows at night to eat anything they can; mainly insects, but also worms, slugs and millipedes.

What does the word *tuatara* mean? (If you already know please do not reveal it to others just yet.) Share your ideas with a colleague(s). Discuss how you went about making sense of this short text, and what you did to work out the meaning of the word tuatara.

You will probably have discovered that you drew on multiple sources to work out the meaning. To begin with, and probably quite unconsciously, you drew on your grammatical knowledge of sentences and identified tuatara as a plural noun – they are things. As you read further you will have drawn on your knowledge of other texts and concluded that this was an information text, not a story, and it was revealing interesting facts that would be helpful in working out what these things called tuatara might be. You were therefore looking for clues in the text to clarify the meaning of a particular word and getting the gist of what the passage was all about.

In considering these clues you drew on your knowledge of the world to infer that tuatara are likely to be living creatures, possibly little furry animals like rabbits as they live in burrows too, but not quite, as rabbits do not eat anything they can get and are not nocturnal. It is likely that you now have a picture in your head of what you think tuatara looks like.

You might also have drawn on your knowledge of languages to conclude that tuatara does not sound like an English word so the creatures might live in somewhere like South America or Australia.

In addition, making sense of this text is supported by understanding individual words in context as well as the ability to recognise and pronounce them.

If you do know what a tuatara is, please now tell your colleagues.

This finally demonstrates that experience and knowledge of the world differs significantly between people and that the way readers make sense of text therefore will be affected by that. Thus there will be many different meanings made – it cannot be assumed that every reader understands the same text in the same way.

Comprehension is fundamentally about what the reader brings to the text as much as it is about what the text offers the reader. In making sense of texts, readers draw on knowledge about how sentences work, how texts are organised, and knowledge of other facts drawn from wider reading/television or film watching. You may also have found it helpful to talk to someone else about your ideas. All this suggests that making meaning from texts – or comprehension – is not just a matter of reading the words on the page but is socially and culturally mediated.

Information about tuataras can be found here: https://en.wikipedia.org/wiki/Tuatara (accessed 1 May 2017).

You might like to compare what you thought with the information found here.

There have been various definitions of reading comprehension, including:

> Retrieving the sense of individual words, combining clauses to make sentences, and make meaning from successive sentences and paragraphs.
>
> (Cain, 2010)

> The skill of reading to extract knowledge or reading with understanding.
>
> (Moyle, 1972)

Pardo (2004) sees it as:

> A process in which readers construct meaning by interacting with text through the combination of prior knowledge and previous experience, information in the text and the stance the reader takes in relation to the text.
>
> (Pardo, 2004: 272)

This last definition reflects the experience of understanding the tuatara passage above. A reader does not depend only on the text itself, as the first two definitions suggest, but what the reader brings to the text is an essential part of the process. Reading is as much about what the reader brings to the text as gets from the text itself. Making sense lies at the heart of reading. However, this is not necessarily a straightforward matter; as reading is a complex system of deriving meaning from print (NRP, 2000) (see also p. 110).

8.2   The components of comprehension

Comprehension is not a single mental process. It is made up of a range of component parts which work together to help the reader understand the text. Tennent (2015) shows that when the reader is directly engaged in the text, comprehension is made up of three areas:

- linguistic processes: including words and sentences; for example, an individual's current understanding of words, phrases and sentences and how these combine together to make meaning
- knowledge bases: including general knowledge, domain knowledge (related to a particular area, e.g., cricket), and pragmatic or cultural knowledge applied to the text currently being read
- cognitive/metacognitive processes: including:
  - short-term and long-term memory. Short-term or working memory ensures that the reader remembers words and sentences that have just been read, or at the very least the gist of them. Long-term memory is used to apply general knowledge to the text to make connections that support understanding.
  - comprehension monitoring or continuous checking that the reading makes sense
  - phonic decoding/word recognition (one of a wide range of components which enable readers to make sense of text)
  - inference making.

> **Cognitive:** related to conscious mental activities such as thinking, understanding, learning, and remembering.
>
> **Metacognitive:** related to reflecting on conscious mental activities.

8.3   Teaching comprehension

Varga (2017) draws on a range of research to suggest teaching strategies which develop metacognition and support reading comprehension. These include encouraging the reader to explain:

- why they want to ask particular questions of a text
- what they think and feel about the text (cognitive as well as emotional processes)
- why they have chosen particular strategies to make sense of the text (and giving feedback about the effectiveness of those strategies or suggesting alternatives)

- what they think of the style of the text and how they respond to it
- how they might use an appropriate metalanguage to explain their ideas in the context of the text

Finally, the teacher gives support to young readers' ability to put their ideas and thoughts into words.

A wide-ranging review in 2010 of the current research on comprehension (Butler *et al.*, 2010) draws together studies of: teacher practice, multiple strategy instruction, instruction in text structure, at-risk learners, technology-assisted instruction and multisensory learning in order to identify the most successful approaches to improving reading comprehension. The summary contains the following findings.

Teacher practice: the most consistent finding was that teachers who emphasised higher-order thinking promoted greater reading growth. On the other hand, routine comprehension exercises resulted in lower growth rates of reading comprehension than teaching children the different comprehension strategies.

Using multiple strategies: one of the most effective approaches is described in work by Guthrie *et al.* (2004, 2006) using concept-oriented reading instruction (CORI) which combines strategy instruction with motivation supports; for example, offering choice, practical hands-on activities associated with texts and texts that engage the reader.

Instruction in text structure: although children find it easier to understand texts about familiar events than texts about unfamiliar events, learning about text structure supports comprehension of both familiar and unfamiliar content, particularly in expository text. However, instruction in a single text structure does not transfer to understanding another text structure (Williams *et al.*, 2004) so that it is important to distinguish explicitly between different text structures.

At-risk learners: amongst the strategies found to support readers who struggle with comprehension were consistency and frequency of instruction, small group work and combining teaching comprehension skills with word recognition rather than focusing on word recognition alone.

Technology-assisted instruction: although there were not many available studies, overall the findings suggest the value of using digital technology because children tend to retain visual and auditory content provided together more successfully than they retain either type of content alone. In addition, learners who are actively engaged in their learning through the use of digital texts have better reading outcomes than passive learners.

Multisensory learning: studies by Glenberg *et al.* (2004, 2007) demonstrated that object manipulation (using puppets, toys, cut-outs) can greatly enhance 5 and 6 year olds' reading comprehension, particularly in small groups.

8.4   Inference

Without inference, reading does not make sense. Williams outlines the main types of inference – anaphoric, global and text-internal:

> Inference is an essential component of reading comprehension. It enables
> the reader to detect implied meaning lying beyond the literal. In reading
> these sentences, you have already made an anaphoric inference by linking
> the pronoun *it* to the preceding noun, *inference*. This occurred

unconsciously at the linguistic level to maintain coherence between the sentences. Continuing to read this article and establishing the main points, you will engage in global inference: drawing on several localised textual details to derive the overall message. Without inferential abilities, no fully coherent understanding of a text can be established. By reaching the end of this paragraph, you may have made a text-internal inference.

(Williams, 2014: 95)

In other words, when reading, inferences are made based on an understanding of text coherence – links between words and ideas which allow a reader to follow the flow of a text (local and text-connecting); wider understanding drawn from knowledge of the world or other texts (global or text-external inferences); and understanding ideas across a whole text (text-internal inferences). These three kinds of understanding work together to enable inferences being made.

Tennent (2015) identifies thirty-two different types of inference but has grouped them into two major categories: coherence inferences and interrogative inferences.

Coherence inference ensures that the reading makes sense. This will include inferring what words mean from their context. For example in the sentences

> *The girl hit the ball. She hit it hard.*

the reader infers that there is a causal connection between the two sentences and that the second sentence refers back to the first sentence. Also, that the meaning of the pronouns *she* and *it* relate to the girl and the ball respectively. A reader might also make inferences from outside the text by picturing the age of the girl and the game she might be playing.

Interrogative inference helps the reader to understand texts at a deeper level. The reader interrogates the text while they are reading and also when reflecting on what has been read, whether it is a sentence or two or a whole text. Readers may not always be aware of the questions they are asking the text as this becomes an automatic process, but slowed down and brought to conscious attention, interrogation might mean something like: *I wonder if this character knows what has happened already?* Reading on will establish the answer to this. Interrogation might also include making inferences about character motivation and personalities, the theme or moral the author might have intended, or expressing opinions about content after reading the full text.

Making meaning from texts requires young (and experienced) readers to apply these processes interactively. The job of the teacher is to help young readers to develop the ability to do so effectively.

8.5 The complexity of comprehension

When developing readers make sense of text, they undertake a cognitively complex process. They have to be able to understand words and phrases, and integrate them across sentences. Whilst they are doing so they have to link this to their background knowledge and fill in any gaps in understanding by way of inference making. Thus even a literal understanding is not necessarily going to be straightforward.

An example of this complexity and the integration of the components of comprehension can be gleaned by reading just the first sentence of a well-known picture book for children.

All the components listed in section 8.2 integrate to support the development of meaning, as shown by analysing the first sentence in *The Gruffalo* by Julia Donaldson (1999):

> A mouse took a stroll through the deep dark wood.

Linguistic processes: a text is made up of words. Young readers have to understand what the words mean individually and in relation with each other. There might be a problem here for the inexperienced reader as the words *took* and *stroll* are not as straightforward to understand as they first look. They could mean to a child that the mouse was carrying something called a 'stroll' through the wood. To do so without asking an adult will mean reading on or drawing on other clues in the text (such as the picture where the mouse is on his own and not carrying anything). By linking it to the context in which it appears, a reader can infer and clarify the meaning of the individual words. Many words in English have more than one meaning (the multiple meanings of the word 'mean' is a good example) and so context and children's knowledge of the multiple meanings of words combine to support making literal sense of the text. This is done on the run as the text is read, and further clues within the text are combined to clarify meaning.

Knowledge bases: significant background knowledge is being applied too. A reader's domain knowledge of books and stories will indicate that this is likely to be a narrative, and the appearance of the phrase 'deep, dark woods' helps predict that it may have elements of a traditional tale. Readers may have domain knowledge related to the author, Julia Donaldson, and the type of texts she writes, drawn from previous reading. Thus the background knowledge draws on the range of knowledge bases, including knowledge of the type of text, the language or literary style, the subject matter of the text, other texts, and any knowledge of the world that can be connected to the text in hand. All this from just the first sentence!

Cognitive/metacognitive processes: once the text has been read to the end, further comprehension takes place through reflection. This reflection enables the reader to engage with deeper layers of meanings in the text (e.g., reflection on the cleverness of the mouse in solving his problem, or the stupidity of the fox: *Aren't foxes supposed to be cunning? – they are in other stories! I wonder if there is a moral that the author has been trying to tell us – cleverness outwits strength, or triumph over adversity.*). Reflecting might require looking for clues, making judgements about characters, evaluating the effectiveness of the text (*did the instructions help to make the bookcase easily?*) or forming other opinions. Reading reflection also depends significantly on inference making, which requires the reader to apply background knowledge as part of their reflection.

The implication for primary teachers is that to teach effectively it is essential to understand how readers have made sense of what they have been reading (as they are reading) and to use this to inform how this understanding of the text can be deepened (through reading reflections).

8.6 Comprehension strategies

Because comprehension is an outcome of a range of cognitive processes, it cannot be taught directly. However, strategies to aid comprehension *can* be taught. Comprehension results from readers applying strategies that support and deepen comprehension and these can be identified and developed.

Figure 8.1 lists the main strategies readers draw on when comprehending text. Teachers can draw attention to, and model, the use of these strategies so that children will develop the ability to use them independently. For example, the questions teachers ask can support children in deepening their understanding of text, offering examples of how to develop the strategy of questioning the text themselves during and after reading.

Strategies	What the strategy involves
Predicting	Making a logically plausible guess as to what will happen next.
Clarifying	Checking how specific words and phrases have been understood.
Questioning	Asking questions about the text to expose different layers of meaning.
Summarising	Stating the main events, actions or ideas in the text.
Connecting	Making connections to previous experience, including other texts.
Noting text structure	Identifying the main linguistic features in a specific text-type.
Visualising	Developing a visual image of written text.
Thinking aloud	Reading a few sentences or a paragraph and verbalizing what has been understood. Then repeating this activity across a text.

Figure 8.1 Comprehension strategies (based on Tennent *et al.*, 2016: 36)

Examples from a group of 7 year olds reading *Black Queen* by Michael Morpurgo (2000) with their teacher, Eleanor, show some of these strategies in action (see the full case study on page 205).

Predicting

> Predicting actions and events that might be forthcoming in the text supports inexperienced readers with comprehension.
>
> (Duke and Pearson, 2002: 212)

Prediction in not simply guessing what a text is going to be about before it is read. When young readers are encouraged to make predictions, they should be based on prior knowledge generally, and if possible, what is already known about the content of the text. Thus, in narrative, it is more productive to ask what might happen, or what a character might do, once some of the story has been read. Inferences to inform prediction can then be encouraged by drawing on knowledge of the character, and action so far, as well as more general knowledge connections.

After reading the first chapter of *Black Queen*, Eleanor asked what the children thought would happen when the door to number 22 is opened and what Billy, the main character, will find out in chapter 2. In doing so, they were able to make connections with the information they had gleaned about Billy and number 22 from chapter 1 as well as reflecting on what they knew about mysterious houses in other stories and perhaps from their own experience.

Clarifying

Clarification involves seeking to find out the meaning of previously unknown words. This encourages readers to monitor how they are making consistent meaning as they read the text and build comprehension (Palincsar and Brown, 1984).

For example, as the children read chapter 2 of *Black Queen*, Eleanor asked them to identify any words or phrases that were unknown and puzzled them. She had also identified a few for a brief discussion after reading. The children identified words such as *high-pitched*, *piercing* and *sheepishly* which were then clarified through discussion by the group and the teacher. Eleanor demonstrated how reading round the word can be a good way of looking for clues about what the word might mean, or if that is not helpful, asking each other or the teacher for help will make the meaning clear.

Clarification is also a good starting point for looking at the meaning of literary features such as simile and metaphor (e.g. *'My mother eyed us both darkly...'*) and discuss why the author chose them and the what the effect on the reader might be. Since all readers are different, teachers may not always be aware which words children will find problematic. As always, it is better to ask children to identify them.

Questioning

The questions that readers can be asked about the text they are reading, or have just read, can help them to access different layers of meaning. Asking questions that require children to make inferential responses deepens comprehension. When teachers model how to ask questions about what they are reading, children can learn how to ask questions of the text when they read independently and the process can be 'handed over' to them. Nystrand (2006) draws attention to the importance of authentic dialogue about what is being read, particularly if it draws on children's personal and cultural experience.

Experienced readers actively engage *with* the text by constantly asking questions *of* the text as they read, even if they are not conscious of doing so. Teachers should be clear that the questions they ask are models for questions the children could be asking when they read and that children's independent questioning should be encouraged, both in and beyond teacher-led sessions. Ultimately it should be children's questions that shape reading comprehension conversations.

There is agreement (Raphael and McKinney, 1983; Raphael and Pearson, 1985; Raphael and Wonnacott, 1985; Duke and Pearson, 2002; Duke, 2005; Tennent *et al.*, 2016) that three main question types support comprehension: 'looking', 'clue' and 'thinking' questions.

Looking questions direct readers to what is explicit in the text. They are designed to develop literal comprehension. Their purpose for teachers is to ascertain whether children have literal understanding of a text. For example: *What did the three little pigs build their houses out of? Can you tell me two interesting facts about blue whales from this film clip?* (Other terms used for this type of question are *literal*, *on the line* and *right here* questions.)

Clue questions ask the reader to think and search; the answer can be found in the text but some level of inference-making will be required. They require young readers to make connections and find evidence in the text to support the development of understanding. For example: *Which was the cleverest little pig? How do you know? Blue whales are enormous. True or false? How do you know?* (Other terms used for this type of question are *inferential*, *between the lines* and *hidden* questions.)

Thinking questions require children to bring their background knowledge (world, domain and pragmatic) to bear on the reading. These questions encourage evaluation of the text, opinions or moral judgements. However, children should be asked to justify their initial observations. For example: *Was the last little pig right to trick the wolf so that he fell in the boiling water and badly injured himself? Is it right that blue whales are hunted? How would you feel if you were in that situation?* (Other terms used for this type of question are *analytical, beyond the lines* and *head* questions.)

These three types of questions can be used to focus of particular aspects of texts. For example, in narrative, questions might focus on character, plot and setting.

Character

- *How many animals did the wolf eat in the story?* (looking)
- *Can you think of a word that describes what this character is like? How do you know?* (clue)
- *Did xxx do the right thing? Why? Why not?* (thinking)

Setting

- *In what places does this story happen?* (looking)
- *When does this story happen? What are the clues to when the story is set?* (clue)
- *What do you think would change if the story was set nowadays?* (thinking)

Plot

- *How does the story begin/end?* (looking)
- *Is it like any other stories you know? How?* (clue)
- *What is the problem that has to be sorted out in this story? Would you have sorted it out in a different way?* (thinking)

Activity 8.2
Formulating questions – pairs/group

Choose a short story or section/chapter from a book you are planning to read with your class (or a book on your 'Texts I Like' list). With a partner, read the text and devise a looking question, a clue question and a thinking question. Share your questions with another pair and reflect on how straightforward they were to formulate.

You will probably have discovered that devising the looking questions were the most straightforward. Consider your looking question. Is it a good starting point for a conversation that will help you check that children have got a reasonable literal understanding of the text as a whole. A question which asks just for a single piece of information retrieval (*What colour was the coat?*) is insufficient to do that job. A better question might be: *What reasons did the woman next door give for getting mad at Billy?* – which can be a starting point for checking understanding more fully.

The other two types of question need more thought. The clue question should focus on finding and integrating information across the text to be able to answer it. (*Why is the woman next door called the Black Queen by everybody?*)

Finally, the thinking question should be open enough for children to draw on their life experience and make connections to the text. (*How would you have planned to find the cat if it was yours? What might have happened in the story if Billy had done that?*)

These planned questions are only the starting point for conversations that develop the range of comprehension strategies. It is how adults respond to children's answers that moves learning forward. Authentic conversations about a text give the teacher an opportunity to extend the questioning. For example: *Why do you think that? Is there any other evidence for that in the story? Does that change as we read on because the character does this later in the story? Would the rest of you agree or have an alternative view?* build a conversation where meaning is made collaboratively and children's agency is encouraged in the process.

(See p. 48 for a good example of how a teacher responds to the answers to an initial clue question *'Can you think of a word that describes what this character is like?'*.)

You may want to improve the questions after discussion with colleagues, but keep them to use as soon as you have a chance to work with the text you chose.

An alternative, but complementary, approach to questioning is suggested by Chambers (2011) as a way of encouraging rich book talk to develop thinking more deeply about and responding to texts read, as well as making connections (see Connecting below). Chambers suggests that after reading a text, the three types of open-ended questions might guide discussion:

Basic questions
- *Was there anything you liked about this book?*
- *Was there anything you disliked?*
- *Was there anything that puzzled you?*
- *Were there any patterns – any connections – that you noticed?*

General questions
- *Have you read any other books like this one?*
- *Has anything that happened in this book ever happened to you?*

Special questions
- *How long did it take for the story to happen?*
- *Who was telling – who was narrating – the story? Do we know? How do we know?*

(See Chambers (2011) for a more extensive list of examples.)

Summarising

Summarising involves encouraging young readers to outline the main points or key events of the text they have just read. This promotes literal comprehension of the whole of what has just been read and supports comprehension monitoring. Children can be asked to summarise the main events with each other and the teacher may then get them to reflect on whether they did cover them all or whether there are more to add. To encourage brevity, a time limit can be useful. For example: *See if you can summarise this part of the story in one minute or less.*

Connecting

Connecting involves finding links in and beyond the text. These may be causal links between events and characters' actions in the text or similarities with other known texts (text-to-text connections) or it could be linking themes to life experience in general (text-to-world connections). Many connections in reading are made through connecting the text to personal experience (text-to-self connections). 'Clue' questions and 'thinking' questions are explicitly formulated to help developing readers to make these connections. Keene and Zimmerman (1997) is a useful text outlining the importance of these connections including practical ideas of how to help children to make them.

Noting text structure

Experienced readers anticipate how they will read a text by their knowledge of text structure. Approaching a narrative, such as a novel or biography, they will expect to read it from the beginning in a linear way, as opposed to an information text which is used for reference where they will come to it looking for specific information and use the contents and/or information pages, or a search engine to find it. They will be aware that sentences may be terser in reference type texts, as opposed to the more literary language of novels, and that technical vocabulary in information texts is highly context specific, for example. These main linguistic features can be highlighted in comprehension activities.

Visualising

Most readers form some kind of visual image in their heads as they read or enact a text; it might be fully formed pictures or seeing the atmosphere or setting in colours. Teachers can ask children to visualise as they read and draw attention, through asking them to describe the images they have in their heads, to the meaning of the text as well as how the images change as they read further. Children might also be asked to encapsulate the text in picture form after the text has been read. They could draw a story map of the main events, or a detailed representation of a character based on the description in the text (Figures 8.2 and 8.3).

Figure 8.2 Visualisation of the main character in *Stitch Head*

Figure 8.3 Visualisation of a key scene in *The Iron Man*

Case study, middle primary: Visualising Cyclops

Alice teaches a highly diverse class of 9 year olds in East London. She planned a sequence of work based on a selection of Greek myths as retold by Anthony Horowitz in *Myths and Legends* (2007). One of the stories was *The Eye of the Cyclops*. In order to see how well they understood the story, Alice asked the class to visualise and then draw a picture of the Cyclops based on the written description.

Figure 8.4 shows Divine's visualisation.

In this picture Divine has drawn on both the description and the action in the story to compose his picture. He has annotated the drawing with some of the descriptive words from the story and the added detail shows that he has very good literal understanding. There are sheep (the Cyclops keeps them) as well as the bloody remains of some of the Greek sailors who have been killed and devoured by the monster. Divine has drawn on his knowledge of ancient Greekcostumes to clothe the Cyclops. Overall this is very good evidence that Divine can use visualising through close reading and use it to develop a detailed literal understanding of the text.

Figure 8.4 Divine's image of Cyclops

Thinking aloud

Thinking aloud involves verbalising thought processes as parts of the text are read. When teachers model how to think aloud, the children can use the model to guide their own think-alouds to support metacognition and strategic reading. For example, a teacher might model how to use a range of strategies to work out to develop their opinions about a character, as Eleanor demonstrates:

When I am trying to get a view about a character I always like to read on a bit and see if there is more information to help me make my mind up about them. So in this chapter I am thinking about the Black Queen and what she is like. When Billy first meets her on page 16 and she opens her front door she gives a really creepy impression, but that could be her being shy as she only opens the door a little way, but then when she speaks she isn't friendly and then shouts at Billy. By this point I think the Black Queen might be a villain in the story and Billy had better watch out! But the book says that she's nervous when talking to Billy so she could be frightened of him but probably not, because on page 18 she starts by wanting to get rid of him and then changes her mind and starts sounding as though she will be helpful and kind. So my view of the Black Queen has changed in just a page or two. I am still a bit confused about her. As Billy says, at one moment she is kind, the next nasty. I will have to read on through the next chapter and see if my opinion of her gets clearer or changes. I will be asking myself whether the Black Queen is kind but strange or scary and strange, or possibly a mixture of both!

So you can see how asking questions of the text as you read helps you to deepen your understanding. I am always asking what kind of character is she? Do I like this character or not? Have I changed my mind about her? What made me change my mind? And so on.

Website resource W8.1 has a series of suggestions for books, films, songs and poems to use for teaching the different strategies outlined in section 8.6 with children aged 4–6.

8.7 Reciprocal teaching

Reciprocal teaching (RT), or reciprocal reading (RR) as it is also called in the specific context of teaching reading, was devised by Palincsar and Brown (1984) as a process for developing and monitoring comprehension with groups of children. Teachers and other adults work with children to develop deeper understandings of texts through focused conversations. The conversations and teaching focus are designed to develop both cognitive and metacognitive awareness. Four specific comprehension strategies, included in the list in Figure 8.1, can provide a sequence for teaching sessions:

- Predicting
- Questioning
- Seeking clarification
- Summarising (Palincsar and Brown, 1984; Brown *et al.*, 1984; Brown and Palincsar, 1989).

Addressing these four strategies creates the context where the full range in Figure 8.1 can be addressed and developed. For example, connections can be encouraged explicitly through prediction – *How do you think it will end? Does it remind you of another text you have read?* – and questioning using the three types of question – *looking, clue* and *thinking*.

Using these four key strategies as the focus for planning a session, a teacher can develop all the components of comprehension through interaction with a group of children.

Case study, middle primary: A small group reading session using reciprocal teaching

This case study focuses on the second of five small group reading sessions planned by Eleanor, a class teacher of 7 year olds, based on *Black Queen* by Michael Morpurgo. She uses reciprocal teaching for group reading focused on developing comprehension and the school devotes 25 minutes every day to this activity.

Before the session Eleanor planned her three questions:

What reasons did Mrs Blume give for not letting Billy into her back yard? (looking)

Why is the woman next door called the Black Queen by everybody? (clue)

How would you have planned to find the cat if it was yours? What might have happened in the story if Billy had done that? (thinking)

Eleanor will use these questions and the text for at least three of the groups in her class. She knows that she can meet the needs of the groups by shaping the conversation arising from the responses to the questions. Currently, with almost all her class, she is supporting their use of making connections with clues in the text; with her most experienced readers she is looking at how authors choose to use similes and the effect this has on the reader.

Eleanor also considered the vocabulary and decided that two of the words would probably need clarifying: *snooty* and *stand-offish*.

At the beginning of the session, Eleanor reminded the children of the reciprocal reading (RR) components which structure the session and explained that they would be reading and discussing chapter 2. The group briefly recapped what happened in chapter 1.

Prediction: the children together then predicted what they thought would happen in chapter 2 based on what they have been read previously. Eleanor occasionally probed by asking for reasons for their answers.

Questioning: Eleanor showed the group the three questions to focus their reading. This was followed by the silent reading of chapter 2 by the children, without interruption. As they read, they noted any words which they would like clarified and also considered the three questions.

Clarification: after reading the chapter, the children were prompted to discuss the words and phrases which puzzled them. The group and Eleanor shared ideas and checked with the text to see which makes sense in the context. One or two of the children had identified *common* as puzzling as they did not understand that it referred to an open space, usually grass land. Eleanor gave them the definition and they checked that it made sense.

Questioning: the three questions were re-read and discussed, and Eleanor asked further questions which probed and challenged thinking. The children and teacher responded to each other by asking for justification, sharing their own ideas which built on what others in the group had said, or suggested alternative ideas. Eleanor monitored the discussion carefully and asked follow-up questions to check the group's literal comprehension to start with. When answering the thinking questions, she checked that they were making connections within the text as well as beyond the text to make inferences. The goal was to ensure that the conversations led to deeper comprehension.

Reciprocal Reading *The Black Queen* by Michael Morpurgo: Session 2			
Thursday: Teaching resources: 6 copies of Black Queen Topic books Laptops Journals	**Learning objective:** I can answer and discuss questions based on a text, giving evidence for my answers, found within the text. **Steps to success:** Read and understand the questions Clarify vocabulary for understanding Discuss questions with group, justify answers and reflect on what I have heard.	**Guided group:** *Prediction*: children to discuss what has happened in chapter 1, to recap, and then predict what they think will happen next. Encourage them to give reasons for their predictions. *Question making*: share the questions with the children ensuring they have a clear understanding of them. Encourage them to consider the questions as they read. *Looking*: what reasons did Mrs Blume give for not letting Billy into her back yard? *Clue*: why is the woman next door called the Black Queen by everybody? *Thinking*: how would you have planned to find the cat if it was yours? What might have happened in the story if Billy had done that? Children to *read* chapter 2 only. *Clarifying*: ask children to think about what they have read. If there are any words they are not sure of or any questions they are wondering about, ask them to record on a whiteboard for discussion (ensure 'snooty' and 'stand-offish' are discussed and clarified) – do not spend longer than 5 minutes on this section.	**Follow up activity:** visualisation Draw Mrs Blume and annotate drawing with quotes. **Before next session:** Read chapter 3 and formulate three questions for the group to discuss
Assessment: Infer reasons for actions and events based on evidence from the text. Comment on the choice of language the author has used and its effect on the reader	**Vocabulary to clarify:** snooty stand-offish darting	Children then discuss the questions. Allow for the children's viewpoints to develop. Ensure the conversation stays on task. Facilitate the discussion encouraging all children to participate. *Summarising*: children to summarise what they have read in this session, focusing on the key points. Pairs or individuals, depending on length of previous discussion.	

Figure 8.5 Plan for group reading session using reciprocal teaching

Summarising: at the end of the session, the children were given some brief thinking time to recall what happened in chapter 2, encouraged to make a mental representation in their heads, and then briefly to tell each other in no more than a few sentences.

After the session: the children were given an activity to complete independently which would consolidate making connections within the text, drawing on evidence and using visualisation to develop a rounded picture of one of the main characters. They were asked to draw Mrs Blume and annotate their drawing with quotes from the chapter.

Many teachers plan for groups to read the text that will be the focus for the teacher-led session before the group session. This enables the children to consider any vocabulary that needs clarification as well as developing initial thinking about the three planned questions. The teacher-led session can then be devoted to the development of the strategies rather than time being taken up by an initial reading.

Teachers then plan a relevant follow-up activity using active strategies to consolidate learning, completed the day after the teacher-led session. These activities need thought as not every text lends itself to every strategy. For example, an emotions graph would work well for the mother or one of the boys in *Zoo* by Anthony Browne but not for the hen or the fox in *Rosie's Walk* by Pat Hutchins. Teachers need to know the texts well in order to plan the most productive activity.

Texts for these group reading sessions can be drawn from across the curriculum. If the class is engaged in a cross-curricular topic, a text can be chosen which would support comprehension in a science or a history text, for example.

Activity 8.3
Planning a reciprocal teaching session – individual/pairs

Choose a short story or section/chapter that you would like to use with your class. Using the planning frame in Figure 8.5, plan a reciprocal teaching-based session with a group of children you have access to using predicting, questioning, clarifying and summarising. The planning sequence is flexible. A session could start by summarising what is known about a character or what has happened so far in the story and end with a prediction about what will happen next. If the focus is on language features, clarification can be incorporated into the questioning.

You will probably have noted how important discussion and dialogue are in this teaching and learning sequence (see section 2.2 about developing dialogue in the classroom). It is essential that children have opportunities to explain their thinking and justify their answers. Prompts from the teacher such as *'How do you know?,' 'Where in the text does it tell you?', 'What reasons can you give me?'* encourage children to reveal their thinking so that teachers and the other children can then respond to develop the collective meaning-making by agreeing and adding more detail, or disagreeing and citing evidence in support.

After teaching the session, reflect on how effective it was in developing comprehension.

Tennent *et al.* (2016) contains twelve detailed case studies of teaching comprehension using variations on this sequence, and illustrates how discussion and dialogue are central to the scaffolding of children's developing competence as meaning makers.

8.8   Fluency and comprehension

Fluency is essential to comprehension. Dudley and Mather comment that:

> When readers are able to mirror the inflections of spoken language, they are demonstrating their abilities to comprehend the text, self-monitor, and self-correct their reading errors.

> (Dudley and Mather, 2005: 22)

When reading aloud becomes effortless, the young reader can settle into understanding what the words are saying rather than just focusing on getting the words off the page. And once reading aloud becomes effortless, the act of reading can slip into the automatic inner process of 'reading in the head'. There is a danger, however, of assuming that children who appear fluent and accurate when they read aloud have understood what they have read. This is not necessarily the case, so conversations about reading are essential to gauge comprehension, whatever the apparent level of fluency. Bayetto describes fluent reading as 'the link or "bridge" between oral language, word recognition and comprehension' (Bayetto, 2013: 11). Once a reader achieves fluency, this increases independence and satisfaction (Pikulski and Chard, 2005; Bashir and Hook, 2009).

Bayetto (2013) lists three components of fluency: accuracy, rate and prosody:

- *Accuracy:* secure phonemic awareness, letter-sound knowledge, knowledge of sight words and high-frequency words help children to become accurate readers (Hudson, 2011). However, if a teacher emphasises word recognition too much, stopping the flow of reading, this can reduce motivation.
- *Rate:* is not about reading quickly but more to do with steady and uninterrupted reading. Developing a sense of the rate (or pace) of a piece of reading benefits from practice in a supportive environment.
- *Prosody:* involves intonation, tone, volume, phrasing, emphasis and pace to express and interpret the author's meaning. Punctuation is the key to reading sentences as they were intended to sound. Knowing when to pause in a sentence (phrasing) is important for prosody. Knowing where the emphasis should be placed on words or phrases also aids understanding, for example, *per*fect (adjective) and per*fect* (verb) or '*I* saw you', 'I *saw* you' and 'I saw *you*'.

Developing the ability to read fluently with accuracy, a steady rate and prosody often means re-reading, either aloud or to oneself. Giving young readers the opportunity to read over what they are to read aloud also helps.

Bayetto suggests reading with a puppet, soft toy or using a mask, reading with a (toy) microphone or reading a text in a group with different children assigned different parts (reading theatre) can support the development of fluency. Digital technology also allows for sound recording/skyping which children may be familiar with from home.

8.9 Using film to support reading comprehension

Film is a highly complex form of text yet it is accessible to those who may find the written word more challenging, or who are beginning to learn written English. Maine comments:

> We have all met children who struggle to comprehend print text at deeper levels. It seems that for some early fluent readers, so much effort is required for them to decode words that they have little cognitive processing energy left for comprehension beyond the literal. However, children come to school armed with vast experiences of other narrative forms of text (Bazalgette, 2010; Levy, 2011; Parry, 2013). As children are often familiar with film narratives, they may have developed an understanding of how these texts work and can decode at a 'technical' level more efficiently, allowing more cognitive resource to be directed to inference, response and engagement. As a result, it is possible to work with quite complex or ambiguous film narratives. These can challenge, excite and motivate young readers who are able to fully engage in discussions, drawing on their experiences of popular culture to approach unfamiliar films (Parry, 2014).
>
> (Maine, 2015: 1)

It is important that teachers model a vocabulary to talk about ideas:

> Much of this talk is comfortably adopted by children and they can readily use language which indicates positioning (such as 'I think', 'I agree'); reasoning or critical thinking '(because', 'why', 'so'); and hypothesis or creative thinking ('maybe', 'would', 'could', 'possibly'). However, some language related to comprehension is trickier and needs careful modelling to ensure it is used to frame high-level thinking. Using the language of making connections can include, 'that reminds me of...'; seeking clarification might be expressed with, 'I was confused when...'. Initially, children might struggle to use these phrases. As teachers we need to listen carefully to the content of children's responses and ensure that there are many opportunities for them to try out the language and practise framing their ideas with it, but not over-prioritise key words and phrases so that the ideas become superficial.
>
> (ibid.: 7)

Questioning was the focus in the following example. The children had been given Talk Prompts to help them frame their ideas including:

> I wonder if, why, what...
> What is it all about?
> Maybe... possibly... perhaps...

Maine explains that films that have some ambiguity are particularly successful because they prompt questions that go beyond the literal, encouraging deeper engagement as children attempt to make sense of what is happening. A group of 7- and 8-year-old children watched *Once in a Lifetime* (Gulledge, 2011) and then used Talk Prompts to generate questions about the film. This is a wordless film, lasting 2 minutes, with poignant music. The scene opens on a ship with an air balloon attached to it. As the captain of the ship notices that he is marooned, a group of turtles fly by. He lassoes one of them and uses it to tow the ship but the rope breaks and it seems he is lost. He notices one turtle that is lagging behind the others, jumps on to its back, leaving the ship behind and they fly off into the clouds.

Maine analyses the children's comments:

Ollie: I wonder why the boat was flying.

Nena: I wonder where the turtles are going to take the man.

Callum: I wonder if erm... at the end when the man jumped on the turtle, I wonder if the turtle come back to save him, or if he was just lucky.

Lenny: I wonder if the man, when the man jumped over onto the turtle, if he made the right decision, because he left everything on his ship.

Ollie's question suggests that he has not picked up the clues from the text (flying boat, flying turtles) that this is a fantasy film. Rather than accept the strange features that might be included in this genre, his question is concerned with the 'trivia' as Palincsar and Brown (1984) might describe, so his attention is not focused on the main point of the story. Nena's question takes her 'beyond the story-world' (Anderson *et al.*, 2001) and into the future, rather than concentrating on the features of the film. Callum's question is an interesting one; it illustrates that he has positioned himself inside the story, and he wonders about plot drivers and character motivation – do the turtles have agency or are they passive? The final question, raised by Lenny, is arguably the one that gets closest to the heart of the film. He has placed himself into the shoes of the pilot and is considering his choices. He shows that he has understood the central dilemma, to leave or stay, to take this 'once in a lifetime' opportunity.

(Maine, 2015: 15)

Teaching Comprehension through Reading and Responding to Film (Maine, 2015) offers a rich resource for teachers wishing to use film as an entry point for reading comprehension. The research project reported significant gains in the children's comprehension of written text as well as teachers' increased enthusiasm for using film as an authentic classroom text.

Film, and all other moving image texts, including digital, are truly multimodal in that many different modes (image, lighting and colour, sound, including music and language) work together to make meaning. Thus when reading moving image and digital texts, teachers and children can look at how the different modes contribute to meaning.

Parry and Hill Bulman draw on Burn to suggest the following practical approach when considering film:

Burn (2013) uses the term *kineikonic*, rather than cinematic, or multimodal, to direct our attention both to the separate meaning-making tools or modes of film and also their combined meaning. In classroom practice this is evident in activities where a teacher might ask children to only pay attention to one aspect of the *kineikonic* (perhaps where the camera is placed) but then to also consider why, what does this mean, what does the filmmaker want us think or feel or understand? By examining one mode, excluding all others, the children are able to really scrutinise meaning in depth. Repeated experiences of this level of analysis helps children make the transition between looking at the specific text in front of them to a broader understanding of, for example, lighting, camera angles, music. If the class is divided into small groups, each with a focus on a different element, then when they share their observations they also begin to consider the ways the elements interact. The teacher's role here is to support the sharing of ideas but also to prompt the children to listen carefully to each other and reflect on how the different elements work together. The teacher can also extend learning by inviting the children to think about other texts they are reminded of and how they are similar or different.

(Parry and Hill Bulman, 2017: 13)

Like the book by Maine cited above, *Literacy and Film in Primary Education* (Parry and Hill Bulman, 2017) is an excellent resource for teachers wishing to explore this area. (See also section 5.4 for a case study focused on reading film.)

8.10 Directed activities related to texts

In an initiative to improve comprehension teaching, Lunzer and Gardner (1979) developed Directed Activities Related to Texts (DARTS) – a series of strategies to help young readers deconstruct (and reconstruct) and analyse texts. DARTS activities have been widely used with non-fiction texts and aid comprehension because they involve the reader in a dynamic relationship with the text:

- *Deletion:* a short text has some key words deleted and children collaborate and decide what words should fill the gaps. This can also be done with a table/diagram which is incomplete.
- *Sequencing:* a text is cut up into sections. Children work together to decide on a sensible order.
- *Comparing texts:* the similarities and differences of two (or more) short texts are identified and discussed, for example, two information texts about volcanoes.
- *Grouping:* children group segments of a cut-up text according to categories.
- *Underlining:* children underline various features in a given text – for example, the advantages of a particular activity (such as air travel) in one colour and the disadvantages in another.
- *Segmenting:* children discuss a long stretch of a text in which the sections or paragraphs have been run together and mark the beginnings and endings of different sections.
- *Disputing the text:* children read a text and discuss whether statements are true or not – for example, in a newspaper article.
- *Alternative representation:* children represent the essential features of a text using a diagram or flow chart, or a drawing of a particular scene or character. They might be encouraged to choose a particular format to suit the type of text they are re-presenting:
  - comparison or contrast – a table or Venn diagram
  - description of a process or a sequence of events – a flow chart

- an explanation of how something might be classified – a branch diagram
- an argument/persuasive text – a mind map or the Explain Everything app.

The Explain Everything app allows the user to 'animate their thinking by presenting ideas visually, or by using audio recording to voiceover presentations' (Kucirkova *et al.*, 2017: 48). Re-presenting ideas like this is an ideal form of comprehension as it not only involves understanding the content but requires metacognition to select what is appropriate to include in a presentation (https://explaineverything.com/ (accessed 1 May 2017)).

8.11 Skimming and scanning

Skimming and scanning are two key strategies that link speed reading with comprehension. Readers use them more when reading for information.

Skimming helps to get the gist of a passage or text; looking only for the main or general ideas.

Skimming strategies include:

- reading the title and sub-headings
- reading the last section (often a summary)
- reading any pictorial information – maps, graphs, diagrams, shaded sections
- reading the first (topic) sentence of each paragraph.

Scanning helps to get key words/specific ideas and information within a text. The reader looks *only* for a specific fact or piece of information without reading everything.

Scanning strategies include:

- identifying as precisely as possible what you want to look for – is it the name of a person or place or perhaps a date?
- looking in the index or contexts page
- looking at headings and sub-headings for clues
- looking only for capital letters (or numbers).

Summary

Comprehension lies at the heart of reading. It has been defined in a variety of ways but essentially involves getting to grips with a text. A highly complex process, comprehension involves a range of components which work together to help readers make sense of what they are reading. Teaching the range of comprehension strategies – *predicting, clarifying, questioning, summarising, connecting, noting text structure, visualising* and *thinking aloud* – aided by reciprocal teaching allows young readers to develop their own inner thought processes. Practical suggestions are made for ways to develop fluency, an important element in developing reading comprehension, using film to promote comprehension of written texts, and directed activities related to texts which support understanding by hands-on manipulation, active analysis and re-presentation of texts.

Recommended reading

Chambers, A. (2011) *Tell Me (Children, Reading and Talk) with the Reading Environment*. Stroud: Thimble Press. A practical guide to shaping productive conversations about texts, particularly narrative.

Elborn, S. (2015) *Handbook of Early Reading: More than phonics*. Leicester: United Kingdom Literacy Association. This book contains a very useful section on teaching comprehension with practical examples focused on 4 to 7 year olds.

Maine, F. (2015) *Teaching Comprehension through Reading and Responding to Film*. Leicester: United Kingdom Literacy Association. Exactly as the title says – clear and concise chapters showing how comprehension strategies can be developed when watching short films.

Parry, B. and Hill Bulman, J. (2017) *Literacy and Film in Primary Education*. Leicester: United Kingdom Literacy Association. An excellent research-informed practical guide to help primary teachers develop and sustain film education, with a particular focus on literacy.

Tennent, W. (2015) *Understanding Reading Comprehension: Processes and practices*. London: SAGE. Tennent reviews international research evidence and makes practical suggestions, including the use of Reciprocal Teaching techniques. **Advanced**

Tennent, W., Reedy, D., Gamble, N. and Hobsbaum, A. (2016) *Guiding Readers: Layers of meaning*. London: University College London, Institute of Education. This book is a lively and very practical handbook for teaching comprehension to 7 to 11 year olds. Full of case studies covering narrative, poetry, information and multimodal texts.

Warner, C. (2013) *Talk For Reading*. Leicester: United Kingdom Literacy Association. A practical guide that summarises comprehension strategies and combines advice on creating a climate for talk for reading with ways which teachers and children can talk productively about texts together.

References

Anderson, R. C., Nguyen-Jahiel, K., McNurlen, B., Archodidou, A., Kim, S., Reznitskaya, A. and Gilbert, L. (2001) The snowball phenomenon: Spread of ways of talking and ways of thinking across groups of children, *Cognition and Instruction*, 19 (1) pp. 1–46.

Bashir, A. S. and Hook, P. E. (2009). Fluency: A key link between word identification and comprehension, *Language, Speech, and Hearing Services in Schools*, 40 (2) pp. 196–200.

Bayetto, A. (2013) Fluency, *SPELD SA Newsletter*, Autumn, 2013. Specific Learning Difficulties Association of South Australia, pp. 11–14.

Bazalgette, C. (2010) Extending children's experience of film, in C. Bazalgette (ed.) *Teaching Media in Primary Schools*. London: SAGE, pp. 35–45.

Brown, A. and Palincsar, A. (1989) Guided, cooperative learning and individual knowledge acquisition, in L. B. Resnick (ed.) *Knowing, Learning and Instruction: Essays in honor of Robert Glaser*. Hillsdale, NJ: Lawrence Erlbaum Associates, pp. 393–451.

Brown, A. L., Palincsar, A. and Armbruster, B. (1984) Instructing comprehension-fostering activities in interactive learning situations, in H. Mandl, N. L. Stein and T. Trabasso (eds) *Learning and Comprehension of Text*. Hillsdale, NJ: Lawrence Erlbaum Associates, pp. 225–281.

Bruner, J. (1996) *The Culture of Education*. Cambridge, MA: Harvard University Press.

Burn, A. (2013) The Kineikonic Mode: Towards a multimodal approach to moving image media. NCRM Working Paper (unpublished). London: NCRM.

Butler, S., Urrutia, K., Buenger, A. and Hunt, M. (2010) *Review of the Current Research on Comprehension Instruction*. Developed by the National Reading Technical Assistance Center, RMC Research Corporation. www2.ed.gov/programs/readingfirst/support/compfinal.pdf (accessed 1 May 2017)

Cain, K. (2010) *Reading Development and Difficulties: An introduction*. BPS Textbooks in Psychology. Abingdon: Wiley Blackwell.

Chambers, A. (2011) *Tell Me (Children, Reading and Talk) with the Reading Environment*. Stroud: Thimble Press.

Dombey, H. with Bearne, E., Cremin, T., Ellis, S., Mottram, M., O'Sullivan, O., Öztürk, A., Reedy, D. (UKLA) and Raphael, T. and Allington, R. (International Reading Association) (2010) *Teaching Reading: What the evidence says*. Leicester: United Kingdom Literacy Association.

Dudley, A. M. and Mather, N. (2005) Getting up to speed on reading fluency, *New England Reading Association Journal*, 41 (1) pp. 22–27.

Duke, N. K. (2005) Comprehension of what for what: Comprehension as a non-unitary construct, in S. Paris and S. Stahl (eds) *Current Issues in Reading Comprehension and Assessment*. Mahwah, NJ: Erlbaum, pp. 93–104.

Duke, N. K. and Pearson, P.D. (2002) Effective practices for developing reading comprehension, in A. E. Farstrup and S. J. Samuels (eds) *What Research Has To Say About Reading Instruction*, 3rd edn. Newark, DE: International Reading Association, pp. 205–242.

Glenberg, A., Gutierrez, T., Levin, J., Japuntich, S. and Kaschak, M.(2004) Activity and imagined activity can enhance young children's reading comprehension, *Journal of Educational Psychology*, 96 (3) pp. 424–436.

Glenberg, A., Brown, M. and Levin, J. (2007) Enhancing comprehension in small reading groups using a manipulation strategy, *Contemporary Educational Psychology*, 32 (3) pp. 389–399.

Gulledge, J. (2011). *Once in a Lifetime*. Sarasota: Ringling College of Art and Design. http://vimeo.com/23805703 (accessed 1 May 2017)

Guthrie, J., Wigfield, A., Barbosa, P., Perencevich, K., Taboada, A., Davis, M., *et al.* (2004) Increasing reading comprehension and engagement through Concept-Oriented Reading Instruction, *Journal of Educational Psychology*, 96 (3) pp. 403–423.

Guthrie, J., Wigfield, A., Humenick, N., Perencevich, K., Taboada, A. and Barbosa, P. (2006) Influences of stimulating tasks on reading motivation and comprehension, *Journal of Educational Research*, 99 (4) pp. 232–245.

Hudson, R. (2011) Fluency problems, in R. E. O'Connor and P. F. Vadasy (eds), *Handbook of Reading Interventions*. New York: The Guilford Press, pp. 169–197.

Keene, E. and Zimmerman, S. (1997). *Mosaic of Thought*. Portsmouth, NH: Heinemann.

Kucirkova, N., Audain, J. and Chamberlain, L. (2017) *Jumpstart! Apps: Creative learning ideas and activities for ages 7–11*. London: Routledge.

Levy, R. (2011) *Young Children Reading: At home and at school*. London: SAGE.

Lunzer, E. and Gardner, W. (eds) (1979) *The Effective Use of Reading*. London: Heinemann.

Maine, F. (2015) *Teaching Comprehension through Reading and Responding to Film*. Leicester: United Kingdom Literacy Association.

Moyle, D. (1972) *The Teaching of Reading*, 3rd edn. London: Ward Lock.

National Reading Panel (2000) *Teaching Children to Read: An evidence based assessment of the scientific research literature on reading and its implications for reading instruction*. Washington, DC: National Institute of Child Health and Human Development.

Nystrand, M. (2006) Research on the role of classroom discourse as it affects reading comprehension, *Research in the Teaching of English*, 40 (4) pp. 392–412.

Palincsar, A. S. and Brown, A. L. (1984) Reciprocal teaching of comprehension-fostering and comprehension-monitoring activities, *Cognition and Instruction*, 1 (2) pp. 117–175.

Pardo, L. (2004) What every teacher needs to know about comprehension, *The Reading Teacher*, 58 (3) pp. 272–280.

Parry, B. (2013) *Children, Film and Literacy*. Basingstoke: Palgrave Macmillan.

Parry, B. (2014) Popular culture, participation and progression in the literacy classroom, *Literacy*, 48 (1) pp. 14–22.

Parry, B. and Hill Bulman, J. (2017) *Literacy and Film in Primary Education*. Leicester: United Kingdom Literacy Association.

Pikulski, J. J. and Chard, D. J. (2005) Fluency: Bridge between decoding and reading comprehension, *The Reading Teacher*, 58 (6) pp. 510–519.

Raphael, T. E. and McKinney, J. (1983) An examination of 5th and 8th grade children's question answering behavior: An instructional study in metacognition, *Journal of Reading Behaviour*, 15 pp. 67–86.

Raphael, T. E. and Pearson, P. D. (1985) Increasing students' awareness of sources of information for answering questions, *American Educational Research Journal,* 22 pp. 217–236.

Raphael, T. E. and Wonnacott, C. A. (1985) Heightening 4th grade students' sensitivity to sources of information for answering comprehension questions, *Reading Research Quarterly*, 20 (3) pp. 282–96.

Tennent, W. (2015) *Understanding Reading Comprehension: Processes and practices.* London: SAGE.

Tennent, W., Reedy, D., Gamble, N. and Hobsbaum, A. (2016) *Guiding Readers: Layers of meaning.* London: University College London, Institute of Education.

Van Keer, H. and Verhaeghe, J. (2005) Effects of explicit reading strategies instruction and peer tutoring on second and fifth graders' reading comprehension and self-efficacy perceptions, *Journal of Experimental Education*, 73 (4) pp. 291–329.

Varga, A. (2017) Metacognitive perspectives on the development of reading comprehension: A classroom study of literary text talks, *Literacy*, 51 (1) pp. 19–25.

Vygotsky, L. (1978) *Mind in Society: The development of higher psychological processes.* Cambridge, MA: Harvard University Press.

Williams, J. C. (2014) Recent official policy and concepts of reading comprehension and inference: The case of England's primary curriculum, *Literacy*, 48 (2) pp. 95–102.

Williams, J., Hall, K. and Lauer, K. (2004) Teaching expository text structure to young at-risk learners: Building the basics of comprehension instruction. *Exceptionality*, 12 (3) pp. 129–144.

Children's books

Guy Bass, illustrated Peter Williamson (2011) *Stitch Head.* Stripes Publishing. ISBN 9781847151834

Julia Donaldson, illustrated Alex Scheffler (1999) *The Gruffalo.* Macmillan Children's Books. ISBN 9780333710937

Anthony Horowitz (2007) *Myths and Legends.* Kingfisher. ISBN 0753415259

Ted Hughes (2005) *The Iron Man: A children's story in five nights.* Faber & Faber. ISBN 9780571226122

Michael Morpurgo (2000) *Black Queen.* Young Corgi. ISBN0552546453

CHAPTER 9

DESCRIBING AND ASSESSING PROGRESS IN READING

This chapter covers:

- Assessing reading
- The problems of testing
- Types of reading assessment
- What is involved in becoming a reader?
- Developing and assessing range and repertoire
  - Case study, middle primary: Group reading non-fiction – *Shackleton's Journey*
- Assessing reading behaviours
- Assessing reading skills and strategies
- Planning and teaching for diversity and differentiation
- Children who experience difficulties with reading
- Diagnostic assessment
- Bilingual readers
- Gender and reading
- Monitoring, recording and assessing progress in reading

9.1   Assessing reading

Reading involves using strategies which need to be carefully developed. Children who know they are readers can choose to re-read books for pleasure, returning to favourites when they feel like it. They can get beneath the skin of a text and empathise with characters and situations; they can use books for their own purposes, talk readily to others about books and look forward to what they can read next. Clearly, then, in considering assessment of what contributes to successful progress in reading, there needs to be a rather wider view than one which simply concentrates on methods of decoding print. Children need to adopt a repertoire of approaches to become effective readers. They need experience of a range of kinds of text and teaching which supports and extends their knowledge of texts and the strategies they use to make sense of them. What is critical is an awareness of the complexities of the process by which children come to be readers so it is important to develop record-keeping systems which will allow for judgements about all aspects of reading, not just skills. But, in contrast to assessing spoken language or writing, assessing reading is rather more complex.

There are four language modes: two are receptive – listening and reading – and two are productive – speaking and writing. When it comes to assessment, it is much easier to find evidence of learning in talk or writing because they are productive and it is possible to take writing away and to record talk for purposes of assessment. Reading presents a different kind of challenge for assessment because it is not possible to see inside an individual's head to measure how their reading is progressing. Reading assessments often depend on tests which require children to answer questions about what they have read, or on children reading aloud to demonstrate that they can decode words, neither of which is likely to provide a full picture of the child as a reader. To gain reliable evidence about a child's reading, such traditional assessment methods need to be supplemented by observation and the children's own reflections on their reading. Before making any assessments, however, it is important to identify just what is being assessed – learning to read, or becoming a reader.

9.2   The problems of testing

For some years, governments have been concerned about comparative reading levels across the world (Twist *et al.*, 2007; OECD, 2016) measuring how, for example, the UK compares with the thirty-four other countries in the study. The Organisation for Economic Cooperation and Development gather data as part of an investigation into the economic potential of countries across the world. It is assumed that levels of attainment in key subjects, including reading, will indicate the possible future economic health of a nation. For this reason, governments take note of reading levels as reported by such international comparisons and develop policy in the light of their findings (see www.oecd.org/pisa/PISA-2015-United-Kingdom.pdf (accessed 1 May 2017)). Two major concerns as highlighted in the OECD report of 2016 (and previously) are the gaps in performance between boys and girls in reading and the differences in performance between children of different socioeconomic groups. These concerns tend to result in governments developing more 'rigorous' testing regimes. However, these have limitations, since the kinds of testing developed (in England, for example, the phonics check for 6 year olds and the reading test for 11 year olds) only measure a narrow range of all the elements necessary to promote lifelong and successful readers. A test that will be relatively easy to mark in large numbers will necessarily only be able to measure a narrow range of skills. Questions tend to involve ranking or ordering events, multiple choice or re-presenting information, for example:

> When did Lucy write the letter to her grandmother?

In the test for 11 year olds, there are more open-ended opportunities for response, for example:

> Look at the sentence that begins "Once upon a time". How does the writer increase the tension throughout this paragraph? Explain fully referring to the text in your answer.

But once again this is specific and focused on language and style; there is (understandably in a test of this type) no scope for personal response. Of equal concern, however, is the fact that a timed test favours quicker readers, although there is no correlation between speed of reading and effective reading for understanding. Some people read more slowly (but equally successfully) than others and they are penalised in a timed test because they may not finish the reading before answering the questions.

There are other, commercially available, reading tests but these, too, tend to measure vocabulary and surface comprehension. Traditional assessment methods may reveal some elements of what a child can do with reading – for example, how they tackle decoding unfamiliar text – but there is more to reading than how an individual lifts the words off the page. Similarly, traditional comprehension tests will only provide information about a child's understanding of the vocabulary and information in the particular text being used. But there is more to being a reader than the ability to answer the relatively restricted questions necessary for a test to be easily marked. None of these summative tests shows the child's preferences and tastes as a reader, the extent to which they can sustain reading or their readiness to tackle difficult texts, their emotional response to particular ideas or themes, their appreciation of the author's representation of character in pursuit of the theme of the narrative, their avid absorption of new information in a topic of interest, their ability to read a variety of texts, including visual texts, their ability to evaluate what they are reading critically – in sum, their commitment and engagement as readers. While tests can be useful for certain summative judgements, different approaches need to be used to develop a full picture of the child as a reader. In addition, it is only possible to assess what has been taught or, in the case of reading, what has been experienced and discussed in the classroom.

9.3 Types of reading assessment

As outlined in Chapters 4 and 15, there are three main types of assessment – summative, formative and diagnostic. Each has its role to play in helping teachers evaluate children's progress in order to move their learning on. National and in-school testing are forms of summative assessment; formative assessment is carried out through guided reading, observations, reading journals and reading interviews; and miscue analysis and running records are used for diagnostic purposes.

> **Summative assessment:** assessment *of* learning, often carried out by testing. Summative assessments are made at the end of a period of teaching to identify what

children have learned: half termly or more frequently. Although some summative assessments can be used formatively, they are generally used to monitor the progress of individuals and groups of children and to identify attainment at ages 7 and 11.

Formative/continuous assessment: assessment *for* learning, used to monitor children's learning at any stage in a teaching sequence. They help to identify strengths and weaknesses so that the teacher can provide feedback that will move learning forward. Formative assessment can also be diagnostic, helping to identify groups of children who may require extra support.

Diagnostic assessment: specifically designed to identify any problems a child might be experiencing or address any causes for concern (see Writing p. 382 – Figure 15.6).

9.4   What is involved in becoming a reader?

Becoming an assured and committed reader means having experience of a range of different texts and learning how to evaluate them critically as well as building the skills of reading and developing reading behaviours, including motivation and engagement and the ability to reflect on what has been read. The reading curriculum in the Introduction to this Part (see pp. 112–113) identifies three areas of becoming a reader:

- Developing range and repertoire
- Developing reading behaviours and reflecting on reading
- Developing reading/language skills and strategies.

Assessing children's abilities across these areas needs to be carried out by observation and recording over a period of time.

Activity 9.1
What a good reader can do – individual journal/blog to pairs/small group

Traves (2015) describes the qualities of good readers. They:

- show versatility, reading different kinds of material in different ways (and sometimes the same material in different ways)
- develop and refine their own preferences for what to read while being open to new possibilities
- find ways to cope with unfamiliar and challenging material
- identify and follow the plot of a piece of writing (whether fiction or otherwise), inferring what is happening and speculating about where it may go next
- interpret ideas, themes and patterns and form questions and comments as they go along

- skim, scan, select and record in order to locate and log what they are after
- appreciate multiple meanings, ambiguities and other twists and turns of language
- connect what they read to their prior knowledge and experience
- cross-refer, combine and compare information from a variety of sources, as well as connecting what they read with their prior knowledge and experience
- make and articulate considered judgements about texts and how they are written
- reflect on the ways in which they go about their reading (Traves, 2015: 10).

He argues that:

Any or all of the abilities listed above can be applied to virtually any kind of text, whether literary or otherwise, long or short, highly imaginative or deeply routine. Nor is there any hierarchy of importance as between these abilities. Development in reading is not a matter of lockstep progress up through any such hierarchy. Younger readers have both the potential and the need to behave like more mature readers, and so can and should use the full range of abilities from the outset.

(*ibid.*)

Working individually at first, reflecting on the class that you are most familiar with, use website resource W9.1 to highlight any parts of this list that the children are already tackling; for example, even early readers can connect what they read to their own experience and begin to show preferences for what they like to read.

Work with a colleague or colleagues who are more familiar with a different age range from you. What do you notice about how they have highlighted this list? Do you agree with Traves that 'younger readers ... should use the full range of abilities from the outset'? What might be barriers for them tackling the full list? Are the difficulties to do with the children themselves or the opportunities offered to them?

9.5   Developing and assessing range and repertoire

It is not possible to assess children's range of reading experience and repertoire of approaches to reading if they are not given access to broad reading experiences in the classroom. A teacher's own knowledge of texts is fundamental in providing for a full range of reading experiences in the classroom (Cremin *et al.*, 2014) (see also Chapter 6). Newly qualified teachers who completed a survey about their own reading tastes and their knowledge of children's texts identified the ingredients of teaching reading successfully as including:

Encouragement, showing interest of reading yourself.

Range of texts to read/choose from.

Focus on inference and breaking down 'tricky' words using phonic awareness.

Enjoyable books, lots of opportunity for discussion, good images.

Vocal expression and engagement with drama.

An interesting text with lots of suspense and action to interest children.

A priority is clearly the kinds of texts they think will stimulate children's interest as readers. Through the survey, they showed that their own reading tastes were varied and they drew on children's recommendations, internet reviews and in-store reviews as well as colleagues' recommendations to select texts for their classes, although very few used the local library or school library service.

Activity 9.2
Range and repertoire: Teacher surveys – individual journal/blog to pairs/group

Have a look at one or two of the website resources teacher surveys: W9.2 (early primary), W9.3 (middle primary) and W9.4 (upper primary) and complete your own survey (website resource W9.5). When you have finished, compare your comments to a colleague's or to several colleagues' (or to those in the website resources). What differences did you find between when you last read something for pleasure, your preferences across the range of texts, the ways you find out about books for children and your priorities for successful reading teaching? What similarities? Discuss the extent to which you think you share your preferences with your class. How wide is your own reading range? Do you provide an equally wide (or wider or narrower) range in your classroom? You might want to have a quick review of your 'Texts I Like' list (website resource W5.4) and see if you can plan to expand the repertoire in your next teaching sequence.

Classroom provision for reading does not always compare favourably with the range of texts that children choose to read at home including magazines, comics, fiction, television, films, books and magazines, signs, poetry and websites (Clark and Foster, 2005; Cremin *et al.*, 2008). Reading perceptions surveys (Figure 9.1) can reveal a great deal about children's reading at home as well as their attitudes to reading as a whole (see p. 394 Survey of multi-modal text experience) and offer a good starting point for teachers to begin assessing range and repertoire.

Children who completed this survey commented on their enjoyment of reading:

I like reading books with naughty people in them. (6 year old)

I don't like reading when I'm told to. (8 year old)

I've always really liked reading. I like books about fantasy. (11 year old)

and on reading as a social act:

I like reading with Sadie. We read at playtime. (6 year old)

I read at home with my brother and help him. (7 year old)

Reading perceptions survey

Do you like reading? Why? Why not?

Do you think you are a good reader? How do you know?

What makes it difficult to read? What makes it easy?

Do you prefer to read silently to yourself or aloud to someone? Why is that?

Do you read a lot at home?

Does anyone read to/with you? What sorts of things do you like to read? What is a recent favourite?

How do you know what to choose to read? Does anyone help you?

Why do you think people need to be able to read?

Figure 9.1 Reading perceptions survey

I don't like reading in a group because I'm not good at reading out loud.
I like silent reading because I can read in my head. (10 year old)

and on choosing books:

There's this programme on CBBC about science and I get books about science.
(7 year old)

I like reading books by a variety of authors so I don't read specific authors like
Enid Blyton or Jacqueline Wilson, I just go for a different range of authors. It
depends on what the book is about. (9 year old)

Other people in the class and my sister recommend books to me. (11 year old)

Activity 9.3
Children's perceptions of themselves as readers – individual/group

This activity uses the reading curriculum list in the Introduction to this Part (pp. 112–114).

As soon as you have a chance, ask some of the children in your class to complete the reading perceptions survey in website resource W9.6. When you have some responses, consider how they help in assessing the child as a reader. For example, do the children show they have experience of reading and being to read to from a range of texts? Do they indicate that they read with some independence for enjoyment and information? Do they see reading as a matter of personal satisfaction or as a matter of getting a job done?

Look at the Reading Curriculum list and see how these kinds of observations contribute to the three aspects of a full assessment profile of a child as a reader:

- range and repertoire
- reading behaviours and reflecting on reading
- reading/language skills and strategies.

Reading circles, journals and blogs

One of the difficulties associated with assessing independent reading is how to discover how a reader has responded to a particular text. Traditionally, children have been asked to write book reviews but these can become a stultifying routine and result in little more than trite comments unless there has been some discussion beforehand. Adult readers tend to talk to friends about what they have enjoyed reading and there are many book groups which provide the shared experience of responding to reading. Book groups in schools, sometimes referred to as Literature Circles (King and Briggs, 2007), can not only offer young readers opportunities to reflect on their reading critically but observations of groups can also provide teachers with insights into the children's responses to reading, particularly if the teacher occasionally joins in the group discussion, modelling possible ways of talking about texts. Typically, groups would choose a book from a range of small sets of books and read it at home and in quiet reading times, deciding on a particular place to stop and come together as a group to discuss it. If only part of the book has been read, the discussion might be related to what members of the group think might happen next (if it is a novel) or how easy they are finding the explanations if it is a non-fiction text. Teachers might provide prompt questions to help discussion; for example, *How well do you think the author creates tension? Which of the characters do you like most? Is there anything you don't understand?* Readers should be reminded to give reasons for any opinions they hold. Once a group has read a book they might provide some of the prompt questions to guide another group's discussions.

Observing and participating in group discussion can give opportunities for a teacher to assess readers' abilities to achieve in a number of aspects of the reading curriculum including, particularly, reflections on reading:

- explaining preferences for certain texts and authors
- sharing ideas about events, characters, setting, structure and theme, supporting their views with evidence from the text
- developing appropriate vocabulary and terminology to discuss, consider and evaluate texts
- using a range of comprehension strategies, both oral and written, to interpret and discuss texts and use evidence to support their views and explain opinions
- reading analytically and critically, comparing and contrast texts, distinguishing between fact and opinion, recognising persuasive language and evaluating the reliability and relevance of sources.

Case study, middle primary: Group reading non-fiction – *Shackleton's Journey*

Every week, Sam's class of 8 to 9 year olds have two regular group reading sessions of 20 to 25 minutes each during guided reading time. The groups usually read and discuss a book every four weeks. They call these 'bookchats' and Sam and Jude, the teaching assistant, organise the time so that one of them joins the group once a week to model response and critical engagement with a text. Groups are from five to six children and the school library provides sets of books in a range of genres for each class. The groups have the chance to select the book they want to read from the list for their class and one group chose *Shackleton's Journey* by William Grill (2014). Fully and strikingly illustrated in a restrained palette of black, blue and brown, this tells the story of Sir Ernest Shackleton's expedition to Antarctica between 1914 and 1916 including all the preparations, recruitment and equipment as well as describing the journey itself and all the hardships the crew encountered. The text includes many facts and quotations from members of the crew.

Sam and Jude provided prompts such as: *What qualities of character did the crew members show? How did you feel when they had to abandon the ship?* And finally: *What did you learn from this book? Would you recommend it to other members of the class?*

Two surprise outcomes from this bookchat choice were that two of the group found YouTube films about Shackleton which soon all the group had looked at, comparing the film versions to the book they were reading. Also, one of the group's parents found a copy of the picture book *Trapped by the Ice!: Shackleton's Amazing Antarctic Adventure* by Michael McCurdy (2002) which was also shared around the group and compared with the Grill version. The children's class blogs reflected their enthusiasm for this non-fiction book, sparking recommendations for other information books and Sam was impressed with the group's avid engagement with the book and particularly by the level of critical reflection they brought to their discussions and comments.

Reading journals or blogs can equally offer teachers opportunities to note children's repertoire of approaches and responses to reading. Sometimes these are used as part of an ongoing personal 'conversation' with a text, or they might be a short recommendation on a specific site. Commercial companies such as Micro Librarian Systems and BugClub not only provide managed computerised library systems but also have a range of opportunities for children to comment on what they have read, make recommendations to others and keep personal records of their reading. Systems like this can also provide links between school and home reading.

9.6   Assessing reading behaviours

One of the key aspects of becoming a reader is to develop long-lasting reading habits or behaviours. A full reading curriculum will provide opportunities for children to:

- read individually and collaboratively
- sustain reading and make discriminating choices
- relate what they have read to their own experience
- retell, re-read and act out a range of texts, representing ideas through drama, pictures, diagrams and digital technology
- explain preferences for certain texts and authors
- share ideas about events, characters, setting, structure and theme, supporting their views with evidence from the text
- develop appropriate vocabulary and terminology to discuss, consider and evaluate texts.

By making several observations over the course of a half term, a term and a year, a teacher can assess children's reading behaviours, in as the following examples.

Do they enjoy sharing reading with others? Do they read independently?

Over a course of time children should show evidence of being able to enjoy both.

Do they actively look for books to read or be read to them – how quickly do they decide?

Deciding quickly can be positive or negative – an indication of clear choices or a lack of discrimination – so that several observations will be necessary to gain a full impression. If a child just picks up the first book to hand and does not settle to reading, then a conversation about how to choose should help.

Do they flick through quickly or read attentively?

Again, flicking through quickly can indicate a precise view of what the reader is looking for or an inability to settle to reading. Several observations over time will be needed and if flicking through is a symptom of not knowing how to choose or not wanting to read, a discussion about choosing might be needed.

What kinds of texts do they choose?

Over a period of time, there should be evidence of children choosing a range of texts, including digital texts. If observations suggest a restricted range of choices, then a conversation about other books they might like will help to broaden their experience of texts.

In guided reading or other small groups for reading, does the child seem happy to contribute or reticent?

A child may be reticent because he/she is thinking before speaking, so that again, observations over a period of time will clarify if there is any need for further support to gain confidence to contribute. Strategies to give reticent readers more assurance can be to provide thinking time before requiring responses, giving questions in writing before a session and paired/collaborative reading.

In whole class settings, how does the child react when being read to?

Usually, children will signal attentiveness by body language, eye gaze and stillness. However, there are some children who are restless but are still concentrating. Discussion is essential to identify if children are engaged when being read to.

In activities like drama or representation through drawing, does the child show understanding of the content or themes of what has been read?

For some children, enacting or drawing can tell the teacher more than their spoken comments.

> *Has the child developed appropriate vocabulary and terminology to discuss, consider and evaluate texts?*
>
> These qualities will be developed by adult modelling/demonstration and opportunities to talk about reading.

Meek highlights the challenges for a teacher of recognising progress in discrimination and deeper understanding:

> The signs of genuine reading development are hard to detect as they appear, and bear little relation to what is measured in reading tests. For me, the move from 'more of the same' to 'I might try something different' is a clear step. So a growing tolerance of ambiguity, the notion that things are not quite what they seem, even in a fairly straightforward tale, say, about a family seaside holiday or the unexpected behaviour of parents …
>
> By the time they are eight or a little later, children are generally expected to choose books for themselves. Those who know that authors help them make sense of the story are more patient with the beginnings of books than those who expect to recognise straight away what they have to understand. The common phrase for this process is 'getting into the story'. Practised readers tolerate uncertainty; they know that sometimes the author is building up suspense and that puzzles will be resolved if they just keep reading.
>
> (Meek, 1987: 30–31)

Observations will show what children are choosing to read and how they make decisions. Videos 3 (section 2), 4 (section 2) and 5 (section 2) (see website) show how children aged between 6 and 10 make choices about what to read. It is interesting that interests out of school feed into the 6 to 7 years olds' reading preferences; that favourite reading for these three 7 to 8 year olds is non-fiction and that the older children are very clear about how they go about making choices.

In Videos 3 (section 5), 4 (section 3) and 5 (section 3) (see website) the children comment on the role of the teacher in advising them about what they might like to read. The prompts below give suggestions about ways of extending and consolidating children's reading repertoire.

Prompts to help children learn to choose books

Teachers might ask:

What have you seen on television recently that you liked?
(Direct towards boxes/shelves with specific topics)

Think of two books that you have liked reading – they could be from when you were younger. Do you think you may like a book by the same author or about the same idea?
(Direct towards books by the same author or in the same genre; for example, fantasy, family stories, etc.)

Do you like books with pictures?
(Direct towards boxes/shelves of picture books suitably complex for the particular reader)

What about comics?
(Direct towards comic/graphic novel box)

You enjoyed reading those poems last week. Why not try a poetry book?
(Direct towards poetry anthology or collection that has some familiar poems)

Have a look in the contents list/index page to find a topic you're interested in.
(Show how to find things in alphabetic lists)

There may also be 'book of the week' or children's recommendations to help guide choice or the teacher might remind children about the book that has been read to them:

Do you remember that book I read that you really liked? That author has written more like that.

9.7 Assessing reading skills and strategies

In order to become readers, children need to learn how to read so that eventually they will be fluent and assured readers who can tackle a range of different kinds of text. To move towards fluency and independence, they will need to:

- use phonic skills
- develop an increasing sight vocabulary
- use knowledge of sight vocabulary, analogy, phonics, context clues, punctuation and grammar to read with understanding, expression and increasing fluency and independence
- identify patterns and recurring structures in language and grammar
- link new meanings to those already known
- develop comprehensions strategies: *predicting, clarifying, questioning, summarising, connecting, noting text structure, visualising* and *thinking aloud.*

All these skills and strategies will be developed through shared and guided reading and guided reading records will provide evidence of learning (see Chapters 7 and 8 for details of teaching and assessing skills and strategies).

9.8 Planning and teaching for diversity and differentiation

Teaching for diversity is another way to describe differentiation. There are diverse children in any class with varied language and literacy experience, levels of fluency as readers, tastes and skills but there are sometimes misapprehensions about differentiation. With the best of intentions, teachers may provide different tasks within an activity to cater for varying levels of perceived ability in reading, sometimes through worksheets: one with mostly pictures and few words for the least fluent readers; one with more words and one picture for the more fluent and assured; and a third with lots of words and no pictures for the high achievers. However, this kind of practice is more like division than differentiation, giving negative messages not only about the abilities of individuals but also about the relative complexity of words and images. It is by no means accurate to see reading images as easier than reading words, as this teacher comments:

> *I try to make sure that I plan to include different kinds of texts – books, films and comics where appropriate – and some drama or role play. Because some children are better at getting hold of ideas visually and others learn best by moving.*

Clearly, it is wrong to assume that 'ability' can only be judged by an individual's level of reading print (Bearne and Kennedy, 2017). Basing differentiated approaches to learning on reading fluency alone is likely to exclude those children who are perfectly able to tackle complex concepts but who find reading a struggle and runs the risk of assuming that reading fluently aloud indicates understanding. The challenge is to find ways of framing tasks that will genuinely stretch all the learners and also provide for the diversity of children, possibly by the choice of text, the level of support given by adults, the kinds of questions asked in class, the pairings and groupings of children or the nature of the task required. Digital texts can often be helpful in creating open access to the ideas being taught and learned without creating any barriers for those who find print literacy more of a challenge.

Teachers can provide for diversity (which is what differentiation is all about) through resources, activities, support and response. In Video 2 (section 4) (see website), Lee explains how he manages differentiation. Teachers' planning for the needs of individual learners depends on observation, assessment and recording progress. In terms of input and activities, once the learning objectives have been identified, it is possible to provide access to ideas through drama, storytelling, film and shared reading, none of which requires the ability to read print. Guided reading groups can tackle text with different levels of support and finding out what children already know about a topic can help plan for teaching new information. Support need not always be seen as adult support; it might also involve the use of digital technology or other tools for learning – for example, prompts, scaffolds, group and paired work. With bilingual learners, support can come from internet sources in home languages or pairing children who speak the same language. For children who are unwilling learners, challenges and short, focused (sometimes time-limited) activities can be a spur to motivation.

Perhaps the most 'open-access' approach to differentiation is talking with children about reading. Warner (2013: 11) recommends a range of ways to strengthen a reading culture and encourage reluctant readers, including:

- setting aside time for children to talk to each other and share and recommend their top reads from home as well as school
- providing children with opportunities to talk about their reading to partners, in small groups, and as part of a class/school book club
- having a graffiti board or book of recommendations in the school entrance hall/library/classroom. Dip into the book regularly

- encouraging every visitor to the classroom to contribute by telling the children what they enjoy reading
- asking teaching assistants and other members of the school staff to talk about the books they read to the children. Display photographs of them with their favourite children's books – put what they have to say about them in speech bubbles
- reading the opening to books that are new to the class book area/school library – giving a taster of what's inside
- asking a different child to recommend a text each day – their turn would come round twice a term. This could be fiction or non-fiction, a poem, website or another electronic text.

9.9   Children who experience difficulties with reading

As reading encompasses a wide range of skills and predispositions, it is tempting to think of struggling readers as those who have not yet got to grips with lifting the words off the page. However, there are different aspects of finding difficulties with reading. Some may be associated with being able to read aloud perfectly accurately but not understanding what is being read, others may be related to children who are competent but reluctant readers. A detailed study of four schools (Hempel-Jorgensen *et al.*, 2017) looking at boys' reading for pleasure found that teachers' perceptions of boys' ability, related to ethnicity and social class, could trap them into roles of 'struggling non-readers'. In addition, attempts at developing their reading were aimed at reading proficiency rather than pleasure or enjoyment (see also section 9.12).

In a multisite ethnographic research project into 7 to 9 year olds' reading, Moss (2007) identified three types of reading commonly encountered in classrooms: reading for proficiency, reading for choice and procedural reading. As children grew older, teacher judgements about proficiency reading tended to separate children into two categories: those who could read well enough from those who could not yet do so. Children in the first group were given greater access to a range of texts and more choice about how they used them. Children in the second group were more closely regulated with teachers tending to select texts for children or have a significant influence on what they read. These separations in practice had an effect on the children's perceptions of their status as readers. However, while girls in the second group were more inclined to accede to the teacher's judgement, the boys were less likely to accept their status as weak readers and engaged in activities to mask their struggles. Displacement behaviours like avoiding tasks or choosing to read highly illustrated information books tended to exacerbate judgements about poor literacy. The level of language in books which have a lot of images might indicate that the children were reading quite well, but they were in fact taking flight from reading by relying on pictures and captions to understand the content. Moss concludes that it is important to consider both how teachers deal with the social status of those left behind and how classroom practice handles distinctions between readers; for example, how children are encouraged to become more independent self-motivated readers. Moss notes that the variation in the ways learners present with literacy difficulties means that they need different kinds of support and identified some elements of best practice: allowing readers to explore all kinds of texts, alongside highly organised opportunities for children to talk and write about their reading together. Teacher input is crucial, including a wide knowledge of children's texts.

Dyslexia

Ehri explains that children who experience dyslexia may have:

> special problems learning the alphabet, processing the phonological level of language, and forming fully bonded connections to remember how to read words so they may need extra time to read. Research has shown that they have greater difficulty learning to segment and blend words into phonemes and to decode words than typically developing readers. These difficulties impair their learning to read words by sight and by analogy ... Their reading is slower and less accurate. They rely more heavily on guessing words from partial letters and context than on fully analysing letter-sounds in words. Remembering the spellings of words is especially difficult.
>
> (Ehri, 2012: 177)

Ehri suggests that to support such children, 'reading instruction needs to be especially intense, explicit and systematic' (*ibid.*) However, Anderson (2008) argues for the combination of this psychological view with a more sociocultural perspective, quoting Burden who discusses how terminology around the word 'dyslexia' reveals different ways of looking at the subject:

> The difference between describing someone as 'having dyslexia', 'being dyslexic' or 'displaying learning difficulties of a dyslexic nature' becomes highly significant. In the first instance, 'dyslexia' is used as a noun and is therefore defined as a 'thing' ... In the second example, the adjectival use of the term 'dyslexic' defines the whole person in a particular way ... [who] may thereby come to be seen as 'handicapped' ... The third example, by contrast, has descriptive and action implications with regard to the nature of the learning difficulties exhibited at a particular moment in time.
>
> (Burden, 2002: 271–272)

In her classroom research into children who experience reading difficulties defined as dyslexia, Anderson (2008: 9) found that children developed a range of coping strategies to minimise the amount of texts they had to tackle independently:

- *inter-person coping strategies* which involved persuading other people, both adults and peers to do reading for them
- *within-person coping strategies* which were used when the support of others was unavailable, and which meant they only attempted to read what they judged as essential text
- *impression management techniques* which were designed to make them appear more competent readers than they really were in order to bolster their self-esteem with their peers.

Observation of children's reading behaviours will help in noticing if any are exhibiting any of the difficulties described by Ehri or the coping strategies identified by Anderson. If a child seems to be exhibiting difficulties such as these, it is important first to carry out a diagnostic miscue analysis (see Activity 9.4), to seek the advice of local learning support services and/or to consult an organisation such as the Dyslexia Association (www.dyslexia.uk.net/) or the British Dyslexia Association (www.bdadyslexia.org.uk/).

Anderson (2008: 20) offers the following advice to support children who experience problems of a dyslexic nature:

- Encourage dyslexic pupils to read non-fiction with its appealing visual design features, in order to increase motivational interest.
- Allow dyslexic pupils to read books related to popular media characters, especially if in cartoon format, as familiarity with storylines will help them to interact more meaningfully with text.
- Make it clear to dyslexic pupils that poetry books are not only an acceptable but a particularly apt choice for silent reading sessions as the repetitive vocabulary and sparse language forms may help them to engage more fully.
- Make sure that 'young reader'-type novels are available that are at a suitable independent reading level. However, care should be taken in their selection as the storylines in such books are aimed at a younger age range, and older dyslexic pupils may shun them if they perceive them at best to be boring and at worst to be demeaning to read.
- Provide a selection of 'high/low', that is, 'high interest/low reading level' books. A number of publishers now include fiction ranges in their lists that have been specially written for middle and upper primary-aged dyslexic pupils and these are often by well-known children's authors.
- Ensure that robust monitoring systems are in place so that staff check regularly that dyslexic pupils are interacting with books set at a suitable independent reading level. If they are found to be choosing texts that are too difficult, support them sensitively in making more appropriate selections.
- Encourage dyslexic pupils to self-monitor for suitability of reading level. Provided books have around one hundred words on each page, pupils can be trained to count how many they are unsure of on the first page, and if it is more than five, allowed to change the book for a different one.

This advice is equally good for supporting children who are struggling with reading for other reasons, too. As children with reading difficulties tend not to choose to read for pleasure, it is crucial to make sure of the quality of provision for reading in the classroom, particularly the kinds of texts available. Texts to support children who are struggling with reading should:

- be varied and of high quality
- be appealing enough to encourage re-reading (often)
- have strong language patterns/rhymes
- offer opportunities for talk, drama, role play and writing.

Teaching children who experience literacy difficulties very often focuses on phonics. Of course, teaching phonics is necessary for any reader, but for children with developmental delay or specific learning difficulties it is important to teach phonics in the context of meaning, not just decoding, and to note whether the use of phonics helps or hinders their ability to read more fluently. A supportive approach for readers who struggle should include attempts to:

- increase motivation and enjoyment of reading, by talking about what children like to watch/read at home and building on that in classroom reading

- teach children about written language, graphophonic relationships, knowledge of frequently used words, letter strings and patterns
- help children to develop knowledge and understanding of the larger elements of texts – meaning, narrative and informational structures, characters and themes
- use a range of cueing strategies to support reading, for example, pictures, context and meaning.

9.10 Diagnostic assessment

There have been two major influences on practice to support readers who find reading difficult: Goodman, working from the USA, and Clay, in New Zealand. Goodman (1973) developed miscue analysis (website resource W9.7), based on the view that the mistakes or 'miscues' that a child makes when reading can tell a teacher a great deal about the strategies a child uses to try to get to meaning in a text. When the miscues are compared with what should have been read, the teacher can analyse how the young reader is using:

- orthographic (print cues or the look of letters on the page)
- phonic (print cues or knowledge of sounds of letters/words)
- semantic (meaning cues or using knowledge and experience of stories or other written texts to predict events)
- syntactic (grammar or the ability to draw on knowledge of patterns in oral and written language to predict text).

Clay (1985) developed a similar observational diagnostic technique – the running record (see Activity 9.4). This refers to three main reading strategies:

- Meaning – this parallels the semantic category in Goodman's framework, Clay asks: *Does the child use meaning?*
- Structure – this parallels the syntactic category: *Is what the child says grammatical?*
- Visual: this parallels the orthographic category: *Does the child use visual cues from the letters?*

Clay also refers to phonic cues and self-correction.

Clay's work is probably best known for her early intervention programme for children who are struggling with reading – Reading Recovery.

Reading Recovery is an intervention programme designed for children experiencing difficulties early in the process of learning to read. Beginning and ending with whole texts, Reading Recovery procedures include:

- learning about the direction of text and pages
- locating words and spaces by pointing/indicating
- looking at and talking about the layout on the page
- writing stories

- hearing the sounds in words
- cutting up and reassembling stories/texts
- learning to look at print
- linking sound sequences with letter sequences
- analysing words for their meaning and links with other known words
- phrasing and fluency
- sequencing
- being careful not to rely too heavily on one strategy
- memory.

For much greater detail about Reading Recovery see:

Clay, M. (2005) *Literacy Lessons: Designed for Individuals: Part One: Why? When? And How?* Portsmouth, NH: Heinemann.
Clay, M. (2005) *Literacy Lessons: Designed for Individuals: Part Two: Teaching Procedures.* Portsmouth, NH: Heinemann.

Although miscue analysis and running records draw on similar features of reading, both linking with the psycholinguistic model of reading, the running record is more likely to be done as part of regular group teaching. It does not need to be sound recorded (as a miscue analysis would be) and because it is a quicker procedure, can be used to monitor the progress of all children in the class once or twice in the year. Running records do not usually involve much discussion of the text as they are primarily aimed at accuracy and are used most commonly with children in the early years of learning to read. Miscue analysis, on the other hand, is a selective procedure, aimed at reaching a detailed diagnostic analysis of a child's reading at any age. A miscue is conducted with a child whose reading gives cause for concern and is sound recorded in order to give the teacher a chance to revisit the reading to focus on details of the kinds of miscues the child might be making. Typically, a miscue interview will involve asking the child to talk about what has been read to give the teacher extra insights into how the child is tackling the text. This is particularly important for older readers who may read aloud accurately, skating on the surface of the text, but not understanding very much of what they have read.

Activity 9.4
Miscue analysis – individual journal/blog

Although reading scores and diagnostic tests such as running records and miscue analysis are often used to identify children who struggle with reading, there are also behavioural clues that can suggest a child is struggling with reading. Spend a short time observing the children in your class as they read to see if you can spot any of the following:

- reading aloud hesitantly, frequently going back and repeating words
- making wild guesses at words they do not know

- for their own reading, always choosing to read books with lots of pictures
- never finishing a book (even a thin book)
- being able to read a picture book/graphic novel well but stumbling with print
- reading aloud accurately enough but not knowing what they have read.

Identify one child in a class you have access to who has not recently had a miscue analysis or running record carried out and use website resource W9.7 to carry out a miscue analysis. If the class is not your own regular class, discuss with the class teacher the summary and possible next steps interventions to support progress in reading.

If the child is still an emergent or early reader, carry out a running record. The school may already use running records in association with guided reading, but if not, for an explanation of how to carry out and analyse a running record go to: http://scholastic.ca/education/movingupwithliteracyplace/pdfs/grade4/runningrecords.pdf (accessed 5 May 2017). Read up to page 8, which is about the basic procedure for running records. The diagnostic reading conferences on pp. 9–11 are useful procedures, very much aligned with miscue analysis, but not centrally part of carrying out running records. It may be worth talking over the analysis process with a colleague who also works with younger readers in order to make sure you are confident about how to go about it.

9.11 Bilingual readers

It is important to remember there is no single category called 'the bilingual reader'. All children who have access to more than one language are individuals with particular experiences that will feed into their learning – and in this case their reading. Some children will be able to read in more than one language (Gregory, 2008), sometimes with different writing/print systems; for example, Hindi and English. Others may have no experience of a written form of their home language. Some children will have had experience of schooling which is comparable to the United Kingdom (Kenner and Ruby, 2012) while others will have had a more limited educational experience or none at all. It is important not to assume that bilingual children will have special educational needs and teachers need to find out about the language resources that bilingual children bring to school and to be aware that children even of the same age will differ in their fluency and confidence (Drury, 2005). Equally, it is important to be aware that some may have experienced trauma or difficulty in arriving in school as a bilingual learner.

In writing of her research into bilingual children's home and community literacy experience, Gregory describes this as 'complex, cultural and personal' commenting that 'home and community practices vary widely in content, language and form' (Gregory, 2007: 52). She stresses, however, that contrasting school and home practices over reading can be brought together but that such syncretism (see p. 121) is likely to be more successful if teachers know about the children's home and community literacy experience in order to build on it in classroom practice. However, it is not only a matter of providing reading instruction or offering experience of a wide range of texts, but of children 'taking hold' of literacy:

'Taking hold' of literacy demands a confidence that extends well beyond any particular method or material of instruction. We now have evidence to show that, throughout the 20th and into the 21st centuries a great deal of literacy practices has provided children with a wealth upon which they may later draw ... ways in which children of all social and educational backgrounds have taken hold of literacy in ways that have usually remained invisible to their teachers in school.

(Gregory, 2007: 52)

Such 'invisibility' is a matter of everyday experience for many bilingual readers. Issa and Öztürk (2007) and Cremin *et al.* (2015) emphasise the value of making home visits to discover:

- the child's language use at home – for example, vocabulary, interaction with parents/grandparents/siblings, whether in the home language or in English
- any games played or favourite rhymes and songs or other imaginative activities
- availability of books in the home language or any examples of storytelling in the home language
- home use of digital texts: television, computer games, internet, etc.

In such home visits it is helpful to stress the importance of developing literacy in the home language and its benefits for learning of English and, particularly, the role that digital texts can play.

Issa and Öztürk (2007: 28) also offer advice for supporting bilingual children's reading in the classroom:

- Choosing interesting, high-quality texts with supportive illustrations; the visual clues will help children to glean meaning from the narrative.
- Including dual texts in the reading repertoire.
- Using bilingual teaching assistants (BLTAs), parents and carers to read aloud the text in the children's home language, translate, or tape-record them.
- Drawing on a range of traditional tales from different cultures, as some of them include repetition.
- Including playground rhymes and games, as well as poetry, from different cultures and in different languages.
- Analysing the language demands of the text to rehearse any difficult vocabulary, phrases or concepts.
- Scaffolding the text by relating it to children's experience.
- Modelling how to read fiction and non-fiction texts, using open questioning to encourage interaction with text.
- Using a range of drama, role-play and hot-seating activities in order to engage the children in higher-order reading and engagement with texts.
- Planning for peer group reading activities – shared reading supports bilingual pupils in extending their skills.

Of course, much of this is good classroom practice for all learners, but other ways specifically to support bilingual children's reading development include encouraging children to write their own bilingual 'identity texts', either as books or digital texts, which can then be used as reading resources for the class (Cummins, 2016) or to compile their own bilingual phrasebook/dictionary (on-screen to help searching), and/or making a classroom display of 'words we know in different languages'; recording stories or information as class podcasts in home languages and finding ways to translate them, perhaps by involving family members (see recommended websites section at end of chapter).

9.12   Gender and reading

For some years there have been concerns that boys' reading attainment have fallen behind girls' scores in national tests (Twist et al., 2007; OECD, 2010), although there are reservations that some of the observed gender differences in the Programme for International Student Assessment (PISA) may be related to the types of tasks and tests used (Shiel and Eivers, 2009). PISA, under the umbrella of the Organisation for Economic Cooperation and Development (OECD), collates data from sixty-five countries; the Progress in International Reading Literacy (PIRLS) study surveys forty-six different educational systems and concentrates the ability to:

- focus on and retrieve information explicitly stated in text
- make straightforward inferences from a text, understanding parts of a text that are not stated
- interpret and integrate ideas and information
- examine and evaluate content, language and features of texts (https://nfer.ac.uk/pirls/).

Both of these major international surveys, as well as research carried out by the Australian Council for Educational Research (ACER) in 2011, which studied a further ten economies, show that girls outperform boys in reading across all the countries involved in the research according to the criteria listed above. According to PISA, the gap has not narrowed between 2000 and 2009 (OECD, 2010: 19–20). However, as with any study about gender and literacy, it is worth remembering that the children in the classroom may not conform to these international norms.

In reviewing the research into gender and literacy, Moss and Washbrook (2016) categorise explanations of the gender gap as ranged along a continuum between Essentialist and Sociocultural explanations. Essentialist explanations consider gender differences to be hard-wired and incapable of change, where as Sociocultural perspectives see gender differences as socially constructed and so capable of change.

Essentialist explanations do not consider differences within the category 'boys' (and there are possibly as many differences between boys as there are between boys and girls) but emphasise differences between the categories 'boys' and 'girls'. Narrowing the gap in performance between boys and girls is seen as a matter of responding to innate differences; for example, by developing 'boy friendly' materials and approaches. Younger et al. (2005) argue that such interventions do not take account of the differences in performance within gender categories. Sociocultural explanations suggest that children's perceptions of what it means to be a 'boy' or a 'girl' vary according to the prevailing attitudes and beliefs in different social contexts. This suggests that once differences in social norms are acknowledged and understood, strategies can be developed to change them; for example, open discussion of perceptions of gendered behaviour and opportunities to develop more 'gender neutral' classroom practice.

In addition to these two different types of explanation for gender differences in literacy attainment, Moss and Washbrook (2016) contrast goals in research, ranging from feminist and social justice perspectives that seek to create greater social equality to technicist perspectives, which prioritise uniformity in institutional outcomes. Feminist perspectives see gender differences as socially and culturally defined, so that they can be changed, but also see the power positions between the two groups 'boys' and 'girls' as maintaining the dominant position of males and marginalising the position of females. Attempts to rebalance these power relations means looking beyond the school system if greater equality and social justice is to be achieved. Technicist perspectives 'prioritise achieving better outcomes from the school system in the interests of (economic) efficiency, with better returns from the monies spent on schooling demonstrated by reducing unevenness in performance' (ibid.: 8). The focus here is mainly on changing aspects of the school system or the support given to families to reach fairer system outcomes, rather than bringing about broader political change.

This large-scale study identified 'where the most effective levers for change might lie and how the resources of school, home and peer cultures could be most effectively mobilised together to minimise gender differences in literacy attainment' (ibid.: 14). Similarly, the Boys' Reading Commission (NLT, 2012) identified boys' underachievement in reading as related to the interplay of three factors: home, school and identity.

The Raising Boys' Achievement project (RBA) (Younger et al., 2005), a three-year enquiry and intervention project, identified strategies which appear to have the potential to make a difference to boys' (and girls') learning, motivation and engagement with their schooling, and consequently to raise levels of academic achievement. Schools whose focus was on literacy adopted a range of ways to raise boys' engagement with reading, some of which mirror the NLT recommendations:

- enhanced and extended provision of books and other texts which invite boys (and girls) to express preferences for what might be bought
- buddy systems, where older boys who have 'barriers to learning' are trained to mentor younger readers (where possible, pairings were matched according to home language)
- reading groups led by members of the school community who are not teachers, where there is emphatically no overt 'teaching' but a general sharing of reading pleasures, based on all kinds of texts
- using reading journals on a regular but not routine basis as a reflective space to record, by choice, response to texts
- explicit attention to teachers modelling ways of responding to the meaning and content of books, not just decoding the text
- homework which specifically encourages students to read all kinds of texts.

In general, the thrust was to encourage a wider view of reading with the emphasis on what is involved in 'being a reader', rather than focusing solely on the skills of reading and there were remarkable individual improvements, but generally, the rate of progress of boys involved in the project was greater than the expected average and the gap between the boys' and girls' reading scores was significantly narrowed or eliminated (Warrington et al., 2006).

Figure 9.2 Reading on screen

9.13 Monitoring, recording and assessing progress in reading

If teaching reading is to be seen as more than instruction in skills, then, as this chapter has shown, regular observation and recording is necessary to track and describe the progress of readers in reading behaviours, their experience and handling of the range and repertoire of texts and their ability to reflect on what they have read. Schools will have agreed recording systems, although individual teachers may want to keep their own records not only of what children have read but also of their attitudes to reading and their progress along the route to independence as readers. Used alongside such records, the Scale of Progression in Reading (Figure 9.3) can be used to track progress and to check coverage of all aspects of the reading curriculum. The scale is derived from discussion with teachers who wanted to establish useful and time-efficient record-keeping systems. It reflects what teachers might expect to see as children develop fluency and assurance in reading and is aligned with the national curricula of England, Northern Ireland, Scotland and Wales. The scale is best seen as a basis for discussion with colleagues, and open to adaptation, as the descriptors may not always reflect particular school circumstances.

An emergent reader	An early reader shows all the features of an emergent reader plus:	A developing reader shows all the features of an early reader plus:
ENGAGEMENT AND RESPONSE		
<ul><li>uses some book language/expressions drawn from books</li><li>knows that print conveys meaning in a range of texts (shopping lists, games, internet, etc)</li><li>knows terminology about books and how they work (cover, front, back, beginning, end)</li><li>understands that print (in English) goes from left to right, including return sweep</li></ul>	<ul><li>gives personal view of characters, events or ideas in texts</li><li>shows empathy with characters through enacting</li><li>retells sequence of narrative or informational content</li><li>identifies general features of familiar text types</li><li>re-reads texts for pleasure</li><li>states preferences about favourite characters, themes, ideas or texts</li><li>uses digital sources to find information</li><li>comments on the main issues raised in the text</li></ul>	<ul><li>expresses reasoned opinions about texts and makes personal choices based on preference</li><li>expresses response through role play/drama</li><li>recognises and responds to the different ways characters are presented, referring to the text</li><li>prefers certain types of reading</li><li>sustains reading with familiar texts</li><li>comments on themes and ideas making reference to the text</li><li>uses different reading techniques for different text types</li><li>retrieves information from books and internet sources</li><li>identifies the point of view from which a story is told</li><li>recognises similarities between stories with similar themes from different cultures/genres or settings</li><li>explains the difference between fiction and non-fiction</li></ul>
COMPREHENSION		
<ul><li>understands literally what has been read</li><li>links poems, stories, film and non-fiction to own experience</li><li>retells stories</li><li>predicts the outcomes of straightforward narratives</li><li>applies language comprehension to words on the page</li><li>recognises the main parts of text</li><li>joins in with poems read aloud and recites some parts by heart</li></ul>	<ul><li>understands literally what has been read and can sequence key events</li><li>makes connections between texts</li><li>identifies key themes/ideas</li><li>infers characters' feelings based on personal emotions as well as the author's representation of the character</li><li>uses some comprehension strategies: retelling, prediction, questioning</li><li>understands and describes information</li><li>uses text layout in books and on screen to locate information efficiently</li></ul>	<ul><li>discusses the actions of main characters and justifies views using general evidence from the text</li><li>draws together ideas and information from across a whole text</li><li>makes plausible predictions about content and narrative development</li><li>identifies imagery in poems</li><li>makes comparisons between texts, noting similarities and differences</li><li>uses text features, to scan and assess for relevance/interest</li><li>recognises that graphic narratives can be serious as well as entertaining</li><li>appreciates the effects of rhyme and rhythm in poetry</li><li>expresses personal preferences about poems/parts of poems</li></ul>

Figure 9.3 Scale of Progression in Reading

An emergent reader	An early reader shows all the features of an emergent reader plus:	A developing reader shows all the features of an early reader plus:
	• gains an overall impression of a text and makes predictions about content/ subject by reference • notices patterns in language, composition or sound • begins to understand how images and words in texts create humour or atmosphere	• recognises differences in style/representation in pictorial text • notices the effects of different elements of composition and how they interact
READING SKILLS		
• discriminates between sounds. • reads and understands simple sentences • recognises one or two words in different contexts • knows the difference between pictures and print • knows that there are letters and that groups of letters can make words • identifies first and last letters in words	• applies phonic knowledge to decode words • recognises a growing number of frequently used words or parts of words automatically • uses onset and rime to generate new vocabulary • checks that reading makes sense when reading aloud and self-corrects	• draws on different strategies when reading unfamiliar material • has a broad and developing sight vocabulary • is beginning to read aloud with intonation and expression • checks that reading is accurate when reading aloud • links (some) new meanings to words already known • knows the difference between statements, questions and exclamations

An increasingly fluent and almost independent reader shows all the features of a developing reader plus:	An experienced and often independent reader shows all the features of increasingly fluent and almost independent reader plus:	An assured and independent reader shows all the features of an experienced and often independent reader plus:
ENGAGEMENT AND RESPONSE		
• explains personal preferences for types of text and subject matter • describes how characters express/represent the theme of a text • reads silently most of the time	• pursues own interest in texts and types of texts chosen, reflecting on personal preferences • makes recommendations, with reasons, of satisfying texts • reads for sustained periods of time and attempts unfamiliar complex texts	• articulates personal responses to a range of texts and text types, analysing own response • interprets and verifies information for oral or written presentation • tolerates ambiguity about narrative endings.

Figure 9.3 continued

An increasingly fluent and almost independent reader shows all the features of a developing reader plus:	An experienced and often independent reader shows all the features of increasingly fluent and almost independent reader plus:	An assured and independent reader shows all the features of an experienced and often independent reader plus:
<ul><li>re-tells narratives and selects information for oral presentation</li><li>quotes from the text and refers to personal experience to support opinions/responses</li><li>discriminates between reading for information and for imagination</li><li>identifies differences in the ways different media texts present the same information or themes</li><li>comments on different text features that contribute to authorial or directorial intent</li><li>makes connections between texts on same topic</li><li>discusses structure of different kinds of texts</li></ul>	<ul><li>prepares poetry/drama for performance</li><li>synthesises information for concise verbal presentation</li><li>identifies and summarises evidence from different elements of the text to support a hypothesis</li><li>perseveres with more challenging texts</li><li>critically evaluates texts by comparing how different text types treat the same information or themes</li><li>identifies the main purpose and viewpoint in a text and shows awareness of the effect of the text on an audience</li><li>draws confidently on a range of book and digital sources for information</li><li>distinguishes between the views of the writer and those expressed by others in the text</li><li>discusses the treatment of social or cultural themes over time</li><li>identifies features common to different texts or versions of the same texts</li><li>uses relevant vocabulary to talk about structure and stylistic features</li></ul>	<ul><li>identifies and describes the characteristics of different genres, styles of individual authors/directors/text type</li><li>makes discriminating choices to expand personal repertoire</li><li>identifies and distinguishes between explicit and implicit points of view in texts</li><li>speculates on reasons for authorial/directorial/editorial decisions and intent in communicating with the audience</li><li>critically evaluates information from books or internet sources</li><li>compares critically how different sources treat the same information, with reference to the texts</li><li>discusses different social, cultural or historical aspects of texts</li><li>uses relevant critical terminology in evaluating texts</li></ul>
COMPREHENSION		
<ul><li>understands that fiction can evoke other worlds</li><li>begins to identify point of view in information material</li><li>retrieves and summarises information on a common theme across different texts</li><li>explores underlying themes and ideas, making reference to different elements of the text</li></ul>	<ul><li>infers reasons for characters' behaviour and motivation referring to specific points in the text</li><li>comments on differences in text types in relation to author's intentions</li><li>identifies themes in novels and poetry</li><li>understands how text sections order and build up ideas, or develop information</li><li>evaluates specific texts with reference to their type</li><li>understands how narrative tension is created in different stories</li></ul>	<ul><li>discusses nuances in character and motivation, relating to personal and text experience</li><li>infers authorial/directorial perspective, commenting on how messages, moods, feelings and attitudes are conveyed by making reference to the text</li><li>explains inferred meanings, drawing on evidence across the text</li><li>compares different types of texts and identifies how their elements interact</li></ul>

Figure 9.3 continued

An increasingly fluent and almost independent reader shows all the features of a developing reader plus:	An experienced and often independent reader shows all the features of increasingly fluent and almost independent reader plus:	An assured and independent reader shows all the features of an experienced and often independent reader plus:
• explains the effects of figurative language in poetry • identifies differences between the structures of fiction and information texts • recognises differences between different types of non-fiction text • uses knowledge of narrative text structure to hypothesise possible outcomes • compares stories/ information in different media • identifies the effects of stylistic features in poetry • compares the effects of figurative language in conveying emotion/ theme	• identifies features of different fiction and non-fiction text types in different media • explores how different texts appeal to readers, recognising how style and composition are linked to the purpose of the text • analyses the effects of interactions between different elements of a text	• uses knowledge of language conventions and organisational features of different types of text to support understanding and confirm predictions • makes judgements about the effectiveness of style and composition in texts • recognises how text elements are used to influence the reader/ viewer
READING SKILLS		
• can scan text for familiar words or phrases • reads own text critically • uses knowledge of sight vocabulary, phonics, context clues and grammar to read with fluency, understanding and expression • identifies some familiar word patterns and affixes, sentence structures and grammatical features • uses dictionary to check accuracy of spelling	• identifies an increasing range of grammatical features • chooses appropriate strategies to read unfamiliar vocabulary • uses thesaurus/internet sources to expand and confirm vocabulary knowledge • shows accuracy and some versatility in reading aloud	• confidently uses grammatical terminology to talk about own and others' texts • shows assurance in reading unseen material • varies pitch, pace and expression for effect when reading aloud

Figure 9.3 continued

These are also available as a printable resource on website resource W9.8.

One way to use the scale is to track individual progress. Records/observations each term can be compared to the statements on the scale. Used in discussions with parents or colleagues, the descriptors can be a useful basis for talking about specific elements of the reading curriculum. Identifying statements which genuinely reflect what individual children can do in reading can provide a very clear idea of the areas they need help with. In addition to reviewing individual progress, at the end of a term or year, the scale might be used to evaluate whole class progress and indicate areas for future planning.

See also CLPE Reading and Writing Scales, which are closely aligned to the national curriculum in England (https://ukla.org/resources/details/clpe-reading-and-writing-scales (accessed 1 May 2017)).

Managing assessment

It can sometimes seem to be a daunting task to manage the reading records/assessments of a whole class. Organisation is key as well as a clear view that not all assessments have to be carried out at once. Many teachers plan to assess and record the progress of their readers over a few weeks, focusing on one or two groups each week. With younger readers, a typical approach would be to carry out running records with one or two groups a week during guided reading time when other adults are available to support the groups not being assessed. The same groups would then be the focus of observational records during independent reading time. This procedure would be repeated in following weeks until all groups have been assessed and observed.

Activity 9.5
Noting achievements in reading – reflective journal/blog to pairs/group

There are three parts to this activity.

1. Watch Video 7 (see website) where Danielle (aged 9) talks about her reading preferences. Using the Scale of Progression in Reading in website resource W9.8, in pairs, note Danielle's achievements in terms of Engagement and response.
   You may have found that she is showing evidence of being an increasingly fluent and almost independent reader as she:

   - explains personal preferences for types of text and subject matter
   - describes how characters express/represent the theme of a text
   - reads silently most of the time
   - retells narratives and selects information.
   - quotes from the text and refers to personal experience to support opinions/responses.

   You might think that she is also showing some evidence of being an experienced and almost independent reader as she:

   - pursues her own interest in texts and types of texts chosen, reflecting on personal preferences

• perseveres with more challenging texts.

You may, also have differing views of her achievements. Discuss them and see what evidence you can find for supporting your opinions.

Consider how she might be moved on, for example, developing more concise verbal expression or developing her vocabulary to talk about texts (she seems not to know the difference between 'realistic' and 'real', although this could be the unfamiliarity of the situation).

Of course, it is difficult to assess a young reader on just the evidence of one observation, but Danielle's comments do indicate that observation over a period of time can give a teacher a very clear idea of children's achievements in engagement and response.

2. Now watch one or two of the interviews with groups of children on Videos 3, 4 and 5. Watch one of the videos once again and using the Reading Progression Scales in website resource W9.8, select one or two children and identify aspects of engagement and response from their comments.

If possible, get together in threes, where each person has analysed a different year group and notice how the children make progress in their reading over time.

3. In the classroom where you are working (or on your next placement), in discussion with the class teacher, select two or three children whose reading interests you and with the teacher note their achievements on the Reading Progression Scale.

If you share the information with anyone outside the school, make sure that you use initials or pseudonyms.

Having noted the children's achievements, how might you move them forward as readers?

Summary

If children are to become successful and committed readers, planning for and assessing reading has to include more than skills. Since it is only possible to assess what has been taught or experienced, the foundation for monitoring and assessing reading must be the provision of a wide and rich range of texts and the introduction and development of a flexible repertoire of reading strategies and behaviours. Teacher modelling and discussion of reading contribute to establishing reading communities and reading circles, journals and blogs offer opportunities for teachers to evaluate children's reflections on their reading. Some children do not find reading easy so the chapter offers suggestions of ways to support struggling readers and gives details of how to carry out miscue analysis and running records. For developing bilingual readers, it is important that teachers find out about their existing language and literacy experience before embarking on any strategies to improve their reading. The issue of gender differences in reading is outlined in terms of effective ways to narrow the gap including the importance of self-esteem. Finally, the Scale of Progression in Reading offers a means of monitoring recording and reporting progress in all aspects of reading development.

Recommended reading

Anderson, R. (2008) *Dyslexia and Inclusion: Supporting classroom reading with 7–11 year olds.* Leicester: United Kingdom Literacy Association. Full of practical advice that will help SENCOs, teachers and assistants to support dyslexic pupils in ways that promote effective learning and ensure inclusion. All the main types of classroom reading encountered are covered, including on-screen texts.

Warner, C. (2013) *Talk for Reading.* Leicester: United Kingdom Literacy Association. This book considers the interplay between three different aspects of talk that can positively influence children's interactions with texts: teacher talk to model and teach reading strategies; classroom talk that promotes a positive climate; and talk that can extend and enrich the way children think when they read together and independently. The examples reflect positive practice observed in schools.

Warrington, M. and Younger, M. with Eve Bearne (2006) 'Now I can read faster': Reading communities and partnerships, in M. Warrington and M. Younger (eds) *Raising Boys' Achievement in Primary Schools.* Buckingham: Open University Press. **Advanced**

Recommended websites

Mantra Publishing www.mantralingua.com (accessed 1 May 2017). A wide range of books including dual language books in many languages.

Milet www.milet.com (accessed 1 May 2017). Books and multimedia resources for children and adults, including translations of books into English.

The National Literacy Trust www.literacytrust.org.uk/search?q=eal and www.literacytrust.org.uk/search?q=community+languages (accessed 1 May 2017). The Trust has many resources to support English as an Additional Language teaching and also accounts of work with community languages.

The Guardian www.theguardian.com/childrens-books-site/2014/oct/13/50-best-culturally-diverse-childrens-books (accessed 1 May 2017). The newspaper publishes reviews of culturally diverse children's books.

Tiny Owl Publishing http://tinyowl.co.uk/ (accessed 1 May 2017). A bookshop which began by publishing stories by Iranian children's authors in English and which has now diversified to publishing from worldwide sources.

The Willesden Bookshop www.willesdenbookshop.co.uk/ (accessed 1 May 2017). A truly massive range of multicultural books.

National Association for Language Development in the Curriculum (NALDIC) www.naldic.org.uk/ (accessed 1 May 2017). This is the national subject association for English as an additional language.

References

Anderson, R. (2008) *Dyslexia and Inclusion: Supporting classroom reading with 7–11 year olds.* Leicester: United Kingdom Literacy Association.

Bearne, E. and Kennedy, R. (2017) Providing for differentiation, in T. Cremin and J. Arthur (eds) *Learning to Teach in the Primary School.* Abingdon: Routledge, pp. 355–371.

Burden, B. (2002) A cognitive approach to dyslexia, in G. Reid and J. Wearmouth (eds) *Dyslexia and Literacy: Theory and practice.* Chichester: John Wiley.

Clark, C. and Foster, A. (2005) *Children's and Young People's Reading Habits and Preferences: The who, what, why, where and when.* London: National Literacy Trust.

Clay, M. M. (1985) *The Early Detection of Reading Difficulties.* Portsmouth, NH: Heinemann.

Clay, M. (2005) *Literacy Lessons Designed for Individuals: Part one: Why? When? And How?* Portsmouth, NH: Heinemann.

Clay, M. (2005) *Literacy Lessons Designed for Individuals: Part two: Teaching procedures*. Portsmouth, NH: Heinemann.

Cremin, T., Mottram, M., Bearne, E. and Goodwin, P. (2008) Exploring teachers' knowledge of children's literature, *The Cambridge Journal of Education*, 38 (4) pp. 449–464.

Cremin, T., Mottram, M., Collins, F., Powell, S. and Safford, R. (2014) *Building Communities of Engaged Readers: Reading for pleasure*. London: Routledge.

Cremin, T., Mottram, M., Collins, F., Powell, S. and Drury, R. (2015) *Researching Literacy Lives: Building communities between home and school*. London: Routledge.

Cummins, J. (2016) Conference keynote speech 'Individualistic and Social Orientations to Literacy Research: Bringing Voices Together?' at the United Kingdom Literacy Association International Conference *Literacy, Equality and Diversity: Bringing voices together*, 8–10 July 2016.

Drury, R. (2005) *Young Bilingual Learners at Home and School: Researching multilingual voices*. Stoke-on-Trent: Trentham Books.

Ehri, L. C. (2012) Why is it important for children to begin learning to read in kindergarten?, in S. Suggate and E. Reese (eds) *Contemporary Debates in Childhood Education and Development*. Abingdon: Routledge, pp. 171–180.

Goodman, K. S. (ed.) (1973) *Miscue Analysis: Applications to reading instruction*. Urbana, IL: National Council of Teachers of English.

Gregory, E. (2007) What counts as reading and learning outside school? And with whom? How? And where?, in E. Bearne and J. Marsh (eds) *Literacy and Social Inclusion: Closing the gap*. Stoke-on-Trent: Trentham Books, pp. 41–52.

Gregory, E. (2008) *Learning to Read in a New Language: Making sense of words and worlds*. London and New York: SAGE.

Hempel-Jorgensen, A., Cremin, T., Harris, D. and Chamberlain, L. (2017) *Understanding Boys' (dis)Engagement with Reading for Pleasure Project Findings*. Buckingham: Open University.

Issa, T. and Öztürk, A. (2007) *Practical Bilingual Strategies for Multilingual Classrooms*. Leicester: United Kingdom Literacy Association.

Kenner, C. and Ruby, M. (2012) *Interconnecting Worlds: Teacher partnerships for bilingual learning*. Stoke-on-Trent: Trentham Books.

King, C. and Briggs, J. (2007) *Literature Circles: Better talking, more ideas*. Leicester: United Kingdom Literacy Association.

Meek, M. (1987) *How Texts Teach What Readers Learn*. Stroud: Thimble Press.

Moss, G. (2007) *Literacy and Gender: Researching texts, contexts and readers*. London: Routledge.

Moss, G. and Washbrook, L. (2016) Understanding the gender gap in literacy and language development. Bristol University, Bristol Working Papers in Education #01/2016.

National Literacy Trust (2012) *Boys' Reading Commission*. www.literacytrust.org.uk/assets/0001/4056/Boys_Commission_Report.pdf (accessed 5 May 2017)

OECD (2010), PISA 2009 Results: Executive summary. www.oecd.org/pisa/pisaproducts/46619703.pdf (accessed 1 May 2017)

OECD (2016) Results from PISA 2015. United Kingdom. www.oecd.org/pisa/PISA-2015-United-Kingdom.pdf (accessed 1 May 2017)

Shiel, G. and Eivers, E. (2009) International comparisons of reading literacy: What can they tell us?, *Cambridge Journal of Education,* 39 (3) pp. 345–360.

Traves. P. (2015) *Reading 7 to 16*. Leicester: Owen Education/United Kingdom Literacy Association.

Twist, L., Schagen, I. and Hodgson, C. (2007) *Readers and Reading: The National Report for England (PIRLS)*. Slough: NFER.

Warner, C. (2013) *Talk for Reading*. Leicester: United Kingdom Literacy Association.

Warrington, M. and Younger, M. with Eve Bearne (2006) 'Now I can read faster': Reading communities and partnerships, in M. Warrington and M. Younger (eds) *Raising Boys' Achievement in Primary Schools*. Buckingham: Open University Press.

Younger, M. and Warrington, M. with Gray, J., Rudduck, J., McLellan, R., Bearne, E., Kershner, R. and Bricheno, P. (2005) *Raising Boys' Achievement*: *Research report No. 636*. London: Department for Education and Skills. http://webarchive.nationalarchives.gov.uk/20130401151715/www.education.gov.uk/publications/eOrderingDownload/RR636.pdf (accessed 1 May 2017)

Children's books

Michael McCurdy (2002) *Trapped by the Ice!: Shackleton's Amazing Antarctic Adventure*. Walker Books. ISBN 9780802776334

William Grill (2014) *Shackleton's Journey*. Flying Eye Books. ISBN 9781909263109

CHAPTER 10

POETRY

This chapter covers:

- Surrounded by poetry
- What is poetry?
- A model for teaching poetry
- The classroom environment for poetry
- The teacher's role
- Performing poetry
- Reading, talking about and writing poetry
- Using personal experience
- Poetry across the curriculum
  - Case study, upper primary: Water cycle rap
- Playing with poetry
- Narrative poetry
  - Case study, middle primary: The Tsunami project – writing narrative poetry
- Responding to poetry

Note: for copyright reasons, many of the examples of poems included in this chapter are 'old but gold'. However, there are recommendations of poets, anthologies and collections in website resource W10.1 and at the end of this chapter.

10.1 Surrounded by poetry

Rhyme and rhythm are all about us. Children and adults sing, chant and rhyme in the playground, at sports events, in religious ceremonies. They listen to popular songs and raps and sometimes even read poems on tube trains and in published texts. Adults recall poems learnt as children and children learn playground rhymes to accompany their play and might even be encouraged to learn poems off by heart themselves. And many of us remember the lyrics of songs that have meant something to us. So forms of poetry are intertwined with daily life. It is difficult to imagine a society where this is not the case.

Poetry is appreciated by the whole body – the eye, tongue, ear, limbs, heart, bones and blood – and also by the mind. In its performance and written forms it depends on the arrangement of sound in space; it has its own choreography on the page and its rhythms, emphases and cadences in the airwaves. The heard and felt experience of poetry is the starting point for writing. The kinds of poetry which surround children at home – lullabies, nursery rhymes, nonsense songs or television advertisements – are often highly repetitive and rhythmic. This means that children's knowledge of poetic forms almost always begins before they come to school. They will be used to rhymes, jingles and songs drawn from their communities, their families, television and tablets. This is what one teacher remembers about her early experience of poetry:

> I remember my nan singing me nursery rhymes; I especially liked See Saw Marjorie Daw, I don't know why. And then there were pop songs. I loved the Spice Girls and used to sing 'I'll tell you what I want, what I really really want' with my friends in the playground at school. I think I just liked the sounds and the repetition. I don't think I thought about what the words said … But we used to sing other songs in the playground: 'Ooh Ah Cantona…' – the next bit is rude – something about knickers and 'my boyfriend's car' – and we used to fall about laughing with no idea of what it was all about! My Mum always chose birthday cards with nice rhymes in them. In school I remember really loving that poem about the Box: 'I will put in my box'. I can't remember much more, there was something about a sari, but I know I wrote a poem I was very proud of.

Activity 10.1
Memories of poetry – reflective journal/blog to group

Think back to your own early years. Can you remember any jingles, rhymes, poems from home? Jot them down. Think about book covers. Can you remember any books that had rhymes or poems in them? What about favourite songs? What did you sing in the playground? What were your favourite advertising jingles?

Share these memories with each other and consider what they have offered you in terms of exploring rhyme, rhythm and language play. How might you use reflections on early experiences of poetry and verse as a starting point for a teaching sequence (or a part of one) with a focus on poetry?

Benjamin Zephaniah describes his own way in to poetry:

> I see poetry as this big tree that has many branches. You can get introduced
> to the tree by climbing up one of the branches, but it doesn't mean to say
> that you can't explore other parts of the tree. I got on to the tree via oral
> poetry, but I've gone on to love all kinds – from nonsense verse to classical
> poetry like Shelley – and I love them all equally.
>
> (Zephaniah, cited in Carter 2010: 18)

With all this implicit experience and enjoyment of rhyme and verse it would seem obvious that it should be built on in school. An Ofsted report (2007) which surveyed over eighty schools found that, particularly in the primary school, teachers lacked confidence in their subject knowledge of poetry and more recent research suggests that poetry is not as much of a focus in primary classrooms as fiction and information texts. Teachers themselves read far less poetry, can name relatively few poets and feel less confident about teaching about poetry than other forms (Cremin, 2013). Cremin points out that:

> poetry needs to be experienced before it can be analysed and deserves to be
> engaged with playfully and actively as a multimodal art form.
>
> (Cremin, 2015: 130)

The following sections are designed to help raise confidence in developing subject knowledge about poetry: the elements that go together to make poetry what it is with some practical suggestions for playful and active classroom experiences with poetry.

10.2 What is poetry?

It is no easy task to define to children what poetry is. There have been many attempts by poets themselves to try to pin down a definition and it can be a useful exercise to consider them and to ask children how they would define poetry.
Famous poets have defined poetry in the following ways:

'the best words in the best order' (Samuel Taylor Coleridge, 1835)
'spontaneous overflow of powerful feelings' (William Wordsworth, 1802)
'the song and dance of words' (Ted Hughes, 1967)
'poetry uses a few words to say a lot and every one of them counts'
(John Mole, 1994)
'little fragments of life' (Michael Rosen, 2006)
'music of being human' (Carol Anne Duffy, 2009)
'a hotwire to our strongest feelings' (Andrew Motion, 2010)

(All quotations cited in Kelly, 2011)

When a group of 9 year olds were asked 'What is poetry?', they commented on meaning:

- every poem has a meaning
- it can be funny and emotional

- it can be about anything
- it needs a title

on structure:

- poems are of various lengths
- new line for a new sentence
- poetry follows a rhythm and a structure
- the first line has to rhyme with the second rhyme and the third line has to rhyme with the fourth line
- you can have acrostic poems
- it has rhyming couplets

on vocabulary and style:

- a poem has rhyming words but a story doesn't
- it has alliteration
- it has repeated words
- it's the vocabulary they use and the style they write it in

and finally:

- it can be a tree – a poet tree!

Activity 10.2
Children's perceptions of poetry – reflective journal/blog to group and classroom

Before teaching children of any age and sharing poems, responding as well as writing them, it is extremely useful to ask children what they think poetry is. This is not only interesting in itself but also provides a really good starting point for making sure that teachers do not have mistaken assumptions about children's thinking.

Start by trying to define poetry yourself and compare your responses with the ideas of others in the group and with the list of what poets have said (see list below). As soon as you have a chance, ask some children what they think poetry is and what the differences are between poems and stories and other kinds of text. Compile an agreed list of what makes a poem a poem.

Then introduce children to a list of definitions from writers:

'the best words in the best order' (Samuel Taylor Coleridge)

'spontaneous overflow of powerful feelings' (William Wordsworth)

'the song and dance of words' (Ted Hughes)

'poetry uses a few words to say a lot and every one of them counts' (John Mole)

'little fragments of life' (Michael Rosen)

'music of being human' (Carol Anne Duffy)

'a hotwire to our strongest feelings' (Andrew Motion)

Do the children agree? Do they think the poets' definitions are better or complementary to the list compiled by the class? Ask if they would want to change or add to the original list as a result of considering the writers' thoughts.

Compile an agreed list of 'What is poetry' and display it in the classroom. This can then be referred to and/or changed as the children read, discuss and compose poetry over the next few weeks.

You may, of course, find, as Dr Johnson said: 'It is much easier to say what it is not' (Boswell, 1776: 38).

The problem with the poets' definitions cited above is that they tend to exclude young children's intimate knowledge of the poetic form through nursery rhymes, pop songs, playground rhymes embedded in 'singing games' as well as the more general playing with language (Opie and Opie, 1985). The project Children's Playground Games and Songs in the New Media Age (2013) explored and recorded children's playground games and the links between poetry and popular cultural texts (see http://projects.beyondtext.ac.uk/playground games/uploads/end_of_project_report.pdf (accessed 30 April 2017)).

10.3   A model for teaching poetry

The elements that combine to make meaning in poetry are:

Sight: the appearance of a poem on the page
including line breaks, lay out and the shape on the page.

Structure: the organisation, including repeated patterning
including the structure of the whole poem including stanzas and verses, combination and collisions of words in sentences/lines, as well as choice of words.

Sound: rhythm and word sounds
including rhythm, patterns of syllables, rhyme, alliteration and other echoes between sounds.

Sense: using the meaning of words and combinations of words to enhance the overall meaning
including images, symbols, allusions, metaphor, simile, connotation, ambiguity, etc.

(Carter (LINC), 1992: 179)

Teachers and children can focus on the above elements to consider poems either when responding to poetry when reading or as points to think about when composing poetry. These aspects of teaching poetry would form part of Phases 1 and 2 of the planning and teaching sequence (see Introduction pp. 6–8) where ideas are explored, texts are closely examined and ideas for personal compositions captured and extended. Explicit teaching about specific elements of a poem can lead to experiments with personal writing which can be polished and prepared for performance or publication (Phase 3).

10.4 The classroom environment for poetry

Creating an environment where reading and writing poetry can flourish often means having anthologies, dedicated poetry walls, picture books of narrative poems, audio files, YouTube, poetry cards, etc. but it also means creating a classroom atmosphere where risks can be taken. This means that discussion of poetry – personal and by published poets – needs to take place openly and thoughtfully. It means planning for performance of different kinds of poetry and opportunities to read poems aloud, share opinions, swap favourites. There should be a good number of different kinds of poetry collections and anthologies in the reading area, classic and modern, serious and humorous, narrative and lyric, and every now and again a new collection introduced, with the teacher sharing some of the poems.

Activity 10.3
Auditing the poetry provision of the classroom – reflective journal/blog to group

Look at the poetry books available in the classroom you work in. How many are there? Are they anthologies (books of poems by many different poets) or collections (books with collections of poems by one poet)? How many poems are there by women? In translation? Humorous? Narrative? Modern? Classic? Are the books colourful and inviting?

Trawl the local charity shops for (good condition if possible) second-hand copies of poetry collections or anthologies and build up your own library.

Search the internet, particularly YouTube, for animated versions of poetry, including poetry in different languages.

Choose a few poems you like that you could just read to the class for pleasure in an odd moment. Start a 'Poetry I Like' file (see website resource W10.1) so that you will remember poems you come across that you like and that you think the children will enjoy. The website resource includes a list of children's poetry collections and anthologies.

For one week, make space to read a poem on each day. You do not need to discuss it in any detail, just see if the children liked it or not. Once you have managed to find time, it becomes easier to find more time to share poetry just for enjoyment.

Make sure you include poetry in the next teaching sequence you plan for English. Again, it need not take a great deal of time but it is interesting how poetry can often echo the themes of books or other texts you are working on.

10.5 The teacher's role

Reading aloud by the teacher models the flow of the text, the distinctive rhythm and the patterns of stress, making the sound of the poem (its tune if you like) explicit to the listeners. It demonstrates how poetry comes alive on the tongue. This modelling is crucial, helping children to become familiar with the sound of the text so that they have a sense of how to read poetry aloud themselves. Reading by the teacher also offers starting points for children to capture their ideas in response to the poem(s) read. Phases 1 and 2 of the teaching sequence might follow this basic structure:

- Read the poem aloud.
- Children in pairs re-read and consider questions such as:
  - *What is happening in the poem? How long did it take to happen? Where did it happen? How do you know?*
  - *Is there anything that puzzles you or is there a question you would like to ask the poet?*
  - *Is there a message for us in this poem or a theme we can identify?*
- To draw attention to particular aspects of sight, sound, structure or sense, ask children to identify rhyming patterns or ask about the effect of a metaphor, for example.
- Use active strategies to deepen understanding – for example, role play/drama, and visualising through drawing or making soundscapes.
- Share and note the responses to the poem.
- Display the poems in full in the classroom once they had been read.

The final element of the teaching sequence, where children might compose their own poems, gives children the opportunity to experiment with language, form and imagery, to express their own ideas and feelings related to the themes of the poems they have read and to choose ways of expressing their own ideas.

Activity 10.4
Close reading of a poem – pairs/group – classroom activity

Another way of exploring meaning is to give a cut-up version of a poem for children to reassemble collaboratively or to give a poem, but not its title, and for children to decide what the title should be. Try it out first with a partner. Read the following complete poem by Alfred, Lord Tennyson. Decide on a title for the poem. Share your ideas.

> He clasps the crag with crooked hands;
> Close to the sun in lonely lands,
> Ring'd with the azure world, he stands.
>
> The wrinkled sea beneath him crawls;
> He watches from his mountain walls,
> And like a thunderbolt he falls.

You will have had to read the poem very carefully and you will have found talking your ideas through with others helpful as you shared your impressions concerning what the poem might be describing. There may have been words that you needed to clarify (e.g. *azure*). You will have looked carefully for clues in the text to infer who 'he' is, speculated and possibly come up with a title such as 'The Dying Hermit'. In passing you may have noted that the poem consists of two stanzas, has a rhyming pattern of aaa, bbb, and enjoyed the alliteration in the first line which follows the stress pattern.

Tennyson's title for the poem was 'The Eagle'. You might now want to read the poem again, as you would with 7 and 8 year olds and discuss how knowing the title changes one's reading of the poem.

When you try out this activity in the classroom, you might ask the children to use visualisation (see pp. 202–203) to draw a picture of the scene the poem describes.

10.6   Performing poetry

Asking children to read poetry aloud and preparing performances is a powerful way of exploring meaning and deepening understanding, as well as being engaging and enjoyable. Such an activity might form part of a longer teaching sequence or be seen as a separate, short 'poetry focus'. Two popular examples – 'First Day at School' by Roger McGough and 'Please Mrs Butler' by Alan Ahlberg – allow exploration through drama with younger children about the feelings of the characters in the poems. When reading 'First Day at School' aloud, the teacher might use a nervous, slightly shaky voice of the little boy as he attends school for the first time. In 'Please Mrs Butler', the reading would bring out the excited and concerned voices of the children in conversation with a world-weary teacher. Then in small groups (twos or fours), children re-read the poems and decide how they will enact them, either after learning the words by heart or as one of them narrates.

Learning by heart and performing is also an engaging way of exploring the 'song and dance of words'. A group performance of, for example, the nonsense poem 'On the Ning Nang Nong' by Spike Milligan can be accompanied by gongs and other percussion instruments by a group of young children. In doing this, the children will implicitly come to understand *sound*; the pleasures and importance of, for example, alliteration, repetition, rhyme and onomatopoeia. It is the group work that gives these examples their power. Similarly, oral poetry – poetry specifically composed to be passed on by word of mouth – is ideal for performance. Dip into *From Mouth to Mouth (Oral Poems from Around the World)* by John Agard and Grace Nichols (2004).

Through discussion, rehearsal and performance, through reading aloud or recitation with actions, children are able to deepen their appreciation and engagement through collective collaboration.

Recently, in the UK, there has been more emphasis on children learning poetry by heart, and in England, The Poetry by Heart initiative has promoted competitions for learning and reciting poetry (see www.poetrybyheart.org.uk/category/primary/ (accessed 30 April 2017)).

The Cambridge Poetry and Memory Project can be found on www.poetryandmemory.com/ (accessed 30 April 2017) (see also Pullinger in Recommended Reading).

Wales has a long tradition of encouraging children to write and recite poetry for local and national eisteddfodau and Scotland hosts a national poetry competition *Poems Aloud* as part of the National Poetry festival: www.poetryoutloud.org/poems-and-performance/listen-to-poetry (accessed 30 April 2017).

In Northern Ireland there are a number of regional feis (very like eisteddfodau) competitions for school children from across all key stages; for example, Feis Ard Mhacha (a County Armagh competition) or Feis Bhéal Feirste (a Belfast competition). Culture Northern Ireland run a variety of poetry competitions: www.culturenorthernireland.org/festivals (accessed 30 April 2017).

10.7 Reading, talking about and writing poetry

Poetry, perhaps because of its compressed form, speaks to a reader's individual experience, so all the following suggestions are intended to evoke different points of view and opinions within a class. Children enjoy being able to discuss poetry critically in groups and encouraging them to explore poems and give their personal responses (rather than just talking about rhyme or rhythm) can be very insightful. Bradley (2017) carried out classroom research into children's attitudes to poetry. They said:

> It settles the mind
>
> Poetry doesn't have to be real
>
> When I feel angry or sad I normally read a poem and it makes me calm
>
> It helps you put energy in your body

They also gave advice to their teachers:

> Let us read it ourselves
>
> Let us choose a poem
>
> Do not tell me what to do or think but give me a theme
>
> Only read it out loud after you have given us time to read it
>
> Get lots of poetry books

(Bradley, 2017: 3)

Many of the following suggestions could form part of the opening phases of a teaching sequence or be part of a special poetry focus.

Poem of the week. Children choose poems they like and put sticky note comments on the poetry wall or on the class blogsite. Time is allocated (perhaps as a treat) for children to share their favourites. Over time, these can be gathered into a class anthology, illustrated by the chooser, with comments beneath each poem by several children. This is a good resource to share with other classes.

Issues raised in poems. Almost any poem can be used to encourage discussion; for example, Michael Rosen's 'Gone' from the collection *Don't Put Mustard in the Custard* (1987), where the reader is not told who 'she' is. At the beginning the reader is told that she 'sat in the back of the van' and that the children waved to her but the van moved off. The poem ends with the poignant words: 'we never reached her / before she was gone'. There is no indication in the poem whether this is a temporary or permanent parting, or what the relationship is between the 'we' of the poem and 'she' who has gone, so there is plenty of space for speculation as well as writing in role.

Writing in role. Narrative poems such as 'The Pied Piper of Hamelin' provide plenty of scope for role play, debate and discussion. After drama exploration, children might write in role as the boy left behind or the Mayor, explaining to the local paper what has happened to the children, or one of the children who has followed the Piper.

Comparisons

A Venn diagram can help in making comparisons (Lambirth, 2007). The chosen poems should have something in common, a theme or setting or character explored in different ways. 'Homework' by Elizabeth Smith and 'Homework! Oh, Homework!' by Jack Prelutsky are ideal for this (see Figure 10.1). Both poems explore the theme in very different ways. The left- and right-hand spaces show the unique features of the two poems in terms of subject, structure, rhyme and so on. The middle space includes the similarities. Discussion over Venn diagrams like this helps children reflect on what each poet is trying to convey through the subject and gives them a basis for more extended reflective response.

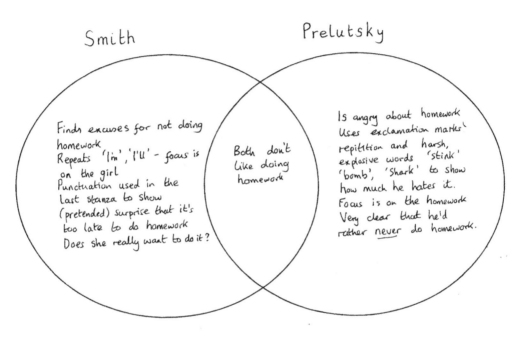

Figure 10.1 Venn diagram comparing two poems

Poetry blogs/forums/wikis

Children can write blog posts about favourite poems that they may have found at home, or by searching the internet or books. Peers, family members and the broader school community can then be invited to read these posts and submit their own comments for moderation by the class teacher. Class forums (a facility of Virtual Learning Environments (VLE)) allow for cumulative comments to be gathered about poetry favourites, and can also be used to support discussions about poems that have been a class focus. Wikis, also often a feature of VLEs, can be used to create online resources, such as webpages about particular poets. This collaborative authorship process might, for example, involve each child starting an entry about a poet and contributing extra information to two of their peers' pages.

Frames

Giving children a frame can support composition, particularly with children who are learning English as an additional language. A simple frame is one which often repeats (e.g. 'The rainbow is...'); offers original poems as stimulus and a kind of frame; starts from personal preferences; and uses what people say.

Frames may be based on anything – not just poetry – that the children may have been reading currently. For example, *Handa's Surprise* offers a good opportunity for a repeating frame asking the children to compose alliterative noun phrases:

> Handa put
> one *prickly pineapple*
> two *bendy bananas*
> three *delicious dates...*
> in her basket

This could be adapted to: I put ... in my basket.

Over-reliance on frames can be restricting but often they can provide just the nudge a young writer needs to express personal feelings or opinions. Any topic, book, film or poem can lead to offering frames for composing. Poems themselves can offer frames; for example, 'Amulet' by Ted Hughes which begins every line with 'Inside...' and provides a challenge to upper primary writers about how to echo such sinewy poetry.

Or Emily Dickinson's 'A Slash of Blue'

> A slash of Blue –
> A sweep of Gray –
> Some scarlet patches on the way,
> Compose an Evening Sky –
> A little purple – slipped between
> A Wave of Gold –
> A Bank of Day –
> This just makes out the Morning Sky.

Simply written, this could be a model for writing about the sky as the children look out of the classroom window, or a frame through which to consider writing about other visible experiences – a local landscape, for example, whether urban or rural.

Benjamin Zephaniah's 'According to My Mood' has the added appeal of varying the typography to add to the meaning.

'The Sound Collector' by Roger McGough offers a frame for thinking about familiar and comforting sounds – or their opposite.

In 'Penguin Complaints' by Jo Shapcott, the layout on the page traces the path of the penguin complaining about the fridge – a frame for experimenting with layout to support a poem's theme.

After reading John Agard's 'Don't Call Alligator Long Mouth' (1996) (and a lot of discussion and modelling), Hillal, a Turkish speaker, and Rosheen, a confident English speaker, were given frames to compose their own poems about Tabby Cat (Figure 10.2 and 10.3).

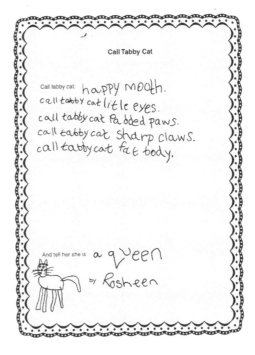

Figure 10.2 'Call Tabby Cat' poem by Hillal
(Bearne, 2002: 109–112)

Figure 10.3 'Call Tabby Cat' poem
by Rosheen (Bearne, 2002: 109–112)

10.8 Using personal experience

Writing about 'what I like'

Touch, taste, smell and memory are often used as starting points for writing poetry but poetry is emphatically not always about 'beautiful things and nature'. Lambirth (2007) offers the following list, drawn partly from Rosen (1989) as possible topics:

- Food – favourites, where it's eaten and how.
- Football – players, games, goals, fights, and injustices.
- Family –loved ones, sibling arguments, worries, moving, changes, days out, days in, conversations.
- Being bored – the fights that result, how parents attempt to help, the reasons.
- School – friends, enemies, teachers, lessons, lunchtimes, playground song.
- Fears – dentists, injections, pain, death, schools, lessons, bullying, global war!
- Loves – boyfriends/girlfriends, mums, dads, pets, foods, places, games.
- Computer games – the games, the consoles, the friends, and the family.
- TV – the shows, the scary ones, the funny ones, the sad ones, the news reports.
- Possessions – pens, pencils, soft toys, football kits, bikes, scooters, clothes.
- Popular culture – pop songs, pop singers, game card collections and characters, films, TV characters, personalities, celebrations like Christmas, Divali, Eid, Hanukkah.

The advantage of a list like this is that it can be used to link with the theme of the current teaching sequence for English or topic in other curriculum work, but can also offer a selection of ideas for personal writing unrelated to any class focus.

Writing about what you hear

It is worth remembering that poetry is meant to be enjoyed by the ear as well as by the eye. Quite often, humorous poetry captures what people say and a class poem can be composed quite quickly to act as a model. Most (if not all) of the children in the class will be able to think of an excuse for not tidying up and these can be listed to become a poem, for example:

Why didn't you tidy up?
> I had to feed the rabbit
> I was doing my homework
> Jack stopped me.

Why didn't you tidy up?
> I was abducted by aliens
> I was just too tired.
> I forgot.

Michael Rosen's poetry offers plenty of models for poems like this as he almost always starts with what people say; for example 'Don't' in the collection *Don't Put Mustard in the Custard*.

Poetry using rap, hip hop or rhythm also echoes what is heard. 'Wha Me Mudder Do' by Grace Nichols uses repetition and a strong beat to celebrate what her mother can do. Korky Paul's *Aesop's Funky Fables* (1999) draw on rap as do Tony Mitton's *Groovy Greek Hero Raps* (2001). Lots of fun to be had with these.

Writing about what you see

Using images from pictures, magazines, films, comic books, video games, dreams can result in precise descriptive writing. Of course, images of country landscapes or seascapes can evoke descriptive vocabulary and ideas but equally, images of urban landscapes can provide stimulus for writing poetry (Figure 10.4).

Figure 10.4 Urban graffiti

Writing for competitions/publication

Local or national writing competitions are often promoted by magazines, supermarkets, local television and radio stations and advertised on the internet. A useful source of information is the poetry library: http://poetrylibrary.org.uk/competitions/ (accessed 30 April 2017) and www.scottishpoetrylibrary.org.uk/learn/teachers/competitions (accessed 30 April 2017).

Children's poetry compositions can also be published in school, of course – in the school magazine, as classroom anthologies shared with other classes or sold to families as part of fund raising for charity. Publishing like this can be very motivational and form part of a whole school focus on poetry.

Inviting poets into the classroom

This can be a most invigorating and inspiring experience. The poet Andy Croft writes:

> The benefits of bringing poets into the classroom are incalculable. Pupils can realise that they are able to write about their own lives in their own words. Working with a writer can help teachers to feel more confident about using poetry in the classroom. They can pick up lots of tricks and collect lots of ideas. And they can soon understand that you don't need to be a published poet in order to encourage children to enjoy reading and writing poetry. Everyone can enjoy themselves. And the world of writing, poetry and books can seem not quite so far away.
>
> (www.childrenslaureate.org.uk/previous-laureates/michael-rosen/poets-in-school/ (accessed 30 April 2017))

(See also: http://poetrysociety.org.uk/content/education/schoolpoet (accessed 30 April 2017).)

If it is not possible to invite a poet into the classroom, these two websites offer many examples of poets reading their own poetry online so they can be 'invited' in virtually.

10.9 Poetry across the curriculum

Poetry can be a good way to introduce or explore any part of the curriculum. For example, try writing a 'recipe' for a historical event – 'Take 1 arrow, 1,000 soldiers, a teaspoon of mist...' – or a haiku about the elements. It is a real challenge to express feelings and ideas about natural events in spare poetry but often startlingly beautiful.

Case study, upper primary: Water cycle rap

Jade planned a geography topic on the water cycle with her 9- and 10-year-old class. But this was a factual project with a difference because the final writing product was to be a rap about the water cycle. She began by asking the class what they knew about raps. At first some said they did not know any raps, but when others shared their ideas, they realised that they did in fact know quite a lot about them – what kinds of things they were about, what they sounded like and some of their favourite rap artists.

With the use of film, books and examples, the class learned that the water cycle can also be called the hydrological cycle and that it describes the continuous movement of water on, above and below the surface of the Earth. Fresh, saline and atmospheric water is in constant movement depending on different aspects of the climate and moves from rivers to oceans or from oceans to the atmosphere by the processes of evaporation, condensation, precipitation, infiltration, runoff, accumulation. The effects of sun and warm weather cause water to evaporate and this rises into the atmosphere where, because it is cooler, it forms clouds through condensation. Clouds then release their loads of water through precipitation and water reaches the seas and oceans or, if it falls on land, reaches rivers and eventually the seas accumulates through run-off, and the cycle begins again as the sun and warm weather once again cause evaporation.

Once the class had a clear picture of the processes of the water cycle, through shared writing, Jade helped them to write a class rap:

Hot sun beating on the sea
That's what evaporation means to me.
Water vapour rises in the air
Condensation happens when there.
Who knows what happens in condensation
Not many in this nation.
Water cools down, clouds are formed
Clouds are pushed up when they are warmed.
Precipitation starts when the clouds are colder
That's when you feel rain fall on your shoulder.
Water runs into rivers and sea
It ends with accumulation
And that's what hydrological means to me.

In pairs, the class then made up their own water cycle raps and performed them to the class (Figures 10.5 and 10.6).

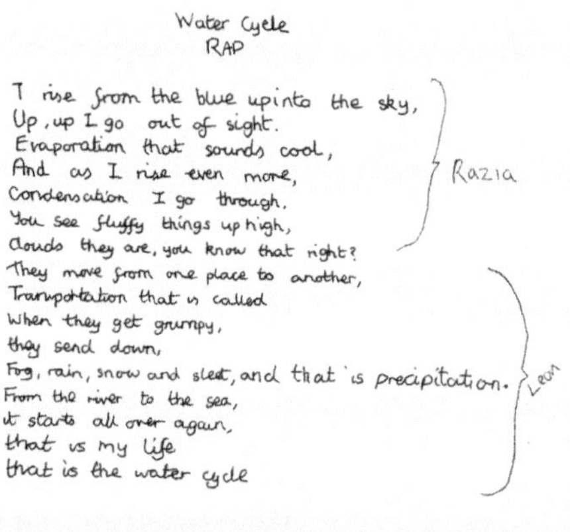
Water Cycle
RAP

I rise from the blue upinto the sky,
Up, up I go out of sight.
Evaporation that sounds cool,
And as I rise even more,
Condensation I go through.
You see fluffy things up high,
clouds they are, you know that right?
They move from one place to another,
Transportation that is called
When they get grumpy,
they send down,
Fog, rain, snow and sleet, and that is precipitation.
From the river to the sea,
it starts all over again,
that is my life
that is the water cycle

Razia
Leon

Figure 10.5 Collaborative rap by Razia and Leon

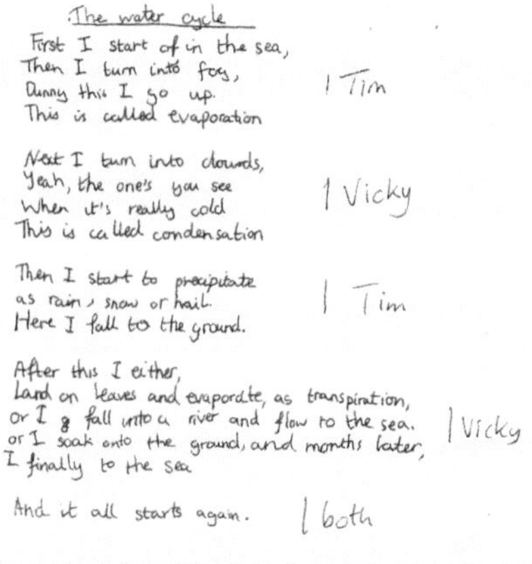
The water cycle

First I start of in the sea,
Then I turn into fog,
Durrny this I go up.
This is called evaporation | Tim

Next I turn into clouds,
Yeah, the one's you see
When it's really cold
This is called condensation | Vicky

Then I start to precipitate
as rain, snow or hail.
Here I fall to the ground. | Tim

After this I either,
Land on leaves and evapordte, as transpiration,
or I fall into a river and flow to the sea.
or I soak onto the ground, and months later,
I finally to the sea | Vicky

And it all starts again. | both

Figure 10.6 Collaborative rap by Tim and Vicky

10.10 Playing with poetry

Orally composed and performed poetry

Find or make up raps, rhyming jokes, jingles for advertisements, questions and answers, repeated refrains, lyrics. Jacqui Harrett's 'Red Riding Hood Rap' (website resource W10.2) is a useful model for children making up their own traditional story raps.

Creating new stories

As part of a longer teaching sequence, a narrative poem like 'The Lady of Shalott' by Tennyson, can be the basis for discussion and writing the prequel explaining how she came to be enchanted and imprisoned in the tower. What was Lancelot's role?

Margaret Atwood's 'Song of the Worms' offers a scary starting point for writing about what happens when the worms do attack.

'From Carnival to Cabbage and Rain' by Julie Holder describes the carnival and what happens after it is over. A good opportunity for writing in role as a spectator during and after a public event.

Transforming poems

Make a storyboard for a 'trailer' for a narrative poem or rewrite a nursery rhyme from the point of view of one of the characters; for example 'I only came to say hello,' by Miss Muffet's spider. Children might be invited to make their own presentations or animations of poetry.

Soundscapes and landscapes

Almost any poem lends itself to being accompanied by sound effects: 'The Listeners' by Walter de la Mare, or 'Welsh Incident' by Robert Graves, for example. Using instruments, other implements or just the voice, ask groups to record soundscapes to capture the mood of the poem. Soundscapes make a good group discussion activity that helps in understanding the poem as the group decide which sounds to use when, in what intensity and for how long.

In addition, any poem can be illustrated, providing a good opportunity for individual response to a poem.

Replying to poems

A letter of apology to the penguin who is complaining about the fridge in 'Penguin Complaints' by Jo Shapcott (using the quirky layout of the poem), outlining how improvements will be made. A text to a friend from Tom the Piper's son about why he is innocent, although the police are charging him with stealing a pig.

10.11 Narrative poetry

Narrative poems provide opportunities for looking at structure and language within the space of a week or so without doing the poem to death – something to be careful about when discussing the technicalities of poetry. Many favourite narrative poems are older and well known, but their quality means that they are worth visiting with every generation of learners. There are some wonderful Charles Keeping illustrated versions of narrative poems such as 'The Highwayman', 'Beowulf' and 'The Lady of Shallot' where the images add immensely to the reading experience. The language of many favourite narrative poems is usually not modern, so provides much meat for rolling it around the tongue, performance and analysis. Importantly, also, narrative poems offer the chance to consider theme in some depth:

- 'The Highwayman' by Alfred Noyes allows discussion of loyalty, self-sacrifice, brutality, the effects of war.
- 'The Song of Hiawatha' by Henry Wadsworth Longfellow can be a chance to explore family, faith and culture.
- 'Flannan Isle' by W. W. Gibson, apart from being a wonderful mystery story, allows scope for considering isolation.
- Robert Browning's 'The Pied Piper of Hamelin' offers an ideal opportunity to explore moral issues about justice/injustice and retribution.
- 'The Owl and the Pussycat' by Edward Lear would be a good basis for writing an account of what happened when they returned from honeymoon.

Case study, middle primary: The Tsunami project – writing narrative poetry

(See website resource W10.3 for a more detailed account of the project.)

Sukhvinder, a class teacher of 8 and 9 year olds at Elmhurst Primary School in the London borough of Newham, and Jane, a visiting consultant, developed an extended multimodal project which aimed to support the language development of bilingual children. They chose to focus the work on a culturally inclusive text (Bednall *et al.*, 2008), the scroll book *Tsunami* (Chitrakar and Chitrakar, 2008), a narrative graphic poem designed by Patua scroll painters from West Bengal, telling of the terrible tsunami that overtook the region in 2004 and dedicated to those who suffered from it.[1] They wanted the children to learn to read 'beyond the literal', seeking the deeper meanings of texts to develop the sophisticated inference and deduction skills involved in reading the multilayers of a text such as *Tsunami*, considering the messages conveyed by the pictures and what the words contribute to the meaning and exploring through drama how sound, movement and gesture add to what is being communicated. The project allowed them to develop the children's reading through visual and word based texts, their writing, layout and art skills by making a class scroll and geography skills by learning about earthquakes, tsunamis and the areas hit by the tsunami in South East Asia. The work was planned for nine afternoon sessions.

Beginning the project

As the children entered the classroom, they saw the *Tsunami* scroll that they would be using as a model for their own work throughout the project, and a Bengali embroidery, intricately designed, hanging at the front of the room. Sukhvinder explained that the children would be making their own class scroll and poem about a tsunami. Using diagrams and photographs uploaded to the digital flipchart, she and Jane explained that earthquakes and tsunamis are natural disasters which affect people's lives and why they happen. Through drama the children recreated the movement of a huge tsunami wave.

Figure 10.7 Tsunami wave

Figure 10.8 Tsunami wave

They discussed how they might show how tsunamis affect people's lives through group freeze framing. In the second session, Sukhvinder read the poem to the class and asked for their thoughts. In small groups the children read three verses and annotated them with questions or comments which were shared with the class, thinking about whether the images make the words easier to

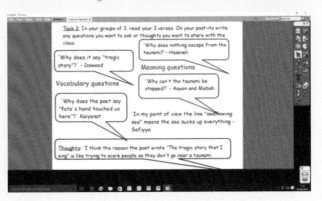

Figure 10.9 Screen capture 1: Vocabulary questions

understand or whether they pose more questions. The session closed by taking suggestions about the meaning of particular verses, images and lines now that the children had been able to look more deeply, which Sukhvinder wrote under headings *Vocabulary questions*, *Meaning questions* and *Thoughts* (Figure 10.9).

Rich descriptive language

The third session focused on developing rich description. Jane told the class about a previous project with a class of 8 and 9 year olds which had used the Bengali poet Jasim Uddin's saga poem 'The Field of the Embroidered Quilt' and images from quilts to create poems and artwork. Jane and Sukhvinder shared some of the poems that the class had written and modelled commenting on examples of rich description they had liked, asking the children to do the same. The focus then shifted to examining artwork carefully. Each table had three images from *The Art of Mithila* by Yves Vequaud (1977)[2] and after Jane and Sukhvinder modelled commenting on the use of pattern, colour and the story/message the artist might be trying to get across, the children chose an image and discussed it with their partners.

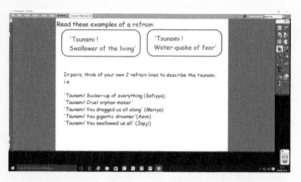

Figure 10.10 Screen capture 2: Refrains

To consolidate the work on poetic language, the next session concentrated in more detail on the words of the *Tsunami* poem. Sukhvinder asked the children to notice the refrain at the end of each verse. In pairs, the children created their own refrains (Figure 10.10).

Sukhvinder and Jane had shown the children how to list the actions in each verse, drawing on both words and images and modelled how to turn these lists into poetic lines. In their groups the children orally rehearsed the descriptive lines of poetry they had based on their lists of drama actions and then wrote them, with the less fluent writers using writing frames.

Creating the scroll

Each child made a block print of wave patterns which would be used as a backdrop to the scroll and Jane and Sukhvinder showed the children complex decorative artwork representative of Hindu art so that they could decorate animal templates in that style.

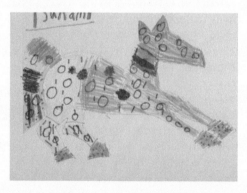

Figure 10.11 Animal templates

With support where needed, the children improved their poems, and copied their verses on plain paper. In the final session the teachers and class assembled the verses and art work on long scrolls.

Extracts show how the children drew on the original poem to make their own moving narrative poems:

Tsunami (corrected spelling; children's own punctuation)
Reporters are coming with huge big cameras ready to talk.
Telling the story across the world.
Orphans there, orphans here, orphans everywhere.
Is this destiny?
Does life have to be like this?
Tsunami!
You life taker of living.

Fame and fortune never lasts
No wishes No dreams
They will never last.
Tsunami!
You stealer of dreams.

(Safiyya)

Helicopters fly to help people
People fighting for food in village and town
I cannot stop the tears in my eyes
Or the Tsunami
The Tsunami broke
Amongst the broken bricks
How much more can I take?
You thief!
Tsunami
You trouble maker.

(Channel)

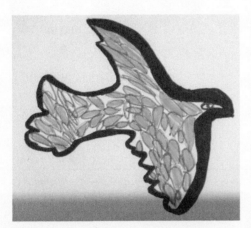

Figure 10.12 Animal templates

Figure 10.13 Animal templates

Figure 10.14 Assembling the scrolls

Figure 10.15 Assembling the scrolls

All religions that are buried line by line
Like a water graveyard.
Friends and family died together
Families died all by themselves.
Tsunami! Who killed us all!

We hold our shoulders tightly together.
Our toes in the centre on top of each other.
The last group hug I think we will have.
No one will break our powerful friendship.
Tsunami!
The killer of the dead!

(Maleka)

A lonely child floats by left behind separated
Who will help them now?
Tears well from my glittering eyes.
Tsunami!!!
You hurt us here.

(Ramisha)

Figure 10.16 The final scrolls

Activity 10.5
Planning and teaching poetry – pairs/whole group

This activity draws on Videos 2 and 3 (see website) where Lee teaches a poetry lesson then talks about his planning.

Watch Video 2 (particularly sections 1–3 and section 5) in which Lee uses a narrative poem as a basis for close attention to language/grammar. You will notice that he begins by recapping on previous work and at the end of section 5 he tells the children what they will be doing in the following session.

Watch Video 8 (see website) where Lee explains his planning (sections 1, 2 and 3) and how he makes decisions about differentiation (section 4). In the later sections (6, 7 and 8) he talks about evaluating the learning, moving the children forward and working as a team.

Make plans for teaching poetry as soon as you can. Identify the language focus you will take and evaluate the children's learning after the lesson or sequence of lessons.

10.12 Responding to poetry

As poetry is so intensely personal and a matter of identity, teachers sometimes feel inhibited about responding to children's poetry writing. This can lead to bland comments such as 'I love your poem', 'Terrific writing' or 'I like the rhyme'. None of which specifies elements that are impressive and areas that might be improved, and so run the risk of disappointing the young writer. An Ofsted survey (Ofsted, 2007) identified some specific and helpful responses:

> Some fantastic metaphors. You need now to think about the rhythm of the lines. Sometimes you will have to add words or leave words out.

> Look at this line. Does it fit the mood of the rest of the poem? Try to write another line, perhaps using a simile, e.g. snow falls like…

> You have tried hard to use interesting verbs like gleaming and chattering. To make the structure of the poem clearer, leave a space between verses.

(Ofsted, 2007: 12)

A study in some London (England) schools, found that many schools had no procedures in place to guide the assessment of poetry (Lambirth *et al.*, 2013). Many teachers found themselves commenting on structural or technical features rather than feeling confident to focus on meaning or style. More specific response to poetry written by children might include suggestions about them editing their poetry to improve atmosphere, mood, suspense, humour, writerly intention and audience awareness.

Anthony Wilson, himself a poet and a teacher, writes about what progress in writing poetry might look like (Wilson, 2009). He suggests that in responding to children's (or adults') poetry it is important to 'identify the genuine' (*ibid.*: 398) and to create an environment of possibility where children can experiment with language and robustly reflect on their own work.

Activity 10.6
Policy about responding to poetry – reflective journal/blog to group

When you can, ask the teachers in your school what guidance the English policy gives for responding to poetry. Bring the information back to the group and draw up a few guidelines or tips for yourselves as a group to help you respond specifically and helpfully to children's poetry writing.

Summary

Poetry is everywhere – in songs, rhymes, jingles, books, films – and children's experience of poetry at home and in their popular cultural interests is a good place to start in teaching poetry. However, defining poetry has been a conundrum for people over the ages and it is worth asking children to add their ideas. Sight, structure, sound and sense are essential elements for reading and responding to poetry and so is an environment which provides rich experience of poetry in all its forms. The teacher's role in critical in sharing and modelling reading and response to poetry, including poetry in performance. Suggestions for many different ways of enjoying and composing poetry together are exemplified by case studies from early, middle and upper primary classrooms.

Notes

1   Patua scrolls are a form of narrative graphic art. Traditionally they would be taken from home to home and presented accompanied by song. As they travelled, the singers would pick up news and carry it on to their next destination. (See www.tarabooks.com/books/books/adults/picture-books--visual-arts/tsunami/ for a description of how the scrolls are made and the words of the English version scroll accompanied by song in Bengali.)
2   Mithila is in North East India. The Mithila women paint scenes from the Ramayana in vivid colours. The pictures form part of family ceremonies and village festivals.

Recommended reading

Lambirth, A. (2007) *Poetry Matters*. Leicester: United Kingdom Literacy Association. This is a book packed with ideas and activities for enlivening poetry teaching.

Lambirth, A. (2011) Poetry is slamming: Different ways to perform poetry in primary schools, in V. Bower (ed.) *Creative Ways to Teach Literacy: Ideas for children aged 3 to 11*. London: SAGE, pp. 55–63. This chapter focuses on performance as a response to poetry, drama from poetry, singing and recitation.

Lambirth, A., Smith, S. and Steele, S. (2013) Responding to children's poetry, in S. Dymoke, A. Lambirth and A. Wilson (eds) *Making Poetry Matter: International research on poetry pedagogy*. London: Bloomsbury, pp. 84–101. It would be well worth reading more in this collection. This chapter outlines research into teachers' knowledge of poetry which influences how they respond to children's poetry composition.

Locke, T. (2010) Reading, writing and speaking poetry, in D. Wyse, R. Andrews and J. Hoffman (eds) *The Routledge International Handbook of English, Language and Literacy Teaching*. Abingdon: Routledge, pp. 367–378. Drawing on work across the Anglophone world, this chapter argues that poetry teaching needs to be revisioned to take into account the place of poetry (in all forms, digital, oral and print) in the lives of contemporary communities. **Advanced**

Obied, V. (2013) Developing poetry pedagogy for EAL learners within inclusive intercultural practices, in S. Dymoke, A. Lambirth and A. Wilson (eds) *Making Poetry Matter: International research on poetry pedagogy*. London: Bloomsbury, pp. 144–153. This chapter explores developing an intercultural perspective through poetry in a UK classroom, drawing on theories of transformative pedagogy. **Advanced**

Pullinger, D. (2012) In living memory: The dying art of learning poetry and a case for revival, *Changing English*, 19 (4) pp. 383–393. A report of research in UK schools which leads to a broader discussion of the value of memorisation.

Wilson, A. (2009) Creativity and constraint: Developing as a writer of poetry, in R. Beard, D. Myhill, J. Riley and M. Nystrand (eds) *The SAGE Handbook of Writing Development*. London: SAGE, pp. 387–401. Research in UK schools about what progress in writing poetry might look like.

Recommended anthologies

John Agard and Grace Nichols (eds) illustrated Annabel Wright (2004) *From Mouth to Mouth (Oral Poems from Around the World)*. Walker Books. ISBN 9780744583830. Poetry intended to be passed on orally and full of delightful rhythms. Ideal for performance.

Julia Donaldson, illustrated by Clare Melinksy (2014) *Poems to Perform: A classic collection chosen by the Children's Laureate*. London: Macmillan Children's Books, ISBN 9781447243397. Delightful collection with varied moods.

Carol Ann Duffy, illustrated Emily Gravett (2012) *101 Poems for Children: A Laureate's choice*. London: Macmillan Children's books. ISBN 9781447220268. Light-hearted and serious poems for children to enjoy, from older poems to the most recent.

Roger Stevens (2013) *Off by Heart: Poems for children to learn and remember*. London: A&C Black Children's and Educational. ISBN 9781408192948. Includes tips for learning by heart and performing.

Morag Styles (1987) *You'll Love This Stuff: Poems from many cultures*. Paperback. Cambridge: Cambridge University Press. ISBN 9780521312752. An absolute must for any poetry corner. Reflective and lively, short and longer, this is an important collection of poems from around the world.

Morag Styles and Susanna Steele (eds), illustrated Jane Ray (1992) *Mother Gave a Shout: Poems by women and girls*. London: Lions. ISBN 9780006741343. Just what it says! Much poetry in anthologies is by men so this is a fine counterbalance.

Recommended websites

http://poetrylibrary.org.uk/competitions/ (accessed 30 April 2017)
www.scottishpoetrylibrary.org.uk/learn/teachers/competitions (accessed 30 April 2017)
http://poetrysociety.org.uk/content/education/schoolpoet (accessed 30 April 2017)
www.childrenslaureate.org.uk/previous-laureates/michaelrosen/
poets-in-school/ (accessed 30 April 2017)
www.poetrysoup.com/poems/for_children (international poems) (accessed 3 May 2017)
www.famousliteraryworks.com/childrens_poetry_resource_index.htm (accessed 3 May 2017)
www.familyfriendpoems.com/poems/famous/children/ (accessed 3 May 2017)
www.storyit.com/Classics/JustPoems/ (accessed 3 May 2017)

References

Bearne, E. (2002) *Making Progress in Writing*. London: Routledge.

Bednall, J., Culora, N. and Fell, S. (2008) *Developing a Culturally Inclusive Curriculum*. London: Mantra Lingua

Boswell, J. (1776) *James Boswell's Life of Samuel Johnson 1766–1776* (1994 edn), M. Waingrow (ed.). Edinburgh: Edinburgh University Press.

Bradley, A. (2017) Developing children's critical response to poetry, *English 4–11*, 60 pp. 3–5.

Carter, J. (2010) *Creating Writers: A Creative Writing Manual for Key Stage 2 and Key Stage 3*. (Revised and updated). London: Routledge.

Carter, R. A. (ed.) (1992) *Language in the National Curriculum: The LINC Project*. Nottingham: University of Nottingham.

Chitrakar, J. and Chitrakar, M. (2008) *Tsunami*. Chennai: Tara Books.

Cremin, T. (2013) Exploring teachers' principles and practices, in S. Dymoke, A. Lambirth and A. Wilson (eds) *Making Poetry Matter: International research on poetry pedagogy*. London: Bloomsbury, pp. 9–19.

Cremin, T. (2015) Playfully exploring poetry, in T. Cremin, D. Reedy, E. Bearne and H. Dombey (eds) *Teaching English Creatively*. Abingdon: Routledge, pp. 118–132.

Hughes, T. (1967) *Poetry in the Making: A handbook for writing and teaching*. London: Faber & Faber.

Kelly, A. (2011) 'Oh, no, we did old poems in year 5!': What is the place of classic poetry in the twenty-first century classroom?, in P. Goodwin (ed.) *The Literate Classroom*. Abingdon: David Fulton, pp. 175–184.

Lambirth, A. (2007) *Poetry Matters*. Leicester: United Kingdom Literacy Association.

Lambirth, A., Smith, S. and Steel, S. (2013) Responding to Children's Poetry, in S. Dymoke, A. Lambirth and A. Wilson (eds) *Making Poetry Matter: International research on poetry pedagogy*. London: Bloomsbury.

Ofsted (2007) *Poetry in Schools: A survey of practice, 2006/07*. London: Office for Standards in Education.

Opie, I. and Opie, P. (1985). *The Singing Game*. Oxford: Oxford University Press.

Rosen, M. (1989) *Did I Hear You Write?* London: Andre Deutsch.

Vequaud, Y. (1977) *The Art of Mithila*. London: Thames Hudson.

Wilson, A. (2009) Creativity and constraint: Developing as a writer of poetry, in R. Beard, D. Myhill, J. Riley and M. Nystrand (eds) *The SAGE Handbook of Writing Development*. London: SAGE, pp. 387–401.

Children's books and film

Roger McGough (ed.), illustrated Sheila Moxley (2001) *100 Best Poems for Children Chosen by Children*. London: Penguin Books. ISBN 9780141310589

Tony Mitton, illustrated Martin Chatterton (2001) *Groovy Greek Hero Raps*. London: Orchard Books. ISBN 9781841217994

Korky Paul, adapted Vivian French (1999) *Aesop's Funky Fables*. London: Picture Puffin. ISBN 9780140562460

Michael Rosen, illustrated Quentin Blake (1987) *Don't Put Mustard in the Custard*. Collins Picture Lions. ISBN 9780006626770

Poems

John Agard (1996) 'Don't Call Alligator Long Mouth', in M. Hanke, J. Leedham and A. Sanderson, illustrated D. Schulman, *Alligator Raggedy-mouth: Making music with poems and rhymes*. London: A&C Black.

Kevin Crossley Holland, illustrated Charles Keeping (2013) 'Beowulf'. Oxford University Press. ISBN 9780192794444

W. W. Gibson. 'Flannan Isle'. www.poetry-archive.com/g/flannan_isle.html (accessed 30 April 2017)

Robert Graves. 'Welsh Incident'. www.poetrybyheart.org.uk/poems/welsh-incident/ (accessed 30 April 2017)

Roger McGough. 'First Day at School'. www.poemhunter.com/poem/first-day-at-school/ (accessed 30 April 2017)

Roger McGough (ed.), illustrated Sheila Moxley (2001) *100 Best Poems for Children Chosen by Children*. London: Penguin Books. ISBN 9780141310589. The following poems are in this collection:

Alan Ahlberg 'Please Mrs Butler'
Margaret Atwood 'Song of the Worms'
Robert Browning 'The Pied Piper of Hamelin' (extract)
Emily Dickinson 'A Slash of Blue'
Julie Holder 'From Carnival to Cabbage and Rain'
Ted Hughes 'Amulet'
Henry Wadsworth Longfellow 'The Song of Hiawatha' (extract)
Walter de la Mare 'The Listeners'
Roger McGough 'The Sound Collector'
Grace Nichols 'Wha Me Mudder Do'
Alfred Noyes 'The Highwayman'
Jack Prelutsky 'Homework! Oh, Homework!'
Jo Shapcott 'Penguin Complaints'
Elizabeth Smith 'Homework'
Alfred, Lord Tennyson 'The Lady of Shalott'

Edward Lear. 'The Owl and the Pussycat'. www.nonsenselit.org/Lear/ns/pussy.html (accessed 30 April 2017)

Alfred Noyes, illustrated Charles Keeping (2013) 'The Highwayman'. Oxford: Oxford University Press. ISBN 9780192794420

Alfred, Lord Tennyson, illustrated Charles Keeping (2013) 'The Lady of Shalott'. Oxford University Press. ISBN 9780192794437

Alfred, Lord Tennyson. 'The Eagle'. www.poetryfoundation.org/poems-and-poets/poems/detail/45322 (accessed 30 April 2017)

Benjamin Zephaniah, 'According to My Mood', https://classyu.wordpress.com/2013/08/30/according-to-my-mood-by-benjamin-zephaniah/ (accessed 30 April 2017)

PART 3
WRITING

In every part of this book you will be asked to keep a journal (or a blog) in which you can jot down reflections, observations and tasks. There are also recommended readings to support your learning.

INTRODUCTION TO PART THREE

P3I.1   What is writing for?

It is easy to take the ability to write for granted. For many it is an everyday feature of life – from making lists to sending emails – but for those who cannot write, it is a precious skill that opens the way to a better life. Being able to write means being able to express one's identity (Cremin and Myhill, 2012; Ryan and Barton, 2012; Cummins, 2016) and to communicate thoughts, emotions and insights. Being able to write is crucial not only to a productive working life but also to a sense of social belonging and self-expression. However, although there are records of writing dating back to ancient times, it is only over the past 150 years that writing has been seen as something that is within the scope of ordinary people and taught in schools (Chamberlain, 2016). More recently, with the introduction of global communications, writing reaches more people throughout the world. In the (very near) past, writing has been seen as a 'basic' requirement and literacy as only necessary to serve the purposes of being able to do a job. Writing is much more than that. It helps to think through ideas, communicate emotions and thoughts, grapple with difficult issues, cement relationships, create different worlds of the imagination, establish a sense of community and express cultural experience. It is useful, creative, communicative. Any writing curriculum should allow for all these different aspects of writing to be developed and nurtured. However, as with other aspects of English, there are differing views and theories. Many of these seem to be in opposition.

Is writing a noun or a verb? Some people who decide what will be included in writing curricula put more emphasis on writing as a noun – a thing that provides either evidence of the content of learning or proof of technical competence. Spelling, punctuation, handwriting and grammar are seen as technical skills which can be tested discretely, separated from a context of meaning. Writing tests are based on the idea of writing as a noun, something completed to satisfy external demands, produced in a set time, on a given topic; a finished product, marked and assessed to establish children's abilities as writers. On the other hand, writing can be seen as a verb – an activity – something in the process of construction which should be read for the meaning it conveys, and an indicator of the writer's ideas and personal intention to convince, entertain, inform or explain. Of course, the verb 'writing' leads to the noun 'writing'; writing results in writing and they are not in opposition to each other, but complementary.

Which is more important: creativity or structure? Writing is profoundly creative. It allows writers to come to understand their own thoughts through making them concrete. As it can easily be revised, it offers opportunities for spontaneous inventiveness, 'shaping at the point of utterance' (Britton, 1980). However, as with any aspect of communication, writing has to follow certain regularities (structures) for it to be understood by others. Even if it is not punctuated, writing follows the expected sentence structure of the language. For example, the words 'went dog The road the down.' do not make a coherent sentence; reorganised into the expected structure of English they become 'The dog went down the road.' So that no matter how inventive and creative writers wish to be, they necessarily communicate their creative thoughts through the expected structures of the language. Creativity and structure are necessarily complementary: creativity depends on the combination of thought, feeling, experience and action with the means to give expression to innovation through making connections, building new structures.

Which should be given more emphasis: transcription or composition? Some current views about writing (notably in the English national curriculum in England) emphasise transcriptional elements: spelling, punctuation, handwriting, grammar. National testing is carried out at ages 7 and 11 to assess children's competence in these elements of writing. This can mean that children's thoughts, imaginings, opinions and ideas can be seen as secondary. However, as with the other dichotomies, the answer is that both are important, especially in producing final versions of texts. The danger is that over-emphasis on transcriptional aspects of writing may stifle creative experiments in children's writing. Sometimes writing does not need to be correctly spelt or punctuated; for example, in personal notes or shopping lists and in early drafts of longer pieces of writing. And transcriptional elements can always be sorted out in the process of proofreading once the content of a piece of writing is shaped to the writer's satisfaction.

The fact of the matter is that balance is essential: a balance between seeing writing as a process (verb) and as a product (noun); between creativity and structure; between compositional and transcriptional elements. Research evidence suggests that learning to write is most effectively achieved through approaches that balance communicative purpose and technical skills (Medwell *et al.*, 1998; Louden *et al.*, 2005). In teaching writing, it is important to keep that balance and build teaching skills through a principled foundation in order to support developing writers.

P3I.2 Principles

Writing is deeply related to reading and spoken language. It is a complex process involving both composition and transcription and a means of communicating and thinking through ideas, as well as a creative and imaginative process. Writing is not always an individual act; it can be social and collaborative and talk is essential at all stages of the writing process. Discussion is also fundamental in encouraging critical conversations about aspects of language and their effects.

Home language and literacy experience is an important foundation for writing development. Children come to school with implicit knowledge of how language works.

Writing in the twenty-first century involves writing on screen as well as on paper, seeing design as part of the writing process.

Fluency in handwriting is important to free mental capacity for compositional skills.

Grammar is one strand of language study and should be taught and assessed for its contribution to expressing meaning, not as a set of rules.

The best writing teachers are writers themselves.

Writing is not just speech written down, but has a specific structure which is different from speech. Unlike spoken language which is absorbed from the environment of the home and community, writing has to be consciously taught and learned (Vygotsky, 1962).

The teacher's role is crucial in:

- modelling writing for purpose and pleasure
- establishing enthusiasm for writing
- creating a classroom environment that engages and motivates children's potential as writers
- exploring and appreciating the writer's craft through familiarisation with texts
- offering opportunities for children to apply writing skills in purposeful contexts
- providing real and imaginary audiences for writing
- encouraging children to be adventurous with writing, helping them to see that taking risks and making mistakes are essential parts of learning
- drawing on children's enthusiasm for playing with language – rhythm, rhyme, alliteration and assonance – to enrich their writing, particularly of poetry
- teaching spelling in purposeful writing contexts and through a range of explicit strategies
- teaching grammar through rich reading experiences allied to investigation and experimentation with language, crafting it to make meaning
- transforming children's implicit knowledge of grammar to explicit awareness
- modelling the use of appropriate terminology to talk about how writing might be improved in the context of purposeful composition.

Composition: (authorial) involves generating ideas, planning what to write, organising the material for a specific purpose and audience, choosing appropriate language and style, monitoring the process and reviewing content, organisation and expression to polish the writing to a finished piece.

Transcription: (secretarial) involves the mechanics of spelling, punctuation, handwriting/typing and layout.

P3I.3 The writing curriculum

The following list draws together key ideas from the national curricula of England, Northern Ireland, Scotland and Wales. In planning for teaching, you may want to refer also to a specific national curriculum.

For effective writing development, children should be given opportunities to:

- experience a language-rich environment where spoken language, reading and writing are integrated
- participate in modelled, shared, guided and independent writing, including composing on screen
- write for a variety of purposes and readers in a range of forms
- write to explore ideas, emotions and opinions, and communicate them factually and imaginatively
- enjoy writing
- play with language – rhythm, rhyme, alliteration and assonance – to enrich their writing
- use writing to help shape ideas for non-written outcomes – for example, drama or presentations

Figure 3I.1 The writing environment

- understand, use and extend their range of vocabulary by investigating and experimenting with language
- talk about and plan what they are going to write
- check their work in relation to specific criteria
- write without prompting, making their own decisions about form and content
- organise, structure, design and present ideas and information using traditional and digital means
- use appropriate vocabulary and terminology to discuss, consider and evaluate their own work and that of others
- develop strategies for editing and proofreading their own writing
- develop increasing competence in using written standard English
- use a variety of strategies to spell accurately
- develop increasing competence in the use of spelling, grammar and punctuation
- use a legible and cursive style of handwriting.

References

Britton, J. (1980) Shaping at the point of utterance, in A. Freedman and I. Pringle (eds) *Reinventing the Rhetorical Tradition*. Conway, AR: L&S books, pp. 61–65.

Chamberlain, L. with contributions from Kerrigan-Draper, E. (2016) *Inspiring Writing in Primary Schools*. London: SAGE.

Cremin, T. and Myhill, D. (2012) *Writing Voices: Creating communities of writers*. Abingdon: Routledge.

Cummins, J. (2016) Conference keynote speech 'Individualistic and Social Orientations to Literacy Research: Bringing Voices Together?' at the United Kingdom Literacy Association International Conference *Literacy, Equality and Diversity: Bringing voices together*, 8–10 July.

Louden, W., Rohl, M., Barrat-Pugh, C., Brown, C., Cairney, T., Elderfield, J., House, H., Meiers, M., Rivaland, J. and Rowe, K. J. (2005) In teachers' hands: Effective literacy teaching practices in the early years of schooling, *Australian Journal of Language and Literacy*, 28 (3) pp. 173–252.

Medwell, J., Wray, D., Poulson, L. and Fox, R. (1998) *Effective Teachers of Literacy.* Exeter: University of Exeter for the Teacher Training Agency.

Ryan, M. and Barton, G. (2012) The spatialized practices of teaching writing in elementary schools: Diverse students shaping discoursal selves, *Research in the Teaching of English*, 42 (4) pp. 387–434.

Vygotsky, L. (trans. 1962) *Thought and Language.* Cambridge, MA: MIT Press.

CHAPTER 11
WHAT WRITING INVOLVES

This chapter covers:

- Theories of writing development
- Teachers as writers
- Teachers' writing histories
- The range of writing: Type, medium, purpose, readership and function
- Pupils' perceptions of writing
- Early writing development
- Diversity and inclusion

11.1 Theories of writing development

As the Introduction to this Part explains, writing serves many purposes. It is both personal and social, reflecting individual ideas and beliefs as well as those expressing the community and culture of the writer. Theories of writing development have sought to explain how individual, social and cultural aspects of writing contribute to the writer's repertoire. Writing development is a complex process and theories reveal different emphases on the inner processes of the mind and social and cultural influences on writing. Some focus is on the role of the teacher and others on text construction.

Cognitive

For cognitive theorists (Flower and Hayes, 1981; Bereiter and Scardamalia, 1987), working in North America, writing is a problem-solving activity. Hayes (1996) developed a model of skilled writing which describes the interaction between the writer's internal thought processes and the context for writing, although he places more emphasis on what happens in the writer's head. Graham (2010) identifies three key aspects of Hayes' model of becoming a competent writer:

1 Developing the strategic processes of planning, drafting, evaluating and revising text.
2 Having a sense of competence and a positive disposition towards writing.
3 Acquiring knowledge of a repertoire of types of writing, the needs of a reader and the topics addressed.

Later, Hayes presented a more developed theory highlighting the importance of working memory to effective writing (Hayes, 2006). For developing writers to attain competence, transcription skills such as spelling and handwriting need to become automatic (see section 13.5) because, until they are mastered, they take up a great deal of mental energy and so get in the way of other thought processes such as planning, evaluating and revising (McCutchen, 1988; Myhill and Jones, 2009). Drawing on developments in neuroscience, Berninger and Richards (2012) also emphasise the role of working memory, although they point out that most neuroscience has focused on sentence-level writing so that further research is needed about composing longer stretches of text. To deal with the problem of working memory getting in the way of fluent composition, teachers may encourage young writers to produce sentences orally before writing or to ask more fluent writers to explain their writing intentions in terms of style, form, genre before committing ideas to paper.

> **Cognitive:** related to conscious mental activities such as thinking, understanding, learning and remembering.
>
> **Sociocognitive:** describes integrated mental and social aspects of processes or systems.

Sociocognitive

Sociocognitive theories of writing see writing development as combining knowledge of social conventions in writing and individual problem solving. So that, for example, while a young writer might know that instructions follow a particular pattern, it is still up to the individual writer to think through how best to present the specific information. To Flower (1994), the skills needed to become effective writers include: being able to understand what the task requires; to plan, organise and revise; to construct meaning; to use or modify conventions; and, when faced with new forms of text, to be able to work out how to make sense of them. Social cognitive theory sees self-regulation as important, working through forethought, performance and self-reflection (Zimmerman, 2000). In self-regulatory theory, feedback is important, so that response from the reader as well as the teacher, and the writer's own reflections, contribute to development.

The writing process

The process approach grew in response to a view of writing as a set of separate skills which could be ticked off on a checklist. The process approach (Graves, 1983; Smith, 1982) saw the environment for writing as crucial, including rich reading resources as models; in addition, publishing, displaying and celebrating writing was an essential part of the process. Donald Graves was a major influence on the adoption of this approach with the idea of the *Writer's Workshop* where children and teachers worked together on composition. The teacher, and the teacher's subject knowledge, was key and the teacher should also be a writer (see section 11.2 below). The process approach influenced the first National Curriculum in England and Wales (DfEE, 1988), which included a writing process of planning, drafting, revising and proofreading leading to presentation of writing. Graves was clear that choice was important for developing writers (Graves, 1983) and that supporting writing should not be a programme of dictated themes but of skilled teacher intervention based on conversations with, and observations of, the young writer.

Smith (1982) made a distinction between composing and transcribing. The compositional skills of writing are related to communicating ideas and making choices about structuring the text and selecting vocabulary – the big shapes of writing. The transcriptional elements are to do with the technical skills associated with handwriting, spelling and punctuation – the smaller details. Chamberlain (2016) sees the connection as when writers 'bring together ideas *about* a piece of writing – *the compositional skills* – and skills *for* the writing – *the transcriptional skills*' (Chamberlain, 2016: 13). In distinguishing between these two aspects of writing, Smith (1982) argued that since over-attention to transcription can get in the way of compositional skills, these, and the creation of meaning, should be the priority for teaching and the transcriptional skills should be taught in the context of the composition.

Genre theory

Australian genre theory developed partly in response to the perceived 'looseness' of the process approach (Freedman and Medway, 1994; Martin, 1997; Christie, 1997) placing writing firmly within the social context. It grew from the work of the linguist Michael Halliday (1978), who describes three kinds of function involved in language: the *ideational* function, which represents the ideas, thoughts and concepts of the speaker/writer; the *interpersonal* function, which reflects social interactions and relationships (audience); and the *textual* function, which puts the ideational and the interpersonal into the shape of a recognisable text. These three elements work together (see Figure 11.1).

IDEATIONAL   **INTERPERSONAL**

TEXTUAL

text form/organisation   sentences/vocabulary

Figure 11.1 Halliday's language functions

The intention of genre theory was to move children away from simply recounting events (do it then write about it) to more developed use of a range of different non-fiction text types: report, explanation, procedure, discussion and narrative. Critics of genre theory argue that tying down types of writing to definitions of specific identifiable characteristics is likely to lead to instrumental teaching (Barrs, 1991; Cairney, 1992). To suggest that there is a catalogue of genres which can be introduced, practised and perfected can lead to the worst kind of checklist approach to teaching writing. One of the key arguments is that learning to write consists not of putting together different 'skills' but of gradual consolidation of experiences which are visited and revisited throughout schooling and, indeed, life. Since writing changes with time, even mature writers continue to learn and develop their expertise as new forms of text emerge; for example, texting, blogging, wikis and other texts associated with digital media.

For a definition of scaffolding see section 2.8.

Writing as design

This approach sees the writer as 'not only a creative thinker and problem solver but also a designer' (Sharples, 1999: 10). A designer who uses materials such as wood, metal, plastics or fabric might start the design process with questions such as: *I want to make xxx. What are the best kinds of materials to use? How do I put it together so that it works?* Then, as the object is taking shape, the designer constantly monitors the process to see if the different parts articulate well together, if the object actually works. When a prototype is produced, the designer tries it out to see if it is fit for purpose and modifies it in the light of those trials. Finally, when all the parts seem to be working well together, the final details are applied and the object is seen as complete and worthy of the attention of others.

When this process is applied to writing, the parallels are clear: *I want to write a set of instructions (or a poem). What is the best way to use words and layout to do that? How can I put it together so that the writing is clear to the reader?* When drafting, the writer constantly monitors the language used, looking back and making small adjustments to vocabulary or punctuation. When there is a finished draft, it might be offered to a friend to read, or the writer reads with a critical eye, to see if it actually communicates what was intended and makes final modifications to enhance the effect. Finally, the writing is proofread and polished so that it can go public. For Sharples, seeing writing as design is liberating. Pushing the design metaphor further, he points out that graphic or product designers work in teams of colleagues who contribute ideas, reactions and evaluations that help move the design process forward, so writers seen as designers work in a collaborative and supportive community. The metaphor of design also carries with it implications of the visual and other multimodal elements of creation (see Chapter 16).

Multimodal

Combining elements of different modes:

- performance – gesture, movement, posture, facial expression
- images – moving and still; photographic, drawn, painted, computer-generated, etc.
- sound – spoken words, sound effects, music and silence
- writing – including font, graphics and layout
- duration – shot length, sequence, rhythm and transitions (Bearne and Bazalgette, 2010: 7).

Multiliteracies

Multiliteracies perspectives (Cope and Kalantzis, 2000; Kress, 1997) see writing or multi-modal composition as matter of transformation where writers take all the resources available to them (personal, cultural and intellectual) and transform them to create new meanings. In an extensive study of children under five making meaning through play, drawing and writing, Kress (1997) describes how children, even at a very young age, use available resources – 'what is to hand' – in their urge to express their ideas. This includes an element of choice: the young writer/multimodal text composer chooses to select, combine and deploy available resources (ideas, vocabulary, knowledge of texts) to create a new text. A multiliteracies approach sees writing as part of situated practice, which is built on a learner's own interests and knowledge. The young writer draws on home, school and community language and literacy experience. The teacher's role is to scaffold learning and give explicit guidance in order to develop young writer's choices and control over their writing.

Situated practice: specific language and literacy practices associated with learners' different roles based on background and experience. It can also apply to ways in which texts are used or developed in different cultural settings (Street, 1993).

Situated practice includes consideration of the relationship between home and school literacies, noting the crucial importance of home experiences of language and literacy; for example, families' 'ways with words' (Heath, 1983), children's funds of knowledge (Moll, 1992) or their language and literacy assets (Cremin et al., 2014). However, Kostouli warns that: 'It is well known that out of school literacies may not always be validated in school contexts' (Kostouli, 2009: 110). Marsh (2005, 2009) has researched children's experience of popular cultural texts since they often act as models and examples for children's writing. She argues that these texts make a greater contribution to literacy development than may be at first thought, since children take a critical stance towards even their most favourite popular cultural texts as they draw on them for their writing:

This is not to suggest that schools should be moving away from a focus on the written word. Far from it. Traditional texts and practices are still a central feature on the lives of many children and young people. Rather, schools need to broaden the writing curriculum to include these multimodal practices if they are to reflect the out-of-school literacy interests and practices of their pupils.

(Marsh, 2009: 319)

Hornberger (2000) emphasises the value of building on children's home languages in the classroom. There is a wealth of knowledge to be drawn from comparing different languages but there is also a great deal to be gained by the learner from knowing that their home language is valued and validated in the classroom.

Critical literacy

There is sometimes a tension between valuing local literacies while keeping an eye on global literacies (Brandt and Clinton, 2002). There are certain literacies that are locally composed but that rely on global networks (Pahl and Rowsell, 2012); for example, emails and texting, presentation software or wikis, blogs. To Janks also, it is not enough to attempt to take account of home language and literacy resources; part of a broader view of language and literacy diversity is to take a critical literacy perspective:

> Unfortunately, there is no point in encouraging writers to exploit all their linguistic resources and to bring their 'community funds of knowledge' (Moll, 1992) and 'ways with words' into the centre, unless simultaneously we work to make the centre more inclusive.

(Janks, 2009: 134)

This has important implications for teachers of writing who seek genuine opportunities for inclusion.

> **Critical literacy:** based on the work of Paulo Freire (1972), it is about education for change, taking into account the relationship between 'the word and the world' – the local and the global – in terms of power, identity, difference and access to knowledge and resources. See Janks (2013) www.lh.umu.se/digitalAssets/122/122861_critical_literacy_in_teaching_eduinq_vol4_no2_june13_225–242.pdf (accessed 1 May 2017).

11.2   Teachers as writers

Although in the UK greater attention is being paid to teachers as writers and their role in demonstrating, modelling and supporting writing is seen as critical to children's writing development, many teachers do not seem confident about their own writing abilities. This is likely to influence their writing identities and may restrain their enthusiasm and motivation to teach writing effectively (Grainger, 2005; Cremin and Myhill, 2012; Cremin and Oliver, 2016). Cremin notes that as a consequence of fear of exposing their writing in the public forum of the classroom, teachers:

may pre-write the haiku or tanka for example in the privacy of their own homes, 'pretending' to demonstrate the act of composition in school. Others may simply avoid demonstration writing, in which teachers compose and think aloud as they do so, preferring rather to engage only in shared writing, when the teacher as scribe records the children's suggestions in a joint composition.

(Cremin, 2011: 10)

Cremin found that 'through writing, sharing, evaluating and publishing their own writing, the teachers came to recognise their vulnerabilities as writers and the essential struggle and perseverance required to craft effective written prose' (*ibid.*).

When teachers write with and for children, they offer a strong model of what it is to be a writer. In talking through the decisions they make as they share writing with the children, they signal that writing is a thoughtful process, and in asking for ideas, that it can be a collaborative process. Most of all, in openly revising and redrafting work they show that writing does not need to be right the first time and that it can be improved and polished over time.

Being a writing teacher in the classroom may involve:

- demonstrating writing to the whole class
- writing alongside children during activities
- scribing for children's compositions (often whole class)
- having writing conversations to support children (individual or small groups)
- talking about personal writing experiences and strategies.

It may not be easy, but being a writing teacher is a powerful way to teach writing – and benefits from admitting to the class some of the difficulties and dilemmas of a writer so that the children see that writing is something that needs to be worked on and does not spring fully formed from the mind or the pen. Some schools have found that setting up writing groups where teachers can talk about and experiment with writing can be beneficial (Smith and Wrigley, 2015) (see also the National Writing Project on www.nwp.org.uk/ (accessed 1 May 2017)). If teachers' confidence and motivation as writers contributes to them being effective writers, then the same must apply to children. Motivation is related to self-perceptions, self-belief, a sense of competence as a writer and ability to cope with the demands of writing tasks (Boscolo and Gelati, 2007). These are critical elements in finding a writing voice (King, 2000; Cremin and Myhill, 2012).

Terri, a newly qualified teacher, explained how she felt when she first started to demonstrate writing with her class of 7 and 8 year olds:

I felt a bit silly at first, talking about what I was writing, and, to be honest, I wasn't always sure why I was choosing a particular word or expression. Gradually, though, I started to get a bit more confident. I think that what helped me was quite early in the term, we were doing poetry and I wanted the children not to come out with rhymes like on birthday cards. We'd been reading poems about families and I could very easily think about my Mum and my brothers! I had thought about it a bit at home but I didn't over-prepare. I just went with the flow, and I was so keen to get the children to help me write something that wasn't rhyming just for the sake of rhyming, that I started to get more confident. I quite enjoy sharing writing now.

For this teacher, taking the plunge and having something to write about helped her to start sharing her writing process with the class. Teachers' writing identity is key in supporting writers in the classroom (Locke, 2017). But it is also worth remembering that there are other adults in school and related to the school who can act as writing models. A survey of parents may well reveal some who spend quite a lot of their time writing, either for work or for pleasure. It might be also worth surveying all the adults in the school to see what different kinds of writing they have to do during the course of a few days (see the Writing Diary on pp. 288–289). Sharing these insights with the children and asking the adults to talk to them about their writing can help young writers understand the range of purposes and audiences for writing.

11.3   Teachers' writing histories

When teachers reflect on their own writing histories and experience, they come to see that they are, in fact, quite experienced writers. A starting point can be creating 'writing rivers' reflecting on their early memories of learning to write and significant experiences both at home and at school. Reflecting on these helps consider the implications for teaching. In Figures 11.2, 11.3 and 11.4, Claire, Charlie and Emma record key experiences in their writing histories.

For Claire, a left-handed writer, handwriting was always a matter of pride to her as well as a high grade for a story written for GCSE. Charlie struggled with reading and writing until she was diagnosed as dyslexic in the later stages of secondary school. For Emma, writing at home was often more rewarding than at school as she was an avid card and letter writer when she was young. All these teacher writers have a range of positive experience to draw on as well as being aware of the negative effects of some school experiences.

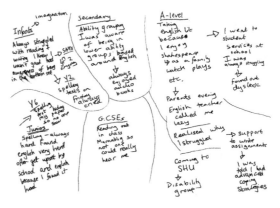

Figure 11.2 Claire's writing river

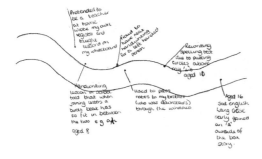

Figure 11.3 Charlie's writing river

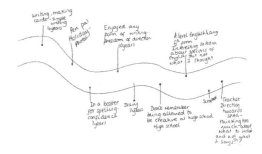

Figure 11.4 Emma's writing river

Activity 11.1
Rivers of writing – reflective journal/blog/pairs/group

Make your own writing river, noting the highs and lows – times when you were proud and pleased with a piece of writing and times when you felt upset or disappointed with response to your writing. It is worth sharing these experiences with others, just to see how similar/different your experiences as writers have been.

Listen to website resources W11.1, W11.2 and W11.3 where Claire, Charlie and Emma talk about their early experiences of writing. Do any of these strike a chord? (There are transcripts in website resources W11.1a, W11.2a and W11.3a.)

Make a few notes about the implications for classroom practice of the experiences you have described, shared and listened to. You might find that, like Emma, there is an over-emphasis on the technicalities of writing, or that, unlike Charlie's experience, you have observed some good practice in supporting children who struggle with writing.

11.4   The range of writing: Type, medium, purpose, readership and function

Despite concerns expressed by teachers, most are accomplished writers, many having written examinations successfully. Also, in everyday writing tasks they make fast and flexible choices about how to use writing to do the jobs they want it to do. A list of personal writing done over a week or so can be a useful way to identify the range of purposes and readers for writing.

Activity 11.2
Writing diary over a few days – Reflective journal/blog /pairs/group

Complete the charts in website resource W11.4 with all the different kinds of writing you have done over a few days – a weekend and a working day can give the widest range. Figure 11.5 gives you a few examples. When you have completed the charts, talk it over with someone else, discussing how the purpose and the readership for writing might make a difference to the way people write. For example, if the writing is to go public, it will be more carefully proofread than a shopping list or a note on the kitchen table. What about punctuation? In a formal piece of writing, there is usually less – and less varied – punctuation. In an email to a friend or family member there may be all kinds of extra punctuation and emoticons designed to show the tone of voice that would be used if the email were spoken.

Have a look at the lists of purposes for writing and the functions of writing below. Note how many of these you have covered in your writing diary for a few days.

Add to your previous notes about classroom implications. What insights have you gained from looking at the range of writing you and your colleagues do over a few days? You may find that the range and the way you have varied the writing according to audience suggest that you may be a more versatile writer than you first thought. You can use this expertise in the classroom when you demonstrate and model writing for the children; for example, when you write an explanation you can voice your thoughts about the best order to put information in – and even show how to insert things you had forgotten at first.

Type of writing	Medium	Purpose	Who read it?
shopping list	narrow strip of paper	reminder	me
email	computer	keeping in touch	my sister
lesson plans	computer and paper	getting organised	me, my teacher, my tutor
note on kitchen table	back of envelope	instructions	the family

Figure 11.5 Writing diary: Types, media, purpose and readership

Looking at writing completed over a few days highlights the different purposes and functions writing serves in social and cultural experience.

Purposes for writing
- *formative:* reflective and exploratory writing helps shape and develop ideas – particularly in group work
- *informative:* explains ideas, conveys knowledge or opinions
- *performative, expressive or presentational:* more 'public' and shaped writing communicates opinions, feelings or what has been learned
- *reflective and evaluative:* writing helps to reflect on learning (and writing) and review progress.

Functions of writing
- *social:* establishing, confirming and changing personal relationships
- *communicative:* helping to shape and share ideas, experiences and feelings
- *cultural:* reflecting home and community experience of texts and media from an early age
- *cognitive:* developing concepts and constructing knowledge.

11.5 Pupils' perceptions of writing

Finding out about what children think about writing – at home and at school – can be powerfully informative to a classroom teacher. Liz Chamberlain (2016) reports on a study of children's perceptions of writing carried out by *Everybody Writes* (www.booktrust.org.uk/programmes/primary/everybody-writes/ (accessed 1 May 2017)). This informed teachers about how to adapt and develop their own approaches to teaching writing in the light of their children's responses. Generally, responses show that children worry about transcriptional skills and the effort of writing, but that getting ideas is also a challenge (see website resource W11.5 for fuller details of the findings).

In a Birmingham school, children from early to upper primary noted what they thought when their teacher asked them to write. Most were very keen and the youngest wrote or drew their responses (see Figures 11.6, 11.7 and 11.8). One 7-year-old girl noted:

> *I think I have to remember all of the information that I need to use. I also think where do I put all of my punctuation?*

While a Year 3 boy responded:

> *I think my teacher feels ever so excited!*

And another 7-year-old boy said:

> *Oh no. My hands are going to ake.*

By upper primary, there was noticeable enthusiasm for writing:

> *What I think is that I feel quite excited because I enjoy writing, especially stories. I enjoy this concept because I like the way we can let out our imagination. English is my strongest subject and our teacher, Mrs Winters always does interesting work. Sometimes we do assessments and sometimes the teacher writes with us.*
>
> *Boy, aged 10*

Another boy in the same class was equally convinced about using his imagination (Figure 11.9).

Children know that their work has to be presentable (Figure 11.10).

Activity 11.3
Discovering children's perceptions about writing – reflective journal/ blog

Using Liz Chamberlain's account of a survey of children's perceptions of writing, and the perceptions survey on the website (see website resource W11.5), ask the class you are working with (or a group of children in the class) about their perceptions of writing. If the children are young, you may want to scribe for them.

Were there any surprises? Reading through the responses, what ideas do they give you about what you might focus on in teaching writing? For example, were there responses which suggest the children think that transcription (spelling, punctuation, handwriting) is more important than the content of their writing? Have a look at the writing curriculum on pages 277–278 and jot down any thoughts so that you can remember them when you are planning to teach writing.

Figure 11.6 What do you think when your teacher asks you to write? Boy, aged 6

Figure 11.7 What do you think when your teacher asks you to write? Boy, aged 7

Figure 11.8 What do you think when your teacher asks you to write? Girl, aged 5

Figure 11.9 What do you think when your teacher asks you to write? Boy, aged 10

Figure 11.10 What do you think when your teacher asks you to write? Girl, aged 10

11.6 Early writing development

Over recent years it has become important to give value to children's home knowledge of language and literacy. It is not just that homes and communities offer print, digital or pictorial experience which can be models of possible future text-making, nor is it just about the important links between early experience of the shapes of spoken texts such as conversation, song, story, explanation and the later ability to write such texts. It is because making meaning is central to writing. This is evident in children's early mark-making, the beginnings of writing. Vygotsky (1962) sees early writing as a development from 'drawing speech' into writing letters and words which carry meaning. Children learn very quickly that writing can do things for them – that it has a function; notes and greetings cards carry messages, for example. They are also fascinated by patterns of language as they learn to write, noticing phonic links or the shapes and length of words. When children see a relationship between the symbols, they write down and the words which people say, they are 'on the path to writing' (Kress, 1997: xviii). Rowe (2009) emphasises young children's writing intentions as being more significant than focusing on the conventions of formal written language, seeing the use of a range of modes as important to children's meaning-making.

Clay (1975), Holdaway (1979) and Ferreiro and Teberosky (1982) give examples of how young children experiment, play with and explore writing, hypothesising about the ways that the letters represent meaning. Lancaster (2007), noting that few studies have been made of children's writing before the age of 3, describes research into children as young as 18 months old discriminating between writing, number and drawing. Goodman (1986) characterises children's early writing as following three principles:

> the *functional* principle: the idea that writing can serve a purpose, has a function for the writer, for example, putting up a notice saying *Keep out of Jo's room!*;
>
> the *linguistic* principle: the idea that writing is a system which is organised into letters and words; even before writing recognisable words children can be seen to separate their letter strings into chunks corresponding to what a word looks like on the page;
>
> the *relational* principle: this is when children begin to make the connection between what they write on the page (or published print) and spoken words, realising that the written system carries meaning.
>
> (Goodman 1986: 15)

Mark, aged 4, left this piece of writing (Figure 11.11) in the classroom and the teacher was astute enough to keep it (National Writing Project 1989: 21–22). Next day she asked Mark what it said and he explained: 'bread, potatoes, eggs, rice crispies, marge and baked beans'. His mother said that he often helped her to make lists at home and that she involved him in deciding what they needed to buy. This single example shows that Mark knows that writing can serve a purpose (functional principle) and has a grasp of linguistic principles because he separates words on his list and he uses initial sounds for his writing and writes letters to represent sounds (relational principle).

Pascalle is a 5-year-old English/Punjabi speaker-writer. She has written a list of washing for the launderette role-play area and a notice signed by the manager (with notes about it written in conversation with her teacher) (Figure 11.12). Her knowledge of the functions of

Figure 11.11 Mark's shopping list   **Figure 11.12** Pascalle's launderette writing

writing are very clear as she writes a list, a notice and a signature – all of which are differently set out – with the flourish of the signature indicating very clearly the kinds of text knowledge which Goodman outlines.

In two carefully researched books, Dyson (1989, 1993) outlines research over three years in two San Francisco schools documenting the writing of children from Kindergarten to Grade 3. She moves discussion about children's early writing from focusing solely on individual development to a more social and collaborative arena, describing how each of the teachers created opportunities for children to learn to write in a classroom community of writers.

It is also worth remembering that many children now come to writing via digital technologies, so that it is important to include keyboarding skills (see section 13.10) in any analysis of children's early writing development (Flewitt *et al.*, 2015). Chapter 16 looks at children's use of digital technology in more detail.

Activity 11.4
From early mark-making to forming accurate words and sentences – pairs/group

Get hold of some early writing by children up to the age of 5. If this is difficult, use the examples in website resource W11.6. See if you can find evidence of Goodman's three principles of writing development: the functional, the relational and the linguistic. Have a look at the curriculum on pages 277–278. Discuss and note (and keep for later) the implications for teaching writing in the early years. For example, how might you provide opportunities for very young writers to write for a variety of purposes, or for them to enjoy writing?

11.7   Diversity and inclusion

Diversity is one of the greatest assets – and challenges – in the classroom. Some of the most obvious aspects are gender, language or cultural differences, but even within those descriptive categories there are differences. For example, boys (or girls) may be reflective, technically oriented, sporty. Children speaking the same community language have their own individual qualities and interests. Some children are physically challenged, find learning easy or have problems with social relationships or have cognitive conditions such as dyspraxia or dyslexia. When it comes to writing, diversity can mean young writers who:

- worry about making mistakes
- love writing
- cannot keep up with their own thoughts (and need a scribe?)
- can write in more than one language
- do not know what to write
- are only beginning to write in English
- do not achieve as well as might be expected
- always finish first
- write accurately but without voice
- find the physical act of writing difficult
- are better at talking than writing
- have problems with the technicalities of spelling and/or handwriting
- write fluently and well.

It can sometimes be tricky to ensure that writers of all kinds feel both secure and challenged. And context will make a difference, too. A child who is unsure in one curriculum area may be very assured and self-motivated in another. Catering for the differing needs of the writers in the classroom means observing and noting individual differences, then providing a flexible enough writing curriculum for all of them to make progress.

Activity 11.5
Identifying diverse needs – reflective journal/blog

Thinking about the class you are most familiar with, using website resource W11.7, note any individuals who might fit any of the categories. Of course, you may not have all of these kinds of writer in your class, or there may be other characteristics not listed here, in which case, add them to the list. Add to your notes about implications for practice, considering what these children's needs mean you have to do to support and extend them.

You might use the children's writing perceptions responses to help decide ways forward. Or you might want to have a writing conference with an individual child, talking about things that help them write or stop them writing confidently and fluently. If you do, try asking them: 'What do you think would help you to get better at writing?' Sometimes they have useful ideas!

You will also find these reflections useful for Chapter 15.

Biliterate (and multiliterate) learners

For any child, acquiring written language is a highly complex matter and it would seem even more so if a child is tackling two script systems at the same time. However, Kenner (2004) gathers a wealth of evidence to argue that rather than children growing up confused by multilingualism, they have particular strengths in dealing with language and literacy. Her research shows that by encountering different language systems, children 'sharpen' their ideas about how language works, explaining that 'biliterate children widen their horizons with respect to the marking and placing of marks on the page' (Kenner, 2004: 73). Kenner argues that babies and very young children develop by looking for and establishing patterns and connections. Rather than seeing bilingual and biliterate children dealing with 'multiple worlds', Kenner prefers to describe them as inhabiting 'simultaneous worlds' as they seek commonalities and differences between the different language systems of home and school literacy.

Longitudinal studies are rare, but Hilary Minns (1990, 1993, 1997), who researched the literacy lives of 4 year olds in the English Midlands, later followed up some of the children when they were 10 and then when they were 15. One of these – Gurdeep – had experienced rich home literacy experiences as a young child: reading the sacred Sikh text, the *Guru Granth Saheb,* with his mother, and hearing her tell folk tales in Panjabi, writing to relatives and having their letters read to him, copying his parents when he saw them writing, and reading stories in English with his father and at school. As a 10 year old, Gurdeep was reading a whole variety of texts from *The Concise Oxford Dictionary* to Teenage Mutant Ninja Turtles comics and his father's engineering books, drawing on both his languages to broaden his literacy learning. At 15, Gurdeep was heavily involved in academic-related reading and writing in English but still found time to read teenage horror novels and write business letters for his mother on the computer. Also, through lessons at the temple, he had already passed GCSE and 'A' level Panjabi by the age of 12 (usually taken at ages 16 and 18 in England).

Gurdeep's strong experience of Panjabi language and literacy had developed alongside his high level of English literacy. Kenner and Gregory comment:

> This development had been made possible by the strength of family and community support as well as mainstream school input. The cognitive and cultural advantages of biliteracy would accrue to Gurdeep, as we hope they could accrue to many other potentially biliterate children.
>
> (Kenner and Gregory, 2003: 187)

They argue that acceptance of biliteracy should be part of mainstream classroom activities, including monolingual children in language exploration. Further, community classes in home languages should support the development of cultural understanding. They point out that when schools see the child as a whole person, with linguistic strengths rather than 'problems', and give status to minority literacies as a valued part of mainstream education, there will be all-round benefits for self-esteem and learning for monoliterate as well as biliterate children.

Boys and writing

In English-speaking countries, concern has been expressed by policy makers about the relatively low performance of boys in writing compared with girls. In England, this led to a three-year government-funded project, *Raising Boys' Achievement* (Younger *et al.*, 2005), taking a detailed look at boys' writing (as well as reading and spoken language). By the end of the project, improved attitudes and performance in writing were shown to develop when children had consistent opportunities for different kinds of talk, including drama, throughout their schooling. Improvements came when teachers:

- organised literacy sessions to incorporate a range of spoken language opportunities – formative, informative, performative and evaluative (see Chapters 4 and 15)
- emphasised talk and time to reflect – finding ways to talk about learning and literacy
- saw the importance of 'companionable' writing through using response partners and group work
- were prepared to take risks in bringing more creativity to literacy sessions
- wrote themselves, modelling writing and showing how it is constructed
- used a variety of activities – at times these might be short, specific, focused writing tasks; at other times they would allow time to return to writing over a period of time
- balanced attention to accuracy and neatness with a sense of writing purpose and knowing when it is important to 'get writing right'
- did not ask the children to do writing for the sake of it – just to prove they had read/learned something – but required less writing, but writing which mattered and was relevant to the learners
- operated more transparent assessment and marking with targets shared and negotiated with the pupils
- had some sense of how literacy is perceived and supported at home.

See website resource W11.8 for more background on boys, girls and literacy and the *Raising Boys' Achievement* project.

Summary

Several major theories have informed current approaches to teaching writing: cognitive theories, focusing on individual development of skills and strategies; socio-cognitive theories, which build on these but emphasise the role of social factors in shaping and developing writing; theories which extend the social elements to include community experience; genre theory, which identifies a range of text types to be taught; approaches to teaching which emphasise the role of the teacher as guide and supporter in the writing process. More recently there has been emphasis on writing as design, seeing the construction of meaning much like the construction of a material object. Similarly, there has been recent focus on teachers as writers and the significance of having a writing teacher as a role model. Most recently, multiliteracies and critical literacy perspectives emphasise the situated nature of writing and its role in transforming experience.

The chapter identifies the range and repertoire of writing: text type, medium, purpose, readership and function. Research into pupils' perceptions of writing can inform teachers about how to shape classroom approaches to writing and a brief outline of early writing development shows how even before they are writing recognisable words, children know a great deal about the purposes and audiences for writing. The chapter concludes with a section on diversity and inclusion, with a short section on boys and writing.

Recommended reading

Cremin, T. and Myhill, D. (2012) Chapter 1: Laying the foundations for teaching writing, in *Writing Voices: Creating communities of writers*. Abingdon: Routledge, pp. 11–26. This chapter outlines a range of theories of teaching writing drawn from international sources, but offers a particularly strong section on Creativity and Writing. **Advanced**

Chamberlain, L. with contributions from Kerrigan-Draper, E. (2016) *Inspiring Writing in Primary Schools*. London: SAGE. Chapters 1–4 of this accessible, practical book, focusing on the UK, gives helpful background to the issues in this chapter.

Dombey, H. (2013) *Teaching Writing: What the evidence says*. Leicester: United Kingdom Literacy Association. This short, comprehensive booklet draws together recent research from the UK and internationally, about effective writing teaching. One of its strengths is the extensive reference list, guiding readers towards the details of specific research projects. **Advanced**

Janks, H. (2013) Critical literacy in teaching and research, *Education Enquiry*, 4 (2) pp. 225–242. This accessible and important online article describes Janks' interdependent framework for critical literacy education, drawing on Mexican and South African experience.

Kenner, C. and Gregory, E. (2003) Becoming biliterate, in N. Hall, J. Larson and J. Marsh (eds) *Handbook of Early Childhood Literacy*. London: SAGE, pp. 178–188. An accessible and thorough international compliation of the issues surrounding the early acquisition of more than one language. **Advanced**

Pahl, K. and Kelly, S. (2005) Family literacy as a third space between home and school: some case studies of practice, *Literacy*, 39 (2) pp. 91–96. The article outlines Family Literacy Projects which included literacy and language activities with parents and children in school and nursery settings in the UK. Parents and children collaborated on joint projects including book making, storytelling, the making of visual artefacts and reading and writing activities. Of particular interest to those working with very young children.

Richmond, J. (2015) *Writing 3 to 7* in the series *English, Language and Literacy 3–19*. Leicester: Owen Education and United Kingdom Literacy Association. This succinct booklet has a detailed analysis of developing writing from 3 years upwards as well as an excellent chapter drawing together recent theoretical perspectives on teaching early writing. While the research is international, the focus is largely on England and Wales. For those working with younger children, Chapters 3 and 4 are particularly recommended.

Rowe, D. W. (2009) Early Written Communication, in R. Beard, D. Myhill, J. Riley and M. Nystrand (eds) *The SAGE Handbook of Writing Development*. London: SAGE, pp. 213–231. Provides comprehensive summary outlines of key theories of early writing development including relevant international research. **Advanced**

References

Barrs, M. (1991) 'Genre theory: What's it all about?', *Language Matters*, 1991–92 (1) pp. 9–16.

Bearne, E. and Bazalgette, C. (eds) (2010) *Beyond Words: Developing children's response to multimodal texts*. Leicester: United Kingdom Literacy Association.

Bereiter, C. and Scardamalia, M. (1987) *The Psychology of Written Communication*. Hillsdale, NJ: Lawrence Erlbaum.

Berninger, V. W. and Richards, T. L. (2012) The writing brain: Coordinating sensory/motor, language and cognitive systems in working memory, in V. W. Berninger (ed.) *Past, Present, and Future Contributions of Cognitive Writing Research to Cognitive Psychology*. New York: Psychology Press, Taylor and Francis, pp. 537–566.

Boscolio, P. and Gelati, C. (2007) Best practices in promoting motivation for writing, in S. Graham, C. MacArthur, and J. Fitzgerald (eds) *Best Practices in Writing Instruction*. New York: Guilford Press, pp. 202–221.

Brandt, D. and Clinton, K. (2002) The limits of the local: Expanding perspectives of literacy as a social practice, *Journal of Literacy Research*, 34 (3) pp. 337–356.

Cairney, T. (1992) Mountain or mole hill: The genre debate viewed from 'Down Under', *Reading*, 26 (1) pp. 23–29.

Chamberlain, L. with contributions from Kerrigan-Draper, E. (2016) *Inspiring Writing in Primary Schools*. London: SAGE.

Christie, F. (1997) Curriculum macrogenres as forms of initiation into a culture, in F. Christie and J. R. Martin (eds) *Genre and Institutions: Social processes in the workplace and school*. London: Cassell, pp. 134–160.

Clay, M. (1975) *What Did I Write?* Portsmouth, NH: Heinemann.

Cope, B. and Kalantzis, M. (2000) *Multiliteracies: Literacy learning and the design of social futures*. London: Routledge.

Cremin, T. (2011) Teachers as writers, in E. Bearne, L. Chamberlain, T. Cremin and M. Mottram (eds) *Teaching Writing Effectively: Reviewing practice*. Leicester: United Kingdom Literacy Association, pp. 7–10.

Cremin, T. and Myhill, D. (2012) *Writing Voices: Creating communities of writers*. Abingdon: Routledge.

Cremin, T. and Oliver, L. (2016) Teachers as Writers: a systematic review, in *Research Papers in Education*, The Open University Open Research Online.

Cremin, T., Mottram, M., Collins, F., Powell, S. and Drury, R. (2014) *Researching Literacy Lives: Building communities between home and school*. London: Routledge.

Department for Education and Employment (1988) www.legislation.gov.uk/ukpga/1988/40/contents (accessed 9 May 2017)

Dyson, A. H. (1989) *Multiple Worlds of Child Writers: Friends learning to write*. New York: Teachers College Press.

Dyson, A. H. (1993) *Social Worlds of Children Learning to Write*. New York: Teachers College Press.

Ferreiro, E. and Teberosky, A. (1982) *Literacy Before Schooling*. Exeter, NH: Heinemann Education.

Flewitt, R., Messer, D. and Kucirkova, N. (2015) New directions for early literacy in a digital age: The iPad, *Journal of Early Childhood Literacy*, 15 (3) pp. 289–310.

Flower, L. (1994) *The Construction of Negotiated Meaning: A social cognitive theory of writing*. Carbondale: Southern Illinois University Press.

Flower, L. and Hayes, J. (1981) A cognitive process theory of writing, *College Composition and Communication*, 32, pp. 365–386.

Freedman, A. and Medway, P. (1994) *Genre and the New Rhetoric*. London: Taylor and Francis.

Freire, P. (1972) *Cultural Action for Freedom*. Harmondsworth: Penguin.

Goodman, Y. (1986) Writing development in young children, in *Gnosis*. Birmingham: Questions Publishing, pp. 10–17.

Graham, S. (2010) Facilitating writing development, in D. Wyse, R. Andrews and J. Hoffman (eds) *The Routledge International Handbook of English, Language and Literacy Teaching*. Abingdon: Routledge, pp. 125–136.

Grainger, T. (2005) Teachers as writers learning together, *English in Education*, 39 (1) pp. 75–87.

Graves, D. (1983) *Writing: Teachers and children at work*. Portsmouth, NH: Heinemann Educational Books.

Halliday, M. A. K. (1978) *Language as a Social Semiotic: Social interpretation of language and meaning*. London: Hodder Arnold.

Hayes, J. (1996) A new framework for understanding cognition and affect in writing, in M. Levy and S. Ransdell (eds) *The Science of Writing: Theories, methods, individual differences and applications*. Mahwah, NJ: Erlbaum, pp. 1–27.

Hayes, J. R. (2006) New directions in writing theory, in C. MacArthur, S. Graham and J. Fitzgerald (eds) *Handbook of Writing Research*. New York: Guildford Press, pp. 28–40.

Heath, S. B. (1983) *Ways with Words: Language, life and work in communities and classrooms*. Cambridge: Cambridge University Press.

Holdaway, D. (1979) *The Foundations of Literacy*. Sydney: Ashton Scholastic.

Hornberger, N. (2000) Multilingual literacies, literacy practices and the continua of biliteracy, in M. Martin Jones and K. Jones (eds) *Multilingual Literacies: Reading and writing different worlds.* Amsterdam: John Benjamins, pp. 253–368.

Janks, H. (2009) Writing: A critical literacy perspective, in R. Beard, D. Myhill, J. Riley and M. Nystrand (eds) *The SAGE Handbook of Writing Development.* London: SAGE, pp. 126–136.

Janks, H. (2013) Critical literacy in teaching and research, *Education Enquiry,* 4 (2) pp. 225–242.

Kenner, C. (2004) *Becoming Biliterate, Young Children Learning Different Writing Systems.* Stoke-on-Trent: Trentham Books.

Kenner, C. and Gregory, E. (2003) Becoming biliterate, in N. Hall, J. Larson and J. Marsh (eds) *Handbook of Early Childhood Literacy.* London: SAGE, pp. 178–188.

King, C. (2000) Can teachers empower pupils as writers, in J. Davidson and J. Moss (eds) *Issues in English Teaching.* London: Routledge, pp. 23–41.

Kostouli, T. (2009) A sociocultural framework: Writing as social practice, in R. Beard, D. Myhill, J. Riley and M. Nystrand (eds) *The SAGE Handbook of Writing Development.* London: SAGE, pp. 98–116.

Kress, G. (1997) *Before Writing: Rethinking the paths to literacy.* London: Routledge.

Lancaster, L. (2007) Representing the Ways of the World: How children under three start to use syntax in graphic signs, *Journal of Early Childhood Literacy,* 7 (2) pp. 123–154.

Locke, T. (2017) Developing a whole school culture of writing, in T. Cremin and T. Locke (eds) *Writer Identity and the Teaching and Learning of Writing.* London: Routledge.

Marsh, J. (ed.) (2005) *Popular Culture, New Media and Digital Literacy in Early Childhood.* London: Routledge.

Marsh, J. (2009) Writing and popular culture, in R. Beard, D. Myhill, J. Riley and M. Nystrand (eds) *The SAGE Handbook of Writing Development.* London: SAGE, pp. 313–324.

Martin, J. R. (1997) Analysing genre: Functional parameters, in F. Christie and J. R. Martin (eds) *Genre and Institutions: Social processes in the workplace and school.* London: Cassell, pp. 3–39.

McCutchen, D. (1988) Functional automaticity in children's writing: A problem of metacognitive control, *Written Communication,* 5 pp. 306–324.

Minns, H. (1990) *Read It To Me Now!* London: Virago.

Minns, H. (1993) Three ten-year-old boys and their reading, in M. Barrs and S. Pidgeon (eds) *Reading the Difference: Gender and reading in the primary school.* London: Centre for Language in Primary Education, pp. 60–71.

Minns, H. (1997) Gurdeep and Geeta: The making of two readers and the nature of difference. Paper given to the IEDPE (UK) Conference, Hidden Europeans: Working with minority language groups in different school systems, London, 17 October.

Moll, L. (1992) Literacy research in community and classrooms: A sociocultural approach, in R. Beach, J. Green, M. Kamil and T. Shanahan (eds) *Multidisciplinary Perspectives on Literacy Research.* Urbana IL: National Council of Teachers of English, pp. 211–244.

Myhill, D. and Jones, S. (2009) How talk becomes text: Investigating the concept of oral rehearsal in early years' classrooms, *British Journal of Educational Studies,* 57 (3) pp. 265–284.

National Writing Project (1989) *Becoming a Writer.* Walton upon Thames: Nelson.

Pahl, K. and Rowsell, J. (2012) *Literacy and Education: Understanding the new literacy studies in the classroom.* London: Paul Chapman.

Rowe, D. W. (2009) Early written communication, in R. Beard, D. Myhill, J. Riley and M. Nystrand (eds) *The SAGE Handbook of Writing Development.* London: SAGE, pp. 213–231.

Sharples, M. (1999) *How We Write: Writing as creative design.* London: Routledge.

Smith, F. (1982) *Writing and the Writer.* Portsmouth, NH: Heinemann Educational.

Smith, J. and Wrigley, S. (2015) *Introducing Teachers' Writing Groups: Exploring the theory and practice.* Abingdon: Routledge.

Street, B. V. (ed.) (1993) *Cross-Cultural Approaches to Literacy.* Cambridge: Cambridge University Press.

Vygotsky, L. (trans. 1962) *Thought and Language.* Cambridge, MA: MIT Press.

Younger, M. and Warrington, M. with Gray, J., Rudduck, J., McLellan, R., Bearne, E., Kershner, R. and Bricheno, P. (2005) *Raising Boys' Achievement: Research report No. 636.* London: Department for

Education and Skills. http://webarchive.nationalarchives.gov.uk/20130401151715/www.education. gov.uk/publications/eOrderingDownload/RR636.pdf (accessed 1 May 2017)

Zimmermann, B. J. (2000) Attaining self-regulation: A social cognitive perspective, in M. Boekaerts, P. R. Pintrich and M. Zeidner (eds) *Handbook of Self-Regulation*. San Diego, CA: Academic Press, pp. 13–35.

CHAPTER 12

WRITING COMPOSITION

This chapter covers:

- The process of written composition
- Finding a writing voice
- Developing voice in the classroom
- Writing journals
- Making space to write
- Professional writers in schools
- Writing narrative
- Making progress in narrative
- Narrative structure
  - Case study, early primary: Using story maps
  - Case study, middle primary: Using stories to support narrative structure
- Writing non-fiction
- Variations on traditional forms of non-fiction
- Making progress in non-fiction writing
- Scaffolds and writing frames

12.1   The process of written composition

Writing is a cognitively, emotionally and creatively demanding process, involving much more than just a range of skills or techniques. Whenever a writer sets out to compose a text, whether it is a note left on the kitchen table or a formal communication, choices have to be made about:

- what has to be communicated
- who is going to read the text
- how formal the piece should be
- what form the writing should take.

In addition, the writer needs to be able to use a pen or digital technology; know how to get the spelling right (if necessary); know how to punctuate writing so that it makes sense; and write in grammatically recognisable sentences. Finally, the writer needs to be able to read over the piece, checking for sense, for fitness for purpose and audience and for technical accuracy. Richmond (2015) describes three facets of the 'personality' of the writer: *composer, communicator* and *secretary* (see also Halliday's language functions, p. 283). For the composer, writing does not just mean writing down ideas already formed in the head; Richmond points out that 'In the act of writing, writers discover what they mean' (Richmond, 2015: 17). As a communicator, the writer needs to know the effects of the writing on the reader. And the writer has to be a secretary, working within the current writing system, but aware that language is always in a state of change; for example, through global communications media.

Teaching writing composition is a progressive move towards young writers being able to make considered choices about form, register and language (see section 1.1 for an explanation of Vygotsky's Zone of Proximal Development, which describes the move from dependence towards independence in learning and p. 137 for details of Pearson and Gallagher's Gradual Release of Responsibility model – a model of reading instruction which similarly moves from inexperience to experience).

Making progress in writing is achieved through teaching approaches which are designed to move children towards independence (see section 15.8 for a fuller description of what is involved making progress in writing).

Shared writing is used to introduce the whole class to a writing experience. Supported by drama, reading and discussion, shared writing can involve:

- teacher demonstration – making explicit the features of the particular text type
- teacher talking through writing choices
- teacher as scribe – where the children are invited to contribute to the composition, particularly choices of words and phrases, to create a shared piece of writing
- supported writing – where the children work in pairs or individually to contribute ideas to the whole class composition.

Website resource W12.1 describes a shared writing session with 5 year olds.

Guided writing is managed in small groups, where children might be grouped according to their stage of achievement or an aspect of their writing which needs to be supported. This kind of grouping gives the teacher and teaching assistant the opportunity to work in some detail on specific learning points. It also allows children to make writing their own, building on the shared work and ideas gleaned from that, but making their composition unique.

Since writing composition is a complex process, it is important that teachers not only reflect on their own experiences as writers (see Chapter 11) but also continue to be writers themselves, particularly in the classroom. In addition, children write most effectively when they are given opportunities to write about aspects of life that have emotional and cultural relevance (Fecho, 2011; Cummins, 2016) so children should be given the chance to write about things that matter to them.

12.2   Finding a writing voice

The notion of 'voice' in writing is a reminder of the important link between spoken language and writing. But it can also refer to a kind of 'essence' of writing – an intangible quality that marks a piece of writing as individual and authentic. This can seem like a 'precious' view of the writer – as an individual, separated from the world, writing in hallowed isolation. At times, of course, this may be true (Cremin and Myhill, 2012) but even if writers are working alone, they draw on the many voices of the people and stories that they have encountered in life, as Mustafa shows:

> The first time Duane saw the green blob he wasn't really scared, he thought something was wrong with the camera screen, but, when the blob made that freaky sound he was shaking nervously, he was frozen with fear and he shrieked like a five-year-old girl.
>
> Duane gulped, "Okay this is one messed up... and ugly dream." He pinched himself but when he saw the blob still in front of him he was shocked. "Oh man, if this isn't a dream then that thing is real." Duane moved back and dropped his camera.
>
> "Aaaargh!" he shrieked, "Guys, where are you?"
>
> (Mustafa, aged 10)

Mustafa's narrative echoes the books, television, action films, comics and probably computer games he has seen or read. All writers, even if they need peace and quiet to compose texts, are not divorced from the world; on the contrary, writers need the world in order to make contact with readers.

Mustafa's writing suggests that voice is not just a matter of 'inner creativity', although this is important. It shows that whilst voice is individual, it is also a social and cultural phenomenon. Any definition of voice in writing needs to include the different 'voices' available through books, plays, poems, films, magazines, television, the internet, etc. Bakhtin (1981) describes texts as *polyphonic* – many tongued – with ideas expressed through different genres and styles reverberating with previously acquired knowledge and experience: cultural, social, linguistic, literary, visual. Every text has echoes and shadows of earlier texts, just like in Mustafa's story.

So writing is deeply personal, but embedded in the social, cultural and historical texts familiar to the writer. Finding a voice as a writer means having a kind of dialogue with others who have written books, made films, told stories. But it also means having a dialogue with oneself, reading writing back and listening to one's own voice; in other words, writing like a reader (Barrs and Cork, 2001). As Cremin and Myhill put it, reading a text aloud helps readers to hear:

> the cadences and rhythms of their writing and evaluate if it is satisfying their authorial intentions; secondly, it helps them to stand in the shoes of a reader and sense how the text might appear to them.
>
> (Cremin and Myhill, 2012: 196)

12.3   Developing voice in the classroom

It is certainly true that the classroom reflects many different facets of writing, often carried out by the teacher: writing on the board, on notes to go home to parents, on children's writing, modelling and talking about the choices made when writing and redrafting stories, information and poetry. All these activities show children that the classroom is a place where everyone can be a writer and that writing takes many forms, including blogs (Barrs and Horrocks, 2016). Young writers benefit from having authentic reasons and audiences for writing, some choice of what they can write and in what form, and freedom to draw on their own cultural experience and expertise (Lambirth and Goouch, 2006). But a supportive environment for writing is more than the physical setting where demonstrations and explorations take place; there also needs to be an environment of possibility – that intangible area of teachers' expertise that informs planning for activities both to challenge and to support writing and which is prepared to foster imagination and each young writer's unique voice.

Activity 12.1
The classroom as an environment for writing – reflective journal/blog

Have a look around the classroom you are working in, or recall the classroom of your last placement. Jot down a few notes about how the physical environment signals support for writers (boys/girls/bilingual learners/children with special educational needs). Does it have a range of different kinds of writing on display? Is it supporting the composer, the communicator or the secretary?

Now for the harder part: think back to a specific lesson or series of lessons you have taken which needed the children to write. How did you convey to the children the sense of an environment of possibility? This can be tricky so you could think about:

- Explanations given to the class about what they were going to learn.
- A clear sense of the audience(s) for the writing.
- Activities to support getting ideas together.
- The amount of time allocated to writing.
- Opportunities for the children to talk to each other about their writing – before and during composition and when it was finished.
- What happened to the writing when it was finished. Was it marked and put away? Responded to and discussed? Published in some way?

● What adjustments (if any) would you make to enhance the environment of possibility the next time you plan and teach a sequence which ends in extended writing.

You may also like to note ways in which the teachers you work with create an environment of possibility for writing to flourish.

Part of the support network of a classroom, however, is the presence of many other writers, all wrestling with words to make their meanings clear. Richmond (2015) describes this as a community of readers and writers, seeing the writing classroom as a place which offers the chance to collaborate with other writers, where reading informs writing and talk is a preparation for, as well as an outcome of, writing. It is a place where the teacher writes, too, where there are opportunities to write for different audiences and which offers various means of publication including making books (Johnson, 2000) reading aloud, classroom displays, class-made books, but also:

> the more recent electronic ones: e-books, websites and blogs, wikis, podcasts and other audio-visual presentations – on whiteboards, tablets and other appliances – in which writing is combined with sound and image.
>
> (Richmond, 2015: 19)

Beck (2010) argues that attention to multimodal composition is essential:

> Compared to composing in an exclusively textual mode, composing in multimodal contexts thus seems to pose new challenges to authors, thus offering a dynamic new context in which to explore the intersection of the cognitive, textual and social dimensions of composition.
>
> (Beck, 2010: 167)

Grainger *et al.* (2005) also make the case for expanding the concept of composition to a more holistic, multimodal experience. They argue that 'mindful, negotiated, interactive, and creative literacy practices which encompass writing' extend children's 'sense of agency in writing and enable them to adopt a more creative stance towards writing' (Grainger *et al.*, 2005: 28). Drama, role play, talk, reading images as well as books, making films, exploring and performing poetry are all shared experiences which can be offered in classrooms to develop children's voices as writers.

12.4 Writing journals

Writing journals have proved to be highly successful in promoting not only a sense of a writing community but of a writer's individual place *within* a community of writers. Graham and Johnson (2012) describe a project where children from 5 to 11 years old were invited by their teachers to use writing journals – to write and draw what they wanted in a book that would not be 'marked'. Some allocated 15–20 minutes every day; others had two sessions each week of about 30 minutes each. In summarising the findings of the project, it was clear that using journals freed up the creativity of many of the children and that they made sensible choices about what to write, where to work and who they worked with. When invited by the children to read their journals, the teachers discovered that many of the children wrote as experts about their own interests, whether about animals, cars, football, fashion, music. The journals allowed the children to behave like professional writers, working at their own pace, and often revising and re-working their journal entries.

It was important to establish ground rules for the use of the journals, but with clear guidance and consistency, all the teachers involved were enthusiastic about the value of making time for a freer kind of writing, as one teacher explains:

> I introduced the idea of writing journals to my Year 3 class with great care and spent the first two sessions discussing the broad range of what they might write, negotiating rules and encouraging them to make their own decorated covers for the books. I emphasised the 'with rights comes responsibility' aspect of the work, taking the time to ensure they were aware of their new found freedom but that they also understood that I expected them to be as focused as usual about their work.
>
> It was a priority to make time at the end of the session for some children to read their work aloud to the rest of the class and I found that this became increasingly popular; children who had been reluctant to read out their writing prior to writing journals were keen to share their written work now.
>
> From the very beginning the children were extremely enthusiastic and wrote in a wide variety of genres including: diaries, comic strips, a novel, episodic stories, letters, short stories and lists. They also enjoyed some copying – mainly jokes from joke books or pop songs and there were some good pastiches on *Star Wars* and other favourites.
>
> (Graham and Johnson, 2012: 37)

12.5 Making space to write

It seems clear, then, that the social nature of writing is an essential ingredient in supporting developing young writers. However, one of the problems facing any teacher who wants to establish the sense of a classroom writing community is that the classroom is not always a conducive place for uninterrupted writing. In talking with professional writers who work in classrooms, Cremin and Myhill found that professional writers 'refer to the privacy of writing and the need to find a mental space for writing' and that 'writing classrooms can be such busy places that privacy and mental space are hard to find' (Cremin and Myhill, 2012: 197). They suggest that it is worth finding alternative tranquil places to write or thinking about how the classroom might be adapted to create tranquil physical spaces for children to write.

Menmuir (2016) writes about a project run in Cornwall with the Kernow Education Arts Partnership and the Learning Institute, specifically designed to help children experience the best conditions in which to develop as writers. The project aimed to provide spaces in which dialogue about authentic writing could take place, to encourage teachers and children to talk about their writing preferences and what inspires and encourages them to write. He argues strongly for creating a supportive environment in the school and classroom:

I challenge the idea there is not enough time in the school day to encourage children to develop as independent writers. I believe without this time, the teaching of writing is incomplete. The children may have the skills if we teach them effectively. They may understand the process of writing if we model it well. But without the time and space to practise these skills and experiment with the writing process, without the time to reflect and share writing in a non-assessed space, our children are less likely to develop into independent, reflective writers who attain mastery over this most complex and vital of practices.

(Menmuir, 2016: 18)

(See website resource W12.2 Space to write: Encouraging independent writers for a full account of the project.)

Children themselves can be useful allies in designing and creating their own writing spaces throughout the school. From a small tent in the book corner to a refurbished shed in the school grounds, children are perhaps the best judges of where to find conducive spaces for writing. Some of those spaces might be at home in preference to school, but one of the key recent insights about children developing literacy has been attention to the 'third spaces' created where school and home practices intersect (Bhabha, 1990; Moje *et al.*, 2004; Pahl and Rowsell, 2012). These can be seen in the opportunities children have to make connections between what they do at home and what happens at school but it can also mean the affordances of digital technology, particularly social media, to make it possible to have a community of writers in the 'third space' offered by blogging, for example. Young writers might be invited to set up writing groups for themselves, within the school or at home either by meeting up or through digital media.

12.6 Professional writers in schools

Initiatives that have involved writers in schools all attest to increases in reflection and learning, often in confidence and positive attitudes and skills (Coe and Sprackland, 2005). Writers in schools can offer not only examples and models of how to write but physical evidence that being a writer is a normal way for someone to spend their time – and earn their living:

> Many pupils have a picture of the writer as a fusty, dusty, grey-haired bore, hunched over an ancient, cobwebby type-writer, ploughing through the fortieth chapter of a worthy, heavyweight novel. Not me. OK, I hardly go marlin-fishing like Hemingway, or live the louche roué existence of Noel Coward but I do ride a Triumph and go to the pub sometimes.
>
> (Dave Smith, comedian and columnist www.wordsmith-features.com/ (accessed 10 May 2017))

> A professional writer can energise creative thinking that can be applied across the curriculum, and can help both pupils and teachers approach subjects from imaginative angles.
>
> (Angel Dahouk, The Poetry Society www.zoominfo.com/ p/Angel-Dahouk/584125464 (accessed 10 May 2017))

A visit from an author is also an inspiration for children to try out ideas for themselves, to take a few more risks with their writing and be more ambitious and adventurous. In website resource W12.3 a teacher reflects on the effects of having a professional writer working with her class.

Organisations which have resources and helpful suggestions for involving professional writers in schools include:

NAWE: www.nawe.co.uk/

Arts Council: www.artscouncil.org.uk/

The Scottish Booktrust: www.scottishbooktrust.com/

Literature Wales: www.literaturewales.org/

Poetry Ireland: www.poetryireland.ie/education/writers-in-schools/

(All accessed 1 May 2017)

12.7   Writing narrative

Narrative is not only to do with imagination; it can also be transparently autobiographical. Every day there are ordinary, unremarkable stories to tell: what happened on the way to school, the shops or the football match; what was on the television last night; what is planned for tonight/the weekend/the holidays. And these narratives are likely to be a mixture of the real and the imagined. Anyone who tells a 'what I did today' story will select and interpret the facts: to make the teller look cleverer or more responsible; to hold the listeners' attention; or to draw a moral. In current terms, there is a 'spin' on even the most innocent of stories to fit with the intentions of the tellers and the decisions about what the audience might find interesting or amusing. But in addition to these everyday stories there are the stories about other people, drawn from newspapers, televisions, books, films. As Chapter 3 suggests, narrative, both invented and real, is profoundly embedded in everyday life. This means paying close attention to what narrative offers to children's learning as a whole. History is, after all, to do with story and, as many television science programmes now show, even the way the solar system has developed is a (very long) story; music, too, often has narrative threads. If writing depends on having models and examples, there are many available models for narrative structures in all areas of the curriculum.

It is not only to do with making up stories; it is not just about recounting experience; nor about structuring the telling in a time sequence which makes sense. It is about mixing all of these elements. Any narrative, whether autobiographical or invented – if it is possible to make a hard and fast distinction between the two – draws on inner and outer experience (see Figure 12.1).

There are suggestions for composing narratives in Chapter 3, although the focus is on oral narratives. The support structures and scaffolds suggested work just as well for constructing written narratives.

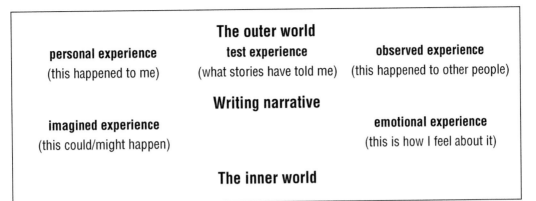

Figure 12.1 Outer and inner experience that feeds narrative writing

Activity 12.2
Children's narratives – individual/pairs/group

Read website resource 12.4 Iyla's story and view her reading her story on website resource 12.5. Iyla comes from a school where storytelling is a valued part of the curriculum and it shows in her clear sense of audience and the story language she uses.

What evidence can you find of this young author drawing on personal, text, observed, imagined and emotional experience (as in Figure 12.1) for her narrative writing?

If Iyla were in your class, what two things would you highlight as strengths of her writing and what two suggestions might you make for improving her narrative writing?

In Chapter 15 (website resource 15.3), Iyla's story is analysed and assessed in some detail.

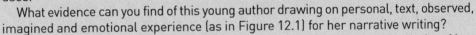

12.8   Making progress in narrative

Making progress in writing (or reading or talk) does not follow a straight line but often goes by fits and starts, 'forgetting' some things when learning something new, doubling back and consolidating knowledge and skills and then building again on what has been learned. Making progress in narrative is about writers developing:

- greater conscious attention about how to shape texts to suit their intentions as writers
- more awareness of how to engage and hold a reader's attention
- greater adeptness at handling the technical aspects and conventions of different kinds of narrative
- increasing facility in choosing language to create effects
- the ability to read their own writing with a reader's eye
- a repertoire of narrative forms to draw on.

All of this depends on writers having opportunities to make decisions about how, when and what to write, who the reader(s) will be and, crucially, having something to write about. (See Chapter 15 for a fuller description of what is involved making progress in writing.)

One of the keys to making progress in writing lies in the teacher's ability to scaffold learning. Dix (2016) describes classroom research which recognises scaffolding as a valued educational practice. In one teacher's work with her 6 and 7 year olds, on character descriptions, some of the strategies and learning opportunities to support/scaffold writing included:

- linking to students' prior knowledge by talking about their favourite book characters
- setting a clear purpose and goals for writing
- students dialoguing – purposeful pair-share talking and responding to each other's thinking and writing
- whole class talk about aspects of character writing
- the teacher sharing students' own writing
- instructional detours – either teacher or student initiated
- a written model for the analysis of the ideas, vocabulary and written structure
- a visualising strategy to deepen description
- role play to act out characters' behaviours
- an illustration to prompt ideas for description
- reading a picture book then modelling how to semantically map words which described the book character
- students mind-mapping their selected character according to three features identified and listed on a template
- a teacher think-aloud demonstration of 'how to' begin writing the introduction that places the character in a setting/context
- students transferring their own vocabulary and phrases from their semantic maps to begin writing their description
- students sharing drafts; giving and receiving feedback from peers
- teacher conferencing with individuals
- students reading/sharing final character descriptions to class (Dix, 2016: 27).

This helpful and comprehensive description of good practice in scaffolding is reminiscent of the kinds of planning and teaching described in section 4.9 (see website resource W4.3) where talk is an essential component of any teaching sequence.

12.9 Narrative structure

The planning and teaching model at the heart of this book firmly places talk as the bedrock of English teaching and learning. Telling stories is an important foundation for story writing, but it is not always necessary to 'tell the story then write it' as an automatic and invariable practice. In addition to potential problems of motivation, if children always have to write their oral stories, there are compositional issues with any 'one size fits all' view which offers a generic story structure. Not all stories follow the 'opening, build-up, problem, resolution, ending' pattern common to many traditional stories. Some do, of course, but others may start with a flash back to the build up to the problem or begin at the end and give hints about what has happened before, gradually revealing the problem, like Iyla's story. Similarly, many highly entertaining stories repeat a 'problem–apparent resolution–new problem–apparent resolution–new problem' structure to build tension and keep the reader involved. Then there are 'framed' stories – stories within stories – and 'caught moments' of experience which may focus on a character's thoughts rather than actions. Using any formulaic structure can act as a straitjacket to a young writer's creativity; it can also become very tedious for the reader! It is better to introduce children to a range of different story structures, some of which may be very like the formula above, but others of which may have different – and more intriguing – structures.

Meek reminds us, in a short booklet which is extraordinarily wise, that:

> The most important single lesson that children learn from texts is the nature and variety of written discourse, the different ways that language lets a writer tell, and the many and different ways a reader reads.

(Meek, 1988: 21)

In the classroom, the books they read and the stories they hear are the essential springboard for young writers' own imaginative excursions. There are many different shapes and sizes of stories, though, and it is worth explicitly drawing children's attention to the variety of story structures they can use for their own narratives.

Case study, early primary: Using story maps

The Year 1 teaching team at this school use story mapping as a way of planning for writing. Class texts are read and re-read, explored and discussed, interpreted and performed through drama. In order to develop the children's knowledge of story – their structures, features and language patterns – the children retell and map known stories. Drawing main events, characters and key elements of stories is part of the planning process in preparation for writing. Vocabulary and story language are added to the story maps following retellings and discussion. These are then used to support the young writers when they come to draft their own compositions. From story maps like these, the children write sequences of sentences composing real and fictional narratives for a range of different purposes and audiences. The purpose for the writing and intended audience underpin decisions about the form of the writing.

'The Sweetest Song', an African-American story taken from *The Story Tree: Tales to Read Aloud* by Hugh Lupton and Sophie Fatus (2005), tells of Little Daughter's trip on the far side of the fence to pick flowers, although her parents have instructed her not to. When she meets a grey wolf, he asks her if she will sing her sweet song to him. As the story progresses, the grey wolf repeatedly asks Little Daughter to sing to him, so sweet is her voice, and by singing the song over and over, the wolf is put into a trance again and again and Little Daughter is able to return safely to her garden and home.

In Figure 12.2, Lizzie has drawn an extended map, adding adverbials to support her oral retelling.

This drawing shows that she knows how to select key events from a story, including important thematic details like the garden gate, which is the marker of Little Daughter's safe return home. Lizzie has drawn the gate at the extreme left and

Figure 12.2 Lizzie's story map of Little Daughter's trip

again before the final drawing of Little Daughter in her garden at the end of the map, showing that she has not only identified key events but also important narrative features: the narrative tension depends on understanding that Little Daughter broke the rules. The musical notes are a delightful example of Lizzie capturing the sweetest song, and the repetitions of that and of the depictions of the wolf emphasise the number of times the wolf is lulled into a trance. The depictions of the main characters also reveal what Lizzie has understood from the story: in the original version, Little Daughter is black, with curly hair – just as in the drawings – and Lizzie's depiction of her as a happy little girl is consistent throughout. The wolf, on the other hand, is seen as threatening, by the inclusion of his fangs and the shift from his happy face in the first four or five depictions to a gloomy expression as Little Daughter reaches the safe side of the garden gate. Lizzie has clearly grasped not only the narrative sequence but also the theme of the story and the characterisation of the key figures in the story.

Maureen Lewis (1999) suggests using groups of books which follow similar distinct and recognisable narrative structures to establish a sense of story structure; for example, cumulative stories, journey stories, turning point stories or problem-resolution stories. In early primary, children can be asked to make and use quite simple story maps, but as children grow older, maps of story structures can be used to develop a sense of character and dialogue.

Case study, middle primary: Using stories to support narrative structure

As a means of rounding off the year's work, Ben planned for his class of 7 and 8 year olds to combine an author study with comparing narrative structures. He chose to focus on *A Narrow Squeak and Other Animal Stories* (1995) and *The Sheep Pig* (2010) by Dick King-Smith. Ben wanted the children to read stories that are structured in different ways in order to fulfil the following objectives for narrative writing:

- plan writing by using stories they have read to support narrative structure
- create settings, characters and plot
- sustain a third person narrative
- punctuate dialogue accurately

- evaluate and edit by assessing the effectiveness of their own and others' writing and suggesting improvements.

After discussion of what the class knew about Dick King-Smith, including the fact that animals are central to his stories, over the first few sessions the teacher read and discussed three stories from the collection, each of which has a different structure. He then drew a story map for each one: 'Norty Boy' is a linear journey story where the central character goes from A to B and back again. Using a linear map, Ben asked the children to attach comments about the emotions of one of the characters (Figure 12.3). 'The Clockwork Mouse' is a circular story where the mouse is taken to one destination after another until it is returned home (Figure 12.4) and 'The Happiest Woodlouse' is a problem-resolution story which Ben used to explore inner and outer dialogue between the two main characters (Figure 12.5).

Figure 12.3 Linear story map 'Norty Boy' with annotations

Figure 12.4 Circular story map 'The Clockwork Mouse'

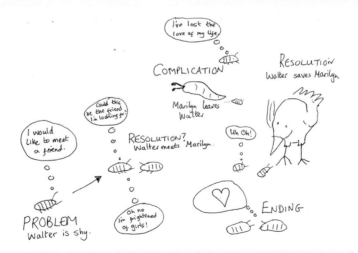

Figure 12.5 Problem-resolution story map 'The Happiest Woodlouse' with annotations

Building on this work on narrative structure, character and dialogue, the rest of the teaching sequence was taken up with reading and responding to *The Sheep Pig* and writing a third person narrative, with dialogue and at least two chapters which, the children were reminded, could be structured in whatever way suits the events being described.

For full details of the teaching sequence, see website resource W12.6 Using stories to support narrative structure. See also Chapter 3 for more story maps.

Activity 12.3
Planning to teach story structure – reflective journal/blog to small group

Find a collection of stories that will fit with a forthcoming English teaching sequence. If your class is upper primary and you choose a novel, you may want to find a complex picture book that follows the same structure. Below are some examples.

Circular stories

In these stories the central character visits a series of places and returns home.

Early, middle and upper primary:
- *Window* by Jeannie Baker (2002)

Early primary:
- *The Snail and the Whale* by Julia Donaldson, illustrated Axel Scheffler (2004)
- *Meerkat Mail* by Emily Gravett (2015)
- *Rosie's Walk* by Pat Hutchins (2009)

Middle primary:
- *Journey* by Aaron Becker (2014)
- *Oliver and the Seawigs* by Philip Reeve, illustrated Sarah MacIntyre (2014)

Upper primary:
- *Shackleton's Journey* by William Grill (2014)
- *Way Home* by Libby Hathorn and Gregory Rogers (2003)
- *Falling Angels* by Colin Thompson (2001)

Returning home stories

In these stories the central character goes from A to B then back to A.

Early primary:
- *Bob, Man on the Moon* by Simon Bartram (2004)
- *The Shopping Basket* by John Burningham (1992)
- *Lila and the Secret of Rain* by David Conway, illustrated Jude Daly (2009)

- *Toys in Space* by Mini Grey (2013)
- *Wild* by Emily Hughes (2015)
- *Where the Wild Things Are* by Maurice Sendak (2000)

Middle primary:

- *The Tunnel* by Anthony Browne (2008)
- *Jemmy Button* by Jennifer Uman and Valerio Vidali (2014)
- *Once upon an Ordinary School Day* by Colin McNaughton, illustrated Satoshi Kitamura (2005)
- *Black Dog* by Levi Pinfold (2012)

Journey stories

In these stories the central character travels from place A to place B.

Early primary:

- *On the Way Home* by Jill Murphy (2007)
- *Suddenly* by Colin McNaughton (2007)
- *Handa's Surprise* by Eileen Browne (2006)

Middle primary:

- *The Promise* by Nicola Davies, illustrated Laura Carlin (2014)
- *Gregory Cool* by Caroline Binch (2012)

Upper primary:

- *The Viewer* by Gary Crew, illustrated Shaun Tan (2005)
- *The Island* by Armin Greder (2008)
- *Rose Blanche* by Ian McEwan, illustrated Roberto Innocenti (2004)

Use the planning and teaching sequence format (website resource WI.2) to jot down some ideas for using two or three of the stories to teach story structure. If you teach younger children it may be best to stick with one or two examples.

Share your plans with the rest of the group and add to them after discussion. (Add them to your Texts I Like file – see website resource W5.4) As soon as you can, take the opportunity to teach the sequence and evaluate how successful it was in helping children structure their own stories.

12.10 Writing non-fiction

In recent years there have been attempts to write 'formulae' for structuring different kinds of non-fiction and informational text, but, as is clear from Chapter 9, much of what is described as non-fiction defies categorisation. Mallett argues that:

> some kinds of non-fiction have an important place in the English curriculum and have, perhaps, not always received the attention they deserve. And yet

the best writing of this kind has qualities which help develop critical literacy and accelerate children's progress in reading and writing.

(Mallett, 2016: 219)

Beautifully illustrated picture books with poetic language, innovative design and typography can give information about the environment; recipe books may tell about the language, customs or history of different countries; persuasive texts can be written as poetry. And newspaper reports, diaries, journals information are often included in fiction. Distinctions between 'fiction' and non-fiction' will depend on:

- the content of the piece
- the implied relationship between the writer and the reader; for example, whether the text is written in the first or third person and whether it directly addresses the reader or takes a more impersonal tone
- whether there is dialogue or reportage
- chronological or non-chronological organisation of material
- the use of verbs – active/passive; past/present/future; action/stative; modal
- the text cohesive devices used – connectives, conjunctions, pronoun patterns, repetition
- features of layout, organisation of material, use of pictorial or diagrammatic detail.

For example, while a short story may be written in the first person, it would be very odd to read a recipe that uses the first person throughout. Similarly, while a poem might use stative verbs such as *dream or believe,* an instruction manual for building a model is more likely to use active verbs such as *cut, attach, fix.* And although a poem or novel may or may not be illustrated by images, visual texts suchas maps, diagrams and photographs are absolutely essential for information or instructional text.

> **Active and stative verbs:** active verbs describe actions; for example, *jump, fly, skate.* Stative verbs describe ways/states of being where there is no action; for example, *trust, imagine, hope, be.*
>
> See also Chapter 14.

It seems clear then, that it is not just the structure of a text that determines its purpose, but also the content and the intention of the writer and the language and organisational features chosen to fit the specific purpose. So 'rules' for 'how to write a non-chronological report', for example, may not be the best way to teach children how to tackle different kinds of non-fiction texts. However, since all non-fiction texts are written with specific purposes and readers in mind, and this influences the language and organisation of the text, there are some definable characteristics of non-fiction texts. These, alongside examples of how these texts appear in everyday life, can help in guiding young writers. As ever, using good models and teacher demonstration will be the most powerful ways of getting to grips with different non-fiction text types. It is worth remembering that fiction can be the springboard for non-fiction writing and that imaginative narratives can include elements of non-fiction; for example, Anne Fine's *The Diary of a Killer Cat* (2009) which is a recount with a fictional context.

The most usual forms of non-fiction which appear in most writing curricula are:

- instruction

- non-chronological report
- recount (including newspaper reports, autobiography, or personal recount, and biography)
- persuasion (usually a one-sided argument)
- discussion (balanced argument and debate)
- explanation
- evaluation.

Figure 12.6 summarises a range of non-fiction texts, the forms they appear in everyday life, and their organisational and language features. This builds on Wray and Lewis (1997), who drew on the work of Australian linguists Martin and Rothery (1980, 1981, 1986) and later Cope *et al.* (2012). However, as mentioned above, not all the elements listed in Figure 12.6 should necessarily be included in any piece of writing in a specific non-fiction text. There are often overlaps between genres of non-fiction, so that, for example, a journal (recount) might include a set of instructions and a poem can be a persuasive piece of writing.

Activity 12.4
Building a library of non-fiction texts – reflective journal/blog to group

A good starting point for teaching a range of non-fiction texts is to demonstrate and use models and examples. Look around at home and gather examples of instructions, non-chronological reports, recounts, persuasive texts, discussion, explanation and evaluation. Think of other places where free leaflets might be found – the vet, the dentist, DIY shops, the doctor, local places of interest – and gather as many examples as possible.

These could be shared as a group resource.

You might then begin to gather examples of information, argument, instruction or explanation which appear in a different form – a poem giving instructions, for example, or a lyrically written information picture book like *Tigress* by Nick Dowson (2015) or *Ice Bear* by Nicola Davies (2015). Marcia Williams' *The Stone Age* (2016) is written as a comic strip packed with facts about early humans. Add them to your 'Texts I Like' file (website resource W5.4).

12.11 Variations on traditional forms of non-fiction

Simply teaching to a set of 'rules' is not the best way for children to learn express their ideas about factual knowledge, as Riley and Reedy put it, such formulae 'attempt to clarify and codify in a linear way a process that is messier and more complicated when it occurs' (Riley and Reedy, 2000: 157). Rather than sticking to formulae, teaching non-fiction depends on providing opportunities for children to speculate, explore and investigate whilst creating different ways to help them gather and shape ideas to suit their preferences for learning.

Mallett describes some principles for teaching non-fiction reading and writing:

> First we need to embed non-fiction reading and writing in strong, lively contexts which, for younger children particularly, include practical and

Non-fiction text	Examples	Text organisation	Language features
Instruction (procedural texts)	• instructions • recipes • manuals • 'how to do it' guides • directions	• states what is to be achieved • lists materials and equipment needed • chronological order of actions • often includes diagrams, drawings or photographs	• present tense often uses imperative verbs: *mix, grate, cut* • often uses 2nd or 3rd person: *you/users*
Non-chronological report	• factual material classifying or categorising information • reference books • dictionaries • maps • diagrams	• opens with general classification • describes object/event: its different qualities/aspects/habits/uses	• present tense • does not follow time sequence • often uses 3rd person: *they/these creatures*
Recount	• newspaper/magazine reports • journals diaries intended for publication • biography	• opens with scene-setting/orientation • recounts events as they happened • closes with a comment on the recount	• past tense • chronological order uses time connectives: *then/afterwards* • newspaper reports and biography written in 3rd person: *she/they* • journals and diaries written in 1st person: *I, we*)
Persuasion	• advertisements • leaflets about local issues • political pamphlets	• opens with a statement setting out a position • often uses bullet points or a statement then an elaboration/example of the view • summarises with restatement of the opening view	• usually in present tense • no specific group is addressed • appeal made to emotions • organisation usually follows a logical rather than chronological path • connectives used to reinforce views: *nevertheless, however, unless*
Discussion	• reports presenting different views, often making recommendations • magazine articles outlining opposing points of view • collections of letters to a local newspaper on a hot topic	• states the matter under discussion • outlines the main arguments • gives arguments for and against (with supporting evidence) • summarises and concludes, sometimes with a recommendation	• present tense • usually 3rd person, referring to people or things • uses logical connectives: *therefore, this means that, and so*
Explanation	• information books, leaflets and online material about how something works or how a natural or physical process operates (weather, digestion) or the causes and effects of historical events	• makes general statement to introduce the topic • follows a series of logical steps outlining how or why something happens • these steps continue until the end of the process or the explanation has covered all key points	• present tense • sentences often start with a noun or noun phrase • uses time connectives: *then, next* and/or causal connectives: *because, so*
Evaluation	• reviews of books or films • report on sports fixture	• opens with general statement describing the matter being evaluated • comments on good and bad points • summarises with a general recommendation	• can be present or past tense : *'This book is… /"The match was…'* • reviews often use stative verbs: *felt, thought, concluded* • sports reports use action verbs: *slotted, smashed, dived* • uses time connectives: *after, following this*

Figure 12.6 Non-fiction texts with examples, organisational and language features

physical activity. Second, we need to encourage and plan for talk and discussion: genuine learning is so often social and collaborative ... The third principle makes the teacher's role central and critical: as an expert on how to help children learn, as an expert on the huge range of texts now available and as an effective and sensitive assessor and recorder of children's progress ... A major theme is the journey children make towards critical literacy in informational kinds of reading and writing ... It is when children feel passionate about the texts they use and become able to articulate their merits that teachers feel they have helped inspire as well as instruct.

(Mallett, 2007: 1–2)

The case study in website resource W12.7 describes a project with 10 and 11 year olds about food and nutrition. After analysing television advertising, the children wrote carefully paragraphed research reports using formal language and passive verb forms.

12.12 Making progress in non-fiction writing

Making progress in writing non-fiction texts means developing expertise in handling:

- the styles and structures of different non-fiction texts
- the typographical and layout features
- the process of gathering and organising material
- the process of composing and recounting, reporting, describing or expressing a personal and analytical view.

In terms of progression, combining these different aspects can be problematic. If the school does not have a coherent and agreed planning framework for progressive non-fiction teaching (or any other texts for that matter), a child might be taught 'how to write instructions' in every year at primary school. Genuine progression and development are likely to be seen in the complexity of the subject-matter and in the growing ability to gather and re-present material independently (see pp. 377–380 for detailed progression statements). If developing writers are progressively to be able to synthesise different information, construct arguments, analyse opposing evidence, then they will need practice in shaping and framing ideas.

12.13 Scaffolds and writing frames

The research work of Wray and Lewis (1997) has been highly influential in developing frames and scaffolds to help children gather and present ideas for non-fiction texts. Although some critics argue that these scaffolds can be potentially restrictive, Lewis and Wray intended them as supports for children who experience difficulties with the complexities of the kinds of language and organisation needed for writing non-fiction texts. The value of their work lies in an approach which never suggests following a set of 'rules' or formulae:

the use of a frame should always begin with discussion and teacher modelling before moving on to joint construction (teacher and child/ren together) and then to the child undertaking independent writing, supported by the frame.

(Wray and Lewis, 1997: 124)

They also stress that 'the frames themselves are not a purpose for writing. The reasons for writing should arise from the work children are undertaking' (*ibid.*: 131) and that 'although some children may need scaffolding for a considerable time, other children may never need a frame or may only need to use one occasionally' (*ibid.*: 132). Scaffolds are, importantly, intended to be taken down as soon as the building is secure. In terms of supporting writing, they should be flexible enough to allow for the individual's point of entry to the subject and jettisoned as soon as the foundations for writing are firm.

In advocating the use of 'graphic organisers' as 'frameworking tools', Steve Moline points out that:

> Our usual practice of 'making notes' tends to focus on details at the risk of overlooking the text's structure and function. Making notes is an excellent way of recording precise and nuanced details, but the notes by themselves lack a 'map' of the text's organising principle, for example, the recursive shape of the water cycle or the classifying principle at work in a report about mammals.

(Moline, 2001: 128)

The point about making notes is critical. Notes are typically written from the top of the page to the bottom, and often the note-maker will use both sides of the paper. This makes it extremely difficult to re-view and synthesise the information. Teachers have long complained about children copying chunks of undigested information and re-presenting it in a topic project. These days, this can be even more evident as children have access to easy cutting and pasting 'information' found on the internet. Much of this information is anonymous and cannot be ascribed to an author or verified, so this makes the ease and accessibility even more of a problem. Children need to be taught how to sift and weigh information to see if it is the most useful and relevant to them. Using diagrams can offer a clearer way of gathering, sorting and summarising information. And pupils whose preferences tend towards the graphic, diagrammatic and spatial have the chance to use their own text experience in a positive way. Apps like Explain Everything (https://explaineverything.com/ (accessed 1 May 2017)) and Skitch (https://skitch-windows-10.en.softonic.com/ (accessed 1 May 2017)) can help in organising, annotating and analysing information.

Activity 12.5
Gathering and organising ideas – reflective journal/blog to group

How do you gather notes and organise your ideas? Have you fallen into the trap of making pages of notes which are then very difficult to select from and summarise, or have you developed your own ways of working, perhaps with frames and diagrams?

Make a note of the most successful ways you have found to gather and organise information and ideas quickly and efficiently.

What about using colour coding, highlighting, sticky notes and other helpful tags?

Share your ideas with the group to build a repertoire of useful frames, scaffolds and diagrams.

Try using some of the scaffolds or frames in Figures 12.7 and 12.8 and website resource 12.8 when you next plan for some non-fiction writing. It could be in any area of the curriculum. Evaluate how helpful they were in supporting children's information gathering and organisation.

It is important to use a scaffold which is designed for the kind of enquiry under way. A non-chronological report may be supported by a note-making wheel (see Figure 12.7) whereas gathering notes for writing a balanced discussion will benefit from a scaffold like that in Figure 12.8.

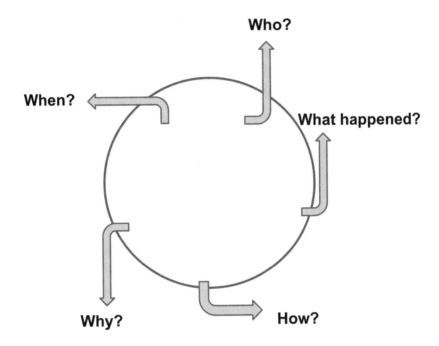

Figure 12.7 Note-making wheel

If children, particularly bilingual children, are to develop their language skills, and particularly their access to academic forms of language, they need learning challenges that are accessible and scaffolded by inclusive teaching and learning approaches (Garcia, 2009; Gibbons, 2015) (see pp. 2–3 for The Planning Access Key for Minority Ethic Learners).

See also the British Council website: https://eal.britishcouncil.org/teachers/great-ideas-scaffolding-learning (accessed 1 May 2017).

Although teacher demonstration and models drawn from text, maps, diagrams, frames and scaffolds are sound supports for children's writing, the individual writer's desire to communicate with authenticity and a clear personal voice has to be central in the act of composition.

In pairs, make notes on different points of view	
For	**Against**

Now think about how you might deal with some of the points made.	
On the one hand....	**On the other hand.....**
Useful words: but however even if although nevertheless	**Useful phrases:** some people think… it might be better if… another point of view… to sum up…

Figure 12.8 Scaffold to organise ideas for a balanced discussion

Summary

Writing composition is a complex combination of gathering and expressing ideas, communicating them to a reader and getting the structure and technicalities right. The individual writer has to find a unique voice but, paradoxically, perhaps, this is often found in the social aspects of composition: the personal within a community of writers. It is tricky for teachers to balance the competing demands of individual development and collaborative endeavour and there are examples of how spaces – both real and metaphorical – can be found to support developing writers. Writers benefit from having models and examples of adults as writers, whether these are the adults in the classroom or visiting writers.

In outlining ways of supporting development of two of the most familiar forms of writing – narrative and non-fiction – this chapter argues for a balance between providing models and examples and the need to be aware that not all narratives of non-fiction writing will or should follow generic formulae. Whilst story maps, frames and scaffolds can be helpful it is important to allow children's written creativity space to breathe.

Recommended reading

Writing composition

Richmond, J. (2015) *Writing 3–7* in the series *English, Language and Literacy 3 to 19*. Leicester: Owen Education with United Kingdom Literacy Association.

Richmond, J. (2015) *Writing 7 to 16* in the series *English, Language and Literacy 3 to 19*. Leicester: Owen Education with United Kingdom Literacy Association.

These short booklets give a comprehensive account of the recent history and development of writing largely in UK schools.

Narrative writing

Cremin, T. (2015) Creatively engaging writers in the early primary years, in T. Cremin, D. Reedy, E. Bearne and H. Dombey (eds) *Teaching English Creatively*. Abingdon: Routledge, pp. 67–83.

Cremin, T. and Reedy, D. (2015) Creatively engaging writers in the later primary years, in T. Cremin, D. Reedy, E. Bearne and H. Dombey (eds) *Teaching English Creatively*. Abingdon: Routledge, pp. 84–100. Both these chapters are packed with examples and practical teaching suggestions drawn from UK classrooms, for helping children to succeed as writers.

Chamberlain, L. with contributions from Kerrigan-Draper, E. (2016) *Inspiring Writing in Primary Schools*. London: SAGE. Chapters 6 and 7 give plenty of practical ideas for teaching sequences creating oral and written narratives with example drawn from UK schools.

Dix, S. (2016) Teaching writing: A multilayered participatory scaffolding practice, *Literacy*, 50 (1) pp. 23–31. This New Zealand-based account of research not only offers a detailed account of sound classroom practice but also a splendidly thorough account of the literature about participatory scaffolding interactions (page 26). **Advanced**

Non-fiction writing

Chamberlain, L. with contributions from Kerrigan-Draper, E. (2016) *Inspiring Writing in Primary Schools*. London: SAGE. Chapter 5 describes a teaching sequence for information writing, with example drawn from UK schools.

Cope, B., Kalantzis, M., Kress, G., Martin, J., compiled by Murphy, L. (reprinted 2012) Bibliographical essay: Developing the theory and practice of genre-based literacy, in B. Cope and M. Kalantzis (eds) *The Powers of Literacy: A genre approach to teaching writing*. London: Falmer Press, pp. 231–247. A comprehensive summary/analysis of Australian genre theory. **Advanced**

Mallett, M. (2016) Non-fiction literature in English lessons, in M. Mallett (ed.) *A Guided Reader to Early Years and Primary English: Creativity, principles and practice*. Abingdon: Routledge, pp. 219–234. A thoughtful chapter with examples of a range of non-fiction literature from UK classrooms, which goes beyond the usual 'information' texts to include 'lyrical non-fiction' and newspapers and magazines for children.

Riley, J. and Reedy, D. (2000) Developing control of the argument/persuasive genre, in J. Riley and D. Reedy (eds) *Developing Writing for Different Purposes: Teaching about genre in the early years*. London: Paul Chapman, pp. 136–160. A chapter with accessible theoretical background and an extensive case study of young children writing argument in an inner-city UK school.

Scaffolding for bilingual learners

Gibbons, P. (2015) *Scaffolding Language Scaffolding Learning: Teaching English language learners in the mainstream classroom*. Portsmouth, NH: Heinemann. This excellent book, based on classrooms in the USA but drawing on experience from around the world, gives a clear rationale and practical suggestions for in-class support for bi-/multilingual learners. **Advanced**

References

Bakhtin, M. (trans. 1981) *The Dialogic Imagination*. Texas: University of Texas Press.

Barrs, M. and Cork. V. (2001) *The Reader in the Writer: The links between the study of literature and writing development at Key Stage 2*. London: Centre for Language in Primary Education.

Barrs, M. and Horrocks, S. (2016) Educational blogs and their effect on pupils' writing. CfBT Educaiton Trust. www.academia.edu/11197640/Educational_blogs_and_their_effects_on_pupils_writing (accessed 10 May 2017)

Beck, S. W. (2010) Composition: Cognitive, textual and social dimensions, in D. Wyse, R. Andrews and J. Hoffman (eds) *The Routledge International Handbook of English, Language and Literacy Teaching*. Abingdon: Routledge, pp. 159–169.

Bhabha, H. K. (1990) The Third Space, in J. Rutherford (ed.) *Identity, Community, Culture, Difference*. London: Lawrence and Wishart.

Coe, M. and Sprackland, J. (2005) *Our Thoughts Are Bees: Writers working with schools*. Southport: Wordplay.

Cope, B., Kalantzis, M., Kress, G., Martin, J., compiled by Murphy, L. (reprinted 2012). Bibliographical essay: Developing the theory and practice of genre-based literacy, in B. Cope and M. Kalantzis (eds) *The Powers of Literacy: A genre approach to teaching writing*. London: Falmer Press.

Cremin, T. and Myhill, D. (2012) *Writing Voices: Creating communities of writers*. Abingdon: Routledge.

Cummins, J. (2016) Conference keynote speech 'Individualistic and Social Orientations to Literacy Research: Bringing Voices Together?' at the United Kingdom Literacy Association International Conference *Literacy, Equality and Diversity: Bringing voices together*, 8–10 July.

Dix, S. (2016) Teaching writing: A multilayered participatory scaffolding practice, *Literacy*, 50 (1) pp. 23–31.

Fecho, B. (2011) *Writing in the Dialogical Classroom: Students and teachers responding to the texts of their lives*. Urbana, IL: National Council of Teachers of English.

Garcia, O. (2009) *Bilingual Education in the 21st Century: A global perspective*. Malden, MA and Oxford: Basil/Blackwell.

Gibbons, P. (2015) *Scaffolding Language Scaffolding Learning: Teaching English language learners in the mainstream classroom*. Portsmouth, NH: Heinemann.

Graham, L. and Johnson, A. (2012) *Children's Writing Journals*. Leicester: United Kingdom Literacy Association.

Grainger, T., Goouch, K. and Lambirth, A. (2005) *Creativity and Writing: Developing voice and verve in the classroom*. London: Routledge.

Johnson, P. (2000) *Making Books*. London: A&C Black.

Lambirth, A. and Goouch, K. (2006) Golden times of writing: The creative compliance of writing journals, *Literacy*, 40 (3) pp. 126–152.

Lewis, M. (1999) Developing children's narrative writing using story structures, in P. Goodwin (ed.) *The Literate Classroom*. London: David Fulton, pp. 79–90.

Mallett, M. (2007) *Active Encounters: Inspiring young readers and writers of non-fiction 4–11*. Leicester: United Kingdom Literacy Association.

Mallett, M. (2016) *A Guided Reader to Early Years and Primary English: Creativity, principles and practice*. Abingdon: Routledge.

Martin, J. R. and Rothery, J. (1980) *Writing Project Report No 1*. Sydney: Department of Linguistics, University of Sydney.

Martin, J. R. and Rothery, J. (1981) *Writing Project Report No 2*. Sydney: Department of Linguistics, University of Sydney.

Martin, J. R. and Rothery, J. (1986) *Writing Project Report No 4*. Sydney: Department of Linguistics, University of Sydney.

Meek, M. (1988) *How Texts Teach What Readers Learn*. Stroud: Thimble Press.

Menmuir, W. (2016) Space to Write: Encouraging independent writers, *English 4–11*, Spring pp. 18–20.

Moje, E. B., Ciechanowski, K. M., Kramer, K., Ellis, L., Carrillo, R. and Colazo, T. (2004) Working towards third space in content area literacy: An examination of everyday funds of knowledge and discourse, *Reading Research Quarterly*, 39 (1) pp. 38–70.

Moline, S. (2001) Using graphic organisers to write information texts, in J. Evans (ed.) *The Writing Classroom: Aspects of writing and the primary child 3–11*. London: David Fulton, pp. 127–122.

Pahl, K. and Rowsell, J. (2012) *Literacy and Education: Understanding the new literacy studies in the classroom*, 2nd edn. London: Paul Chapman.

Richmond, J. (2015) *Writing 7 to 16*, in the series *English, Language and Literacy 3 to 19*. Leicester: Owen Education with United Kingdom Literacy Association.

Riley, J. and Reedy, D. (2000) *Developing Writing for Different Purposes: Teaching about genre in the early years*. London: Paul Chapman.

Wray, D. and Lewis, M. (1997) *Extending Literacy: Children reading and writing non-fiction*. London: Routledge.

Children's books

Jeannie Baker (2002) *Window*. Walker Books. ISBN 9780744594867

Simon Bartram (2004) *Bob, Man on the Moon*. Templar. ISBN 978840114911

Aaron Becker (2014) *Journey*. Walker Books. ISBN 9781406355345

Caroline Binch (2012) *Gregory Cool*. Francis Lincoln Children's Books. ISBN 9781847802583

Anthony Browne (2008) *The Tunnel*. Walker. ISBN 9781406313291

Eileen Browne (2006) *Handa's Surprise*. Scholastic/Walker. ISBN 9780744536348

John Burningham (1992) *The Shopping Basket*. Red Fox. ISBN 9780099899303

David Conway, illustrated Jude Daly (2009) *Lila and the Secret of Rain*. Frances Lincoln Children's Books. ISBN 9781847800350

Gary Crew, illustrated Shaun Tan (2005) *The Viewer*. Hodder Children's Books. ISBN 9780734411891

Nicola Davies, illustrated Laura Carlin (2014) *The Promise*. Walker Books. ISBN 9781406355598

Nicola Davies, illustrated Gary Blythe (2015) *Ice Bear*. London: Walker Books. ISBN 9781206364644

Julia Donaldson (2004) *The Snail and the Whale*. Macmillan Books. ISBN 9780333982242

Nick Dowson, illustrated Jane Chapman (2015) *Tigress* (Nature Storybooks). London: Walker Books. ISBN 9781206365429

Anne Fine (2009) *The Diary of a Killer Cat*. Puffin. ISBN 9780140369311

Emily Gravett (2015) *Meerkat Mail*. Two Hoots. ISBN 9781447284420

Armin Greder (2008) *The Island*. Allen & Unwin. ISBN 9781741752663

Mini Grey (2013) *Toys in Space*. Red Fox. ISBN 9781849415613

William Grill (2014) *Shackleton's Journey*. Flying Eye Books. ISBN 9781909263109

Libby Hathorn and Gregory Rogers (2003) *Way Home*. Andersen Press. ISBN 9781842702321

Emily Hughes (2015) *Wild*. Flying Eye Books. ISBN 9781909263628

Pat Hutchins (2009) *Rosie's Walk*. Random House. ISBN 9781862308060

Dick King-Smith (1995) *A Narrow Squeak and Other Animal Stories*. Young Puffin. ISBN 9780140349634

Dick King-Smith (2010) *The Sheep Pig*. Puffin. ISBN 9780141332352

Hugh Lupton, illustrated Sophie Fatus (2005) *The Story Tree: Tales to read aloud*. Barefoot Books. ISBN: 978–1905236121

Ian McEwan, illustrated Roberto Innocenti (2004) *Rose Blanche*. Red Fox. ISBN 9780099439509

Colin McNaughton, illustrated Satoshi Kitamura (2005) *Once Upon an Ordinary School Day*. Andersen Press. ISBN 9781842704691

Colin McNaughton (2007) *Suddenly*. Andersen Press. ISBN 9781842706213

Jill Murphy (2007) *On the Way Home*. Macmillan Children's Books. ISBN 9780230015845

Levi Pinfold (2012) *Black Dog.* Templar. ISBN 9781848777484

Philip Reeve, illustrated Sarah MacIntyre (2014) *Oliver and the Seawigs.* Oxford University Press. ISBN 9780192734884

Maurice Sendak (2000) *Where the Wild Things Are.* Red Fox. ISBN 9780099408390

Colin Thompson (2001) *Falling Angels.* Hutchinson. ISBN 9780091768171

Jennifer Uman and Valerio Vidali (2014) *Jemmy Button.* Templar Publishing. ISBN 9781848776159

Marcia Williams (2016) *The Stone Age: Hunters, gatherers, and woolly mammoths.* Walker Books. ISBN 9781406370836.

CHAPTER 13
SPELLING AND HANDWRITING

This chapter covers:

- The complexity of English spelling
- What good spellers do
- Teaching spelling
- Spelling development
- Developing a repertoire of spelling strategies
  - Case study, upper primary: Investigating morphemes
- The spelling environment
- Spelling homework and spelling tests
- The continuing importance of handwriting
- Teaching handwriting
  - Case study, early primary: A handwriting lesson
- Keyboard skills
- Children who experience difficulties with handwriting

SPELLING

13.1   The complexity of English spelling

Spelling correctly has a high status in the English-speaking world. If someone produces a piece of writing with spelling errors, readers may make negative judgements about their intelligence and literacy skills. Clearly there are strong pressures to be seen to be spelling conventionally. However, the English spelling system is not straightforward. Writing in English has had a varied and complex history and thus the spelling system is also based on a variety of different principles. It is no wonder that many people find spelling tricky. English is a polyglot language and its history over the last 2000 years has influenced both the words we use and their spellings. English is still borrowing and making up new words. It is a dynamic, ever-changing language. Not only is the history complex but also the spelling system, and how we spell words continues to change; for example, text messaging has opened up further conventions for spelling words in the context of the ubiquitous use of mobile phones. Nevertheless, it is possible, and enjoyable, to teach children how to spell conventionally. This chapter suggests that a repertoire of knowledge about words and spelling strategies is needed if young people are to be shown how to develop as competent spellers. This repertoire includes looking at writing holistically through language study as well as paying explicit attention to the development of a range of spelling strategies.

People are different in the way that they approach spelling as they write. For example, one teacher struggled with spelling all the way through his school days and was removed from class on a regular basis to have a one-to-one intervention in upper primary focused upon his poor spelling. In secondary school, his reports were littered with disparaging comments about spelling mistakes infecting all his written work. It was only at college, when more substantial writing had to be completed, that spelling seemed to fall into place. He still has to think carefully about some spelling patterns, such as the one found in 'necessary' (*one collar and two socks* is the mnemonic he uses to remember this) but has had no significant problems with spelling since that time. For this teacher, it seems that confidence was a significant factor. Some people use visual cues for spelling correctly (e.g. they see the whole word and are able to spell it). Others draw on auditory cues, such as splitting words into syllables. There is no one strategy which works for everyone and for every word. As Kress points out:

> Children have many routes into spelling, and all children always use more than just one. Meaning, however, is an absolutely essential element in all of these routes, and unless we realize this we cannot understand children's spellings.
>
> (Kress, 2000: 5)

Spelling is deeply related to meaning so that any approach to teaching spelling needs to have an interest in language and word meanings at its heart.

Activity 13.1
Our history as spellers – reflective journal/blog/pairs/group

Note down any memories you have of how you learnt to spell and your experience of being taught spelling in your school days.

How did (do?) you feel about spelling difficulties if you had any? What helped? Discuss your history with someone else. Do your experiences or feelings differ? Discuss what you think makes a good speller and the experiences needed to become one. As a whole group, make a list of the features and the strategies you think collectively would aid spelling development.

13.2   What good spellers do

When completing the above reflection you will probably have come up with a list outlining what good spellers are capable of. This would have included some or all of the following areas of knowledge that O'Sullivan and Thomas (2000) found, through observation and research with many hundreds of children, to be essential in the teaching and learning of spelling:

- extensive experience of written language
- phonological awareness
- letter names and alphabetic knowledge
- known words which can form the basis of analogy making and deducing rules
- visual awareness
- awareness of common letter strings and word patterns – for example, -at, -ad, -ee, -ing, -ough
- knowledge of word structures and meanings – for example, prefixes, tenses, compound words, word roots and word origins
- growing independence – where and how to get help, using dictionaries, spell checkers, etc.

In a similar study, O'Sullivan stresses the importance of extensive experience of written language:

> Writing played a key role in promoting spelling development. In all the case studies, spelling development was supported by a wide range of writing experiences. As the children wrote widely, and at increasing length, their spelling noticeably developed.

> (O'Sullivan, 2000: 10)

Importantly, she adds:

> Where children's writing experiences were limited for various reasons, their spelling development was adversely affected.

> (*ibid.*: 10)

13.3 Teaching spelling

Spelling: Caught or Taught? by Peters (1985) is one of the most influential books on the teaching of spelling. She argues that spelling is a set of skills that requires explicit teaching and that if children are not taught spelling well, there is a significant danger that they will develop a lack of self confidence in their writing as a whole and, for example, be reluctant to be adventurous in word choice. More recently Adoniou has stated:

> A review of the literature in the field reveals the following as fundamental understandings teachers should have about spelling:
>
> - Spelling is a learned skill, not an innate ability and therefore it can and should be taught. English spelling is systematic, contrary to popular perception, and therefore it can be taught.
> - Spelling is a linguistic skill that develops through, and for, interactions with others. It is an integral component of reading and writing, allowing us to make meaning from, and with, texts.
>
> (Adoniou, 2014: 144)

By combining the insights of Adoniou, Peters and O'Sullivan, teaching spelling should be approached through extensive opportunities to write *and* be explicitly taught as part of the teaching of writing. These comments have implications for teaching writing generally. Moreover, O'Sullivan's research strongly suggests that a critical factor in developing conventional spelling is to do with the reasons children are being asked to write. When they recognise that their writing is going to be read for its interest, in the same way as a printed book is read, then they can see the point of being careful about spelling. Similarly, if children are occasionally asked to write for a readership outside the classroom, emphasising, as Adoniou does, the social nature of writing, then they can see the importance of learning how to proofread for spelling and to get it right.

Therefore developing writers have to see spelling in the context of writing for a clear purpose and an intended audience and realise why it is important to spell conventionally. For teachers the implications are clear: spelling should be taught making connections to the teaching of writing as a whole and to the ongoing writing that children compose.

Thus when teachers are planning a sequence of work where children will write, they need to consider when explicit attention to spelling will be most effective. In the planning framework outlined in the introduction to this book (Figure I.3) attention to spelling would fit into the third phase of this framework and would include the specific modelling of the application of spelling strategies by the teacher when engaged in the act of writing as well as carrying out focused spelling investigations (see below).

13.4 Spelling development

Gentry (1982) proposes five stages of development for spelling which occur over a long period of time:

1 Pre-communicative. In this stage the child knows that symbols can be used to say something and uses a range of invented letter or number-like symbols to do so. There

are no sound-symbol connections being made. It is therefore unreadable by an independent reader.

2   Semi-phonetic. In this stage the child is beginning to make sound-symbol connections, shows some knowledge of the alphabet and knows about word boundaries and leaving gaps. Some words are likely to be abbreviated.

3   Phonetic. In this stage the child uses sound-symbol connections consistently to represent all the sounds they can hear in words. They are beginning to develop a sight word vocabulary and can cope with simple letter strings such as -ing.

4   Transitional. In this stage children develop visual strategies and are less dependent on sounding out. They are using many of the conventions of the English writing system and have a larger sight word vocabulary.

5   Conventional (or correct). In this stage the child has a basic knowledge of the spelling system, its patterns and rules, has a wide spelling sight word vocabulary and can use spelling supports efficiently. Correct spellings are being produced almost all the time.

This is a useful outline, and has been cited regularly since publication, but does come with some words of caution – it is based on a case study of one child. Also it gives no indication of how long each stage lasts, and implies that development is linear through the stages when experience reveals that there is significant overlap.

The Education Department of Western Australia (1997) identifies the following phases of development:

1   Children know that print has meaning; they experiment with writing-like symbols and try to represent written language, assigning meaning to their own writing.

2   Children attempt spellings using some sound-symbol relationships. They can copy, recall and invent words, representing words by using one or more letters, usually consonants.

3   Children can match letters and sounds. Although they may have limited understanding of conventional spelling patterns, they will make meaningful attempts. They may use self-constructed rules and are likely to develop a large bank of words which they can read, write and spell.

4   Children tend to move more towards meaning-based strategies, relying less on phonetic strategies. They use visual strategies more and classify words by patterns.

5   Children are independent spellers with a large bank of known words. They use both visual and sound patterns, attempt unknown words, predict likely spellings and make generalisations. They proofread and use dictionaries successfully.

The research also identified critical factors in supporting spelling:

- an interest in words;
- a positive view of themselves as spellers;
- a sense of responsibility towards the reader of their writing;
- seeing spelling as problem-solving;
- being prepared to take some risks with spelling.

(EDWA, 1997)

Successful spelling depends on more than strategies. It involves hand/eye coordination, making relationships between symbols and sound, seeing patterns, knowing about spelling supports such as dictionaries, having an interest in words, but, importantly, it begins with the attitudes held by adults and children about spelling.

13.5   Developing a repertoire of spelling strategies

The following strategies can be used when a teacher is working one-to-one with a child discussing their writing, or with a group of children, teaching strategies explicitly for them to use when they are writing.

Phonological (What does it sound like?)

The majority of all the words in English are phonically regular and children can be helped to encode by demonstrating how to start with a word they wish to write and then segment it into its constituent sounds. Each sound can then be represented by a letter or group of letters. A practical strategy for this would be using a word grid.

For example, a child wants to spell the word *leg*. She would say the word slowly, splitting it up, and identifying there were three sounds to represent. A grid of three spaces could then be drawn representing the three sounds identified:

Into each box the appropriate letter would be entered:

More complex phonically regular words can be encoded in this way – for example *bring*:

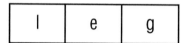

This emphasises one of the principles of the English spelling system that a sound can be represented by more than one letter.

However, if children depend solely on phonological strategies, they will never spell very many words accurately. Fewer than half of the most common English words have regular sound-symbol correspondence. Also if children rely on how they say words in order to spell them, they will always have difficulty in spelling accurately. For example a 7 year old wrote the following two words in her writing task:

e chuffer

You might have some trouble working out that the two words are intended to be *each other* but they accurately represent the way the child pronounced them.

A further complaint might be made that if this child pronounced those words 'properly', there would not be a problem. This ignores the fact that even speakers who use a 'received pronunciation' accent do not pronounce words exactly as they are spelled; for example, the majority of people do not pronounce the 'd' in *sandwich* or *handbag* and recently more people are not pronouncing 't' at the ends of words like *lot* or *but*. This means that attention to what the word looks like is essential for correct spelling.

Visualisation (Does it look right?)

Peters (1985) emphasised the importance of acquiring visual strategies as well as auditory cues (phonics) and particularly recommended the use of the 'Look–Cover–Say–Write–Check' strategy for developing visual and kinaesthetic approaches to spelling, as well as drawing attention to common and familiar letter patterns including prefixes and suffixes. The teacher would *identify* a word or words from children's writing or a group of words that need to be taught that have letter pattern in common and *draw attention* to the part of the word(s) that has the error or contains the letter pattern in common. Then the children would:

- *Look* carefully at the word(s) paying attention to the identified particular part/feature, and memorise it by saying the whole word again quietly to themselves, thinking of its meaning and attempting to see it in their minds as a whole word.
- *Cover* the word up and *say* the whole word before as well as whilst writing it.
- *Write* the word from memory, continuing to picture it and remembering the specific feature.
- *Check* that the spelling is accurate by looking back at the original and matching it. If the spelling is incorrect, repeat (some teachers ask children to repeat three times even if the first attempt is correct, in order to consolidate).

The learnt words could then be written into a personal spelling dictionary, which would be kept to hand to refer to when writing.

This reflects one of the most common strategies expert spellers use when they are unsure – they write the word and then ask: 'Does it look right?'

Analogy (What other word is like this one?)

This knowledge comes through seeing that words can be grouped by letter pattern. So, for example, children realise that if you can spell *ball*, you are also likely to be able to spell *call, wall, fall, tall* and *stall*.

To develop this strategy teachers ask questions such as, 'Is the word you are trying to spell like another word that you know?' In addition children can, with a partner, be word detectives and look for words which have the same letter string/pattern.

Activity 13.2
Generating correct spelling using onset and rime – individual/pair/group

Note: If you have read Chapter 7, you will have already come across onset and rime and tried out the one-minute challenge. It is worth trying again to see if you can beat your total and to link reading with spelling.

Website resource W13.1 is an extract from a book on teaching reading which shows how new words can be formed by using onset and rime. In the space of one minute, see how many words you can generate from the figure in W13.1. What does this suggest about how children might be helped to generate correct spellings by using the analogies offered by onset and rime?

Onset and rime: a syllable can normally be divided into two parts – the *onset*, which consists of the initial consonant or consonant blend, and the *rime*, which consists of the vowel and any final consonants.

For example: simple onsets and rimes are:

rime *in* onsets *pin bin tin*

rime *at* onsets *cat sat bat*

Slightly more complex are:

rime *ain* onsets *train brain gain*

rime *ight* onsets *fight light bright*

Analogy does not always work in English, particularly for vowel sounds. For example, if I can spell *meet* I can probably spell *greet* but might have difficulty with *heat*, therefore, analogy is useful but not foolproof and children will need to have other strategies to draw on.

Meaning links (Why is it spelled like that?)

Activity 13.3
Morphemes – group discussion (very brief)

Say the following words out loud and consider:

- the way the ending of each word sounds
- the meaning of the last two letters that the words have in common
  - shouted
  - joined
  - jumped.

Although the ending of the three words are spelled the same, they are pronounced differently (*id, d* and *t* respectively). What they do have common is they are all the past tense of the verb and the –ed ending shows they are common in meaning.

English is a *morphophonemic* language. Morphological knowledge is essential for accurate spelling. This knowledge involves understanding that words are made up of morphemes. In the word *eggs* there are two morphemes: *egg* and /*s* where /*s* indicates the plural and *egg* something laid by birds. Roots or base words (or base morphemes) suffixes and prefixes are all morphemes and when added to a root or base word (or morpheme) they create new meanings.

> **Morphophonemic:** a combination of morphemes and phonemes.
>
> **Morpheme:** the smallest meaningful unit in a language.
>
> **Phoneme:** the smallest unit of sound in a word.
>
> **Root word:** a word that makes sense on its own but can be changed by adding prefixes or suffixes – for example, *happy – unhappy; happiness*.
>
> **Base morpheme:** a single syllable which is the root of the word but which does not make sense on its own – for example, *rupt – erupt; disrupting*.

Nunes and Bryant (2006) argue that morphological knowledge is the least understood and least exploited spelling knowledge. Teachers can develop children's morphological understanding in a range of ways. With younger children they can play games such as the 'happily/unhappily' story. The teacher starts by beginning a story by saying something like; 'On Saturday I went to the shops to buy some clothes. Happily I had pockets full of money to spend.' A child then starts the next sentence with 'unhappily', for example 'Unhappily my pocket had a hole in it.' The next child then begins the next sentence with 'Happily...'. Turns are taken in pairs or in larger groups. This activity helps children to understand how adding a prefix *un-* changes the meaning of the base word to its opposite.

Case study, upper primary: Investigating morphemes

A teacher with a class of 9 and 10 year olds developed the habit of challenging children to become spelling detectives. In investigating morphemes and how they are combined, he gave the children the base morpheme *rupt*. They then had to generate and find, in the reading material in the classroom, and from their heads, as many words that they could which had that base morpheme in common.

They came up with the following list:

interrupt	disrupt
rupture	disruptive
disrupted	nondisruptive
interrupted	uninterrupted
erupt	erupted
eruption	bankrupt
corrupt	corrupted
incorruptable	

In discussion with the class, the teacher then divided the words into a table where the children could select prefixes and suffixes that combined with the base morphemes to make new words; for example, *nondisruptive*:

Prefixes		base morpheme	suffixes
non	inter	rupt	ive
un	dis		ed
	bank		able
	cor		ure
	e		ion

The children discussed how the morphemes combined to make meaning and how the meaning changed when each prefix or suffix was added. Finally the children were given two challenges: find the longest word with *rupt* as base morpheme and decide on the common meaning of all the words generated (which is contained in the *rupt* morpheme).

This activity helped the children to understand how words are related in meaning, how adding morphemes changes the meaning each time and that more than one morpheme can be added at the front of the base or root.

Orthography (Do I know a rule that might help me?)

There are some spelling rules that are worth knowing. Most work fairly well most of the time and children enjoy being word detectives. Any of the following could be investigated by challenging children to find as many examples as they can from reading materials at home as well as at school and, in pairs or small groups, coming up with a 'rule' about how to spell them:

- 'Q' is followed by 'u' and another vowel.
- Prefixes never alter the spelling of the root word.
- If a word ends in a vowel (e.g. *like*), you often drop the vowel before adding a suffix (e.g. *ing* – *liking*).

> **Orthography:** the conventional spelling system of a language.
>
> **Etymology:** the study of the origin of words and how their meanings have changed throughout history.

Etymological knowledge (Where do the words come from?)

Children enjoy investigating word origins. They can be challenged to collect 'borrowed' words and then investigate where they come from using a dictionary. Words such as *sushi*, *pyjamas*, *berserk* can be used as a starting point. Young investigators may guess that *sushi* has been borrowed from Japanese, but not realise that *pyjamas* comes from Hindi and *berserk* from Icelandic. Parts of words can also be used. The prefix bi- comes from Latin and children can collect words containing it, derive the meaning and then find out which Latin word it draws on.

Activity 13.4
Investigating language – reflective journal/blog to pairs/group

Try to think of some other spelling challenges you could offer the age group you are most familiar with. They might be about adding prefixes or suffixes or to do with the derivation of words. Younger children will need support but can look for words with regularities as part of their phonics learning.

When you have a chance, try out some of the challenges, including the examples given.

Kinaesthetic (Bodily memory of muscle movements)

Spelling accurately is supported by handwriting and keyboard practice. As letter strings in words are repeatedly written, the hand movements associated with them become internalised and the spelling of the practised words becomes automatic, enabling the writer to focus on composing and spelling more unfamiliar words.

Other strategies for spelling (I have tried all the above. What do I do now?)

Good spellers know where to go if they need further support. They know they can use dictionaries, though you need to know the first few letters if you are going to find the target word. They also know you can ask friends and adults. Good spellers are aware of the few words that always cause them trouble and have devised ways to help them remember them. Some of these might be *mnemonics*, others might be rhythmic or visual. For example, a common misspelling in primary schools is *'because'* which can be remembered by '**b**ig **e**lephants **c**an **a**lways **u**nderstand **s**mall **e**lephants'. Similarly, *address* can be remembered by visualising the two double letters. Children enjoy identifying their own tricky words from their writing and making up ways to help them remember the correct spelling. Some might be visual, some auditory. What is important is to remember is that there are differences in the ways people remember spellings and that no one method will suit everyone, so it is important for the teacher to provide a variety of strategies and supports for spelling accurately.

Mnemonics: a method for assisting the memory.

13.6 The spelling environment

A supportive environment for spelling will include all sorts of prompts and aids to spelling but an essential element of the environment is the teacher's own attitude. Some people find spelling accurately easier than other people do and often people who find spelling difficult are made to feel ashamed. The most important thing to remember is that spelling needs to be right in the final draft of any writing. Before that, any errors should be dealt with tactfully and with support for finding the right spelling. Alongside an atmosphere of encouragement, a supportive environment for spelling might include:

- word banks
- key words on display – this week's phonics/spellings
- dictionaries, thesauruses and the knowledge of how to use them
- alphabet books/posters/displays; alphabet friezes (for all ages)
- class (own made) alphabet/spelling/word books or dictionaries
- spelling baskets with different cards and support material – e.g. 100 high-frequency words; time phrases and joining words; different words for *said*; adding *ing* to words
- laminated sheets and display of 'what to do if you don't know how to spell a word'
- spelling games
- computer programs for spelling
- reminders about strategies (Look, Say, Cover, Write, Check)
- posters of commonly misspelled words (compiled by the pupils)
- handwriting activities related to the week's spelling patterns
- books/posters about words
- word webs showing relationships between words
- challenges – related to subject specific vocabulary or different language roots (e.g. 'words we've borrowed from Greek')
- crosswords and word searches; word matching activities
- words related to particular topics or subjects – displayed or in folders
- word of the week – inviting children to add words with identical letter clusters, similar prefix/suffix to the list.

If an individual child seems to be struggling with spelling, it may be worth carrying out a miscue analysis (see section 15.9) to identify any patterns in error and plan systematically to support spelling development.

13.7   Spelling homework and spelling tests

The discussion above has shown that learning to spell accurately in English is not a simple process. Thus the development of a repertoire of spelling strategies needs to be encouraged. The 'traditional' view of teaching spelling was that all you need to do is to give children lists of words to learn every week and then to test them on a Friday, seeing how many words each child could spell correctly. All teachers who have used this method know from experience that broadly speaking, the same children get the words right and the same children always seem to struggle with getting 10 out of 10. In addition many children who do well in traditional spelling tests then make errors with the same words in their ongoing writing. This shows that this 'traditional' approach is unlikely to help many children become good spellers.

However, many parents and carers are keen to help their children with spelling. They know that accuracy is important. Thus homework for spelling should be planned but the activities should be ones which encourage an interest in words and close attention to spelling patterns and meaning connections. Activities suggested in this chapter can be used as homework. Children can complete word searches, investigate and collect words with identical letter patterns, explore the rules for pluralisations or adding suffixes, for example, and look for exceptions (sheep?), which can then be discussed in follow-up lessons.

Further examples include children and their families being encouraged to find words from the week's word work in newspapers or magazines, cereal and other food packets at home, play spelling snap; see how many syllables there are in everyone's name in the family; make alphabetic lists of friends' names, animals, toys, etc.

Children can ask their parents how they remember how to spell tricky words and bring them back to the classroom to make an anthology of techniques.

Summary

English spelling is highly complex and, starting with what good spellers do, this section of the chapter outlines the repertoire of spelling strategies and knowledge that writers need to spell conventionally in English. Spelling should be taught as well as being caught through the experience of plenty of authentic writing experiences. Children can be shown that there are many sources of information that they can draw upon as spellers and no one strategy will ever be enough. Young spellers will thrive best in an environment where spelling accurately is seen as something that is necessary in a final draft and there are plenty of supportive materials and strategies on offer.

Recommended reading

Adoniou, M. (2014) What should teachers know about spelling, *Literacy*, 48 (3) pp. 144–153. A concise and readable recent overview of international research into spelling and the implications for teachers. **Advanced**

Bourassa, D. C. and Treiman, R. (2010) Linguistic foundations of spelling development, in D. Wyse, R. Andrews and J. Hoffman (eds) *The Routledge International Handbook of English, Language and Literacy Teaching*. Abingdon: Routledge, pp. 182–192. Taking a deeper look at spelling strategies, this chapter outlines recent international research into spelling, arguing that much of what has been learned about spelling in 'typical' children also holds good for children with dyslexia. **Advanced**

Kress, G. (2000) *Early Spelling: Between convention and creativity*. London: Routledge. A thoughtful and thought-provoking argument about children making their own sense of spelling through experimentation and how this leads to conventional orthography. **Advanced**

Martin, T. (2014) *Talk for Spelling*. Leicester: United Kingdom Literacy Association. A highly practical book with plenty of suggestions for teaching spelling and encouraging children to become self-reliant spellers.

O'Sullivan, O. and Thomas, A. (2000) *Understanding Spelling*. London: Centre for Language in Primary Education. An account of an in-depth study carried out in the UK of what children do when spelling, how spelling can be taught and assessed, including a suggested methodology for analysing spelling errors and difficulties.

Scharer, P. L. and Zutell, G. (2003) The development of spelling, in N. Hall, J. Larson and J. Marsh (eds) *Handbook of Early Childhood Literacy*. London: SAGE, pp. 271–286. Supported by thorough coverage of international research literature, this chapter argues for a developmental approach to teaching spelling which rejects 'one-size-fits-all' approaches to teaching spelling. **Advanced**

Recommended websites

Support for Spelling http://webarchive.nationalarchives.gov.uk/20110809091832/teachingandlearn
ingresources.org.uk/collection/35326 (accessed 1 May 2017). Primary National Strategy Spelling
Scheme.

Spelling bank http://dera.ioe.ac.uk/4831/1/c4b989c553cc6dd6f2b6fab92f6cb310.pdf (accessed 1 May
2017). Specifically for KS2 spelling activities and investigations.

First Steps file:///C:/Users/Windows%2010/Downloads/FIRST007.pdf (accessed 1 May 2017).
Resources for writing include suggestions for teaching spelling in context.

References

Adoniou, M. (2014) What should teachers know about spelling?, *Literacy*, 48 (3) pp. 144–153.

Education Department of Western Australia (EDWA) (1997) *Spelling Developmental Continuum* (First
Steps). Melbourne: Rigby Heinemann.

Gentry, J. R. (1982) An analysis of developmental spelling in GYNS AT WRK, *The Reading Teacher*, 36
pp. 192–200.

Kress, G. (2000) *Early Spelling: Between convention and creativity.* London: Routledge.

Nunes, T. and Bryant, P. (2006) *Improving Literacy through Teaching Morphemes.* London: Routledge.

Peters, M. L. (1985) *Spelling: Caught or taught: A new look.* London: Routledge and Kegan Paul.

O'Sullivan, O. (2000) Understanding spelling, *Reading*, 34 (1) pp. 9–16.

O'Sullivan, O. and Thomas, A. (2000) *Understanding Spelling.* London: Centre for Language in Primary
Education.

HANDWRITING

Activity 13.5
Handwriting – individual/pairs

Write your name and address in your best joined handwriting but with your eyes closed!

Hopefully you have in front of you a legible, reasonably well formed (and spelled)
and set out name and address.

This illustrates that once the purpose of a piece of writing has been decided, the
body has to then set to work to physically turn the idea into a text. Although vision is
important, the essential component of turning a composition into a text is through
muscular movement. You have learnt the muscular movements associated with the
sequence of letters that make up your name and address and can make those
movements even with your eyes closed. This has come from being taught those
movements and having regular practice through writing a wide range of texts. People
who can touch type essentially are doing the same. They do not have to look at the
keyboard in order to know how to move their hands and fingers to create the words
on screen. Handwriting supports the compositional process and involves flexing the
fingers and nodding the wrist in predetermined ways.

Discuss what implications this might have for teaching handwriting.

13.8   The continuing importance of handwriting

Teaching handwriting continues to have an essential place in the curriculum. Even with the rise of keyboards and on-screen composition, handwriting is not an anachronism. Indeed, the development of a legible, fluent and comfortable handwriting style is important for success at school; for example, it affects performance in tests and exams, as well as being a useful life skill.

Studies have shown (Berninger and Amtmann, 2004; Medwell and Wray, 2007) that children who write more easily write better texts and that poor handwriting can have an impact on motivation as well as compositional skills. As Christensen (2009) notes, speed and fluency underpin writers' ability to produce high-quality written text. Speed and fluency indicate automaticity in handwriting, which enables the writer to concentrate on other elements in writing, particularly the compositional. Christensen states:

> Automaticity in handwriting is an essential prerequisite to the production of high quality, creative and well-structured written text. Indeed, over the last 20 years, in addition to theoretical analysis, there has been a steady accumulation of empirical support for the notion that handwriting plays a central role in allowing the production of high quality written text.
>
> (Christensen, 2009: 285)

Like spelling, handwriting should be explicitly taught as well as embedded in plenty of opportunities to write and handwriting should be taught right from the beginning.

Learning to handwrite and join the letters of the alphabet in their varied combinations quickly, so that writing can be read by the writer and others, is a complex *perceptuo-motor process*. It involves gross and fine muscle control, including a comfortable pencil/pen grip, posture and the formation of evenly sized letters and joins. All these elements can be developed through the direct teaching of handwriting.

> **Perceptuo-motor process:** the combination of perception (usually visual perception) and muscle movement.
>
> **Gross motor control:** control of large muscular movements such as swinging the arms.
>
> **Fine motor control:** control of small muscular movements such as threading a needle.

13.9   Teaching handwriting

Gross and fine motor skills

Gross and fine motor skills are important in developing hand/eye coordination and the muscular movements that will be essential in handwriting. Handwriting depends on sequences of small muscular movements; essentially nodding the wrist allied with flexing the fingers.

Before and during early formal schooling, activities should be planned to help develop gross and fine motor skills before teaching handwriting formally:

- paint walls or the ground with water and large house painting brushes to develop strength and coordination with large sweeps and circular movements (Figure 13.1)
- roll balls at objects
- scramble over cargo nets and use parallel bars to build upper body strength
- use ropes to skip, jump, tug, pull and wiggle
- use pegs and boards, geo boards and rubber bands
- construct with Lego and other challenging equipment
- complete a changing range of inset and interlocking jigsaws
- thread beads with fine laces and copy a simple bead pattern (Figure 13.2)
- draw in damp, dry or coloured sand with finger and tools
- sort and handle coins and buttons
- mould, squeeze, flatten, cut, roll and shape a range of different textures to develop tactile awareness and discriminatory skills
- promote activities that encourage eye gaze – for example, tracing with a finger, completing dot to dot activities, tracking toy cars on a road
- provide diverse materials and scissors to cut and stick in mixed media collage.

Figure 13.1 Developing gross and fine motor skills

Figure 13.2 Developing gross and fine motor skills

Pen/pencil grip

Holding a pen or pencil with the most comfortable grip enables the wrist and fingers to move freely and to not strain the hand. The tripod grip is the recommended grip to learn for both right- and left-handers. The hand shape for the tripod grip can be made by pretending to pick up a £1 coin. For right-handers the pen/pencil top should point slightly away from the shoulder and for left-handers the pen/pencil top should point towards left shoulder or heart.

Posture, sitting and paper position

To be able to write over a period of time, a comfortable sitting position is important.

This consists of being able to sit at a table or desk with the chair well under the table. The writer should be leaning slightly forward, bottom well back on the chair, knees at a right angle and feet flat on the floor. There should be good light. The paper or book should be slightly away from the nearest table edge and, for a right-hander, angled at approximately 30–40 degrees. It should be in front of the writer, not to one side.

The other hand should be used to steady the paper/exercise book.

> **Ascenders:** the vertical lines that rise above the midline on letters such as *d*.
>
> **Descenders:** the vertical lines that go below the baseline on letters such as *y*.
>
> **Entry stroke:** where the writing of a letter starts.
>
> **Exit stroke:** where the writing of an individual letter ends with a movement which may be extended to join it to the next letter.
>
> **Horizontal join:** the join between letters such as between *o* and *a*.
>
> **Vertical join:** the join between letters such as *a* and *t*.

Developing handwriting

A suggested sequence for teaching handwriting:

- writing patterns related to the letter families (see below)
- unjoined letters (but with exit strokes), related to writing patterns, taught in families (see below)
- horizontal joins
- diagonal joins
- tricky joins
- building speed and accuracy.

Letter formation and sequence

Jarman (1989) and Sassoon (1990) suggest that letters should be taught in families that are related in by their patterns of movement. There are two common types of movement: clockwise and anticlockwise. Making the correct movement is fundamental to legible and fluent handwriting. Sassoon suggests the following letter families, which have common movements, should be taught in this order:

1   i l t u y j (these start with a downstroke)
2   r n m h b p k (downstroke followed by a clockwise arch movement)
3   c a d g q o e (anticlockwise arch movement)
4   s f (anticlockwise but depends on style taught)
5   v w x z (starts with a slanting down stroke – although *z* is a bit of a anomaly).

Sassoon also suggests that children should have experience of handwriting patterns related to each of the main families which would introduce children to the movements associated with each one, as shown in Figure 13.3.

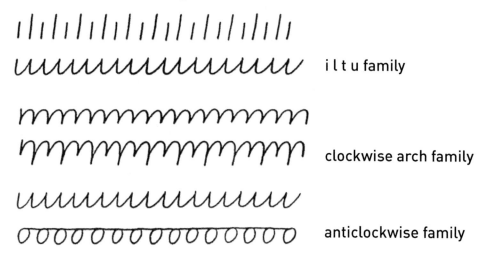

i l t u family

clockwise arch family

anticlockwise family

Figure 13.3 Handwriting patterns

Joining

Once children have been taught the letters and their exit strokes in a cursive style joining should not be too problematic. Children should be shown how to make the four main types of join (or ligature) by extending the exit strokes to join with the next letter.
The four types of join can be taught in the following sequence:

1 Vertical join to letters without ascenders (e.g. *a* to *o*)
2 Vertical join to letters with ascenders (e.g. *a* to *b*)
3 Horizontal joins (e.g. *o* to *c*)
4 Horizontal joins to letters with ascenders (e.g. *o* to *l*).

Jarman suggests that it is sensible to leave some letters unjoined such as b g j p q and y when they are next to vowels.

Speed and fluency

Once children have learnt letter formation and joins, they can practise developing speed and fluency. Much of this will come from engaging in regular and wide-ranging writing activities. However, handwriting challenges, individually or with a partner, can be helpful and fun; for example, practising writing sentences quickly which contain all the letters and joins with no loss of quality and legibility and monitoring time and quality, then trying to beat the best time.
   Sentences which include all letters and joins include:

   The quick brown fox jumps over the lazy dog.

   The five boxing wizards jump quickly.

Left-handedness

A significant number of children have a preference for using their left hand for writing. As the writing system in English is biased towards right-handedness, teachers will need to make adjustments to ensure that they help left-handers develop a fluent cursive style. These adjustments include:

- Sitting left-handers to the left of others so elbows do not interfere with each other.
- Monitoring grip. Left-handers can get in the habit of holding the hand like a claw so that they can see what they have written and not smudge if they are writing in ink. The tripod grip should be taught and left-handers should be encouraged to point the pen/pencil top towards their left shoulder or heart. The paper should be slanted 30–40 degrees to the right. This will ensure what has been written can then be seen and a more comfortable and less painful grip established.
- Provide a sloping desk or aid so that children do not have to lean over the paper or exercise book.
- Monitor letter formation carefully as left-handers may find clockwise movements easier and so reverse letters.

Case study, early primary: A handwriting lesson

Nat, who teaches 5 year olds, carries out regular dedicated handwriting sessions. A typical 15–20 minute lesson focused on basic letter formation would include:

- Teacher demonstration by writing in the air, talking through the letter formation: *'To form the letter b I am going to start at the very top of the ascender, go straight down to the baseline, then up and all the way round.'*
- Children copying the model writing in the air using their index finger and copying the way the teacher talks through the letter formation.
- Teacher demonstration using paper and pencil and a visualiser to project onto the screen showing the hand movements and continuing to talk through the formation as it is demonstrated.
- One or two children coming to the front and demonstrating via the visualiser in the same way.
- Guided and individual practice by the children of the targeted letter with the teacher checking and intervening as necessary.
- Recapitulation and final plenary assessing progress together.

Handwriting patterns, joins, letter strings related to spelling patterns and the relative size of letters can be taught using a similar multisensory process.

Importantly, the taught letters and joins should be reinforced when children are engaged in writing activities through reminders of letter formation on display in their classroom and adults commenting positively when they see children using the taught formations.

Teaching handwriting should occur both in context and in handwriting skills-focused sessions. Teachers should model how the taught movements, letter formations and joins are applied when writing a variety of texts, both in whole class shared writing and in small groups and with individuals. Feedback can be given to children about how well they are applying handwriting skills 'on the run'.

13.10 Keyboard skills

Little research has been completed which examines effective teaching and learning of keyboard skills in primary classrooms. In one of the few pieces of research, Connelly *et al.* (2007) compared keyboarded and handwritten compositions of primary-age children. They found that:

> Handwriting speed was consistently faster than keyboarding speed across all ages. Only a small minority of children in years 5 and 6 [9 to 11 year olds] had faster keyboarding than handwriting speed. Results showed that children's compositional quality was superior in the handwritten scripts as opposed to the keyboarded scripts. Keyboarded scripts were up to 2 years behind handwritten scripts in development.

> (Connelly *et al.*, 2007: 479)

They recommended that: 'Explicit keyboarding instruction (touch-typing) is needed to develop keyboarding fluency and unlock the full potential of the word processor for children's writing' (*ibid.*). Connelly *et al.* suggest that explicit instruction in keyboarding would improve the quality of composition, but in addition, James and Engelhardt (2013) suggest that keyboarding instruction, particularly at early ages, can have a significant impact on the development of reading. However, it is unlikely, even if keyboard skills are taught systematically in schools, that handwriting will wither away in the future. Handwriting is very convenient. Unlike word processing, handwriting materials are cheap, widely available, light, portable and very flexible.

Currently there is little research about what the balance should be between teaching handwriting and keyboard skills or when the formal teaching of keyboard skills should begin.

13.11 Children who experience difficulties with handwriting

Many children in primary schools experience difficulty with handwriting. Medwell and Wray (2007) cite evidence that up to 20 per cent of children, with boys outnumbering girls in this group, have difficulties in achieving automaticity in handwriting and that this undermines both handwriting and composing competences. Medwell *et al.* (2009) report how an intervention which targeted handwriting automaticity with groups of boys at 7 and 11 significantly improved levels of composing as well as the quality of handwriting.

Wyse *et al.* (2013: 249) list a range of reasons that children may be having difficulties with handwriting including motor coordination problems, hesitancy and lack of confidence in spelling, psychological problems such as bullying and bereavement, weak auditory, perceptual and memory skills, poor eyesight, fatigue, physical disability, poor posture and/or pencil grip. Teachers will need to be aware of these factors when assessing difficulties and plan to meet these specific needs, sometimes in consultation with other professionals.

Summary

This section of the chapter outlines factors that lead to legible and fluent handwriting; for example, explicit attention to handwriting is necessary to support children in producing high-quality writing. Practical approaches to teaching handwriting include teacher demonstration and modelling. Although handwriting remains an essential skill, there is a significant gap in research and advice on teaching keyboard skills which needs to be filled. There are many reasons why children experience difficulty with handwriting and teachers need to be observant and tactful if they are to help children develop fluency and legibility in handwriting.

Recommended reading

Christensen, Carol A. (2009) The critical role handwriting plays in the ability to produce high-quality written text, in R. Beard, M. Myhill, J. Riley and M. Nystrand (eds) *The SAGE Handbook of Writing Development*. London: SAGE, pp. 284–299. A thorough overview of the most recent international research into the importance of teaching handwriting and developing automaticity. **Advanced**

Dinehart, L. H. (2015) Handwriting in early childhood education: Research and future implications, *Journal of Early Childhood Literacy*, 15 (1) pp. 97–118. A comprehensive summary of international research into early childhood handwriting, arguing that practitioners should develop and implement best practice programmes in teaching early handwriting and handwriting 'readiness' skills. **Advanced**

Medwell, J. and Wray, D. (2007) 'Handwriting: What we know and what do we need to know?', *Literacy*, 41 (1): 10–15. An accessible report of research carried out in UK schools about the role of handwriting in promoting fluency and composition skills.

References

Berninger, V. and Amtmann, D. (2004) Preventing written expression disabilities though early and continuing assessment and interventions for handwriting and/or spelling problems: Research into practice, in L. Swanson, K. Harris and J. Graham (eds) *Handbook of Research into Learning Disabilities*. New York: Guilford, pp. 345–363.

Christensen, Carol A., (2009) The critical role handwriting plays in the ability to produce high-quality written text, in R. Beard, M. Myhill, J. Riley and M. Nystrand (eds) *The SAGE Handbook of Writing Development*. London: SAGE, pp. 284–299.

Connelly, V., Gee, D. and Walsh, E. (2007) A comparison of keyboarded and handwritten compositions and the relationship with transcription speed, *British Journal of Educational Psychology*, 77 pp. 479–492.

James, K. H. and Engelhardt, L. (2013) The effects of handwriting on functional brain development in pre-literate children, *Trends in Neuroscience and Education*, 1 (1) pp. 32–42.

Jarman, C. (1989) *The Development of Handwriting Skills: A resource book for teachers*. Oxford: Basil Blackwell.

Medwell, J. and Wray, D. (2007) Handwriting: What we know and what do we need to know?, *Literacy*, 41 (1) pp. 10–15.

Medwell, J., Strand, S. and Wray, D. (2009) The links between handwriting and composing for Y6 children, *Cambridge Journal of Education*, 39 (3) pp. 328–344.

Sassoon, R. (1990) *Handwriting: A new perspective*. Leekhampton: Stanley Thornes.

Wyse, D., Jones, R., Bradford, H. and Wolpert M. A. (2013) *Teaching English, Language and Literacy*, 3rd edn. Abingdon: Routledge.

CHAPTER 14
GRAMMAR AND PUNCTUATION

This chapter covers:

- Research into teaching and learning sentence grammar
- Word classes
- Phrases, clauses and sentences
- Teaching grammar in context
  - Case study, early primary: Explicit grammar teaching – present and past tense
  - Case study, upper primary: Explicit grammar teaching – active and passive verbs
- Punctuation
- Sentence punctuation
  - Case study, middle primary: Explicit punctuation teaching

14.1 Research into teaching and learning sentence grammar

Arguments concerning teaching grammar in primary classrooms have been raging for more than fifty years (Locke, 2009), with some arguing that teaching grammar impacts positively on young people's writing development and others that teaching children to name the parts of a sentence has no effect on how well they communicate through speech and writing and is a waste of time. There are also misunderstandings about what 'grammar' means.

Activity 14.1
Definitions of 'grammar' – reflective journal/blog/pairs

What do you think when you hear the word 'grammar? Jot down a few notes. Some teachers gave the following responses:

> Panic... worry... tests...
>
> *My grammar isn't very good – I don't speak Standard English.*
>
> *Little punctuation marks jumping up all over the place!*

The first response is quite common; many people worry about grammar. The second sees grammar as to do with accent and the third sees punctuation as the same as grammar. These views probably represent the most general responses. Talk with a partner about your school experiences of learning grammar. Did you learn about language in the context of reading and writing? As naming and defining parts of speech? Through decontextualised grammar exercises? Or not at all?

How successful do you think the teaching was? Were there any times you were confused? What made you feel like that? How have you come to learn about elements of grammar or punctuation?

Make a few notes about the implications for your own teaching. What does it tell you about how/how not to approach teaching grammar?

Grammar is the study of how to make sense in speaking, reading or writing in order to understand people who use the same language. It is no more mysterious than that. As Crystal puts it: 'Grammar is the business of taking language to pieces, to see how it works' (Crystal, 2000: 1). Many adults feel insecure about aspects of grammar but in fact all adults (and many children) know a lot about grammar. By the age of 5 many children can speak in sentences when necessary, and adults certainly can. This is all implicit knowledge.

Activity 14.2
Implicit knowledge about language – individual/pairs

Try filling in the gaps in the sentences below with one word for each space (there are no correct answers):

I crawled to the _____ and bumped into a _____. It was _____. Terrified, I ___ .

What could I _____ now?

In the first sentence, for the first gap you might have chosen words like 'door' or 'window' and 'chair' or 'table'. These are nouns. No other kind of word would fit. It just would not sound right if you put 'yellow' or 'packed' in either of those gaps. (Have a go!) In the second sentence you may have put the adjective 'painful'. It would not have made sense if you had put 'cat' or 'bicycle' there. In the third sentence, you would not have put the adjective 'small'. 'Terrified, I small.' just does not make sense, but adding a verb such as 'cried' or 'whimpered' would. And similarly, in the final space you would not put a noun or an adjective but another verb like 'do' or 'hope'.

Being able to fill in the gaps in these sentences shows that implicitly you know a lot about how language works and the choices you can make. It is worth remembering that children will have implicit knowledge too. Explicit knowledge about language, or grammar, means bringing what is under the surface – implicit – out into the open and making it explicit.

Two significant large-scale studies (Hillocks, 1986; Andrews *et al.*, 2006) found no evidence that formal teaching of grammar out of context has any beneficial effect on either reading or writing. However, the key phrase in the last sentence is 'out of context'. When grammar is taught in the context of reading and writing, it can be very beneficial to young writers. A large-scale study by Myhill *et al.* (2013) in secondary schools found significant positive effects for teaching grammar in the context of teaching about writing. The key teaching principles are that:

- grammatical metalanguage is used, but it is explained through real examples
- links are always made between the feature introduced and how it might enhance the writing being tackled
- discussion is fundamental in encouraging critical conversations about language and effects
- the use of 'creative imitation' offers model patterns for pupils to play with and then use in their own writing
- activities support pupils in making choices and being designers of writing
- language play, experimentation, risk taking and games are actively encouraged (Myhill *et al.*, 2013: 105).

See: http://keenkite.collins.co.uk/articles/videos/David%20Reedy%20On%20Deborah%20Myhill.mp4 (accessed 1 May 2017) and http://keenkite.collins.co.uk/articles/videos/David%20Reedy%20Grammar%20in%20Context.mp4 (accessed 1 May 2017).

When it comes to teaching, it is easier to help children be more reflective readers and writers if teachers and pupils have a shared language to talk about how language works.

This is the approach that this chapter takes: that grammar is a resource, serving writers' and speakers' purposes as they work to express meaning in the texts they create. This approach also takes a *descriptive* perspective to grammar as opposed to a *prescriptive* approach. Prescriptive grammarians believe that there are fixed rules that should be adhered to and that if features such as double negatives are used, they should be corrected and expunged. A descriptive approach looks at language in use, whether spoken or written, and is interested in understanding the features as they are used and the effect they have on meaning.

> **Metalanguage:** a language used to discuss or describe the structure of language; grammatical or linguistic terminology.
>
> **Prescriptive grammar:** a set of rules about language based on a view of how people think language should be used. In this view, language use can be deemed 'right' or 'wrong'.
>
> **Descriptive grammar:** a set of rules about language based on how language is actually used in everyday social contexts.

Many people feel anxious when confronted with the word 'grammar', but essentially grammar is about syntax: it gives an account of how sentences are constructed to make sense so that users of the same language can understand each other. It is no more complicated than that. Grammarians look for patterns of words in use in sentences, categorise those patterns and give them names, such as *adverb*, *phrase*, *multiclause sentence* and so on. Some patterns are simple and some are more complicated but grammarians try to give each pattern a label and a definition.

> **Syntax:** sentence structure.

Grammatical terminology, or metalanguage, is very useful because it gives teachers and children a shared vocabulary to talk precisely about language in use and reflect upon it. Some teachers feel confident with the terminology, some do not. Bearne *et al.* suggest that:

> If you feel confident, then it suggests that you were taught first about how language works and then given the grammatical terms to describe language features. You used the grammar first, to make meaning, then used the grammatical terminology. That kind of knowledge and experience helps you to make sense of language and shape language to say what you want to say. If you feel a tingle of fear when you hear particular terminology, then it suggests that you were only taught the names of grammatical parts, rather than how they work to create meaning – or you weren't explicitly taught grammar.
>
> (Bearne *et al.*, 2016: 4)

All speakers and writers of English have a wide implicit understanding of grammar otherwise they would not be able to understand each other. When teaching grammar in primary classrooms, teachers need to decide what grammatical features to make explicit through looking at and discussing language in use, using appropriate grammatical terminology, in order to help children reflect on and develop their own language in use.

Activity 14.3
Grammar quiz – individual

Fill in the grid on website resource W14.1. Check out your answers with the definitions and examples in section 14.2.

14.2   Word classes

This chapter focuses on syntax: the grammar of sentences. Sentences are structured hierarchically: words go to together to make phrases, phrases go together to make clauses and clauses go together to make sentences.

Words can be *nouns, pronouns, adjectives, verbs, adverbs, prepositions, determiners* and *conjunctions*.

A word is defined by the job it does in a sentence. So the same word can be a different word class if it has a different function in the sentence. For example, the word *run* acts as a verb in this sentence:

I *run* down the street.

and a noun in this sentence:

I scored a *run*.

Another example would be green. It acts as a noun in:

They played cricket on the village *green*.

and as an adjective in:

It was a *green* door.

Nouns

Nouns are words for things, people, animals, or states of mind or existence: *frog, wood, woman, tiger, toad, sorrow, fear, love, humility, hunger, coronation, palace, queen, envy, courage*. These are often referred to as common nouns. Proper nouns, which need a capital letter, are names of people, places, days and months; for example, *Siobhan, Aberdeen, Tuesday* and *December*.

Compound nouns are made up of two or more words, sometimes an adjective and a noun or a noun and a noun which keep their original spelling when joined together:

breakwater, snowfall, toothbrush.

Adjectives

Adjectives are words which modify nouns: *red*, *tall*, *ugly*, *small*, *cheerful*, *open*, *old*. They tell us what the noun is like; for example, a **red** car, a **tall** cupboard.

Verbs

Verbs are words for actions; for example, action verbs – *jump*, *climb*, *drop* – or states of mind (stative verbs) – *think*, *decide*, *hope*, *be*.

Auxiliary (helping) verbs

The auxiliary verbs *do*, *be* and *have* help in the formation of the tenses of main verbs:

> Do you like sweets? (*like* is the main verb; *do* is the auxiliary)
> I am going. (*going* is the main verb; *am* is the auxiliary)
> They have appeared. (*appeared* is the main verb; *have* is the auxiliary)

Do is common for asking questions, emphasising points or making negatives:

> Do you want to sit down?
> I do like this book.
> I don't think that is fair.

But it can also be a main verb, as in: I do the washing.

Be and Have

As auxiliary verbs, *be* and *have* help to form several tenses of other verbs:

> She *is* going. (continuous present/present progressive)
> They *were* dreaming. (continuous past/ past progressive)
> I *have been* running. (continuous present perfect/progressive present perfect)
> We *had been* hoping. (continuous past perfect/progressive past perfect)
> You will *be* leaving. (continuous future/future progressive)
> They will *have been* waiting for three hours. (continuous future perfect/future perfect progressive)
> We *have* decided. (present perfect)
> We *had* decided. (past perfect)

Modal verbs

Modal verbs are a type of auxiliary verb that indicate belief that something is certain, probable or possible. They modify or add meaning to other verbs; for example, *can*, *will*, *may*, *shall*, *must*, *ought*, *need*, *could*, *might*, *would*, *should*.

Regular verbs

Regular verbs follow the same pattern using '-ed' in the past tense (plus 'have' for the past perfect) and the present tense form plus 'will' or 'shall' for the future tense:

> I *like* ice cream.
>
> I *liked* ice cream the first time I tasted it.
>
> I **have** *liked* ice cream since I was young.
>
> I **will** like ice cream forever.

> I *pass* that house every day.
>
> I *passed* the library on the way to the shops.
>
> I **have** *passed* that bus stop every day for years.
>
> *I* **will** pass the station at 6 o'clock.

Irregular verbs

Irregular verbs do not use the '-ed' ending in past tenses, as most verbs in English do.

> *I see, I saw, I have seen*
>
> *I run, I ran, I have run*
>
> *I speak, I spoke, I have spoken*
>
> *I know, I knew, I have known.*

Adverbs

Adverbs modify verbs, adjectives or other adverbs, telling you how the verb is carried out; for example, *strangely, very, often, well, quickly, soon.*

> She was acting *strangely.*
>
> I *very often* go there.
>
> I'm feeling *well.*
>
> It was *quickly* done.
>
> I'll be there *soon.*

Many adverbs can be placed in different places in the sentence and still make sense:

> Quickly, it was done.
>
> It was quickly done.
>
> It was done quickly.

The placing of the adverb depends on what the writer wants to emphasise.

Determiners

These are small but very important words that tell us something about a noun. The most common are *a* and *the*, although there are others such as *this, that, some, any, my, your, its, whose, which* and numbers (*three, hundreds*).

Prepositions

Prepositions are words or groups of two or more words which come before nouns or pronouns to indicate place, time or position:

> *opposite* him
>
> *before* lunch
>
> *between* the trees.

Sometimes prepositions link two nouns or pronouns; for example, 'She went *into* the house.' Some prepositions can also act as conjunctions if they link clauses rather than single nouns/pronouns; for example, 'I'm leaving *before* I say something I shall regret.'

Prepositions include: *about, above, across, after, against, around, before, behind, beyond, by, down, in, into, near, off, on, opposite, out, over, round, through, towards, under, up, in front of.*

Pronouns

Pronouns are words which stand in for or refer to nouns: *I, mine, who, anyone, she, her, ours, myself, itself, those, who, whoever*

Types of pronoun:

- personal – *I, me, he, him, she, her, it, we, us, they, them*
- possessive – *my, mine, your, yours, his, her, hers, its, our, ours, their, theirs**
- reflexive – *myself, yourself, himself, herself, itself, ourselves, yourselves, themselves*
- demonstrative – *this, that, these, those*
- relative – *who, whom, whose, which, whoever*
- interrogative – *who? whom? whose? what? which? whoever? whichever? whatever?*
- reciprocal **–** *each other, one another* (used to express a two-way relationship).

* NB: *possessive pronouns* never need an apostrophe; for example, 'The cat licked *its* paws.'

Conjunctions

Conjunctions link two words, phrases or clauses together. There are two main types:

1   Coordinating: linking two words, phrases or clauses together as an equal pair (*and, but, or, so*)
   - *This band is very well known **and** the venue is sold out.*
   - *It's getting late **and** I'm tired.*

- *I like coffee **but** I don't like tea.*
- *We can eat now **or** we can wait till later.*

2 Subordinating: introduces a subordinate clause, using *when, if that, because, until, where.* For example:

- *We worked all night **because** you wanted the report.*

14.3   Phrases, clauses and sentences

Phrases

Words go together to make phrases. There are two types of phrase:

- Noun phrases (made up of a determiner + noun(s) plus an adjective(s)).
  For example:

	the	*iron*	*man*
	determiner	adjective	noun

- Verb phrases (made up of a verb plus another word that might indicate tense or sometimes mood).
  For example:

  smashed

  was smashed

  was entirely smashed

  was being smashed

  would have been smashed

Clauses

Phrases go together to make clauses. A clause contains a noun, or noun phrase, and a verb or verb phrase. For it to be a clause it has to include a verb.
  For example:

- *the Iron Man smashed into the rocks*

noun	verb phrase

- *falling from the top of the cliff*

verb	noun phrase

Some clauses, such as the first example, make sense on their own and are called *main clauses*. Some clauses only make sense when read in relation to the main clause, such as the second example above. These are known as *subordinate clauses*.

Sentences

Clauses go together to make sentences. A main clause can stand on its own (usually) and is called a single-clause sentence (sometimes called a simple sentence, although a single clause sentence can actually be quite complicated), once punctuated with a capital letter and a full stop, for example:

> The Iron Man smashed into the rocks.

A main clause and one or more subordinate clauses can go together and make a multi-clause sentence (sometimes known as a complex sentence):

- *The Iron Man, falling from the top of the cliff, smashed into the rocks.*
- *Falling from the top of the cliff, the Iron Man smashed into the rocks.*
- *The Iron Man smashed into the rocks, falling from the top of the cliff.*

The subordinate clause is distinguished from the main clause by the use of commas. As can be seen a subordinate clause can be placed in three different places in relation to the main clause depending on the writer's intentions.

Multiclause sentences can also contain more than one main clause where the clauses are joined together with conjunctions such as *and*. An example would be *I went to the park and I played football*. (This type of multiclause sentence is sometimes termed a *compound sentence*.)

> **Subject:** the subject in a sentence carries out the verb; for example, The boy dropped the cake. Here, *The boy* is the subject because he dropped the cake.
>
> **Object:** the object is on the receiving end of the verb – in the sentence above, *the cake* is the object because it was dropped by the boy.
>
> **Complement:** a complement completes the meaning of a sentence, particularly when part of the verb 'be' is used; for example, The boy was *ashamed*. The cake was *ruined*.

Sentences can be statements, questions, exclamations or instructions/commands. They can be *simple*, just containing one clause, or *compound* where two main clauses are joined with conjunctions such as *and*. Finally they can be *complex*, with a main clause and one or more subordinate clauses:

> Simple sentence: *I went home.*
>
> Compound sentence: *I went home and I had a bath.*
>
> Complex sentence: *As I went home I was thinking about having a lovely warm bath.*

14.4 Teaching grammar in context

The evidence from the latest research shows that explicit attention to grammar is likely to be effective when it is approached within a broader sequence of activity focused on text.

Reedy and Bearne have argued strongly that:

> Good writing is what works to do the job the writer wants. And studying how language works – grammar – should help young writers to say what they want to say as effectively as they can.
>
> (Reedy and Bearne, 2013: 4)

Using the planning and teaching sequence in the Introduction to this book, grammar can be addressed at crucial points in the three phases of the sequence. Phase one starts with reading a chosen text which has good examples of the kind of grammatical and literary features the teacher wants to focus on. The text is read and discussed, investigating the specific grammatical feature being taught. Children have the chance to familiarise themselves with the author's style and to capture ideas for their own writing. Phase two involves explicit teaching including the introduction and use of grammatical terminology and teacher modelling of the grammatical feature in use. At the beginning of phase three, which prepares for writing, through discussion and experimentation with the grammatical feature, the children begin to apply the feature and see how they might use it themselves for a given effect. After support and modelling, they are in a position to make more controlled and informed writing choices as they pursue their purposes for writing.

Reedy and Bearne (2013) refer to the pedagogical process of explicit grammar teaching in context: reading and investigation supported by explicit teaching of the specific language feature under consideration; discussion about how this piece of language works; experimenting with it in use; finally, practising its use by making informed and controlled choices in writing. They summarise this as the REDM sequence – the process of teaching grammar in context (Figure 14.1).

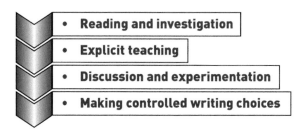

Figure 14.1 REDM sequence (Reedy and Bearne, 2013: 7)

Case study, early primary: Explicit grammar teaching – past and present verbs

(For a more detailed case study of explicit grammar teaching in context, see also website resource W4.3.)

As part of a unit of work on superheroes, a teacher planned a 'verb week' with her 6- and 7-year-old class, where the children collected action verbs and put them on a special word wall called 'action corner'. After talking about their favourite superheroes, and films they had all enjoyed, she began reading *Traction Man is Here* by

---

Mini Grey (2006). On the board she put the title with the 'action' bit of 'Traction' highlighted and explained that this week the focus would be on actions.

After hot-seating Traction Man's friend Scrubbing Brush, and imagining new scenarios for the two friends, reading and enjoying the books, the action verb list was growing well. By the third day, the teacher was able to select a series of verbs that she planned to use to help the children learn about past, present and future tenses. She first of all explained that the children were going to write their own Traction Man (TM) and Scrubbing Brush (SB) adventure and in preparation for this they were going to look at some of their action verbs. The children would later choose to write an adventure in the present or past tense.

The teacher had prepared a grid on the Interactive White Board (IWB) with a few action verbs, carefully selecting verbs with regular past tenses ending in '-ed':

Yesterday (past)	Today (present)
	TM jumps
SB climbed	
	SB shouts
TM explained	

She did not mention the words in brackets first of all but asked the children to tell her what they would say if 'Traction Man jumps' happened yesterday. They didn't find it too difficult to provide 'jumped'. After the class had filled in the first three lines of the grid, she asked them to talk to their partners to come up with a verb that was either past or present. She then asked the children in pairs to think of another adventure Traction Man and Scrubbing Brush could have. Once they had come up with some ideas she gave them planning sheets with two columns headed 'past' and 'present' and asked the children to choose one or the other column and to get down a few of their ideas for the next TM and SB adventure before they forgot them. With support, in groups, they decided on whether their stories would be in the present or past tense. They would start drafting their stories tomorrow.

The next day, after a quick recap looking at the saved chart on the IWB, the teacher asked the children to use either past or present verbs to start drafting their adventures. She and the teaching assistant worked with each group and dealt with any confusions, although she was pleased and surprised to find that there were not many. Most of the children were keeping to their chosen tense and where they veered off, just a reminder helped them to get back on track. On the following day, the teacher chose one story in the present and one in the past and read them to the class. At this stage she began to bring in the word 'tense' but didn't explain or labour it.

One child's story began:

Traction Man is sitting in the kitchen. He looks out of the window. He decides to go outside so he climbs down the tea towel on to the floor.

Another had written:

Yesterday Scrubbing Brush was sad because Traction Man hadn't played with him all day. He decided to go for a walk, but ...

When the stories were finished they were published in a class book called 'The Further Adventures of Traction Man and Scrubbing Brush'.

Source: Reedy and Bearne, 2013: 16–17.

Case study, upper primary: Explicit grammar teaching – active and passive verbs

In a sequence of work where the outcome was a class newspaper, Kem, the teacher, decided it would be a good context to explore further active and passive verbs with his 10 and 11 year olds. The class had already covered this area previously and had identified that a verb is active when the subject is doing it (*The girl kicked the ball.*) and passive when the object of the sentence is having something done to it (*The ball was kicked by the girl.*). The class were aware that passive constructions usually consisted of one of the forms of the verb 'to be' and a past participle and that it many cases the subject of the verb might not be indicated (*The ball was kicked.*). The children looked in a few local newspapers for examples of the use of the passive and noticed that many headlines used the passive and sometimes omitted the form of the verb 'to be'; for example, *Pet found after two weeks. Car abandoned in layby.* The children then used this new understanding of the passive to compose their own headlines for the class newspaper.

14.5 Punctuation

Punctuation is essential in writing. Punctuation shows the reader how to read the words and sentences in the text: when to pause, when to make the voice rise to indicate a question, when to be emphatic. Punctuation reveals the meaning in a piece of writing and it really matters. It shows which chunks of words go together and which are more separate. Without attention to punctuation, a reader could take a completely opposite meaning to the one intended. For example, a notice might say:

**PRIVATE
NO
ACCESS
ALLOWED**

If it contained the following punctuation it might have a very different message:

PRIVATE?
NO.
ACCESS
ALLOWED

Just as with grammar, knowing about punctuation is helpful in that a writer can decide what punctuation to choose to make the intended meaning absolutely clear. The choice of punctuation depends on what the writer wants to say, so looking carefully at where published writers have used punctuation can help young writers to see how they can vary punctuation to create the effect they want in their own writing.

Although punctuation is very important in making the message of writing clear, it is one of the least researched (but most complained about) aspects of language development, in respect of how children come to understand punctuation (Hall, 2009). Teachers' experience of helping children develop their understanding of the use of punctuation would suggest that it can be a problem. Hall points out that punctuation has always been the site of contestation and this is particularly marked in education:

> For while language and punctuation continually evolve, so government and other agencies attempt to lock it down and keep it fixed. Unfortunately, children are taught the rules whilst at the same time popular culture and advertising play havoc with them.

> (Hall, 2009: 272–273)

Further:

> Defining punctuation and its marks has become increasingly difficult. As punctuation has shifted from a more elocutionary nature to a more grammatical nature, so definitions have become more flexible.

> (*ibid.*)

All this adds to the formidable challenge for a young writer of orchestrating all the complex elements that are needed to make meaning in written language.

There seems to be a division in the way that children understand punctuation (Hall and Robinson, 1996; Hall, 2009). First, there is *pre-linguistic punctuation.* In this phase children have been taught about punctuation but they do not habitually use it (unless reminded). They seem to see these marks as not very important when they are engaged in the act of composing. Children in this phase seem to understand sentence punctuation as a graphic device – full stops marking the end of lines or the end of the piece as a whole. Children do eventually begin to become aware that punctuation is more than just graphical and begin to enter the second phase of *linguistic punctuation*, where the punctuation marks semantic units within the composed text. Children slowly take on the grammatical use of punctuation as they move through primary school. However, although children increase their understanding, Hall suggests:

> As written language use progresses so the punctuation problems that children have to solve increase in difficulty. Older children may make

punctuation errors, but this is often because the problems they have to solve by using punctuation have become much more complex.

(Hall, 2009: 281)

> **Semantic units:** sections of text which make sense on their own; for example, a sentence.

In order to solve those problems, children need plenty of opportunity to explore and discuss the use of punctuation in real texts and then reflect on how they are going to use them in their own.

The parallels with teaching grammar are very close indeed and therefore the teaching sequence outlined above for grammar is highly appropriate for approaching the understanding of sentence punctuation.

14.6 Sentence punctuation

Sentence punctuation marks that are likely to be addressed in primary schools are: full stops, capital letters, question marks, exclamation marks, commas to mark lists, commas to mark phrases and clauses, apostrophes of omission, apostrophes of possession, speech marks, colons and semicolons, ellipsis, parenthesis and, possibly, bullet points.

(See www.youtube.com/watch?v=My6oGvkHnfY for an animated film about the use of apostrophes (accessed 1 May 2017).)

Activity 14.4
Punctuation – individual/pairs

Looking at the list of punctuation marks above, highlight any that you are unsure about. Talk to a partner about them and see if you can come up with examples of their use. Now take a few books or magazines that are handy and explore them to see if you can find examples of the punctuation you have highlighted. Can you explain what the particular punctuation mark does? It does not matter if you are not quite right. Just making it explicit helps – and shows where you need to look further.

Check out your highlighted punctuation marks with website resource W14.2.

Case study, middle primary: Explicit punctuation teaching

Eleanor, who teaches 7 and 8 year olds, decided to focus on the punctuation of direct speech.

This was part of a sequence of work based on a work of fiction which contained plenty of direct speech: *Black Queen* by Michael Morpurgo (2000).

After reading and responding to the text for a while, the children were asked to look at the way the book sets out and punctuates direct speech. Eleanor asked questions to focus their investigations:

- What do the speech marks look like?
- When is a new line started?
- Where do the speech marks/inverted commas go?
- Where do you put the punctuation at the end, for example, a comma, full stop or question mark?

Looking in *Black Queen*, in twos and threes the children investigated other stories in the class library and were challenged to devise their own set of rules for how to punctuate direct speech. Each group shared what they had found out and discussed some of the complications found in the text, such as the introductory comma that comes when a sentence introduces a speech (Billy shouted, "Go away!") and what goes on when a speaker's dialogue is split ("Like bats," I quipped. "Like vampires, like witches. She's got a black cat too. A witch! Maybe she's a real witch.")

Once the guidelines were formulated and agreed, they were displayed and referred to when needed. Children then used the agreed guidelines when using direct speech in their writing of an additional episode for *Black Queen* and in subsequent writing activities, including stories and newspaper reports.

Summary

Grammar and punctuation are tools to make meaning clear for speakers and writers of a common language. Fluent users of a language have considerable implicit knowledge of language structure and how to make meaning clear to themselves and others. Teachers have to plan to decide what aspects of sentence grammar (or syntax) to make explicit to children so they are more aware of the choices they can make, particularly in their writing, to get better at creating the messages and text they want to or are asked to compose. Grammar and punctuation are best learned in real reading and writing contexts. There is no evidence that the decontextualised learning of rules and definitions lead to improvements in children's spoken or written language.

Recommended reading

Bearne, E., Kennedy, R. and Reedy, D. (2016) *Teaching Grammar Effectively at Key Stage One*. Leicester: United Kingdom Literacy Association. Based on the premise that grammar should be taught in context (Reading, Explicit teaching, Discussion and Making language choices – REDM), this book deals with all aspects of grammar, spelling and punctuation required at early primary stage in England.

Hall, N. (2009) Developing an understanding of punctuation, in R. Beard, D. Myhill, J. Riley and M. Nystrand (eds) *The SAGE Handbook of Writing Development*. London: SAGE, pp. 27–283. A succinct summary of international research about punctuation. **Advanced**

Hall, N. and Robinson, A. (eds) (1996) *Learning About Punctuation*. Cleveden: Multilingual Matters. Despite its age this is still the most comprehensive resource for punctuation.

Locke, T. (2009) Grammar and writing: The international debate, in R. Beard, D. Myhill, J. Riley and M. Nystrand (eds) *The SAGE Handbook of Writing Development.* London: SAGE, pp. 182–193. This chapter summarises the key international debates about teaching grammar. **Advanced**

Reedy, D. and Bearne, E. (2013) *Teaching Grammar Effectively in Primary Schools.* Leicester: United Kingdom Literacy Association. Based on the REDM process (see Bearne *et al.*, above), this book covers all the English national curriculum requirements for spelling punctuation and grammar for children up to 11 in England.

References

Andrews, R. C., Torgerson, S., Beverton, A., Freeman, T., Lock, G., Low, G., Robinson, A. and Zhu, D. (2006) The effect of grammar teaching on writing development, *British Education Research Journal*, 32 (1) pp. 39–55.

Bearne, E., Kennedy, R. and Reedy, D. (2016) *Teaching Grammar Effectively at Key Stage One.* Leicester: United Kingdom Literacy Association.

Crystal, D. (2000) *Rediscover Grammar.* London: Longman.

Hall, N. (2009) Developing an understanding of punctuation, in R. Beard, D. Myhill, J. Riley and M. Nystrand (eds) *The SAGE Handbook of Writing Development.* London: SAGE, pp. 27–283.

Hall, N. and Robinson, A. (eds) (1996) *Learning About Punctuation.* Cleveden: Multilingual Matters.

Hillocks, G. (1986) *Research on Written Composition: New directions for teaching.* Urbana IL: National Council of Teachers of English.

Locke, T. (2009) Grammar and writing: The international debate, in R. Beard, D. Myhill, J. Riley and M. Nystrand (eds) *The SAGE Handbook of Writing Development.* London: SAGE, pp. 182–193. (This chapter summarises the key international debates about teaching grammar.)

Myhill, D., Jones, S., Watson, A. and Lines, H. (2013) Playful explicitness with grammar: A pedagogy for writing, *Literacy*, 47 (2) pp.103–111.

Reedy, D. and Bearne, E. (2013) *Teaching Grammar Effectively in Primary Schools.* Leicester: United Kingdom Literacy Association.

Children's books

Mini Grey (2006) *Traction Man is Here.* Red Fox. ISBN 9780099451099

Michael Morpurgo (2000) *Black Queen.* London: Corgi. ISBN 9780552559010

CHAPTER 15

RESPONDING TO AND ASSESSING WRITING

This chapter covers:

- Response, feedback and assessment
- A note about differentiation
- Assessment, 'correcting' and response
- A note about correcting
- Self-evaluation, self-assessment and self-regulation
  - Case study, early primary: Proofreading and self-correcting aged 6
- Managing response
- Planning, teaching, writing, reviewing, planning
- Monitoring progress
  - Case study, upper primary: Responding to and assessing writing throughout a teaching sequence
- Diagnosing difficulties with writing
  - Case study, middle primary: Amy, a 9-year-old writer

15.1   Response, feedback and assessment

This chapter draws a distinction between response, feedback and assessment, with response and feedback being the 'conversation' the teacher (or other reader) has, either verbally or in writing, with the young writer. Response can happen at any time during the composition of a piece of writing: as it begins, when it is in draft form and when it is ready for the reader. It can be spoken or written and responders might be other children as well as the adults in the classroom. Formative assessment will be fed by the teacher's insights gained during the process of responding to writing. This kind of assessment, as the name implies, leads to the teacher making decisions about how best to help the individual or group move forward. Summative assessment is a more formal matter which happens at national, local, school, classroom and individual levels. Nationally, assessment data are used by governments to develop testing and accountability measures and to demonstrate the effectiveness of their educational policies. Locally, assessments are used to judge school effectiveness and compare provision between schools. Within a school, assessment can lead to initiatives to address specific development needs. In the classroom, assessment is associated with daily observation, weekly, half termly and termly record keeping; individual records; and assessment of the curriculum. In order to assess writing (or any other aspect of English) a teacher needs to have some idea of what progress looks like (see section 15.8).

> **Formative/continuous assessment:** assessment *for* learning, designed to monitor children's learning at any stage in a teaching sequence, allowing teachers to address gaps in understanding. Formative assessment also helps to identify children's strengths and weaknesses and provide feedback that can move learning forward. Formative assessment can also be diagnostic, identifying groups of children who may require extra support.
>
> **Summative assessment:** assessment about what children have learned made at the end of a period of teaching. This could be termly, half termly or indeed more frequently. Although summative assessment can be used formatively, it is generally used to monitor the progress of individuals and groups of children and to predict age-related attainment. Summative assessment can be defined as assessment *of* learning and is often carried out by testing.
>
> **Diagnostic testing**: specifically designed methods used with children who present cause for concern; for example, a full reading or writing miscue analysis, or an assessment of specific learning difficulties.

Assessment allows teachers to evaluate their provision for progression (how all the children move on during the course of a year) and differentiation (how individual learning needs are catered for). As well as being formative and summative, assessment can be diagnostic, to help support children whose learning needs are beyond the usual. When it comes to writing, however, the matter of assessment becomes a little more complicated because writing is used both as an *object* of assessment and as a *means* of assessment. Writing is assessed through English tests; it is also the means of showing what pupils know in every other subject so that science, history, art, music, all depend on writing to show what pupils have learned. This makes it all the more important to establish clear principles and practice in assessing writing – and in using writing to assess.

15.2   A note about differentiation

There are many ways to interpret differentiation. At its most basic, teachers may provide different tasks within an activity to cater for varying levels of perceived ability based on assessments of reading (see pp. 227–228), often represented by worksheets with an increasing number of words in relation to illustrations. However, this can often be more like division than differentiation, giving negative messages not only about the potential of individuals but also about reading being seen as the most effective measure of a child's intellectual capacity. Although teachers use such approaches with the best of intentions to try to cater for the range of pupils, it is wrong to assume that 'ability' can only be judged by an individual's ability to read (Bearne and Kennedy, 2017). It is the teacher's role to move all learners on, and offer the appropriate support at whatever stage they are at in their learning. Assuming that certain children or groups can only cope with a limited amount of information can mean that those who struggle with literacy but are conceptually perfectly competent (children with dyslexia, for example) will be excluded. The challenge is to find ways of framing tasks that will genuinely stretch all the learners.

These teachers describe their approaches to differentiation in planning and responding to writing:

> I think it's important to plan for different kinds of work according to where the children are in their learning. For instance, when children are working in writing groups, I might ask one child to write a paragraph about the setting, another to retell the story we'd read, and another to invent a story, depending on their level of writing.

> The way you do feedback is crucial to move learning forward. When I'm marking children's work I look for things they're doing well and for areas of improvement and my feedback and comment specifically on those. Of course I focus on the learning objective but the development points are personal. I always identify part of the writing that could be improved and either talk about how it might be worked on when we have small group writing or I make a written suggestion. When I've marked the work, if there is a group of children who all need the same support, I'll teach a guided session with that group.

Effective differentiation can be provided through resources, activities, support and response. And response and assessment certainly provide a teacher with useful information to help plan for the needs of individual learners. Video 9 (see website) shows how Lloyd assesses and responds to pupils' writing. Section 3 looks at how he challenges the most able writers, in section 4 he describes supporting bilingual writers and in section 8 he explains his approach to differentiation.

Activity 15.1
Differentiation – reflective journal/blog

Ask the teacher you work with most closely how s/he provides for diversity – or differentiates resources, activities, support and response. When you plan your next teaching sequence, check that in your planning you have catered for the needs of all the learners. As you respond to the children's work and assess it, select two or three children whose progress interests you and note how you will be able to cater for their different needs when you next plan a teaching and learning sequence.

15.3 Assessment, 'correcting' and response

Assessment carries with it the flavour of judgement against certain criteria since it is the teacher's job is to help children 'get better at it', whatever 'it' is – in this case, writing. That means having some idea of what success or achievement looks like. In terms of writing this will include judgements about how well the writer communicates with the reader, the organisation of the piece and how effectively it conveys meaning. It will also include marking vocabulary, spelling, punctuation and grammar. But even formative assessment, intended to build achievement progressively, can get bogged down and lose the broader focus of judging writing in terms of meaning and focus solely on 'correcting errors'. Huot and Perry (2009) cite the example of Joseph Williams (1981), himself a teacher of composition in Chicago, USA, who carried out a small-scale experiment to determine if teachers treat writing by their pupils and by published authors differently. He took a piece from *1984* by George Orwell, inserted about a hundred errors into it and asked readers to comment on the piece. Most of the errors went unnoticed. Huot and Perry ask: 'What would happen if you sat down to enjoy and learn something from your [pupils'] writing? How differently would you respond?' (Huot and Perry, 2009: 431). They go on to consider what kinds of questions might be asked of a young writer if the teacher were not focused on 'correcting' but read the writing in the same spirit as reading a published writer.

Activity 15.2
Reading children's writing like a reader – reflective journal/blog to group

When you have the opportunity, find a few pieces of children's writing that you have not seen before and, ignoring all errors, read them as if they were by published authors. (It helps if you read them aloud.) Quickly note down what each piece is saying and any questions you would like to ask the author. What did that feel like?

Share your reactions with the group and consider the implications for your own response to children's writing.

The prime aim of response to writing is to demonstrate readership – to read children's work like a reader as well as like a teacher. Through this kind of purposeful modelling, young writers will learn to become readers of their own work, developing a sense of self-awareness and self-efficacy. If they understand that writing is meant to be read for the meaning it conveys, they will be able to improve their writing so that reviewing, redrafting and self-editing become well-practised, familiar and satisfying aspects of being a writer.

15.4 A note about correcting

All schools will have a marking and feedback policy because, of course, it is the job of a teacher to correct errors, but it is important to be clear about what is being corrected and why. A 'scattergun' approach, where a teacher marks some spellings as inaccurate and leaves others, or marks some punctuation and leaves other errors, can only confuse the young writer. A teacher can easily explain to the class what will be the focus for correction and that as well as correcting, s/he will respond to the content of the piece. For example, if the focus has been on using consistent past tense in a piece of writing, or the use of speech punctuation, then it is essential to let young writers know how far they have succeeded. But this needs to be accompanied by opportunities to put things right and a comment on the content. A useful approach is something like:

There are four places where you haven't used the past tense /speech punctuation correctly. Can you find them and put them right? I really like the way you have...

Similarly, correcting spelling should be focused and purposeful. If a young writer is showing a pattern in their errors – for example, misspelling words which have double consonants before adding a suffix, or using 'w' instead of 'wh' – the most productive kind of response is to say something like:

I have highlighted/circled some spellings that need double letters/adding 'h' to make 'wh'. Write the words correctly and find three more words that use the same pattern and ask me to have another look.

Or, if the spellings don't follow a particular pattern:

I have highlighted/circled five words that aren't spelt correctly. Look them up or ask someone to help you correct them and I'll check in group work.

In this way, the writer gets involved in the correcting and the teacher then can check that the errors have been detected and remedied. This kind of error checking is often best done during small group writing time when it is possible to have a conversation with the writer about the errors.

15.5 Self-evaluation, self-assessment and self-regulation

Children need to learn that it is not just the role of the teacher to read and comment on writing. They need to learn how to evaluate their own and others' writing – how to identify the value in it. Key to formative assessments are self- and peer-evaluation (Black and Wiliam, 1998) sometimes referred to as self-assessment, self-rating or self-grading (Nielsen, 2014). However, there needs to be deliberate and progressive planning towards effective self-evaluation. In a survey of research on assessing writing, Nielsen summarises findings about strategies for effective implementation of self-assessment methods

(Nielsen, 2014: 13). According to the research, as well as modelling, the teacher should plan specifically to teach children how to self-assess and:

- make time for practice
- involve pupils in developing criteria for self-assessment
- ensure that pupils are engaged and motivated to evaluate their own work
- only use self-assessment for formative purposes, never for summative assessment
- support and monitor during self-assessment, providing feedback, including dialogues about writing
- ensure that self-assessment is used for different purposes – to assess the grasp of specific skills as well as more holistically to look at content and effect
- provide feedback on the effectiveness of pupils' self-assessment
- provide time for pupils to revise their work after self-assessment
- regularly evaluate classroom methods for self-assessment to gauge effectiveness in helping pupils improve their writing.

One of the most important strategies is making writing the focus of talk, both with the class and with individuals. This may begin with the teacher's writing, the children's drafts or a published text, but should be designed to provide a model for evaluation and give young writers the experience of the kind of vocabulary they might use to identify strengths and weaknesses in a text. The teacher's verbalisation of thoughts during shared writing gives pupils an insight into the thought processes of an adult writer and this stage of the teaching sequence can be designed to include terminology focused on specific objectives. However, there is a potential problem in that 'thinking talk' might tend towards just talking about transcription and choices of vocabulary, so talking about 'what' as well as 'how' is important:

> Modelling, re-reading and reviewing one's writing should be introduced gradually and reinforced throughout the primary years. In the process, writers can usefully consider the following prompts:
>
> - What am I trying to say?
> - How does it sound so far? Why did I choose...? How else could I say this?
> - What do I want to say/do next?
> - How could I express...?
> - What will my reader be thinking/feeling as they read this?
>
> (Cremin *et al.*, 2015: 93–94)

When a teacher demonstrates like this, it gives developing writers a frame to look at their own work, to try out ideas and discuss what they want to say.

Helping learners to evaluate their own writing means providing models, examples and teacher demonstrations of planning, drafting, editing and proofreading as well as examples of response designed to help writers improve their writing. Frameworks to help children ask each other questions about a particular piece of writing and reading children's work aloud to them at all stages of composition also support them as they learn how to self-evaluate. And, at all stages, it is important to offer chances to discuss writing, to make criteria explicit and to agree targets for improvement.

Using response partners can be an effective way to involve pupils in their own learning as well as developing some independence. However, they need to have models of helpful response and this is not achieved overnight. The teacher's own use of language will show what kind of comment is likely to be most helpful. A planned programme for developing response partners might begin in group writing sessions where the teacher or teaching assistant has the opportunity to model response. To start with, children might be asked to read over their work and highlight parts they like, then explain to a partner why they like it (Rooke, 2013). This can lead to a more general discussion, guided by the adult, about what kinds of comments are helpful.

A frame to help support the beginnings of partner response might be:

- What parts of the writing did you like? Why?
- Were there any parts that you did not understand? What might have been missing?
- What would you suggest to improve the beginning or end?

Once children become more experienced in commenting they will not need the frame.

Case study, early primary: Proofreading and self-correcting aged 6

When children learn that writing is about making choices to express ideas as well as possible, the process becomes more automatic, more of a self-regulating process. Emily, aged 6, shows clearly how she can proofread and self-edit as she writes, making choices about the best way to express her ideas. In her recount of the visit from Zoolab (Figure 15.1) she self-corrects for spelling, capital letters and to express exactly how much she enjoyed the visit when she crosses out 'fabulous' and replaces it with 'brilliant'.

In the diary written as Bog Baby (Figure 15.2) again she self-corrects for spelling but also for legibility.

In her adventure story about Bog Baby (Figure 15.3), she clearly proofreads as she writes: for punctuation (amending lower case letters to capitals for the beginning of sentences); for meaning (replacing 'out' with 'off') and for spelling (tea, coffee). But she also shows that after she has written, she reads over her writing and makes considered choices about improving what she has written, inserting 'crash' to make 'and he fell' more vivid.

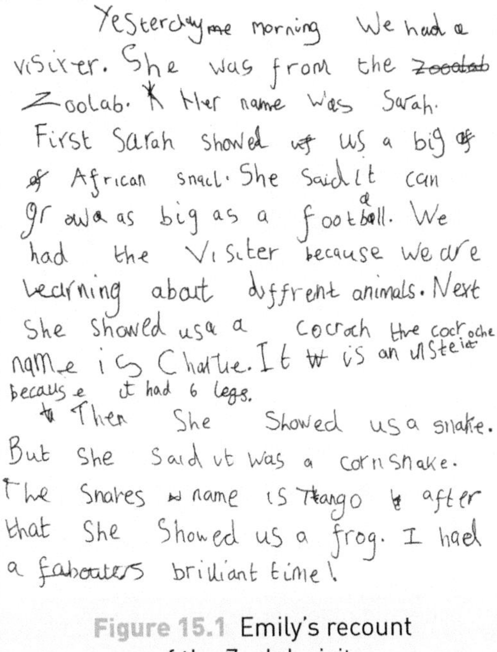
Yesterday ~~me~~ morning We had a visiter. She was from the ~~Zooalab~~ Zoolab. Her name was Sarah. First Sarah showed ~~us~~ us a big ~~of~~ ~~of~~ African snail. She said it can grow as big as a football. We had the visiter because we are learning about diffrent animals. Next She showed us a cocroch the cockroche name is Charlie. It ~~is~~ is an insect because it had 6 legs. Then She showed us a snake. But she said it was a cornsnake. The snakes name is Tango after that She showed us a frog. I had a ~~fabouters~~ brilliant time!

Figure 15.1 Emily's recount of the Zoolab visit

Remarkable as this example is, Emily could only reach this level of proofreading and improving her work through consistent good teaching.

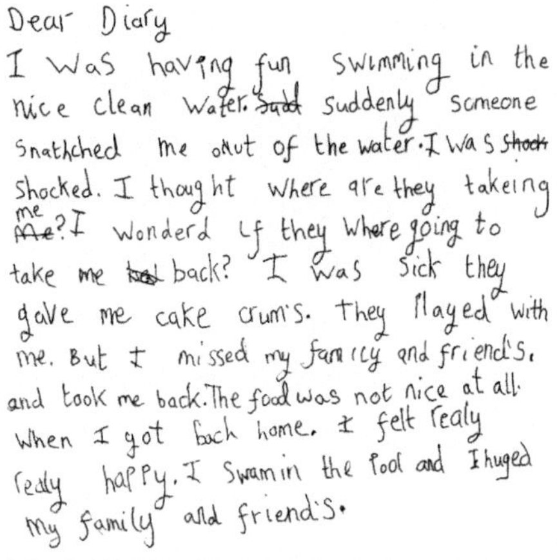

Dear Diary
I was having fun swimming in the nice clean water. And suddenly someone snatched me out of the water. I was shocked. I thought where are they taking me? I wonderd if they where going to take me back? I was sick they gave me cake crum's. they flayed with me. But I missed my family and friend's. and took me back. The food was not nice at all. When I got back home. I felt realy realy happy. I swam in the pool and I huged my family and friend's.

Figure 15.2 Emily's diary written as Bog Baby

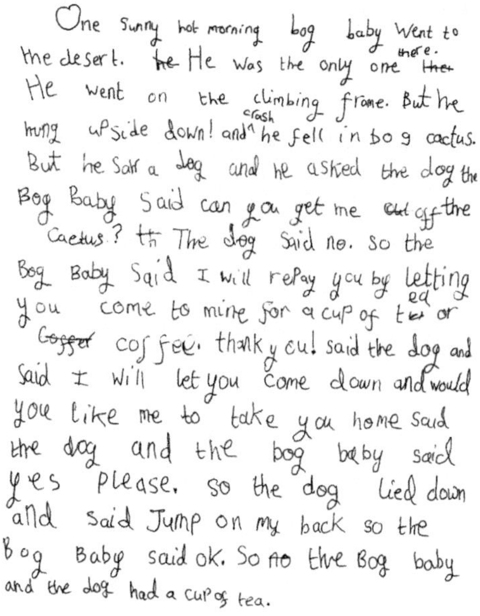

One sunny hot morning bog baby went to the desert. He was the only one there. He went on the climbing frame. But he hung upside down! and he fell in bog cactus. But he saw a dog and he asked the dog the Bog Baby said can you get me off the Cactus? The dog said no. so the Bog Baby said I will repay you by letting you come to mine for a cup of tea or coffee. thank you! said the dog and said I will let you come down and would you like me to take you home said the dog and the bog baby said yes please. so the dog lied down and said Jump on my back so the Bog Baby said ok. So so the Bog baby and the dog had a cup of tea.

Figure 15.3 Emily's adventure story about Bog Baby

Helping children to develop self-regulation in writing is crucially important for those children who finding writing difficult. However, teaching strategies specifically to aid composition and to read over their own work in order to improve it can prove successful in supporting struggling writers (Tracy et al., 2009). The online article by Harris et al. (n.d.) gives practical details of how to support writers in the planning, drafting and proofreading process.

15.6 Managing response

Wyse et al. suggest selecting writing from the range planned for the term to respond to in some detail:

> So if on the last occasion you marked a story, a piece of non-fiction might be appropriate next time. Or if on the previous occasion you had commented on the presentation of a final draft, you might want to comment on an early draft. It is worth remembering that appropriate written comments can be collected together to form the basis of an assessment profile for a child.

One of the difficult aspects of marking children's work relates to the range of choices that are available for your response. One possible way to think about these choices can be to have a system for responding:

- A specific positive comment about the writing.
- A specific point about improving something that is individual to the child's writing.
- A specific point about improving something that relates to a more general target for writing.

(Wyse *et al.*, 2013: 268)

An example of this kind of specific feedback is from Karl's class of 10 and 11 year olds. The class had been reading *Rose Blanche* by Ian McEwan and Roberto Innocenti. Karl asked them to write a third person narrative from where the child comes out of the truck. Kayleigh wrote:

> *Quickly but silently Rose followed the giant trucks. Rose followed the trucks because she wanted to know where they were going. Whilst following the trucks she had to go under fences and barriers, go through ditches and around frozen puddles. By the time she arrived, she was exhausted. She was shocked when she saw faces looking directly at her. They all looked hungry and tired. The children asked her if she had any food to eat. She gave them some food as they had nothing else to eat.*

In response, Karl wrote:

> *I enjoyed your use of adverbials and themes to build cohesion across and between paragraphs. For example, 'A promise was made' and 'Rose kept her promise.' It helped me to follow the plot of the story.*
>
> *Be careful not to simply recount events but to balance description with action.*

Recently, there has been a move towards selective response and feedback, rather than marking every error in a piece of written work. The basic idea is to colour code aspects of a child's work, either to indicate 'good stuff' (highlighted in green) or to suggest 'this is a part that needs some attention' (highlighted in pink) and to make a written response to the content of the writing. What is important about this procedure is that when the child has acted on the pinked sections, the teacher makes some further comment, because feedback is of no use unless writers have a chance to act on it and be assured that they have improved their work. However, this style of response needs to be time-managed. It is best to be selective: either select a few children's work – for example, a writing group – to respond to in depth at any one time, or select one piece of writing from each child during every teaching sequence. It is also worth bearing in mind that any writer who receives work back with a lot of highlighting or marking on it, may feel discouraged. As with all other elements of response, balance is essential.

Website resource W15.1 shows Dan's response to book reviews written by two fluent writers.

By responding to the content, structure and style of the writing and by asking genuine questions to push the girls' ideas further, this teacher shows that selective response can be a powerful teaching tool and may not take any more time (perhaps even less) than detailed 'red pen' marking, which, as many teachers will attest, often falls on barren ground, with errors being repeated time and again. Focused, specific response and the opportunity for writers to reply and improve their work in a way that makes sense to them, is an efficient way to use teacher time. Details of spelling, punctuation and grammar can be dealt with in an equally focused way, at different times. Small group teaching, discussion and response can be more effective than 'marking' for many technical aspects of children's work.

> ## Activity 15.3
> ### Approaches to responding and marking – reflective journal/blog to group
>
> What good ideas for responding and marking have you observed in your classroom or placement school? What implications might this have for time-management?
>
> Watch Video 9 (see website) where Lloyd explains how he uses marking to help children make progress with their writing. After watching it once, choose one of the sections to review, noting anything that Lloyd does that is something that you might want to do yourself. It might be to do with making time for children to act on corrections (section 2), challenging the most able writers (section 3), supporting bilingual writers (section 4), monitoring learning through feedback (section 5), peer assessment (section 6), making time for marking (section 7) or how he manages differentiation (section 8).
>
> Discuss with each other ways in which you could make effective responses to children's writing without spending too much time. How might you make sure that the children act on your response to their work?

15.7   Planning, teaching, writing, reviewing, planning

As the early part of this chapter suggests, response to writing should not only be concerned with transcription but also with judgements about how far writers have managed to fulfil their intentions in writing composition: Does the text meet the purpose it is intended for? Does it take account of what the reader needs to know? If teachers are to provide clear and specific feedback, then these features need to be included in written and spoken comments. In fact, much of the response to writing happens during the course of shared and guided writing, quite a while before any writing is finished and, it is worth remembering, some writing will be done as part of getting familiar with a text and exploring ways of shaping writing. To be able to respond in a focused way throughout the teaching sequence and consider whether the writing has fulfilled objectives for teaching and learning, the criteria need to be clear from the outset. Assessment of writing starts with planning for teaching writing. The planning and teaching sequence (see Figure 15.4) begins with identifying what the teacher wants the children to learn and leads to a completed, revised and edited writing outcome, allowing the teacher to assess how far the teaching – and learning – have been successful for the whole class and for individuals.

15.8   Monitoring progress

One of the easiest ways to keep records of progress is for each child to have a portfolio of writing accompanied by some brief notes about the context for the piece of writing. Children can be asked to choose a piece work every half term that they are pleased with and the teacher can also select work which shows particular strengths or weaknesses. If the school is in the habit of using children's writing books as records, this can equally well act as a

Case study, upper primary: Responding to and assessing writing throughout a teaching sequence

Leigh planned for her class of 10 and 11 year olds to engage in a variety of kinds of writing throughout a four-week teaching sequence, designing ways of responding to the writing which would move the children's ideas further, but would not create a burden of marking for her. Informal assessments of the children's grasp of key concepts were made throughout the teaching sequence. The written outcome was for the class to write multimodal mystery stories for the class of 8 to 9 year olds. Reading and writing objectives were selected to fit with the outcome:

Reading:

- Reading books that are structured in different ways: using the complex picture books *The Wolves in the Walls* by Neil Gaiman (2005) and *The Red Tree* by Shaun Tan (2012) to discuss how the modes of writing and image interact to make meaning.
- Reading film for atmosphere, creation of tension and point of view/perspective.
- Identifying how language, structure and presentation contribute to meaning.
- Comparing characters, considering different accounts of the same event and discuss viewpoints of authors and fictional characters.

Writing:

- Use of the first person in writing diaries and autobiographies.
- Use of technical terms such as *mode, perspective, implication, effect.*
- Identifying the audience for and purpose of the writing, selecting the appropriate form and using other similar writing as models for their own.
- In narratives, describing settings, characters and atmosphere.
- Careful choice of language for effect.

Figure 15.4 shows the opportunities planned for response and assessment throughout the teaching sequence. There are different kinds of writing, each treated differently according to the purpose of the writing:

- responded to by response partners
- used to gather ideas
- responded to in small groups by Leigh and Leyla, the teaching assistant
- displayed in the classroom for general comment.

Finally, a multimodal book assessed by the teacher according to her planning and responded to by the target audience.

For a full account of the teaching sequence see website resource W15.2 Responding to and assessing writing throughout a teaching sequence.

Narrative: Writing a multimodal mystery story
Complex picture books: *Wolves in the Walls* (set of books) and *The Red Tree* (using visualiser)
Film clip: 'We are being attacked…'

4 weeks

Reading discussions – Wolves: How does the author create atmosphere?

What do the words do? What do the images do? Introduce 'mode', 'perspective' and 'point of view'.

Assess use of terminology in discussing words and images. Follow up in small group work.

Model voicing Lucy's thoughts. Demonstrate difference between diary and autobiography.

Introduce *The Red Tree*. Read to 'where you are' discussing combination of words and image.

Read to end of book. Re-read, paying close attention to leaves of the red tree on each double page spread. What is the author saying here?

Show words on IWB. Discuss the use of simple, direct language.

Remind about point of view and perspective in moving images. Watch 'We are being attacked…' Discuss creation of tension and mystery and hopeful resolution. Re-view clip several times. Establish criteria for successful mystery for slightly younger children.

Remind about storyboarding. Demonstrate planning 7 key events to make 7 double page spread storyboard: model sketching scenes and drafting first person narrative. Talk about what the images will do and what the words will convey and how atmosphere will be created.

Reading and investigation
Becoming familiar with text type

↓

Capturing ideas

↓

Explicit teaching and modelling

Discussion and experimentation

↓

Shared and supported writing/composition

↓

Making controlled choices about writing/composition in independent work

Annotate double page spreads with sticky notes: What questions do you want to ask the author? What do the different modes contribute to the meaning?

Writing in role (diary entries) to express point of view.

Peer support and response.

Autobiographical writing in role as Lucy.

Assess (in small group work) grasp of writing from an individual's point of view.

In pairs, jot down response to double page spread. Individually, draw own image with a few words (as in the book) to express the feelings represented; indicate sound effects.

Share double page spreads in small groups, commenting on effectiveness of combination of word and image. Display spreads.

Write own poems about 'feeling lost' and finding hope. Display.

Small groups discussing how the film created tension.

Start deciding on criteria for a successful mystery story.

Storyboarding own first person mystery story with hopeful ending.

7 double page spreads (plus front and back covers). Story to include dialogue and narrative and create tension and show point of view. Sketch first and draft dialogue and narrative.

Check out with response partner. Teacher and TA circulating to support development of story.

Written outcome: Multimodal first person mystery story for younger readers.

Assessment: Success in:

- creating setting, atmosphere and tension
- showing character's point of view
- hopeful resolution
- awareness of how to convey meaning through images and words
- using spare, effective language.

Reading books with small groups from younger class.
Response from readers.

Figure 15.4 Opportunities for response and assessment throughout a teaching sequence 'portfolio' record with the children's and teacher's comments added on sticky notes. The crucial part of this is to review the work with the children every so often, asking them to notice how they are (or maybe are not) making progress. This can be done over a week or so by talking through progress with each writing group. Involvement in their own progress is invaluable for the development of children's critical abilities and having portfolio-type records can also be very helpful for informing parents, governors, inspectors or other visitors.

It is also important, however, to make sure that all aspects of children's writing development are being monitored including writing behaviours and choices. Used alongside portfolios, the Scale of Progression in Writing/Composition (Figure 15.5) can be used to track progress and to check coverage of all aspects of the writing curriculum. The scale is derived from discussion with teachers who wanted to establish useful and time-efficient record keeping systems. It reflects what teachers might expect to see as children develop assurance and versatility in writing and is aligned with the national curricula of England, Northern Ireland, Scotland and Wales. The scale is best seen as a basis for discussion with colleagues and open to adaptation, as the descriptors may not always reflect particular school circumstances. The statements are not arranged in any order of importance but are loosely grouped according to the following categories:

- technical features
- writing to help form ideas
- responsive/reflective writing
- informative/communicative writing
- performative/expressive writing.

An inexperienced writer:

- spells familiar and key words correctly using phonics and word recognition
- with support, applies a range of strategies in attempting spelling
- joins handwriting
- uses basic punctuation consistently
- uses direct speech but does not always punctuate it correctly
- drafts and redrafts/redesigns with help
- from jottings, deliberately chooses words for own poems for variety and interest
- with guidance, finds and notes information from texts
- adapts, synthesises and expands ideas from a range of sources
- enjoys using newly discovered language for poetry
- draws on known language and story patterns in independent writing/composition
- is beginning to comment independently on own and peers' writing/composition
- shows awareness of a reader's needs in sequencing a story or writing non-narrative
- uses known poetic structures to write own poems independently, noticing the effects of the language
- can write stories with a character/event, beginning, middle and end and some dialogue
- increasingly varies connectives in own writing and is more adventurous with sentence structure
- uses time connectives to help structure story sequence
- writes consistently in 3rd person when narrating events
- can write a 1st person sustained narrative
- draws on own imaginative world for expressive texts

Figure 15.5 Scale of Progression in Writing/Composition

- with guidance, writes sequenced instructions using diagrams and illustrations
- writes longer report of experience, showing features of known non-chronological reports
- constructs texts using words and images
- uses digital technology to design (multimodal) texts

An increasingly assured and experienced writer:

- spells familiar words correctly
- independently applies a range of strategies in attempting spelling
- experiments with a wider range of punctuation
- is gaining speed and fluency in handwriting
- can identify errors when proofreading own text
- uses reader response to help guide revisions of own text
- generates ideas/jots before writing
- finds and notes information from familiar text
- can use a variety of planning strategies
- summarises longer passages of familiar text
- chooses to work individually or in a team
- comments on and experiments with sound and visual effects in writing
- usually makes secure choices of mode for specific readers/listeners/viewers
- wants to write to express personal meaning
- uses language and structures from different text types for own writing/composition
- uses sequenced plans to help shape writing
- writes consistently in 3rd person when narrating events
- can write a 1st person sustained narrative, including dialogue
- uses known layout to write dialogue and playscripts
- uses language and story knowledge to create settings and character
- sustains stories, incorporating setting and characterisation
- shows some awareness of what a reader needs to know
- uses time connectives to help structure text
- uses paragraphs to organise material
- independently writes non-chronological report (at own level of experience) using information from texts read
- composes accurate well-sequenced instructions with appropriate diagrams/flowcharts
- uses a range of organisational devices and diagrammatic text for presenting sequenced information
- tries out different layouts and designs for poetry, fiction and non-fiction texts, using known software as appropriate

A more experienced and almost independent writer:

- usually spells correctly using a range of strategies
- writes fluently and at speed
- uses a range of punctuation accurately (most of the time)
- with guidance, improves cohesion of written instructions/explanations using known range of organisational devices
- sets out direct speech correctly
- independently uses sequenced plans/maps or notes to help shape events in stories
- in reports, selects and orders information into paragraphs
- after modelling, makes short notes, selecting key points from an unfamiliar passage

Figure 15.5 continued

- distinguishes between fact and personal view when using sources
- collaborates productively with others over writing/composition
- in poetry writing, comments on and experiments with sound, shape and vocabulary
- responds helpfully to other people's writing
- redrafts and practises poetry for performance
- uses language to engage the reader
- can select specific style and mode for different readers
- gains satisfaction from shaping writing for others to read, showing organisation, imagination and clarity
- uses paragraphs to organise narrative
- begins to use chapters to organise narrative
- independently writes non-chronological report using information from texts read
- uses structure drawn from known texts
- presents personal point of view in an ordered way
- imaginatively extends content from other sources
- makes choices about when to compose using words and images and when to write
- uses a range of organisational devices and diagrammatic text for presenting sequenced information, instructions or explanations, choosing digital technology or paper as appropriate to the task, purpose and readership

An experienced and often independent writer:

- spells correctly most of the time in final drafts
- sets achievable targets for presentation, adapting handwriting to a range of tasks
- looks more for content/style/vocabulary when redrafting rather than technical features alone
- improves the cohesion of written instructions/explanations using familiar organisational devices
- writes grammatically correct sentences
- can write direct and reported speech
- collaborates well with a partner over writing/composition
- with support, can plan, compose and edit reports/explanations modelled on known text
- composes text from notes, paying attention to style
- can evaluate own writing for its effects on readers
- increasingly uses writing as a means of reflection on novels, stories, plays and poems
- increasingly experiments with language for effect
- usually chooses an appropriate style for writing purpose and readership
- comments thoughtfully on own and others' writing/composition, suggesting improvements
- continues to want to write to express personal meaning
- with help, begins to use knowledge of story structure and theme to write own versions of known stories
- can depict atmosphere, character and setting
- begins to use implication to suggest character, mood, theme in writing
- writes own poetry showing awareness of language effects, and prepares it for performance
- uses known layout to write dialogue and playscripts
- presents personal point of view for known and unknown readers
- justifies own views in writing
- knows how to vary the use of images and words for specific effects
- writes clear and concise non-chronological texts
- makes considered choices about mode, design and presentational effects for specific purposes/audience

Figure 15.5 continued

An assured, experienced and independent writer:

- independently drafts, edits and proofreads
- revises structure of text with purpose and readership in mind
- makes decisions about when to handwrite and when to use digital technology
- works collaboratively in groups for a writing outcome
- uses notes, charts, other planning devices to gather ideas
- independently organises writing
- uses reflective writing to note personal ideas
- comments on style and language features in own and other writing/composition
- experiments with language, particularly in poetry: sound, shape, rhythm, rhyme and figurative language
- uses collaboration and response to further own writing
- develops plot with clear events and resolution
- finds different ways to resolve the complication created in plot
- uses evocative language to create mood/atmosphere
- shows awareness of different aspects of character, using language to evoke sympathy or dislike
- uses action, direct description or dialogue and indirect suggestion to show character and motivation
- varies sequencing to unfold a narrative, e.g. flashback
- begins to use implication and allusion to draw a reader into the narrative
- constructs coherent multimodal text
- writes clear and concise non-chronological texts, including relevant detail
- takes account of reader when informing, explaining and presenting ideas/information
- writes to persuade the reader by providing examples/reasons
- writes reports balancing two opposing sets of ideas
- can use a variety of applications of digital technology to present non-fiction texts, e.g. databases and graphics
- uses digital technology for all stages of the writing process, making discriminating choices about modes, language and effects for communication

Figure 15.5 continued

The statements are not intended to be all-inclusive nor exclusive, and might form the basis for school discussion of how best to describe progress in writing and communicate that progress to others.

One way to use the scale is to track individual progress. Reviewing the portfolio each term, observations can be checked against the statements on the scale. Used in discussions with parents or colleagues, the descriptors can be a useful basis for talking about specific elements of the writing curriculum. Identifying statements which genuinely reflect what individual children can do in writing can provide a very clear idea of the areas they need help with. In addition to reviewing individual progress, at the end of the year, the scale might be used to evaluate whole class progress and indicate areas for future planning (website resource W15.3).

Website resource W15.4 shows how the Scale of Progression can be used to describe the achievements of writers at early primary and at upper primary stages, the ages when national tests are often administered.

Activity 15.4
Noting achievements in writing – reflective journal/blog

Read website resource W15.4 which uses the Scale of Progression in Writing/ Composition to identify the writing achievements of Sam (aged 6) and Iyla (aged 10), whose story was featured in Chapter 12 (website resources W12.4 and W12.5).

In the classroom where you are working, or on your next placement, and in discussion with the class teacher, select two or three children whose writing interests you and with the teacher, note their achievements on the Scale of Progression (website resource W15.3).

If you share the information with anyone outside the school, make sure that you use initials or pseudonyms.

Having noted the children's achievements, how might you move them forward as writers?

15.9 Diagnosing difficulties with writing

Monitoring individual progress can help to draw attention to those pupils who are not making the kinds of progress that might be expected. These may not just be children who seem to be falling behind but can also be those who seem unwilling to take risks and who opt for conformity rather than imagination; those who might be described as 'Gifted and Talented' but who are unmotivated about writing; those who simply do not seem to be fulfilling their potential. The writing miscue analysis is intended for just those kinds of pupils. It gives a teacher the chance to talk with them about their writing in an unthreatening, non-testing environment and to look closely at one piece of writing as a way of finding areas for future development.

The analysis covers more than just the technicalities of writing such as text construction, vocabulary choice, spelling and punctuation. It also helps focus on writing behaviour, the process of writing, and awareness of purpose and audience. In a similar way to a reading miscue, this diagnostic process involves looking at the piece of writing for meaning (semantic features) at the level of the text as a whole; for sentence construction (syntax); and for phonetic, visual and analogic features at individual word level (see Chapter 7). A first analysis might be followed up six months later to note progress in the areas identified for development. Of course, it is not suggested that any teacher should carry out a writing miscue on every pupil. Diagnostic writing miscue should only be used where there seems to be a specific problem or difficulty.

The flow chart in Figure 15.6 summarises the process of carrying out a miscue analysis of writing. The teacher is looking at:

- writing behaviour
- the process of writing
- the purpose/intention of the writer and the writing
- awareness of the needs of an audience/readership
- ability to structure/form writing according to intention
- patterns of correctness/error in technical features.

The aim is not only to analyse but also to note areas for development/improvement. Some of these will be related to the individual writer, but a miscue analysis can also point to areas that the teacher may want to focus on with the class as a whole.

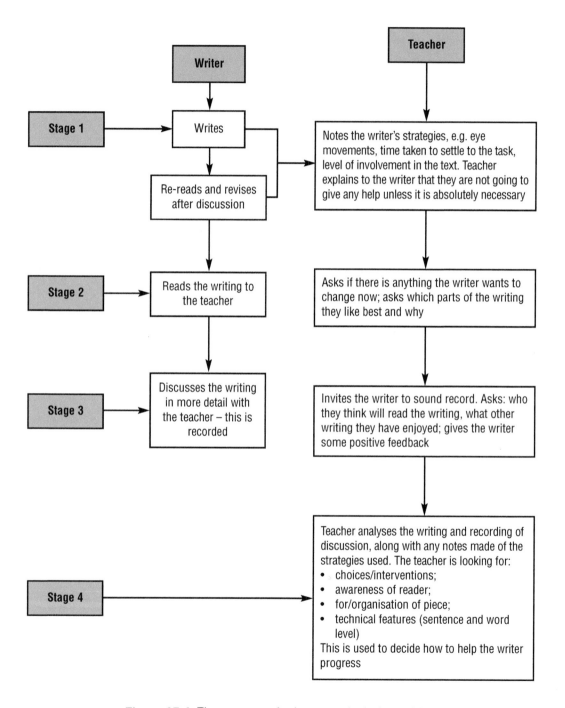

Figure 15.6 The process of miscue analysis for writing

Case study, middle primary: Amy, a 9-year-old writer

Bethan, a student teacher, carried out a writing miscue analysis with Amy, a bilingual 9 year old, then planned strategies to help move her forward as a writer.

Issues revealed by the writing miscue analysis

Amy lacks confidence in her ability as a writer, both in Spanish and in English. As a result of this, she is not a fluent writer. She engages in distraction activities and can take 5 minutes or more to complete a single sentence, often spending longer rubbing out than writing. As a result of the lack of fluency in her writing, Amy's sentences can often be constructed awkwardly. She does not write for pleasure and views writing as something that is done for the class teacher to mark. Amy seems to have anxiety over the content of her writing and repeatedly checks with friends if her writing is similar to theirs. Amy lacks the confidence to include original ideas in her writing. She is slowly beginning to experiment with using exclamation marks and question marks in her writing. She chooses very simple vocabulary and can be confused over the use of plurals. Amy is able to use her knowledge of phonics to attempt phonetic spellings of unfamiliar words.

Next steps for Amy

- To write more fluently.
- To use original ideas in her composition.
- To move towards writing more independently.
- To feel pride in her writing.
- To use a wider vocabulary in her work.

Strategies chosen to help Amy

My first aim was to reduce the anxiety that Amy felt about writing. Prior to the sessions planned to improve Amy's writing, I used her knowledge of Spanish to ask her and Bella [Amy's Spanish friend] to write a Spanish chorus for an existing poem. Amy enjoyed reading this to the class and being applauded for it. She needed to experience success with a trusted friend, before being confident enough to write independently. This also allowed her to recognise that her input as an individual is valued and unique. I planned to give the class time to explore the issues they would be writing about in drama and in class discussion before asking them to write.

To move Amy away from the distraction techniques she employs when faced with a blank piece of paper, I chose a structure for the poem which took away her initial anxiety of how to start. I decided not to suggest 'levels of attainment' as I marked the poems, to move Amy away from her concern over her level of achievement. It seems unsurprising that Amy has low self-esteem as a writer when she is made aware at the start of every lesson that she is working at a lower level than her peers.

I used Amy's work as a good example to the class.

I sat with Amy and talked through the decisions she made as a writer. I used this time to question some of her decisions and lead her to extend her writing.

Using a netbook to write freed Amy from the necessity of sharpening pencils and rubbing things out – some of her favoured distraction techniques.

I deliberately gave Amy an authentic reason to write – so that her poem can be sent to Tom Bolton, the author she welcomed to the class when he visited the school.

Evaluation

Amy responded well to the first lesson. The use of drama and class discussion clearly gave her plenty of ideas to use in her writing – this allowed her to progress towards a fluency in her writing. When I sat with her I had to explain the structure of the poem, but once she had understood that, she got satisfaction from following the structure and adding her own ideas. Amy was tentative at first, asking me if it 'was ok' to write certain things. However, by the time she had written her first verse she was visibly pleased with what she had achieved and asked for much less support as she was writing her second verse.

Amy wrote her own simile at the end of verse 2, 'could I say as shiny as a mirror?' I was able to read this to the class as an example of a simile that should be used in the final line of each verse. I found it interesting that Amy did not ask me how to spell certain words; she usually asks how to spell words in every lesson. I was pleased that she was concentrating on her ideas and using her knowledge of phonics to have a best guess at spelling. During the second lesson Amy made a clear effort to extend the vocabulary she had originally chosen.

On the third day, despite the fairly fast pace of the lesson Amy was able to complete her poem. She also added adjectives to her work to improve it – for example, 'leaves' became 'autumn leaves'. She wrote a four-verse poem containing personification, onomatopoeia and similes using entirely original content, simple but effective vocabulary and worked with far less distraction than usual. I would say that this piece of work – and Amy's attitude to writing – shows a significant improvement on what she has written previously.

Activity 15.5
Writing miscue analysis – reflective journal/blog to group

In discussion with a teaching colleague, select a child whose writing is giving concern and use website resource W15.5 to carry out a writing miscue analysis. Note the points in the resource about organisation and timing. Read website resource W15.6 as an example of a final analysis report. (This will be particularly useful if you are working with children in the younger age range.)

Carry out the analysis and discuss your findings with the teacher, deciding on a plan of action to support the young writer's development and a time when you might review the effectiveness of your interventions.

It will be helpful to share your work throughout the analysis and support stages to maximise the value of your insights.

Summary

Assessment happens throughout any teaching sequence – indeed it forms part of the process where a teacher plans to move the class forward to the next learning objectives. The chapter defines and clarifies the different facets of assessing writing: marking, correcting, responding, describing progress and final assessment, taking into account how teachers can allow for differentiation. Pupils' self-assessment or evaluation need to be included in any provision for assessment and the chapter gives examples of children responding to their own and other people's writing. There are sometimes concerns about the amount of time a teacher may have to spend on marking or responding to writing and case studies outline how to manage selective and effective response throughout a teaching sequence. The chapter provides a descriptive framework for monitoring progress in children's writing with examples of how this can be used and ends with details of how best to diagnose and plan to support children who experience difficulties with writing.

Recommended reading

Dix, S. (2006) 'What did I change and why did I do it?' Young writers' revision practices, *Literacy*, 40 (1) pp. 3–10. This classroom-based study from New Zealand demonstrates that young writers (aged 8 to 10 years old) can be thoughtful and reflective readers of their own writing. It argues that this gives stronger evidence of writing achievement than contrived tasks imposed, controlled and assessed from outside of the learning classroom. **Advanced**

Huot, B. and Perry, J. (2009) Towards a new understanding for classroom writing assessment, in R. Beard, D. Myhill, J. Riley and M. Nystrand (eds) *The SAGE Handbook of Writing Development*. London: SAGE, pp. 423–435. Supported by extensive synthesis of international research literature, the authors argue for a strongly conceptualised approach to formative classroom writing assessment. An accessible research chapter addressing practical classroom matters. **Advanced**

Parr, J. M. and Limbrick, L. (2010) Contextualising practice: Hallmarks of effective teachers of writing, *Teaching and Teacher Education*, 26 (3) pp. 583–590. This study identifies practices of effective teachers of writing in Australian schools. Common features of successful teaching were: a commitment to formative assessment practices; supportive classroom environments; and consistent and systematic teaching and response. **Advanced**

Rooke, J. (2013) Appendix 2 *Transforming Writing: Final evaluation report*. London: National Literacy Trust. www.literacytrust.org.uk/assets/0001/9256/Transforming_Writing_Final_Report.pdf (accessed 1 May 2017). Drawn from research in the UK, Appendix 2 provides a practical and useful guide about response to writing.

References

Bearne, E. and Kennedy, R. (2017) Providing for differentiation, in T. Cremin and J. Arthur (eds) *Learning to Teach in the Primary School*. Abingdon: Routledge, pp. 355–371.

Black, P. and Wiliam, D. (1998) *Inside the Black Box: Raising standards through classroom assessment*. London: Kings College.

Cremin, T. with Reedy, D., Bearne, E. and Dombey, H. (2015) *Teaching English Creatively*. Abingdon: Routledge.

Harris, K. R., Schmidt, T. and Graham, S. (n.d.) Strategies for composition and self-regulation in the writing process. www.ldonline.org/article/6207/ (accessed 1 May 2017)

Huot, B. and Perry, J. (2009) Towards a new understanding for classroom writing assessment, in R. Beard, D. Myhill, J. Riley and M. Nystrand (eds) *The SAGE Handbook of Writing Development*. London: SAGE, pp. 423–435.

Nielsen, K. (2014) Self-assessment methods in writing instruction: A conceptual framework, successful practices and essential strategies, *Journal of Research in Reading*, 37 (1) pp. 1–16.

Rooke, J. (2013) Appendix 2 in *Transforming Writing: Final evaluation report*. London: National Literacy Trust. www.literacytrust.org.uk/assets/0001/9256/Transforming_Writing_Final_Report.pdf (accessed 1 May 2017)

Tracy, B., Reid, R. and Graham, S. (2009) Teaching young students strategies for planning and drafting stories. The impact of self-regulated strategy development, *Journal of Educational Research*, 102 (5) pp. 323–331.

Williams, J. (1981) The phenomenology of error, *College Composition and Communication*, 32, pp. 157–168.

Wyse, D., Jones, R., Bradford, H. and Wolpert M. A. (2013) *Teaching English, Language and Literacy*, 3rd edn. Abingdon: Routledge.

Children's books

Shaun Tan (2012) *The Red Tree*. Sydney, Aus.: Lothian Children's Books. ISBN 9780734411372. See also *The Red Tree* on YouTube www.youtube.com/watch?v=PrmMFFpKxgw (accessed 1 May 2017)

Neil Gaiman illustrated Dave McKean (2005) *The Wolves in the Walls*. Harper Trophy. ISBN 9780380810956

Ian McEwan, illustrated Roberto Innocenti (2004) *Rose Blanche*. Red Fox. ISBN 9780099439509

CHAPTER 16

MULTIMODAL, MULTIMEDIA AND DIGITAL TEXTS

Although the focus is on teaching English in relation to twenty-first century technologies and cultural practices, much of the relevant research uses 'literacy' as a key term rather than 'English' so this term will be used in this chapter.

This chapter covers:

- Modes and media
- Children's experience of digital technology
- The New Literacy Studies
- Children's cultural and literacy assets or funds of knowledge
- Critical literacy
- Children's digital practices at home and school
  - Case study, early, middle and upper primary: Surveying children's use of multimodal texts at home and at school
- Computer games
  - Case study, upper primary: The Barnsborough project – virtual worlds in the classroom
  - Case study, early, middle and upper primary: Composing with wikis, blogs, pods and vlogs
- Reading on screen
  - Case study, early primary: Using apps for reading
- A note about children who experience difficulties with on-screen reading
- Using film in the classroom
- Describing progress in reading and composing multimodal texts

16.1 Modes and media

Rapid technological change has meant that everyday practices surrounding reading and writing have shifted significantly. Most homes have access to a range of digital devices and children are brought up in a world where they expect screens to be their companions, toys, entertainers, information givers and means of social communication. However, the visual and graphic elements of texts are not confined to screen-based texts; books, magazines, comics, newspapers and leaflets are now far more likely to include images than texts of twenty years ago. Of course, multimodality is not new. For many years people of all cultures have used a range of ways (modes) to represent ideas and communicate meaning through speech, writing, gesture, image, movement, music and sound. Even the most familiar and everyday communications are made up of complex combinations of modes. Talk, whether in face-to-face meetings or viewed on screen, is accompanied by movement and gesture; television and film combine moving images and sound to create an overall text. Any multimodal text might combine elements of:

- performance – gesture, movement, posture, facial expression
- images – moving and still; photographic, drawn, painted, computer-generated, etc.
- sound – spoken words, sound effects, music and silence
- writing – including font, graphics and layout
- duration – shot length, sequence, rhythm and transitions (Bearne and Bazalgette, 2010: 7).

These elements will be differently weighted in any combination of modes; for example, mime has no verbal dialogue, a photograph is a still image and a piece of instrumental music is just sound but film includes all the modes – performance, image, sound, movement, gesture, words and duration. The multimodal shift offers significant challenges to traditional forms of English/literacy education so that in the classroom, children need to be helped to identify the contributions made by each mode to any text.

> **Modes:** the different ways that people communicate: sound (including speech, music and sound effects); images (moving and still); gesture/posture (sometimes referred to as body language); writing in all its forms.
>
> **Media:** the means through which communications are conveyed: books, magazines, screens, airwaves, etc.

In addition to using different modes to represent and communicate ideas, messages are relayed and distributed through different media of communication. These might be traditional media such as books, graphic novels, magazines and leaflets, but digital technology now offers the medium of the screen in its various forms as well as sound files. Children now type as well as write by hand and use screen navigational facilities; mobile phones transmit images as well as words, can be used to play games, access the internet and much more – the number of applications is quickly expanding.

Activity 16.1
Analysing the role of different modes – pairs/group to class

You will need some sticky notes for this. Before asking children to think about the different contributions made by words, images, sound or movement, try analysing some multimodal texts yourselves. Start with a complex picture book; for example, Anthony Browne's *Gorilla* (2013) or Gary Crew and Shaun Tan's *Memorial* (2017) (any good picture book will do). Choose a double-page spread with words and pictures and add notes about what the words tell you and what the images convey (notice the posture and gestures of the figures, the colours used, the typeface, the design of the page as well as the words). Are the words and images saying the same thing or does one add to the other – or even contradict each other? What is the overall message of both words and images combined?

Plan to include an opportunity for your class to analyse the contributions made by different modes to a text – a comic book, graphic novel or picture book. Ask them:

- What did the words tell you?
- What did the images add to the meaning?
- Would the text have been as interesting if there had only been the words or the images?

The important thing for them to understand is that different modes carry different aspects of any text and that the meaning of a text is created by how the modes interrelate.

In a project using complex picture books, when the children were asked what advice they would give to someone about reading multimodal texts, Tania said:

> *Look at the pictures carefully. If they can't read they have to look at it really carefully and look at the colours and what the person is doing – the facial expression and the body language. You have to look at the picture and the colours and the person's face really carefully to ask yourself a few questions: 'How is the person feeling? What sort of state is he or she in?' or maybe a few more questions. But I think that they should look at the picture really carefully ... the colours and the face represent something.*

See website resource W16.1 for more examples of children's comments on multi-modal texts.

Asking children to talk about how images carry meaning gives valuable insights into how children are reading for inference. Wordless (or almost wordless) picture books such as *Tuesday* by David Wiesner (2013) or Aaron Becker's *Journey* Trilogy (2014) are an excellent starting point for imaginative narrative writing as they help in understanding narrative structure. Multimodal information books provide plentiful opportunities for focused reading and non-fiction writing. Equally, film and television – either fictional or factual – are a strong support for talk, reading and writing (see section 5.4 Reading on screens).

16.2 Children's experience of digital technology

Even before they enter school, many children have experience of operating a range of digital devices (Childwise, 2012), often using them in their play and for entertainment (Marsh *et al.*, 2015). In a longitudinal, in-depth study of children's digital technology use, Broadbent *et al.* (2013) describe extensive and confident use of PCs, laptops, tablets, games consoles and smartphones. But although many children experience digital texts and environments from a very early age (Merchant, 2015), their access to technology varies considerably. It is not simply a matter of whether families can afford digital devices, but the different ways in which they use the resources (Stephen *et al.*, 2013; Marsh *et al.*, 2015). Digital practices vary according to social, cultural, personal and economic factors so that in thinking of how best teachers can respond to the digital experience of their children, focusing on skills is not enough.

It is not only the texts and their take-up in homes and schools which have changed but also the ways in which they are composed, produced and distributed have undergone a fundamental change. The new textual landscape (Carrington, 2005; Carrington and Robinson, 2009) has led to attempts to (re-)define literacy from different theoretical standpoints. New types of text require changes in language to describe them and imply reconsideration of definitions of 'reading', 'writing', 'depicting', 'literacy', 'literature' – and 'English'. In particular, the dominance of the screen means that there is now a need to 'look beyond the linguistic' (Jewitt, 2005: 315) for ways of understanding representation and communication. Lankshear and Knobel (2006) explore different kinds of literacy but settle on 'new literacy'. It may be that 'literacy' or the school subject 'English' are not sufficient to describe twenty-first century texts, contexts and practices: the combination of the representational modes of speech and sound, writing, image, gesture, with the communicative media of book, magazine, computer screen, video, film, radio. The challenge for teachers is how to include within such school subject titles as 'English', 'language and literacy' or 'language arts' the different modes and media of representation and the dimensions of time and space through which they communicate meaning. A further challenge is to cope with continually evolving digital technologies.

16.3 The New Literacy Studies

'Digital literacy' is a common term and includes many of the texts and social practices developed over the last few years. However, as new kinds of text are not always digitally created or transmitted, the New London Group (1996) moved thinking about literacy from a focus on books and writing and the skills associated with them, to a view of 'multiliteracies' (Cope and Kalantzis, 2000) which encompasses a range of social practices and modes of representation. The New Literacy Studies (NLS) sees literacy as something practised every day in homes, communities, schools and workplaces and which ranges from formal to informal; for example, sticky notes left attached to computer screens in offices, records of goods as they are checked in a warehouse, drawings made by parents for their children, messages on social media, online petitions to government, letters to insurance companies. All of these have specific social and cultural significance and have purpose in getting something done in the world, whether it is keeping the workplace ticking over, sharing pleasure with children, keeping friendships going, expressing political opinions or dealing with financial matters. This view recognises the complexity and fluidity of literacy practices. Leander (2009) suggests there should be a parallel pedagogy which recognises that whilst the products of composition may be represented in different media – paper or screen – the processes of composition have similarities.

Central to New Literacy Studies is the importance of reflective critical analysis of texts related to the contexts of culture and situation in which they are used. Texts may be social in nature but so are the social practices which surround texts (Street, 1993; Barton *et al.*, 1999; Cope and Kalantzis, 2000). However, what counts as valid or valuable English/literacy is often determined by policy makers and government departments, who create curricula, inspect schools and assess children's progress where English/literacy is often seen as a set of skills to be mastered rather than seeing communication as part of the social and cultural fabric of life. Cummins (2016) describes this division as the 'individualistic' acquisition of skills as contrasted with social orientations towards literacy. For Cummins, whose focus is English language learners (children who are acquiring English as an additional language), individualistic views tend towards seeing children as 'in deficit' (see Chapter 1) when they do not reach expected levels of standardised testing, rather than acknowledging the language and cultural assets they bring to learning.

16.4 Children's cultural and literacy assets or funds of knowledge

This book is founded on a theory of teaching and learning which from the earliest years acknowledges children's existing language and literacy experience and consciously builds on those assets and recognises the importance of all partners in the learning process: families, teachers, adults and children (see the list of principles in the General Introduction I.1). The view of 'assets' brought into the schools is related to the idea of 'funds of knowledge' (Moll *et al.*, 1992; Gonzalez *et al.*, 2005) which describes the cultural and family experiences and expertise which children can draw on in the classroom. For example, Marija moves between the discourse communities of home and school: at home she is very knowledgeable about how to navigate digital texts, often communicates with family abroad and helped her grandmother learn how to text on her phone; in school, none of this experience is recognised because she is a beginning English language learner and struggles with the demands of the reading she is asked to do. In conversation with her teacher, Marija is able to show what she knows, thus bringing together the separate spaces of home and school into a third space (Moje *et al.*, 2004) where they overlap and she is able to draw on her funds of knowledge.

Funds of knowledge: this term is derived from the work of researchers and teachers in Tucson, Arizona, who sought to offset deficit views about certain families and children by getting to know more about their home lives. It was based on the idea that people gain knowledge from their life experiences (Moll *et al.*, 1992; Gonzalez *et al.*, 2005). The term is now more widely used to refer to the knowledge and expertise that children bring to school from their home and community experience.

Third space theory: drawing on the ideas of Bhabha (1990), Moje *et al.* (2004) and Wilson (2000), this theory describes the interlinking of home and school experience. It helps in thinking about how children inhabit both the worlds of home and school, often not making distinctions in their own minds about the reading, writing, listening,

> viewing, drawing, talking they use in either place. They may draw on school experiences when they write for their own pleasure at home or bring their knowledge of computer games or film to bear in reading or writing at school. The challenge for the teacher is how best to use the children's cultural resources and assets to help them get to grips with the school curriculum.

16.5   Critical literacy

Critical and inclusive literacy are key features of the New London Group's view of the possibilities for transformation and change offered by education (New London Group, 1996). According to this view, teaching should make a difference. However, as Barbara Comber points out:

> Despite theoretical and policy moves in literacy education that acknowledge the complexity and plurality of literacy practices, internationally, what constitutes classroom literacy is frequently colonised by standardised testing and scripted programmes.

> (Comber, 2007: 116)

Such a focus can drive teachers into providing a narrowed and often formulaic approach to literacy. In addition, although testing and highly prescribed curricula are intended to raise standards, often in 'high poverty locations' they have the opposite effect and result in deficit descriptions of children's (and families') literacy (*ibid.*). Critical literacy requires not only sharp analysis of what is read – for example, carefully weighing the truthfulness (or otherwise) of information on the internet (Carrington, 2009)– but it also implies a process of critical reconstruction and transformation. Janks (2010) sees literacy as central to identity formation and argues that teachers have a responsibility to create opportunities for children to think critically about their world so that they can act in ways, however small, that will 'make a positive contribution to the creation of a humane and hopeful future' (Janks, 2006: 25).

Critical digital literacy (Dowdall, 2009) emphasises the socially situated nature of children's on-screen text production and consumption and highlights the importance of an 'asset model' of what children know about and can do with digital texts when they use them at home. Understandably there are concerns about safety when children are online (Marsh *et al.*, 2015; Kucirkova and Littleton, 2016), but advice to parents and other adults having care of children often starts from the point of view of danger (Plowman *et al.*, 2010). Whilst recognising the need to safeguard children from predators and from their own naïve postings on social media which might have harmful effects on them and others, developing children's critical digital literacy is essential.

Part of becoming a successful reader is the ability to read evaluatively and critically. This is not something which happens automatically as children become more fluent readers, but needs to be deliberately modelled and taught. The following activity offers a starting point for a teaching sequence which focuses on reading critically and evaluatively.

Activity 16.2
Critical reading: Magazines – reflective journal/blog to pairs/group to class

Collect a few magazines that you like to read. Take just one and choose four or five adverts and consider:

- What do the image and the text convey? What happens if you only have a picture or only have the text?
- What is the story behind the advert? Who is the product aimed at and how do you know?

Now have a look at a few others:

- Hunt for adverts masquerading as articles.
- List the adverts in one magazine and look for patterns. What kinds of adverts are included? What does that tell you about the readers of this magazine?
- Consider the placing of whole-page adverts on double spreads. Why is this placing used?

You will already be aware that no text is 'neutral' but what have you gleaned about the way magazines work? You may feel that you are not influenced by advertising, but large multinationals spend a lot of money on it and social media depend on it.

If you have a chance, possibly in guided reading sessions, ask the children to bring in magazines they like and, using some of the suggestions in website resource W16.2, encourage them to analyse their magazines, remembering that these are things read for pleasure (just as any adult reads magazines) so that the idea is not to suggest that their reading is in any way deficient but to give them the means to be aware of how texts are constructed for particular purposes.

You could equally well examine advertisements on screen.

Section 5.5 has a list of websites of magazines and newspapers for children.

16.6 Children's digital practices at home and school

Recent studies of children's home and school literacy and digital experience (Broadbent *et al.*, 2013; Marsh *et al.*, 2015; Cremin *et al.*, 2015) indicate that many children have access to games consoles, laptops and PCs, internet-enabled tablet computers or smartphones and extensive experience of popular cultural texts. From a very young age, mobile devices are used for play, communication and documentation of everyday life (Merchant, 2015). These are valuable assets to build on in the classroom, but before assuming what children know and can do with digital technology and texts, it is worth finding out the facts. A primary school in south-east England decided to survey its children to find out about their use of multimodal texts, including digital technology, at home.

Case study, early, middle and upper primary: Surveying children's use of multimodal texts at home and at school

This primary school in an industrial town in south-east England has 325 pupils, many of whom are learning English as an additional language. The school wanted to review its use of digital technology and other multimodal texts in the classroom, so they asked all classes to complete the survey (see website resource W16.3) about children's use of the following types of multimodal texts at home and at school:

- comics
- magazines
- newspapers
- television programmes
- computer games
- films/DVDs
- internet texts
- emails
- phone texts
- e-books
- books with words and no pictures
- books with pictures
- audio books.

The survey also asked about ownership of an iPhone or iPad.

The picture of the whole school

Figure 16.1 shows a comparison for the whole school: boys and girls, ages 5–11. The graph is based on percentages of the responses from the total number of children who completed the survey. Of course, these responses only represent the text experience of children in this school. They are not intended to indicate any general trends.

When the teachers reviewed the responses, they noted that the children's popular cultural home reading of magazines and comics does not feature so highly in the classroom, although the figures for reading newspapers are about the same at home and at school. Understandably, television and computer games are more likely to be used at home than at school, although the figure for using computer games in school is about half that of home use. Only one teacher used computer games as part of the curriculum, so the teachers wondered if the relatively high response might partly be because over half the total number of children at the school have iPhones or iPads and report that they use them mostly for playing games and taking photographs. Screen-based texts on the television and internet seem equally regularly used at school and at home and emails and texts, again, understandably, hardly feature at school. Where children use e-books and audio books at home these are much less common in school, although books, with and without pictures are equally prevalent at home and at school.

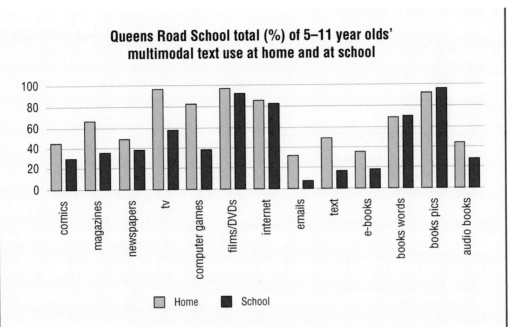

Figure 16.1 5–11 year olds' multimodal text use at home and at school

Gender differences in multimodal text use

When it comes to looking at gender differences (see Figure 16.2), in this school, at least, there seem to be relatively few major differences in multimodal text use between the boys and the girls. More boys than girls read comics, and more girls than boys read

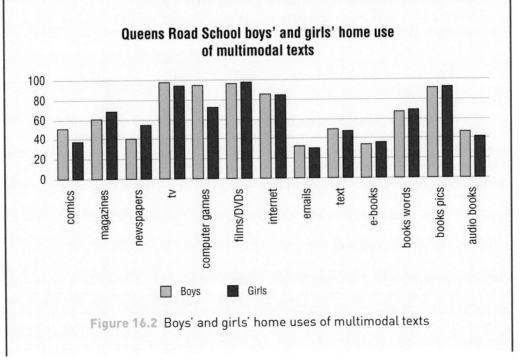

Figure 16.2 Boys' and girls' home uses of multimodal texts

magazines and newspapers. Television viewing is almost the same between boys and girls with the boys slightly higher and where 96 per cent of the boys play computer games, the number of girls reporting playing games is 73 per cent. There are few major differences in the use of all other types of text between boys and girls. (These figures again are based on percentages of the total responses to the survey.)

Looking at each year group

There were some differences between the age groups (see website resource W16.3) but more revealing was that it seems that the particular class teacher's planning for using multimodal texts – both on screen and off – is a key factor in whether the children's home expertise is fully built on in the classroom. Gaps in provision were found in the reading material and technologies associated with reading; for example, home reading of comics, magazines, e-books and audio books was noticeably higher than at school. There were some interesting spikes in the responses about emails and texting but since these seem to be frequently used at home, the teachers felt it may be useful to build on this epxertise in school.

Reviewing the information as a whole, the teachers decided on the following actions:

- Widen the range of reading material in classrooms to include children's preferred comics, magazines, audio and e-books.
- Set up staff training sessions to look at how computer games might be used in the curriculum (particularly as so many girls also report playing computer games; see Figure 16.2).
- Plan to use emails and texting as part of English teaching.
- Plan to use film more deliberately as text to be studied, not just watched.

(See website resource W16.3 for full details of the survey results.)

The teachers at this school decided to develop their classroom uses of a range of multi-modal texts as a result of carrying out this survey and to have more conversations with the children about their digital and multimodal experience. However, it is by no means common that children's text experience and expertise is built on in schools. Many teachers have no idea of the range of home literacy practices children are engaged with (Arrow and Finch, 2013; Cremin *et al.*, 2015), often underestimating children's home reading and writing practices.

16.7   Computer games

Computer games are an important feature of the lives of many children (and adults) but rarely enter the space of the classroom. There may be very good reasons for this, but as part of children's popular cultural experience, it seems perverse to ignore what games have to offer to learning, and to English/literacy learning in particular. Computer games have been examined as effective learning tools (Downes, 1999; Gee, 2003) because playing

Activity 16.3
Surveying digital and multimodal experience – reflective journal blog to pair/group to class

There are several parts to this activity.

1   It is sometimes suggested that teachers lack confidence in using digital technology in the classroom (Graham, 2012; Cremin et al., 2015) but in fact, many teachers and student teachers have considerable experience in using digital technology for their own purposes. The trick is to find ways of using this expertise in the classroom. Read website resource W16.4 Teachers' experience of using digital technology at home and at school. Do you identify with either of the teachers? Make a quick list of your use of digital technology at home and plan to use this experience in the classroom. A good place to start would be with your own knowledge; for example, computer games can be a good springboard for imaginative writing. Or enjoyment of television soap opera can be the basis for talking about characterisation. Plan to start a teaching sequence talking about your own knowledge of popular cultural texts.

2   Watch the talk by Sonia Livingstone 'How children engage with the internet' about current research into children's internet use (www.youtube.com/watch?v=Syjb DUP1o0g (accessed 30 April 2017)). She is arguing that there needs to be a more informed and thoughtful approach to children's use of the internet. What are the implications for classrooms? For example, should there be more discussion about internet use? Or about the use of social media? Sonia Livingstone suggests that adults should listen to children's views in order to help them become more adept and resilient internet users. How might you make opportunities for children to discuss their own preoccupations, fears and enjoyment of internet use?

3   When you have a chance, ask a class of children to complete the survey in website resource W16.5. What experience do they have from home that is not being used in the classroom? Building on their experience may be a long-term matter, but in a forthcoming teaching sequence for English, plan to include some use of digital technology that will make use of the children's funds of knowledge.

4   As the use of the internet, YouTube, games and apps are all part of a fast-moving area, it is worth compiling a list of websites and apps that children have said they like – and to look out for some that you think are useful. Website resource W16.6 'Digital Texts that I Like' is a starting point. Add your own favourites.

reinforces exploratory learning. Learning through game play is seen as more effective because skills are learned in a context of activity and because, by their nature, games scaffold learning.

Practice in games playing can be seen as valuable cultural capital to be drawn on to enhance learning (Marsh and Millard, 2003) and as a model for literary study (Burn, 2008). In a review of research into games in the classroom, Perrotta et al. (2013) identify a common theme that video games contribute to personal and intellectual development as young people join 'affinity groups' where 'players share "cheats" … and "modding" groups who use game development skills to modify how games are played and experienced' (Perrotta *et al.*, 2013: 6). Another frequent theme was that video games provide effective contexts for learning through virtual worlds because acting in such worlds allows learners to develop social practices and take on the identities of genuine professional communities. Such possibilities are seen are as more valuable than some of the more traditional forms of schooling (Shaffer, 2006; Bogost, 2011).

Computer games have also been seen to contribute to more effective narrative writing (Beavis, 2001; McClay, 2002; Bearne and Wolstencroft, 2006). What children know about computer game narratives can have a beneficial effect on children's composition. The narrative structure of many games provides a good model for learning how the action of a narrative moves from place to place or time to time. In addition, game playing models the use of dialogue while the multimodal dimension of the game experience encourages young writers to draw on sound, location and action to enliven their written stories. Computer games often involve challenges or quests (Beavis, 2014) which are familiar to children through their experience of myths, legends and folk stories in films, television series or books. There is scope for a whole variety of fiction and non-fiction reading and writing through virtual worlds; for example, Futurelab's Savannah project which investigates the life of a pride of lions through mapping a virtual savannah on to a real place which is navigated using a hand-held device (Facer, 2004). With the rapid development of technology, such virtual world experiences should become a more common means of building on children's home experience of gaming.

Equally, computer game knowledge can support non-fiction reading and writing. There are often quite complex instructions to follow, quite possibly more challenging than some of the explanatory texts used in the classroom, and children can be asked to make presentations (and film them) about, for example, how to construct worlds in Minecraft or SIMS (Apperley and Walsh, 2012).

Case study, upper primary: The Barnsborough project – virtual worlds in the classroom

This collaborative research project investigated how virtual worlds might be used within school literacy.

In a classroom in South Yorkshire, children aged 8–10 are exploring a secure virtual world: Barnsborough,[1] accessible only to the pupils and their teachers, and designed to provide opportunities for children to engage in reading and writing within a meaningful and motivating context (Merchant 2009, 2010). Children can enter and explore the world individually, represented by avatars on screen. They can visit various locations including the sewers, park, town square, town hall, internet cafe, military headquarters, castle. Apart from them, the world is deserted and the children's task, on entering, is to find out why this might be the case. Barnsborough is laced with clues about what could have happened. Dropped notes, internet sites, graffiti, posters and so on suggest various possibilities – an alien invasion, a nuclear explosion, an insurrection – and children can piece together the clues they find in all sorts of ways. They also have access to an online chat function, which enables them to post comments and questions to other avatars on-screen.

The activity raised many questions for us about how we might work with virtual worlds in classrooms in future. We had given the children a very open brief and they responded to this with purpose and commitment. Whilst they took different pathways and arrived at different conclusions, all engaged with the world, reading and writing along the way. While it would have been possible to give precise assessment criteria, the children seemed to be learning so much about the world, about each other, about the texts they were encountering, that went beyond the originally defined objectives.

A literacy focus could be developed within the virtual world through specific reading and writing experiences 'plotted' by the teacher or by the writing of a blog. As 'wrap-around' tasks, plans could be devised and written up, dialogue between avatars annotated as play-scripts or short films created in response, with the children re-enacting part of their journey or key discovery points (e.g. the Helipad, Barnsborough) could be used as a stimulus for narrative writing, with avatars used at specific points to look around and describe what they could see with the teacher modelling possibilities in terms of use of literary features, extending vocabulary and visualisation techniques. Ensuring pupils engage with reading and writing opportunities in a way that extends them appropriately would require the teacher to set specific challenges both within and outside the virtual world – this virtual environment would appear to have the flexibility and the potential to support and extend both more and less able through the teacher's in-role interactions.

Source: Adapted from Chris Bailey, Emma Gill, Jemma Monkhouse, Julie Rayner, Cathy Burnett, Karen Daniels, Guy Merchant and Roberta Taylor (2013) Zombie Apocalypse: Children's problem solving in a virtual world*English 4–11*, Summer, pp. 7–10.

Case study, early, middle and upper primary: Composing with wikis, blogs, pods and vlogs

This school has set up a virtual learning environment (VLE) to enable children from 5 to 11 years to explore a variety of digital texts securely. The 5 and 6 year olds have been reading Emily Gravett's books. Focusing on *Meerkat Mail* (2015), Gemma planned a collaborative writing project using wiki pages to write more adventures of Sunny the meerkat. She modelled using a wiki page (imported on to an interactive flipchart) to compose Sunny's account of the beginning of a new adventure, talking about her choices and decisions about what to write in exactly the same way as she would if the medium were to be a version on paper. One of her objectives was to encourage the children to be attentive readers of each other's work and to learn how to improve their writing. The children composed their stories in guided group time so Gemma and the teaching assistant, John, could help them proofread and work on their texts. They noticed that although the composition took longer than a hand-written piece, there was a lot of discussion about what to write and that most of the children had found reading and improving the stories much easier than redrafting handwritten text. They accompanied the online writing with postcards from Sunny, modelled on those in the book, about his latest adventures.

As part of a teaching sequence on the Caribbean, a class of 8 and 9 year olds used blogs to respond to a variety of poems they read in class. Peter chose a selection of anthologies collected by John Agard and Grace Nichols (see entries in Children's books section) and after sharing some poems as a class on the theme of friends and family, in group reading time each group chose two anthologies to select more poems that they liked. After discussion, the children chose one poem per group and wrote blogs about why they liked it. As the teaching sequence progressed, the children were invited to make individual choices of poetry and blog about them and to add comments about the poems on other people's blog entries. They became so engrossed in poetry blogging that they carried it on in their own time in computer club.

The 10 and 11 year olds had been reading *Skellig* by David Almond (2013) and Jenny wanted to focus on the speaking and listening opportunities offered by the different themes in the book. As part of the drama activities associated with the beginning of the novel, they had improvised discovering Skellig. Using a video camera, Jenny filmed their improvisations and as a class they edited them and uploaded them as vlogs. As their exploration of the text continued, groups of children filmed their own improvisations then edited and uploaded them to the class interactive flipchart. Jenny used these as an opportunity to reflect further on the themes of the story as well as using it as an opportunity to comment on the effect of their improvisations. When they had finished reading the novel, the teacher asked them in groups to debate the merits of home-based education and being educated at school. This was to be the basis of persuasive writing but before they began to write, the groups made their own podcasts stating their views on the relative merits of being taught at home and at school. These were shared and discussed before the class wrote their persuasive texts. Jenny was particularly impressed with the maturity and conviction of the arguments, which were much more developed than when they had written persuasive pieces without detailed exploration of the issues.

A research study carried out to assess the effects of blogging in school on children's writing (Barrs and Horrocks, 2016) found that blogging had a positive effect in terms of the children's greater awareness of audience, increased sense of 'voice' as a writer and an enhanced sense of belonging to a writing community. This seemed particularly true for children learning English as an additional language.

16.8   Reading on screen[2]

The skills associated with reading are under greater scrutiny as digital sources offer information, communication and entertainment. One of the implications for teaching is the amount of text: there is far more visual information to process in a variety of forms and media. The texts are designed to be navigated differently from the usual direction of reading a printed page of continuous text. In a book, the reading pathway is (in Anglophone countries) usually from top to bottom and left to right. On screen, the eye moves more radially, selecting what to read according to preference and interest. Also, screen texts often invite interaction, moving between screens through hyperlinks. However, it is not only that the screen and its associated hypertext possibilities offers different – and perhaps more 'open' – navigational pathways but also that the reader has to make decisions about what Kress terms 'criteria of relevance' (Kress, 2003). This suggests that young readers have extra demands on them in terms of knowing what they are looking for when reading on screen.

Figure 16.3 Navigating texts on screen

Figure 16.4 Navigating texts on screen

In addition, there are issues of authorship and provenance to be considered. Screen-based texts do not have to go through an editorial process. Blogs, websites, wikis, zines and chat sites are not susceptible to any critical scrutiny and 'information' which is little more than unconfirmed assertion can appear on any site. This means that attentive and critical reader-ship is even more important as part of the young reader's repertoire (Lankshear and Knobel, 2006; Janks, 2010). There are many texts specifically designed for screens which are part of children's home reading experience (Broadbent *et al.*, 2013; Marsh *et al.*, 2005; Marsh, 2010) and whilst there is some indication that these are seen as important for the classroom, they do not often form part of the reading curriculum in school (Burnett, 2016).

Certainly, children enjoy interaction with iPad stories and quickly learn the 'choreography' (Merchant, 2014: 135) of holding, balancing, tapping, swiping in much the same way as they learn the pointing, stroking, tapping and turning movements that accompany reading paper books.

Case study, early primary: Using apps for reading

With a class of 5 and 6 year olds, teachers Hannah and Richard, and Natalia, a University researcher, tried out the app *Flip Flap Safari*.

This app enables users to create safari creatures with a simple slide of the finger. There are eleven animals that can be mixed and matched to create 121 possible combinations of imaginary safari creatures and their mixed names. The pages of the digital book are split into top and bottom halves of the animals and, when flipped, produce funny hybrid animals. 'What do you get when you cross a zebra with an antelope? Why, a zebelope, of course! What about a buffalo with a flamingo? Well, that would be a buffingo, naturally!' The text beneath each animal introduces children to many new adjectives, nouns and verbs. The app has a 'read to myself' option or an option to have the poem beneath each animal read aloud, with original sound effects, safari music, and text highlighting.

We used *Flip Flap Safari* within guided reading and found this really effective. Children were completely engaged in the activity as it was different from the usual books that they would use. We were concerned that the children would be distracted by the 'flipping and flapping' and therefore recommend that children are given the opportunity to play with the app before the guided reading session. We decided to make this our pre-reading task where we gave the children the opportunity to become familiar with the app and choose their favourite new animal and explain why this was their favourite. After the guided reading session, children created their own new animal and those children working at a higher level were challenged to write a verse of a poem to describe it.

The resources can be used with the whole class thanks to the option to have the app read the poem to the children. This allowed children who were less fluent readers to access the app as well as the children working at expected or higher. The fact that the voice used was that of a child's was something we all really liked. We also liked the vocabulary used within this app which extended our children's understanding of words. This made a direct improvement in their writing with lots of the children choosing to use some of the new words within their literacy and cross-curricular work.

Source: Walker, H., Kucirkova, N. and Gould, R. (2016) UKLA Digital Book Award: Teachers' perceptions of the winning apps in 2015, *English 4–11*, Summer.

Apps can be as useful as books in developing all the skills of comprehension – inference, deduction, questioning, predicting, making links between texts and between texts and personal experience. They can also be used for gathering information, classifying and creating non-fiction texts as well as composing multimodal and written texts (see Kucirkova *et al.*, 2017).

16.9 A note about children who experience difficulties with on-screen reading

Although there is evidence that on-screen reading in the classroom can contribute to children's enthusiasm and knowledge, there are questions about how screen-based classroom reading, particularly perhaps on the interactive whiteboard/digital flipchart, may suit a diverse range of readers. In an extensive observation of children with dyslexia in mainstream classrooms, Rosemary Anderson (2008: 26) suggests:

- Light reflection can be a problem in bright conditions, and as the reading of dyslexic pupils is disproportionately affected by indistinct print, their seating position in the classroom should be carefully chosen.
- As some dyslexic pupils are very sensitive to print/background contrast and will experience dazzle if the screen is too bright, they should be consulted about their preferences with regard to this aspect of readability.
- When studying internet material originally designed to be viewed on a small screen, it is important to be aware that there may be readability issues and problems with visual features.
- Because of the dominance of the screen, there is a tendency for the presence of an IWB in the classroom to lead to an increase in instructions and information being provided only in written form, but this should be guarded against in order to avoid marginalizing dyslexic pupils.

However, she recommends that children experiencing difficulties with reading should be encouraged to take an active role in screen-based activities with a partner and other suitable support.

16.10 Using film in the classroom

Film is one of a range of media used to engage children in the classroom and is now an expected part of the teacher's toolkit. However, film is often used as an adjunct or comparison to a written narrative text or for information about different curricular areas, but rarely studied for its own sake (Bazalgette, 2010). Parry and Hill Bulman put it like this:

> We do not see the central role of film to be to teach aspects of school-based literacy such as grammar or paragraphing and would even suggest that this may be counter-productive ... We would argue that to ignore children's experiences of film and television risks excluding them from participation in literacy learning. Where children's understandings of narrative, based on

the moving image, are valued in the classroom, there is clear evidence of engaged and meaningful progression in relation to literacy.

(Parry, 2013, 2014; Hill Bulman, 2017)

There is evidence that drawing on children's popular cultural experience in the classroom reveals a wealth of knowledge of characters, themes and issues drawn from the narratives of films, games and television (Willett, 2005). Potter (2012) also shows that when children produce digital texts, they combine their media experiences to express their identities as learners.

Another drawback to teaching film as a text in its own right is the lack of a sense of what it means to make progress in reading (or making) film. In a four-year study, Hill Bulman (2017) identified a series of steps of progression, which teachers could use to track progress and inform next steps in learning. This spiral framework of progression of reading film is based on children's experience, not levels of ability:

- Progression in reading film – related to print
  - Comprehension of film
  - Characterisation
  - Plot structures
  - Genre
  - Intertextuality and connections
- Progression in reading film
  - Camera
  - Colour and light
  - Sound
  - Editing
- Vocabulary development and the metalanguage of film.

Bulman's study shows that it is important to think more widely about the term 'text' in order to meet the needs of learners and create a curriculum that is fit for purpose in a twenty-first century globalised community.

Activity 16.4
Analysing film – pairs/group to class

Although children have extensive experience of watching and enjoying film, they need to be taught how to analyse film in the same way as they might any other text. Before trying this out with a class, it is worth analysing some film yourself. Find a short extract from a film where the sound and camera work contribute to the meaning, characterisation and atmosphere. *The Iron Giant* is good for this kind of activity and a clip of the trailer is available on: www.youtube.com/watch?v=OTnu-cGP17w.
Watch it first with the sound off.

- Make notes about the use of camera:
  - Whose point of view does the camera show?
  - Why has a long shot been chosen as opposed to a mid-shot?

- Why is a close-up particularly powerful at a certain point? (Parry and Hill Bulman, 2017)
- What does the lighting and colour convey?
- What do the characters' postures, gestures and facial expressions show? (Although the Iron Giant does not have a mobile face, he certainly expresses emotion.)

Now watch it with the sound. What do the dialogue and sound effects add to the meaning?

Once you have analysed some film yourself, plan to include film as a text in a forthcoming English sequence. Using or adapting the prompt questions, create opportunities for children to analyse extracts in the same way that you have to explore characterisation, setting, the creation of atmosphere or narrative structure.

Equally, good-quality information films, such as the BBC Natural World series, can be used to enhance cross-curricular topics, or non-fiction writing.

BFI's free downloadable publication *Look Again* has a wealth of ideas for using film and television in the primary classroom: www.bfi.org.uk/sites/bfi.org.uk/files/downloads/bfi-education-look-again-teaching-guide-to-film-and-tv-2013–03.pdf (accessed 25 May 2017).

See also Chapter 8 for accounts of how film can aid comprehension.

16.11 Describing progress in reading and composing multimodal texts

Arising from the research project *Reframing Literacy*,[3] Bearne and Bazalgette (2010) developed a set of progression statements to describe progress in reading/viewing multimodal texts across the dimensions of:

- engagement, understanding and response to text
- inference and deduction (including modality)
- structure and organisation of texts
- style and composition (including diegetic and non-diegetic sound)
- purpose, viewpoint and effect of text on the audience
- social, cultural and historical context.

Whilst the Scale of Progression for Reading (see Chapter 9) includes elements of multimodality, the Scale of Progression in Multimodal Reading/Viewing is specifically designed to cover screen-based and paper-based multimodal texts (see website resource W16.7 for the full Scale of Progression in Multimodal Reading/Viewing).

Modality (in film terminology): judgement about how real a text is meant to be based on signals from the text; for example, a live television broadcast has high modality because it shows what is really happening at the moment. A story about an ogre living in a swamp has low modality because it cannot happen in reality. However,

> even in a story with low modality, there are realistic elements; for example, the ogre's (Shrek's) love for Fiona. Thinking about modality allows discussion about how real a story is supposed to be and whether this makes a difference to the reader/viewer's enjoyment.
>
> **Diegetic and non-diegetic sound:** diegetic sound is part of the 'world' of the TV programme or film; for example, voices, cars revving, animal noises. Non-diegetic sounds are added to evoke atmosphere; for example, background music or sounds that the character might be imagining.

In terms of composition of multimodal texts, the Scale of Progression in Multimodal Text Composition (see website resource W16.8) developed from three research projects: *The Essex Writing Project* (2002–2005),[4] the UKLA/National Strategy *Raising Boys' Achievement in Writing* project (2003) and *More than Words* 1 and 2 (QCA 2004–2006). Whilst the Scale of Progression in Writing (see Chapter 15) includes elements of multimodality, the Scale of Progression in Multimodal Reading/Viewing specifically describes text making on screen and on paper.

Progression in multimodal text composition is marked by increasing ability to:

- Decide on mode and content for specific purpose(s) and audience(s):
  - choose which mode(s) will best communicate meaning for specific purposes – for example, deciding on words rather than images or gesture/music rather than words
  - use perspective, colour, sound and language to engage and hold a reader's/viewer's attention
  - select appropriate content to express personal intentions, ideas and opinions
  - adapt, synthesise and shape content to suit personal intentions in communication.
- Structure texts:
  - pay conscious attention to design and layout of texts, use structural devices (pages, sections, frames, paragraphs, blocks of text, screens, sound sequences) to organise texts
  - integrate and balance modes for design purposes
  - structure longer texts with visual, verbal and sound cohesive devices
  - use background detail to create mood and setting.
- Use technical features for effect:
  - handle technical aspects and conventions of different kinds of multimodal texts, including line, colour, perspective, sound, camera angles, movement, gesture, facial expression and language
  - choose language, punctuation, font, typography and presentational techniques to create effects and clarify meaning
  - choose and use a variety of sentence structures for specific purposes.
- Reflect:
  - explain choices of modes(s) and expressive devices including words
  - improve own composition or performance, reshaping, redesigning and redrafting for purpose and readers'/viewers' needs

- comment on the success of a composition in fulfilling the design aims
- comment on the relative merits of teamwork and individual contribution for a specific project.

See website resource W16.8 for the Scale of Progression in Multimodal Text Composition and website resource W16.9 Analysis of Max and Caroline's storyboards – analysed examples of two multimodal texts.

Summary

This chapter acknowledges the ways in which English teaching will need to develop to answer to an increasingly global and digitised world. It covers multimodality, critical literacy, digital texts, children's cultural and literacy assets or funds of knowledge, their digital practices at home and school and how each of these relates to more traditional forms of English. Students and teachers vary in their assurance about using digital technologies and a reflective task focuses on how their own experience can enhance their pedagogy. Examples of children using new forms of text (blogging, emails, social media) are examined as relevant to a continually evolving English curriculum and the place of film and reading on screen are considered as new developments in English teaching. The chapter ends with a section offering scales of progression for describing progress in reading and composing multimodal texts.

Notes

1   Barnsborough was built by virtuallylearning.co.uk in the Active Worlds Educational Universe (www.activeworlds.com) and developed by a group of educators, researchers and consultants.
2   In Northern Ireland, Scotland and Wales, digital, multimedia and multimodal texts are included in the speaking and listening, reading and writing national curricula. In the national curriculum in England there is no explicit reference to multimodal/multimedia texts. In Northern Ireland, the phrase 'traditional and digital resources' is repeated in both the reading and writing curriculum, as are 'multimedia presentations', 'representing ideas through ICT', 'composing on-screen' and 'combining text, sound or graphics' (http://ccea.org.uk/curriculum) (accessed 30 April 2017). In Scotland, children are expected to read, watch and compose different kinds of text, including CVs, letters and emails, films, games and TV programmes, text messages, blogs and social networking sites and web pages (https://education.gov.scot/Documents/literacy-english-pp.pdf (accessed 30 April 2017)).
    The Welsh curriculum includes frequent mention of 'on-screen and web-based materials', locating information, developing a critical view of what is read and composing on screen (http://gov.wales/topics/educationandskills/schoolshome/curriculuminwales/arevisedcurriculumforwales/?lang=en (accessed 30 April 2017)).
    In England there is no mention of any texts other than books and no suggestion that writing might include writing on screen. This lack of explicit mention of visual or digital texts can offer a challenge to teachers. However, as can be seen from the case studies in this book, many teachers in England take an innovative and enlightened view of how best to equip children for the literacy demands of the twenty-first century.
3   The *Reframing Literacy* research project was funded by the Qualifications and Curriculum Authority (QCA) in 2007–8 and carried out by a team of researchers from the British Film Institute (BFI), the UK Literacy Association (UKLA) and the Centre for Literacy in Primary Education (CLPE).

4   The Essex Writing Project involved 430 teachers over four years and was originally set up to support boys' literacy through the use of visual texts then developed into a more comprehensive multimodal action research project.

The United Kingdom Literacy Association in association with the Primary National Strategy worked with forty-eight teachers in three local authorities in England on an action research project designed to raise boys' achievements in writing through drama and visual texts.

The Qualifications and Curriculum Authority funded researchers from the United Kingdom Literacy Association to work with small groups of teachers to develop descriptors for multimodal text composition in line with descriptors for progress in writing.

Recommended reading

Apperley, T. and Walsh, C. (2012) What digital games and literacy have in common: A heuristic for understanding pupils' gaming literacy, *Literacy*, 46 (3) pp. 113–167. Australian researchers offer a model to support teachers in using games in the classroom. **Advanced**

Arrow, A. and Finch, B. (2013) Multimedia literacy practices in beginning classrooms and at home: The differences in practices and beliefs, *Literacy*, 47 (3) pp. 131–141. Research article from New Zealand with fascinating details about 5 year olds' home and school literacy experience and an analysis of teachers' and parents' perceptions of the literacy demands of home and school. **Advanced**

Carrington, V. (2009) From wikipedia to the humble classroom wiki: Why we should pay attention to wikis, in V. Carrington and M. Robinson (eds) *Digital Literacies: Social learning and classroom practices.* London: SAGE/UKLA, pp. 65–79. **Advanced**

Janks, H. (2002) Critical literacy: Beyond reason, *Australian Educational Researcher*, 29 (1) pp. 7–27. www.researchgate.net/publication/225485710_Critical_Literacy_Beyond_Reason (accessed 30 April 2017). In this article, Janks draws on her experience in South Africa and Australia to argue that critical literacy is essentially rational and does not sufficiently consider the non-rational elements that readers bring to texts. She uses playful advertising texts to consider the role of pleasure in contrast with reason. **Advanced**

Janks, H. (2006) The place of design in a theory of critical literacy. Keynote address presented at the AATE/ALEA conference: *Voices, vibes, visions*, 8–11 July, Darwin, Australia. http://hilaryjanks. co.za/wp-content/uploads/2015/01/aate-design-darwin-2006.pdf (accessed 30 April 2017). Janks' synthesis model for critical literacy sees domination or power, access, diversity and design/ redesign as interdependent theoretical concepts in the field of critical literacy. In this article, she draws on research in Australia and South Africa to focus on design/redesign. **Advanced**

Marsh, J. (2010) The relationship between home and school literacy practices, in D. Wyse, R. Andrews and J. Hoffman (eds) *The Routledge International Handbook of English, Language and Literacy Teaching.* Abingdon: Routledge, pp. 305–316. This is a 'must read' where Marsh first of all outlines theoretical perspectives that inform the literature on home and school literacy practices, reviews international research about how digital literacy practices are embedded across the domains of school and home and suggests areas for further research. **Advanced**

Parry, B. (2014) Popular culture, participation and progression in the literacy classroom, *Literacy*, 48 (1) pp. 14–22. This article draws on data from a media literacy research project in the UK to argue for the relevance of popular culture experiences in literacy teaching, including film making. **Advanced**

Perrotta, C., Featherstone, G., Aston, H. and Houghton, E. (2013) *Game-based Learning: Latest evidence and future directions* (NFER Research Programme: Innovation in Education). Slough: NFER. www.nfer.ac.uk/publications/GAME01/GAME01.pdf (accessed 30 April 2017). This review of international research into game-based learning sets out to define game based learning and to consider the impact and potential impact of game-based learning on learners' engagement and attainment and the implications for schools.

References

Anderson, R. (2008) *Dyslexia and Inclusion: Supporting classroom reading with 7–11 year olds.* Leicester: United Kingdom Literacy Association.

Apperley, T. and Walsh, C. (2012) What digital games and literacy have in common: A heuristic for understanding pupils' gaming literacy, *Literacy*, 46 (3) pp. 113–167.

Arrow, A. and Finch, B. (2013) Multimedia literacy practices in beginning classrooms and at home: The differences in practices and beliefs, *Literacy*, 47 (3) pp. 131–141.

Bailey, C., Gill, E., Monkhouse, J., Rayner, J., Burnett, C., Daniels, K., Merchant, G. and Taylor, R. (2013) Zombie Apocalypse: Children's problem solving in a virtual world, *English 4–11*, Summer, pp. 7–10.

Barrs, M. and Horrocks, S. (2016) Educational blogs and their effect on pupils' writing. CfBT Education Trust. www.academia.edu/11197640/Educational_blogs_and_their_effects_on_pupils_writing (accessed 10 May 2017)

Barton, D., Hamilton, M. and Ivanic, R. (eds) (1999) *Situated Literacies.* London: Routledge.

Bazalgette, C. (ed.) (2010) *Teaching Media in Primary Schools.* London: SAGE.

Bearne, E. and Bazalgette, C. (eds) (2010) *Beyond Words: Developing children's response to multimodal texts.* Leicester: United Kingdom Literacy Association.

Bearne, E. and Wolstencroft, H. (2006) *Visual Approaches to Teaching Writing.* London: SAGE/UKLA.

Beavis, C. (2001) Digital culture, digital literacies: Expanding the notions of text, in C. Beavis and C. Durrant (eds) *P(ICT)ures of English: Teachers, learners and technology.* Adelaide: Wakefield Press, pp. 145–161.

Beavis, C. (2014) 'Games as text, games as action', *Journal of Adolescent & Adult Literacy*, 57 (6) pp. 433–439.

Bhabha, H. K. (1990) The third space, in J. Rutherford (ed.) *Identity, Community, Culture, Difference.* London: Lawrence and Wishart, pp. 207–221.

Bogost, I. (2011). *How to Do Things with Video Games.* Minneapolis, MN: University of Minnesota Press.

Broadbent, H., Fell, L., Green, P. and Gardner, W. (2013) *Have Your Say: Listening to young people about their online rights and responsibilities.* Plymouth: Childnet International and UK Safer Internet Centre. www.saferinternet.org.uk/content/childnet/saferinternetcentre/downloads/Safer_Internet_Day/2013/Have_your_Say_survey_-_Full_Report.pdf (accessed 30 April 2017)

Burn, A. (2008) The case of rebellion: Researching multimodal texts, in J. Coiro, M. Knobel, C. Lankshear and D. J. Leu (eds) *Handbook of Research on New Literacies.* Abingdon: Routledge, pp. 151–178.

Burnett, C. (2016) *The Digital Age and its Implications for Learning and Teaching in the Primary School: A report for the Cambridge Primary Review Trust.* CPRT supported by Pearson. http://cprtrust.org.uk/wp-content/uploads/2016/07/Burnett-report-20160720.pdf (accessed 30 April 2017)

Carrington, V. (2005) New textual landscapes, information and early literacy, in J. Marsh (ed.) *Popular Culture, New Media and Digital Literacy in Early Childhood.* London: RoutledgeFalmer, pp. 13–27.

Carrington, V. (2009) From wikipedia to the humble classroom wiki: Why we should pay attention to wikis, in V. Carrington and M. Robinson (eds), *Digital Literacies: Social learning and classroom practices.* London: SAGE/UKLA, pp. 65–79.

Carrington, V. and Robinson, M. (eds) (2009) *Digital Literacies: Social learning and classroom practices.* London: SAGE/UKLA.

Childwise (2012) *The Monitor Pre-school Report 2012: Key behaviour patterns among 0 to 4 year olds.* Norwich. www.childwise.co.uk/preschool.html (accessed 30 April 2017)

Comber, B. (2007) Assembling dynamic repertoires of literate practice: Teaching that makes a difference, in E. Bearne and J. Marsh (eds) *Literacy and Social Inclusion: Closing the gap.* Stoke-on-Trent: Trentham Books, pp. 115–131.

Cope, B. and Kalantzis, M. (eds) (2000) *Multiliteracies: Literacy learning and the design of social futures.* New York: Routledge.

Cremin, T., Mottram, M., Collins, F., Powell, S. and Drury, R. (2015) *Researching Literacy Lives: Building communities between home and school.* Abingdon: Routledge.

Cummins, J. (2016) Conference keynote speech 'Individualistic and Social Orientations to Literacy Research: Bringing Voices Together?' at the United Kingdom Literacy Association International Conference: *Literacy, Equality and Diversity: Bringing voices together*, 8–10 July.

Dowdall, C. (2009) Masters and critics: Children as producers of online digital texts, in V. Carrington and M. Robinson (eds) *Digital Literacies: Social Learning and Classroom Practices*. London: SAGE, pp. 43–62.

Downes, T. (1999) Playing with computing technologies in the home, *Education and Information Technologies*, 4 pp. 65–79.

Facer, K. (2004) *Savannah: A Futurelab Prototype Research Report.* www.nfer.ac.uk/publications/FUTL45/FUTL45.pdf (accessed 30 April 2017)

Gee, J. (2003) *What Video Games Have to Teach Us about Literacy and Learning.* New York: Palgrave Macmillan.

Gonzalez, N., Moll, L. and Amanti, C. (2005) *Funds of Knowledge: Theorizing practices in households, communities and classrooms.* Mahwah, NJ: Lawrence Erlbaum Associates.

Graham, L. (2012) Unfolding lives in digital worlds: Digikid teachers revisited, *Literacy*, 46 (3) pp. 133–139.

Hill Bulman, J. (2017) *Children's Reading of Film and Visual Literacy in the Primary Curriculum: A progression framework model.* London: Palgrave Macmillan.

Janks, H. (2006) The place of design in a theory of critical literacy. Keynote address presented at the AATE/ALEA conference: Voices, vibes, visions, 8–11 July, Darwin, Australia. http://hilaryjanks.co.za/wp-content/uploads/2015/01/aate-design-darwin-2006.pdf (accessed 30 April 2017)

Janks, H. (2010) *Literacy and Power.* London: Routledge.

Jewitt, C. (2005) Multimodality 'reading', and 'writing' for the 21st century, *Discourse: Studies in the Cultural Politics of Education*, 26 (3) pp. 315–331.

Kress, G. (2003) *Literacy in the New Media Age.* London: Routledge.

Kucirkova, N. and Littleton, K. (2016) *A National Survey of Parents' Perceptions of and Practices in Relation to Children's Reading for Pleasure with Print and Digital Books.* http://booktrustadmin.artlogic.net/usr/resources/1407/digital_reading_survey-final-report-8.2.16.pdf (accessed 30 April 2017)

Kucirkova, N., Audain, J. and Chamberlain, L. (2017) *Jumpstart Apps: Creative learning ideas and activities for ages 7–11.* London: David Fulton.

Lankshear, C. and Knobel, M. (eds) (2006) *New Literacies: Everyday practices and classroom learning*, 2nd edn. Maidenhead, Berkshire: Open University Press.

Leander, K. (2009) Composing with old and new media: Toward a parallel pedagogy, in V. Carrington and M. Robinson (eds) *Digital Literacies: Social learning and classroom practices*. London: SAGE, pp. 147–162.

Marsh, J. (2010) The relationship between home and school literacy practices, in D. Wyse, R. Andrews and J. Hoffman (eds) *The Routledge International Handbook of English, Language and Literacy Teaching*. Abingdon: Routledge, pp. 305–316.

Marsh, J. and Millard, E. (2003) *Literacy and Popular Culture in the Classroom.* Reading: National Centre for Language and Literacy, the University of Reading.

Marsh, J., Brooks, G., Hughes, J., Ritchie, L., Roberts, S. and Wright, K. (2005) *Digital Beginnings: Young People's Use of Popular Culture, Media and New Technologies.* Sheffield: University of Sheffield Literacy Research Centre. www.digitalbeginnings.shef.ac.uk/DigitalBeginningsReport.pdf (accessed 30 April 2017)

Marsh, J., Plowman, L., Yamada-Rice, D., Bishop, J. C., Lahmar, J., Scott, F., and Winter, P. (2015) *Exploring Play and Creativity in Pre-Schoolers' Use of Apps: Final Project Report.* www.techandplay.org/reports/TAP_Final_Report.pdf (accessed 30 April 2017)

McClay, J. (2002) Hidden 'treasure': New genres, new media and the teaching of writing, *English in Education*, 36 (1) pp. 46–55.

Merchant, G. (2009) Literacy in virtual worlds, *Journal of Research in Reading*, 32 (1) pp. 38–56.

Merchant, G. (2010) 3D Virtual worlds as environments for literacy teaching, *Educational Research*, 52 (2) pp. 135–150.

Merchant, G. (2014) Young children and interactive story apps, in C. Burnett, J. Davies, G. Merchant and J. Rowsell (eds) *New Literacies around the Globe: Policy and Pedagogy*. Abingdon: Routledge, pp. 128–139.

Merchant, G. (2015) 'Moving with the times: How mobile digital literacies are changing childhood', in V. Duckworth and G. Ade-Ojo (eds) *Landscapes of Specific Literacies in Contemporary Society: Exploring a social model of literacy*. London: Routledge, pp. 103–116.

Moje, E., Ciechanowski, K. M., Kramer, K., Ellis, L., Carrillo, R. and Collazzo, T. (2004) Working towards third space in content area literacy: An examination of everyday funds of knowledge and Discourse, *Reading Research Quarterly*, 39 (1) pp. 38–70.

Moll, L.C., Amanti, C., Neff, D. and Gonzalez, N. (1992) Funds of knowledge for teaching using a qualitative approach to connect homes and classrooms, *Theory into Practice*, 31 (2) pp. 132–141.

New London Group (1996) A pedagogy of multiliteracies: Designing social futures, *Harvard Educational Review*, 66 (1) pp. 60–92.

Parry, B. (2013) *Children, Film and Literacy*. New York: Palgrave Macmillan.

Parry, B. (2014) Popular culture, participation and progression in the literacy classroom, *Literacy*, 48 (1) pp. 14–22.

Parry, B. and Hill Bulman, J. (2017) *Film Education, Literacy and Learning*. Leicester: United Kingdom Literacy Association.

Perrotta, C., Featherstone, G., Aston, H. and Houghton, E. (2013) *Game-based Learning: Latest evidence and future directions* (NFER Research Programme: Innovation in Education). Slough: NFER. www.nfer.ac.uk/publications/GAME01/GAME01.pdf (accessed 30 April 2017)

Plowman, L., McPake, J. and Stephen, C. (2010) The technologisation of childhood? Young children and technology in the home, *Children and Society* 24 (1) pp. 63–74.

Potter, J. *(2012) Digital Media and Learner Identity: The new curatorship*. New York: Palgrave Macmillan.

Shaffer, D. W. (2006) *How Computer Games Help Children Learn*. New York: Palgrave Macmillan.

Street, B. (1993) Introduction: The new literacy studies, in B. Street (ed.) *Cross Cultural Approaches to Literacy*. Cambridge: Cambridge University Press, pp. 1–21.

Stephen, C., Stevenson, O. and Adey, C. (2013) Young children engaging with technologies at home: The influence of family context, *Journal of Early Childhood Research*, 11 (2) pp. 149–164.

Walker, H., Kucirkova, N. and Gould, R. (2016) UKLA Digital Book Award: Teachers' perceptions of the winning apps in 2015, *English 4–11*, Summer.

Willett, R. (2005) Baddies in the classroom: Media education and narrative writing, *Literacy*, 39 (3) pp. 142–148.

Wilson, A. (2000) There is no escape from Third Space Theory: Borderline discourse and the 'in between' literacies of prisons, in D. Barton, M. Hamilton and R. Ivanic (eds) *Situated Literacies: Reading and writing in context*. London: Routledge, pp. 54–69.

Children's books

John Agard and Grace Nichols (1992) *No Hickory, No Dickory, No Dock*. Puffin Books. ISBN 9780140340273

John Agard and Grace Nichols (eds) illustrated Christopher Corr (2002) *Under the Moon and Over the Sea: A collection of Caribbean poems*. Candlewick Press. ISBN 9780763618612.

John Agard and Grace Nichols (eds) illustrated Annabel Wright (2004) *From Mouth to Mouth (Oral Poems from Around the World)*. Walker Books. ISBN 9780744583830

John Agard and Grace Nichols (eds) illustrated Satoshi Kitamura (2010) *Twinkle, Twinkle, Firefly*. Collins Big Cat. ISBN 9780007336142

John Agard and Grace Nichols (eds) illustrated Satoshi Kitamura (2011) *Pumpkin Grumpkin*. Walker Books. ISBN 9781406308884.

John Agard and Grace Nichols (eds) illustrated Cathie Felstead (2011) *A Caribbean Dozen: Poems from 13 Caribbean poets*. Walker Books. ISBN 9781406334593

David Almond (new edition 2013) *Skellig*. Hodder Children's Books. ISBN 9780340944950

Aaron Becker (2014) *Journey*. (Journey Trilogy 1). Walker Books. ISBN 9781406355345

Anthony Browne (2013) *Gorilla*. 30th anniversary edition. Walker Books. ISBN 9781406352337

Gary Crew, illustrated Shaun Tan (2017) *Memorial*. Little, Brown Books for Young Readers. ISBN 9780734417206

Emily Gravett (2015) *Meerkat Mail*. Pan Macmillan Two Hoots. ISBN 9781447284420

David Wiesner (2012) *Tuesday*. Andersen Press. ISBN 9781849394475

Film resources

BBC Natural World series. This has a wealth of short films. www.bing.com/videos/search?q=Natural+World+BBC+YouTube&FORM=RESTAB (accessed 30 April 2017)

Starting Stories 2. Twelve short films between 2 and 10 minutes long, aimed at children aged 3 and over drawn from international sources. British Film Institute. www.bfi.org.uk/ (accessed 30 April 2017)

Story Shorts. Five short films for 7 to 11 year olds accompanied by notes for teachers. British Film Institute. www.bfi.org.uk/ (accessed 30 April 2017)

The Windmill Farmer (2010) Joachim Baldwin. Los Angeles: UCLA Animation Workshop. A farmer is in danger of losing his crop as he struggles against the forces of nature. https://vimeo.com/12377177 (accessed 30 April 2017)

Bridge (2010) Ting C Tey. Academy of Art University. A moral tale about how animals try to cross a bridge and become obstacles to each other, showing how compromise may be better than conflict. https://vimeo.com/27299211 (accessed 30 April 2017)

Studio Ghibli. Japanese animation films. Haunting and beautifully made, find details of all films from this studio on http://studioghibli.net/links.htm (accessed 30 April 2017)

Howl's Moving Castle (2004) (dir. Hayao Miyazaki; Studio Ghibli). Based on the novel by Diana Wynne Jones. Sophie Hatter, a bookworm, the eldest of three daughters, is doomed to an uninteresting life as a hat maker until she finds her way to the moving castle inhabited by the wizard Howl, said by all to eat the souls of young girls.

Spirited Away (2001) (dir. Hayao Miyazaki; Studio Ghibli). A fantasy adventure with a 10-year-old girl, which starts in everyday Japan but young Chihiro and her family follow a mysterious tunnel which leads to the Land of Spirits, inhabited by gods and monsters and ruled by the greedy witch Yu-baba.

The Literacy Shed. Curated by Rob Smith, a former teacher, and provides a wealth of visual resources, organised thematically, for example, The Fantasy Shed, The Great Animations Shed, The Robots Shed. www.literacyshed.com/ (accessed 30 April 2017)

Film websites

https://ataleunfolds.co.uk/

https://theclipclub.co.uk/

www.englishandmedia.co.uk/

www.ecfaweb.org/ (European film)

www.filmeducation.org

www.intofilm.org

www.learnaboutfilm.com (All accessed 30 April 2017).

Apps

Flip Flap Safari. Axel Scheffler (2017) Nosy Crow. http://nosycrow.com/product/axel-schefflers-flip-flap-safari/ (accessed 10 May 2017). There are so many others that it is impossible to list them here, but the best resource for using them in classrooms is: Kucirkova, N., Audain, J. and Chamberlain, L. (2017) *Jumpstart Apps: Creative Learning Ideas and Activities for Ages 7–11.* London: David Fulton.

www.theguardian.com/technology/2012/aug/04/50-best-apps-chidren-smartphones-tablets (accessed 30 April 2017). Reviewing the best apps for children.

http://nosycrow.com/apps/ (accessed 30 April 2017). For a range of story and information apps for children.

http://booksforkeeps.co.uk/issue/202/childrens-books/articles/picture-book-apps-the-best-new-titles (accessed 30 April 2017). Lucy Russell reviews the best picture book apps.

https://ukla.org/awards/ukla-digital-book-award (accessed 30 April 2017). In a move to involve teachers in using apps in the classroom and give recognition to digital books which support children's reading for pleasure and enjoyment, the United Kingdom Literacy Association (UKLA) has set up a two yearly Digital Book Award.

INDEX

Page numbers in italics refer to figures.